The Real Estate Market in the Roman World

As it is today, the property market was a key and dynamic economic sector in Ancient Rome. Its study demands a deep understanding of Roman society, of the normative frameworks and the notions of wealth, value, identity and status that shaped individual and collective mentalities. This book takes a multisided insight into real estate as the subject of short- and long-term economic investments, of speculative businesses ventures, of power abuses and inequalities, of social aspirations, but also of essential housing needs.

The volume discusses thoroughly relevant and new literary, legal, epigraphic, papyrological and archaeological evidence, and incorporates comparative historical perspectives and methodologies, including economic theory and current, critical sociological debates about the functioning of modern real estate markets and issues linked to its commodification and regulation. In pursuing this line of enquiry, the contributions that make up the book investigate the impact of ideas such as profit, risk, security and trust in transfers, management and use of residential houses, commercial buildings and productive estates in urban and rural contexts. The work further evaluates the legal responses to and the public enforcement strategies concerning such activities, the high mobility of fortunes and unstable property-rights that resulted from one-off but also structural, political, financial, economic and institutional crises that marked the history of the Roman Republic and Principate.

This book aims to demonstrate the relevance of the study of pre-modern real estate markets today, and will be of significant interest to readers of economic history as well as Roman law, Roman archaeology, the history of urbanism and social history.

Marta García Morcillo is an Ancient Historian and Research Fellow at Durham University.

Cristina Rosillo-López is Associate Professor of Ancient History at the Universidad Pablo de Olavide, Seville.

Routledge Explorations in Economic History

Edited by **Lars Magnusson**, *Uppsala University, Sweden*

Paper and the British Empire
The Quest for Imperial Raw Materials, 1861–1960
Timo Särkkä

Institutions and Chinese Economic Development
A Comparative Historical Approach
Li Tan

Port-Cities and their Hinterlands
Migration, Trade and Cultural Exchange from the Early Seventeenth-Century to 1939
Edited by Robert Lee and Paul McNamara

The Economy of Renaissance Italy
Paolo Malanima

The Decline of British Industrial Hegemony
Bengal Industries 1914–46
Indrajit Ray

Industry and Development in Argentina
An Intellectual History, 1914–1980
Marcelo Rougier and Juan Odisio
Translated by James Brennan

The Real Estate Market in the Roman World
Edited by Marta García Morcillo and Cristina Rosillo-López

An Economic History of the First German Unification
State Formation and Economic Development in a European Perspective
Edited by Ulrich Pfister and Nikolaus Wolf

For more information about this series, please visit: www.routledge.com/Routledge-Explorations-in-Economic-History/book-series/SE0347

The Real Estate Market in the Roman World

Edited by
Marta García Morcillo and Cristina Rosillo-López

Routledge
Taylor & Francis Group
LONDON AND NEW YORK

First published 2023
by Routledge
4 Park Square, Milton Park, Abingdon, Oxon OX14 4RN

and by Routledge
605 Third Avenue, New York, NY 10158

Routledge is an imprint of the Taylor & Francis Group, an informa business

British Library Cataloguing-in-Publication Data
A catalogue record for this book is available from the British Library

ISBN: 978-1-032-03533-8 (hbk)
ISBN: 978-1-032-03538-3 (pbk)
ISBN: 978-1-003-18780-6 (ebk)

DOI: 10.4324/9781003187806

Typeset in Bembo
by Taylor & Francis Books

Contents

Illustrations

Figures

Tables

Contributors

Jean Andreau is Emeritus Professor of Roman History and Research Director at the École des Hautes Études en Sciences Sociales (Paris).

Maria Letizia Caldelli is Professor of Roman History at the Università degli Studi di Roma, La Sapienza.

Luigi Capogrossi Colognesi is Emeritus Professor of Roman Legal and Economic History at the Università degli Studi di Roma, La Sapienza.

Marta García Morcillo is an Ancient Historian and Research Fellow at Durham University.

Dennis Kehoe is Professor of Classical Studies at Tulane University (New Orleans).

Paul V. Kelly is an Economic Historian specialised in Roman Egypt. He holds a PhD from King's College London.

Max Koedijk is an Ancient Historian and Economist. He holds a PhD from the Ruhr-Universität Bochum.

Annalisa Marzano is Professor of Roman Archaeology at the Università di Bologna.

Dominik Maschek is Professor of Roman Archaeology at the Leibniz-Forschungsinstitut für Archäologie of the Römisch-Germanisches Zentralmuseum Mainz and at the Universität Trier.

Emilia Mataix Ferrándiz is a María Zambrano Postdoctoral Fellow at the University of the Basque Country.

Sofia Piacentin is Lecturer in Ancient History at the Università di Verona.

Francisco Pina Polo is Professor of Ancient History at the University of Zaragoza.

Cecilia Ricci is Professor of Ancient History at the Università degli Studi del Molise (Campobasso, Molise).

Cristina Rosillo-López is Associate Professor of Ancient History at the Universidad Pablo de Olavide (Seville).

1 Embedded, Eclectic, Elusive

The Real Estate Market and the Roman Economy

Marta García Morcillo and Cristina Rosillo-López

Abstract

The introduction examines the particular characteristics of immovable goods and their central role in the socioeconomic strategies and institutions that shaped notions of wealth and property rights in ancient Rome. In addition to direct transfers of properties and renting practices both in urban and rural contexts, the editors highlight the embeddedness of this singular commodity in different types of economic relationships, financial and commercial enterprises. The rich, albeit heterogenous corpus of available evidence illuminates the Romans' deep engagement with notions of risk, security and trust, with the complex and often symbiotic relationship between profit and speculation, valuation and pricing, as well as with the challenges and limits of the state's regulation of private affairs concerning immovables. The problems of housing and social inequalities that affected ancient, but also modern real estate markets, and the interactions between financial and non-financial motivations of actors are discussed in relationship to methodological approaches. The chapter includes an insight into contemporary debates, such as the limits of neoclassic economics, and the possibilities of applicability in studies of pre-modern societies of tools and frameworks of analysis developed from the dynamic field of economic sociology, such as economics of information and behavioural economics.

★★★

The possession, valuation, and transfer of immovable properties played a fundamental part in the economic and social life of ancient Romans. Real estate, broadly speaking, refers to land and any building or structure permanently attached to it. These forms of property can be primarily used for residential and commercial purposes, but they can also be part of more complex economic and financial enterprises, including speculative and credit transactions. As a non-homogeneous commodity that undergoes physical transformations, changes of uses and users, and that is also exposed to external damage throughout time, immovable goods are particularly challenging to appraise. In the case of residential properties, personal and emotional attachment to a particular house or building, but also subsistence needs turn these objects into complex subjects of economic and social analysis. These considerations are valid for both ancient and modern estate markets.

DOI: 10.4324/9781003187806-1

Real Estate and Elite Mentality

In ancient Rome, the investment in real estate, above all in productive rural properties, grounded a notion of private wealth that was largely forged by an elite mentality. This line of thought was substantiated by the relative economic security and long-term perspective of stable growth traditionally associated with farming-estates. This upper-class ideological discourse, which also permeated other social strata, was reinforced by a certain disregard towards the insecurities and the high risks of maritime trade, financial adventures, and other speculative businesses.[1] The second century BC treatise *On Agriculture* (*De agri cultura*), by Cato the Elder, is considered to be one of the seminal texts of this mentality.[2] In this influential work, Cato shapes a portrait of the ideal moral man, the *vir bonus*, who, as a worthy representative of the propertied class, effectively applies his social virtues and skills to his commitment as a good "farmer." The Catonian *dominus* and *pater familias* is an entrepreneur and economic actor who, in an era of expanding markets for Italian land products, searches for profit and surplus via capital investment, while nonetheless firmly observing a settled ecosystem of social and moral values that avoids unnecessary risks, wasteful expenditures, and dangerous temptations. *On Agriculture* reads as a very detailed guidance to landlords who are expected to be not only efficient managers and marketers of their produce, but also to have a good eye as purchasers of properties: "When you are thinking of acquiring a farm, keep in mind these points: that you be not over eager in buying nor spare your pains in examining, and that you consider it not sufficient to go over it once."[3] Cato further recommends to observe the suitability of the neighbourhood, the good climate and location, its accessibility, the supply of water and workers, as well as the condition of the buildings and equipment of the farm. Other important factors to bear in mind as a buyer are the history of earlier transactions of the property and the avoidance of farms that were sold too often in the past. The final advice is to buy from a good farmer and from a good builder (*de domino bono colono bonoque aedificatore melius emetur*).[4] The author confers relevance on good, well-built storage rooms for products such as oil and wine, as these could be very valuable when prices went up and had a favourable impact on the reputation of the landlord.[5]

Cato's depiction of the ideal landlord, which is largely replicated in later agronomic works, such as those by Varro and Columella, is thus that of a socially bounded manager who searches for sustained profitability, either via direct exploitation or by means of tenancy agreements. In these accounts, however, transfers of properties, although necessary, remain as a relatively secondary activity in relation to the main objective of acquiring and preserving a suitable estate, as well as securing and gradually expanding its productivity. In Cato's mindset, a landlord who voluntarily and frequently sells his estates to profit from such transfers cannot be a good, reliable *dominus*.

From a phenomenological perspective, and as a contrast to this rather one-sided picture of the landowner as gross-farmer, Cicero's and Pliny's letters provide invaluable first-hand testimonies for the active involvement of late republican and early imperial upper-class Romans in more diversified businesses activities involving sales, letting arrangements, and other kinds of property transfers, such as legacies and inheritances. These reflected not only a very dynamic and multifactual mobility of fortunes, but also wider financial and economic interests in which immobile assets played a central role, both as objectives of transactions themselves, and as forms of security for credit and other operations. Ancient letters also permit the rare opportunity to explore the reasoning, decision-making mechanisms and socioeconomic motivations, including self-justification, that informed the actors' investments in and engagement with residential, productive, urban, and rural properties. One of the objectives of the present volume is precisely to try to understand the embeddedness of activities revolving around this singular commodity within larger economic and social frameworks and relationships.[6]

Take, for instance, an epistle in which Pliny acts on behalf of his friend, the famous historian Suetonius. The letter is addressed to the friend of the seller of an estate, Baebius Hispanus, asking for a fair price that would avoid a bad deal for the purchaser, as appears to have happened before, due to (according to Pliny) a reproachable foolishness (*stultitia*) of the previous *dominus*.[7] In this way, Pliny ensures that his addressee, Baebius, and the unnamed seller, are accurately informed about his knowledge of the wrongdoings of the previous transfer of the *praedium* (implicitly, an unjustifiably high price), as well as his familiarity with the property itself, its convenient location near Rome (*vicinitas urbis*), its medium size, and ideal conditions for the modest purpose of the interested potential purchaser, a schoolman searching for a well-connected and pleasant farm. The need to meet an agreed fair price is alluded to twice more in the short letter, which reinforces Pliny's position as an informed party in the future negotiation.[8] This affair shows how the letter becomes an instrument for Pliny's negotiation of a favourable deal that is in his and Suetonius' interest. It issues the author's construction of what he thinks to be an ideal market price for the estate. This argument is backed by information that demonstrates his own knowledge of the property and the market.

Other than his role as expert agent, the letters show Pliny's direct engagement in the purchase of properties, as well as his acquaintance with factors that conditioned the deals. A letter in which he asks for the expert advice of his friend Calvisius Rufus provides a precious testimony of Pliny's own reasoning concerning the advantages and inconveniences of acquiring a property adjacent to his own that has been put up for sale. Among the first, the author refers to the costs that would be saved in labour, equipment, and maintenance. A potential inconvenience for this merging operation would be a hypothetical natural disaster that would damage the estate, the costs of which would certainly be minimised if the possessions were located in different places.[9] Pliny admits, however, that the main reason for his hesitation to purchase the estate lies in the pauperisation of the tenants (*coloni*) who, due to their inability to make a profit from the fertile estate in the past, were decapitalised by the previous owner, who sold the pledged property (*pignus*) that the renters had given to him as security (Plin. *Ep.* 3.19.4–6). This capital loss conditioned the perspective of profit for the tenants and for the future owner of the estate. Pliny shares his plan of recapitalising the tenants again, provided he could acquire the property for a reduced price of three million sestertii, instead of the five million sestertii it had once cost. The devaluation of the property is seen by Pliny as the result not only of the poverty of the tenants (*penuria colonorum*), but of the general inequality of the times (*communi temporis iniquitate*) that has provoked the fall in yields (*reditus agrorum*) and of prices (*Ep.* 3.19.7). Finally, Pliny explains to his addressee how he would raise the cash for the operation. Even if almost all of his capital is invested in land (*in praediis*), he admits having some money from loans (*aliquid tamen fenero*) and having no problem borrowing cash from his mother-in-law, as he could use it as if it were his own (*Ep.* 3.19.8).

This letter shows the direct effect of the productivity of an estate – and its fall – on its valuation and sale price, as well as other considerations concerning risks. Pliny also traces a normalised picture of lending and borrowing as a regular, acceptable strategy to fund such transfers, which often appeared as unexpected opportunities of the market.[10]

Pliny's familiarity with the price of estates was not only based on his own experience, but also on his understanding of the broader economic and political context. This is the theme of a letter to his friend Marcelinus Nepos, in which Pliny alerts him to the sudden rise of the price of land, particularly in the Roman suburbs – a very attractive residential area for upper-class Romans.[11] The reasons for this increase are identified by Pliny in a series of political measures undertaken by Trajan to stop candidates for the senate using their money for bribery. These imperial regulations included the obligation for anyone (e.g. provincials) who aspired to be eligible for a senator's position to invest at least one third of their patrimony in land in Rome and Italy, instead of using the country as a mere inn (*hospitium*) or lodging-stable (*stabulum*) as travellers do (*Ep.* 6.19.2–4). Accordingly, adds Pliny, the candidates "bid against each other for every estate they hear is for sale, and thus bring more into the market."[12] Finally, Pliny encourages Nepos – ironically or not – to sell any *praedia* he may own in Italy, as it is the right time to do so, whilst it is also a good moment to buy in the provinces, "for those same candidates are selling there, in order to buy here."[13] Trajan's political measure was certainly also linked with other socioeconomic initiatives, such as the *alimenta* programme and the associated loans to farmers, which were destined to revitalise the Italian land, help depauperated families, and boost the economy of Italy in the longer term.[14] A passage from the *Life of Marcus Aurelius* from the Historia Augusta mentions that the Antonine emperor reduced the imposed obligation for senators to invest in Italian land to one-fourth, thus confirming the continuity and impact of these regulations on urban and sub-urban estates, and implicitly on related industries and activities, such as the building sector and other subsidiary markets.[15] This later reform would have been a reaction to the unviable inflation of the price of estates, particularly in Rome and the *suburbium*.

Either way, this case study is particularly relevant not only to attest the effects of the interventionism of the state in private transactions, but also to trace the reactions to such regulations by those – like Pliny and his circle – who were directly or indirectly affected by them as prominent actors in the market. The breadth and depth of the state's interventionism – as external regulator or as interested party – in the real estate market is not just the topic of heated debates of twenty-first century economists but, as Pliny and other sources show, also impacted mentalities and conditioned behaviours in ancient Rome.[16]

Immobile assets were frequently transferred, divided, and reunified as the outcome of inheritances and legacies, a practice that was well established in society beyond the boundaries of close and extended family relationships. The introduction of a perceptual inheritance tax of 5 per cent (the *vicesima hereditatium*) by Augustus, which has managed to survive in varying forms through to the present day, signals the vitality of such transactions, which impacted heavily on the reputations of citizens, but also evidenced the long-term need of such regular cash incomes for the public finances of the state.[17] Both Cicero's and Pliny's correspondence, as well as legal literature, are enlightening and complementary documents that help to deepen our understanding of this social practice and its large impact on the continuity, but also the fragmentation, of fortunes.[18] This later outcome was common in cases of divided inheritances and legacies, as is discussed by Pliny himself in a letter to Calpurnius Fabatus, in which the senator feels obliged to justify his withdrawal from an agreement between coheirs to auction a property as a single unity (*Ep.* 7.11). Instead, Pliny decided to sell his part of the property (five-twelfths of the share) to Corellia, the sister of a good friend, to whom he felt morally compromised to help in her search for an estate in Comum, near to his own. Pliny's letter is a reply to a previous critical note by Fabatus, who appeared surprised that Pliny would have rejected a joint auction of the whole estate, which would have theoretically resulted in a large profit for Pliny and the rest of the coheirs.[19] Pliny's insistence on his social bonds of friendship against his perspectives of individual and collective wealth in the letter illustrate plainly that inheritances involving attractive real estate tested and challenged the balance between economic opportunities, social expectations, and the reputations of individuals. All in all, the evaluation of these documents deepens our understanding of the mentalities and mechanisms of decision making that shaped the engagement of upper-class Romans with immovable wealth.[20]

Immobile Properties, Housing, and the Intersectional Rental Market

Beyond this valuable, yet partial picture of the Roman real estate market from the perspective of the elite, other types of documents provide a more socially chromatic picture of economic activities linked to immobile goods. This is the case in particular with the rich papyrological evidence.[21] These documents fill important knowledge gaps about economic activities in Roman Egypt, including pricing, and agreements on the sale of houses, estates, and buildings, both in cities and villages and in rural contexts. They also bring to light a very dynamic rental market for residential houses and rooms, and for industrial and commercial buildings and facilities.[22] Contracts, receipts, letters, and other preserved public and private documents show interesting intersections between the real estate market, labour, and other economic sectors, as well as aspects such as demography, social mobility, and the impact of institutional enforcement and regulations on private businesses.[23]

Documents concerning the provincial census in Roman Egypt, for instance, which aimed principally at controlling, as accurately as possible, the population distribution for tax purposes, counted individual residents per house, e.g. they required declarations of the exact people who regularly lived in them, including the landlord, his household, and any tenants. Other than attesting the frequent residential rentals of houses and rooms, these documents also identified a significant mobility of population within and between regions of the vast Egyptian territory, mostly for work- and business-related purposes. An example of such a census return from Oxyrhynchus, dated on 25 November, 132 CE, includes an oath in the name of the emperor Hadrian in which the landlord declared that the house was uninhabited and that no foreigner, Roman, Alexandrian, Egyptian, freedman, or anyone else lived or was registered there (*P. Oxy.* III.480). Another document mentions the oath by the landlords of a vacant house, declaring that the tenant, an artisan, had left it and that no other property was linked with that person.[24] A census roll from Philadelphia (Arsinoites) (*P. Corn.* 22), dated during the first quarter of the first century CE, provides a long list of men living in the city yet registered in other places, including the profession of the majority of them (potter, flute-player, coppersmith, donkey-driver, water-guard, embalmer, etc.). The control of such a very dynamic seasonal rental market must have been a big challenge for the regional officers of the census.

As in the case discussed above regarding the rising price of properties in Rome and Italy following Trajan's impositions upon new senators, we find in the papyri similar signs of political decisions impacting the market. Take for instance the case of the city of Antinoopolis, which records a rather high average house price compared with other cities. This phenomenon appears to have been linked to the particular attractiveness of this city for non-residents, as the authorities granted special privileges to its citizens, including immunity from poll-taxes, since its foundation by Hadrian.[25] Public interventionism – in the form of tax impositions, exceptions, restrictions, privileges, control institutions, etc. – was thus, as it is today, a relevant factor to understand the dynamics of price formation, of supply and demand in the ancient Roman real estate market. Papyri also provide fertile ground for the use of solutions that aimed to overcome the problems of asymmetric information in contract arrangements, an issue that was aggravated by the high mobility of the working population in Roman Egypt. This is the case with recommendation letters required, as they are today, by lessors from tenants.[26] A long, highly detailed third-century (AD

240) financial account by the manager of a large private estate in Arsioites (Fayum) belonging to Valerius Titanianus, a high-ranked equestrian officer in the Severan period, lists the letting of rooms and facilities within the property to specialised workers for six months, until the end of the low water season.[27] The document mentions different payments, as well as rent-free agreements in some specific cases, for different types and numbers of rooms let. Rent-costs are specified in drachmae, but also in pigs, an important commodity for the estate and for the Egyptian economy.[28] The length of the contract can at times give us an indication of the specific use of the building. This is the case with a leasing agreement, from an unknown location, for a fish-shop for the duration of 62 days, which might coincide with the fishing season on the Nile.[29] Not surprisingly, the documents show on average that the rent of workshops and facilities for economic use tended to be higher than residential rent, or even than the sale price of houses in certain urban areas.

The study of the abundant papyrological material concerning the credit market shows that land and real estate, as an alternative to payments in kind or slaves, became the most common form of security in loans attested in Roman Egypt from the second half of the first century CE.[30] This coincides with a remarkable growth in attested loans and has also been linked to the creation, between 68 and 72 CE, of a public, administrative institution, the "archive of acquisitions" (*bibliotheke enkteseon*), which held registers of individual property rights over real estate and slaves. This institution played a fundamental role in clarifying property rights in sales and mortgages, and thus contributed to notably reducing transaction costs and information asymmetries in the real estate market.[31] It is also a relevant source of information on the important role of women as protagonists in the real property and credit markets.[32] The widespread use of real property as security for loans is further attested in antichretic loans, a popular formula that allowed creditors to occupy and use the pledged properties as replacement for interests owed by the debtor. This kind of agreement worked in practice as an alternative to cash circulation, and again attest to the vitality and variability of the rental market in Roman Egypt.[33]

The examples above allow us to merely scratch the surface of a vast theme that was fundamental to the understanding of the Roman's legal, social, and economic notion of individual wealth and property rights. Despite the problem of limited sources that often silences these activities, the evidence preserved illustrates how real estate fulfilled a great variety of uses that permeated social strata and economic sectors and activities. Both Pliny's letters and the Egyptian papyri demonstrate that real estate was a multi-layered commodity, which articulated social and economic investments, aspirations, and ambitions, whilst for the majority of the population – as is the case today – it primarily fulfilled the essential need of housing, whether permanent or temporary. As we will see throughout this volume, trust, security, and risk are crucial underlying concepts that shaped the Romans' mental and practical engagement with immobile goods, but also the construction of individual and collective identities.[34]

Real Estate: Historical and Methodological Perspectives

More than 40 years after the classic, collective work edited by Moses I. Finley, *Studies in Roman Property* (1976), the relevance of land and property tenure and ownership in Roman law, economy, and society is widely recognised in scholarship. However, it is remarkable that the enormous and transversal impact of the real estate market on Roman society has traditionally been studied mostly from particular angles rather than comprehensively, when it is not marginalised in economic research. This volume aims to redress this oversight, while offering an integral insight into this multisided socioeconomic sector, as well as incorporating literary, legal, epigraphic, papyrological, and archaeological sources. Furthermore, the book addresses a historiographical gap, namely the lack of a joint study of both residential and commercial real estate in the Roman world. Ultimately, this collective volume aims to provide tools and ideas that will hopefully inspire future research into historical perspectives of "real estate studies".

Previous scholarship regarding real estate in Roman antiquity has mainly concentrated on three areas. First, studies that focus on the renting of houses and apartments primarily cover landlords and tenants and the management of properties.[35] From a social inequality perspective, scholars have investigated the figure of the poor urban tenant and homeless people, namely those who could not even access the rental market.[36] Rental properties in Pompeii, Herculaneum, and Rome have been analysed from a social and architectural perspective, focusing not only on houses but also shops (*tabernae*) and rooms (*cenacula*).[37] These works have demonstrated the need to approach the topic of residential renting from an intersectional perspective that also integrates the information provided by material culture and archaeological evidence.

The second large area of past and present scholarly interest is the Roman villa in its various forms, from the suburban residential villas of the elite to large productive rural estates that played a central part in the Roman economy.[38] The importance of archaeology in understanding the functionality of slave-run *latifundia* and their economic impact has greatly influenced the study of this topic.[39] These studies have considered *villae* as independent entities, with no connection to the real estate market as a whole. An integrated evaluation of different types of evidence for the study of rural properties and the activities and actors linked to them, such as those proposed in the present volume, could contribute to reformulating traditional ideas concerning the division between urban and rural economies. Related to this aspect, the economic exploitation of estates, as well as questions of landownership and tenancy, have also been the subject of scholarly attention.[40] Further work has proposed the integration of *villae*, houses, and warehouses to form a more nuanced perspective.[41]

Finally, Roman law has been the focus of remarkable studies concerning property rights and its regulation, as well as the resolution of conflicts that affected different kinds of transfer, management, and the tenure of immobile assets. The law of ownership has been studied both for the late Roman

Republic and the Roman Principate.[42] Questions such as the concept of *familia urbana*, the division of property, co-ownership, legal conflicts, and the law of inheritance and its impact on the strategies of transmission of property have also been covered, together with the regulations of private buildings.[43] Tenancy from a legal perspective has also been extensively investigated.[44]

Another fruitful field of research has been the study of the complex legal framework of rural properties.[45] Related to this topic is the study of the economic impact of the transformation of land tenure and property rights during the Roman Empire and the spread of the colonate system.[46] A relevant subject that blurred the boundary between the public and private sphere, and which heavily impacted the Roman economy and the market of specific products, was the expansion, both in Italy and the provinces, of properties that ended up in possession of the Emperor.[47] The *Oxford Handbook of Roman Law and Society* (2016), and most recently the double volume *Roman Law and Economics* (2020) include some highly valuable contributions on regulations on immovable properties in Roman law, on possession in Roman Egypt, urban landlords and tenants, and the regulation of land tenure.[48] Finally, tenancy and price setting have recently been studied from the point of view of Roman law and, more specifically, regarding rent control measures established in the 40s BCE in Rome and Italy.[49]

The present volume builds upon these important contributions, as well as upon relevant research on transaction cost theory and the ancient economy.[50] Our work also stands on the shoulders of a recent collective monograph devoted to the economics of information, including the impact of uncertainty and information asymmetry on real estate.[51] This previous groundwork joins other critical approaches in questioning the narrow conception of markets as being exclusively shaped by supply and demand and by actors that always take rational decisions in order to maximise their profit.[52] Despite valid criticism, neoclassical economic models remain influential in areas such as valuation theory in the real estate sector today. The impact of non-financial motivations on housing decisions, for instance, is still surprisingly underrepresented in studies of price formation. Even if empirical research in areas such as economic sociology warned for years about the failures of a property market that is too reliant on inaccurate and limited systems of information, it was not until the subprime mortgage crisis of 2007 and the ensuing Great Recession that the fundamental deficiencies of a highly illiquid real estate market worldwide were exposed to the public.[53] The frequent misunderstanding of risks by overconfident investors and consumers, but also by external evaluators and appraisers using inappropriate models, has been identified as a major structural issue.[54] The crisis also revealed the extent to which this financial and economic sector suffers from a lack of effective institutional check-and-balance regulations to assure fairness and prevent dangerous price bubbles with devastating consequences, particularly for householders. A fundamental lesson from the previous decade is thus that a study of the real estate market needs to be approached and understood from a social and behavioural perspective.[55]

Phenomena such as the development of prices – and this is also applicable to historical research – cannot be fully comprehended without looking beyond rationalised normative models. Factors such as money illusion, confirmation bias, loss aversion, social expectations and pressure, and mental accounting are subjects of analysis of economic behavioural studies that have also gained weight in empiric and theoretical research of the real estate market.[56] Recent sociological research has also revealed the utility of social and historical perspectives in understanding this complex activity, as well as the multifaceted functions of immovable property for those involved in their transactions and management.[57]

The twenty-first century financial crisis and the Great Recession have also spurred historical perspectives of housing, especially those related to real estate prices and the cost of living. An analysis on the freehold property market in England between 1300 and 1500 has for instance revealed the large impact of speculative practices on real estate investments and transfers.[58] The availability of sources for the early modern period has allowed detailed studies for cities as diverse as Beijing, Toledo, Amsterdam, Milan, Old Warsaw, and Edirne.[59] These studies share the objective of putting the housing price boom of the previous decades into historical perspective, contradicting and offering valuable alternative interpretations to previous conceptions of housing prices as a "hockey stick," that is, a long stagnation followed by a sharp increase during the late twentieth to early twenty-first century.

Another relevant recent sociological trend regarding the real estate market, very much linked to the experiences of the Great Recession, focuses on the impact of housing policies on inequality. The specific impact of eviction, the lack of affordable housing and extreme poverty on families struggling to pay rent during the financial crisis of 2007–2008, has been also the focus of ethnographic research that has exposed the structural problem of inequality in the sector.[60] The housing crisis has been also studied as a way to reject the understanding of housing as commodity and call for an overhaul of the concept of the contemporary housing landscape.[61]

Beyond the obvious differences between capitalistic and ancient societies, Romans often faced similar problems and challenges in their engagement with urban and rural properties. The responses by public institutions reveal, for example, the ancient Romans' extraordinary capacity to offer effective solutions to complex issues concerning property rights, and to provide clear frameworks that distinguished and protected public and private property, as well as the ability to identify and regulate abusive and speculative practices. A diversified insight into the Roman real estate market provides fertile ground for tracing a wide variety of evidence that reveals different forms of investment, contractual arrangements, and notions of value, including sophisticated forms of abstraction attached to immobile assets.

As we have seen in the examples unpacked above, the ancient evidence shows the frequent interaction between real estate and other markets. This is the case for credit and other financial practices, as well as for the profitable hosting of commodities in warehouses – which was a popular business in major cities and harbour towns, but also, as shown in Cato's *De agri cultura* as well as by other sources – in productive rural properties. The challenges of urban housing and the importance of the rental market in Roman antiquity offer a valuable, comparative historical framework of analysis for similar problems faced within modern societies.

An Essential Good and a Multilayered Commodity: This Volume

The contributions that shape this volume offer different perspectives and methodological approaches to this inexhaustive area of study. The primary objective of our work is to demonstrate, through discerning case studies and a wide-ranging framework of analysis, that Romans of all social ranks had an intensive engagement with real estate and that this interaction defined not only their wealth and legal status, but also their identity as private individuals, as well as in relation to the community and the state. The study of property as being the subject and instrument of economic activity also offers the opportunity to deepen our understanding of the Roman economic mentality and of fundamental emotional, moral and legal concepts such as property rights, risk, fear, speculation, security, and profit.

The book is divided into five Parts. The first (Concepts and Control) offers two overarching chapters that discuss two fundamental aspects of ancient and modern real property markets. Rosillo-López (Chapter 2) addresses the question of the degree of intervention of the Roman state within the real estate market, both under the Republic and the Principate. Even nowadays, state intervention remains a taboo topic in many countries, and many economists believe it will have negative consequences. However, the Great Recession of 2007 and beyond saw a change in many of these considerations; thus, a re-consideration of the role of the state from a historical perspective is needed. This chapter studies three instances of government intervention regarding private real estate, specifically residential, considering whether the intervention was exceptional or structural: 1) taxation on real estate; 2) laws limiting real estate speculation; and 3) expenditures by emperors. Finally, it addresses how the jurists considered that the government had an interest in the protection of real estate. The author argues that throughout its history, the Roman government made a clear point of upholding a set of laws and procedures that promoted real estate as a financial and private sphere. Roman law recognised real estate as a sector with special and specific needs, which differed from other areas of law, and which the government had a particular interest in protecting.

The next chapter, by García Morcillo (Chapter 3), investigates the Romans' conceptualisation of different notions of value attached to non-homogeneous and specifically immobile properties. It also evaluates the challenges of applying such concepts of worth in practical situations, such as the valuations required for measuring individual wealth, property transfers, credit activities, and conflicts of property that required concrete solutions by judges and public authorities. The author discusses value theory from different angles, including behavioural economics, and reflects upon how the ancient paradigm can contribute to a better understanding of current debates about the credibility of valuers and valuations in modern real estate markets.

Part II (Land, Property, and Law) encompasses two chapters that focus on economic strategies linked to land and rural estates. Considering B. Shaw's influential article "Did the Romans Have a Future?", which argues that the Romans' perception of the future made them incapable of engaging in strategic long-term economic planning, Kehoe (Chapter 4) studies how economic actors (both the *fiscus* and private property owners) used land to achieve specific financial goals, i.e. how land acted as a resource for long-term financial objectives, and which factors limited their ability to do so. Such strategies are relevant because they affected the market for agricultural land and other forms of real estate. Land was the most important financial resource for both the imperial government and for private landowners because of its capacity to provide stable revenues. When property owners pledged their land to secure credit, this was in all likelihood a last resort when there was no alternative (such as savings or cutting back on spending) to meet a financial obligation. Furthermore, property owners were unwilling to commit their land to leverage long-term loans; the Egyptian papyri show that land was mainly employed as a collateral for short-term loans. Despite those limits, the Roman government used land to fund in the long-term its alimentary foundations or for private property owners to support towns, trusts, and private foundations. This study shows how, in an economy with limited options for investing wealth and minimal economic growth from one year to the next, land represented the most important financial resource for securing the future.

Capogrossi Colognesi (Chapter 5) investigates how legal sources discuss the strategies by large-estate proprietors of expanding their domains through accumulative mechanisms, rather than through the substantial modification of their existing production structures, considering what might be called "minor exchanges," i.e. those involving only portions of large estates. These *fundi* in Imperial times are conceived as a set of *partes*, resulting from the progressive acquisition of neighbouring parcels of land, combined to form larger units and considered to be various estate units of the same owner as separate entities, even in cases where land units were adjacent to each other. The autonomous management of various properties is also confirmed by the particular emphasis that Roman jurists placed on internal distributions within larger estates, as well as on the single *partes fundi*. An analysis of this topic through the Trajanic Table of Veleia, which lists numerous landed properties in the two *municipia* of Placentia and Veleia that were pledged as security for loans made by the imperial administration to its owners, allows us to clarify the organisational system of landed properties and its economic and administrative implications. The lack of transformation into larger land units for the majority of single *fundi* likely facilitated the quantity and speed of land estate circulation.

Andreau (Chapter 6) investigates the unique information concerning real estate transfers and management in the Campanian Wax-Tablets during the middle of the first century CE. These documents regard the Pompeian archive of the banker Jucundus, the tablets from the Sulpicii, financers from Puteoli, and the private archives of individuals found in Herculaneum. The latter are particularly useful to identify properties in the region. It is remarkable that rentals are barely present, while there are records of the sale and auction of *fundi*. At Herculaneum, the market for the sale of agricultural land and land for stock-raising was relatively active.

The third Part of the volume (Social Status, Forms of Investment, and the Roman Elite) discusses the engagement of the Roman elite with real estate both as an objective of investments, but also as spatial platforms of economic information and activity. Two chapters are set in the late Republic. Koedijk (Chapter 7) ponders the lack of estate agents in the ancient world, an absence that, Finley thought, prevented a property market from emerging. Koedijk surveys the process of property exchange in the letters of Cicero and argues that the information problem created by the absence of estate agents was overcome in part by social relations that may have usurped many of the functions of estate agents, and which consequently played a major role in how properties were found, how the price was determined, where the money came from, and how the quality was assessed. However, even if many of an estate agent's functions could be otherwise fulfilled, this does not mean that the Roman property market operated along the same lines as markets with estate agents (such as modern markets) do. The Romans faced much higher levels of uncertainty, which affected the efficiency of the market and their rate of success.

Pina Polo (Chapter 8) considers Italian *villae* of the Roman elite as an expression of status and self-representation, since they afforded them contact with eminent neighbours, making it possible to develop an intense social life, almost as if the holidaymaker lived in a miniature Rome. In moments of political crisis, access to reliable information and a continuous flow of news was relevant, as was the possibility to have face-to-face meetings, to talk and discuss in person. A study of the period of April–July 44 BCE shows the constant mutual visits and invitations to each other's homes, which meant long conversations that, as with the letters, dealt with both personal matters and current political issues. Such meetings allowed for first-hand information, but also for an exchange of views and attempts to directly or indirectly influence a certain trend of opinion. The underlying idea that permeates the chapter is that the intensive personal and social interactions generated by the location, use, and connectivity of these villas not only turned information into a valuable commodity, but would have also inevitably impacted the economic value of these properties.

Marzano (Chapter 9) critically revisits the concept of luxury villas and their economic rationality, focusing on the case of the luxury maritime villa of Positano, on the Amalfi side of the Sorrento Peninsula. This villa was built without relevant natural resources, presented very little land that could afford only limited agriculture, and could be reached only by sea. Pondering the logistics of construction and the shipping of building materials, Marzano discusses the Positano villa in the broader context of the real estate market along the Bay of Naples and the Sorrento Peninsula, in comparison with rural properties in Campania, and in relation to coastal connectivity.

In their chapter, Caldelli and Ricci (Chapter 10) propose a long-term analysis through the history of a relevant Italian senatorial family, the Neratii, and their engagement with real estate. The chapter studies the acquisition, maintenance, and consolidation of properties by the Neratii in central and southern Italy throughout the second and third centuries CE. The Neratii followed the habitual pattern of high-ranking families of combining rural land holdings with large urban real estate properties. Furthermore, the Neratii remained loyal and present to their home territory, Samnium, and were active in municipal public life and patronage activities, which contributed to consolidating their real estate investments, and in turn allowed them to gather support and resources in order to re-emerge as relevant players in Roman politics during the fourth century.

Part IV (Urban Businesses) discusses profitable investments in productive real estate in the city. Maschek (Chapter 11) analyses the financial opportunities of the rental market in Late Republican Central Italy from the perspective of "predatory urban practices" by financial elites. How, on a structural level, did investment in urban development create both wealth and destitution, and what, if any, was the systemic link between the two? Maschek focuses on *tabernae*, that is, spaces for production, retail, and rental accommodation, as a relevant factor in real estate development and investment, and estimates the necessary net profits, prices, and rent to create a good return on investment for the owner. An estimation of a 'subsistence basket' and its relationship to earnings sheds light on the economic potential of predatory urban practices: many of the people who lived in rental accommodation bought goods in *tabernae*, and consumed food and drink in local bars, and thus generated a significant amount of surplus capital.

Mataix (Chapter 12) addresses the role of warehouses in the real estate market and the legal responses to these multifunctional facilities. In addition to storing goods, warehouses had a wide variety of functions: retail and wholesale outlets, as well as other complex operations, also revealing the changes in the cycles of trade and storage. Recent excavations carried out at Portus, the imperial harbour of Rome, have revealed archaeological anomalies in one cell of the group of warehouses constructed during the reign of Trajan, suggesting that activities other than storage were perhaps carried out in this cell. This would imply the development of legal remedies in the contract of *locatio conductio* (lease and hire) to take these other activities into account.

The fifth and final Part (Properties Beyond Italy) concerns real estate in two very different regions of the empire: one well-attested and with abundant sources (Egypt), and another with fewer sources of information (the north-western provinces of the Roman Empire). Piacentin (Chapter 13) studies patterns of acquisition and exploitation of imperial property in the north-western provinces of the Roman Empire (Gallia Narbonensis, Gallia Lugdunensis, Aquitania, Belgica, Germania Inferior, Germania Superior, Britannia), examining a number of property transactions (i.e. confiscations and inheritance) between the emperor, his property (*patrimonium*), and individuals. The chapter also discusses whether the emperor had an active role in the provincial estate markets. From an analysis of epigraphic, literary, and archaeological evidence, it emerges that the emperor rarely intervened in the provincial real estate markets, and rather exploited pre-existing economic activities such as the rich mineral resources of these provinces.

Kelly (Chapter 14) describes the real estate markets of Roman Egypt (1 to 274 CE), dealing with both agricultural land and housing, examining market data on the demographics and locations of the participants, the seasonality of transactions, the formats of prices and rents, the transactional costs, and the likely investment return to the owner. He argues that there is little to no evidence for the exercise of financial rationality (as opposed to actions based on reciprocity and redistribution) in real estate, in contrast to the market for agricultural land, which was driven by financial rationality. The real estate market had several institutional constraints, such as the level of taxes and other frictional costs, such as legal or registration fees, and the difficulties with regard to information exchange, which made it a less attractive market than leasing land (which had low frictional costs and sufficient information exchange).

The multisided research on real estate as both commodity and as an economic and socially embedded investment and resource discussed in this volume suggests some captivating ideas about the ways Romans expressed, negotiated, and projected notions of short-term and permanent possession, of wealth and business ventures, and of protection and security in the long term. The conceptualisation of immovable property, particularly land and productive estates, as the essential expression of personal fortune was, despite its exposure to risks, devaluations, and destruction, inevitably linked to the desire to transcend the possessor's ephemeral existence. And yet, at the end of the day, as Charon reminds us in Lucian's implacable dialogue about the inexorability of death and its aftermath: "Nothing of the pomp of this world will endure; nor can any man take anything hence when he dies. He will go naked out of the world, and his house and his lands and his gold will be another's, and ever another's."[62]

Notes

1 The acquisition of real estate as a social aspiration, and the radical contrast to the risks of sea trade, are central themes in Roman literature. The fictitious freedman Trimalchio from Petronius' *Satyricon*, who enriched himself through the investment in trade ventures and later embraced the economic stability and more acceptable lifestyle of the landlord, embodied the typical traits of this ideological discourse on social ascension, see Veyne 1961; D'Arms 1981: 97–119; and Grosdemouge 2008. This discourse is also explored in Lucian's *Navigium* 20.

2 In the famous Preface of *De agri cultura*, Cato labels moneylending as a profitable, yet hazardous and morally dubious activity, in contrast to the virtues of farming. Cicero develops this ideological contraposition in *Off.* 1.150–151.

3 Cato, *Agr.* 1: *Praedium quom parare cogitabis, sic in animo habeto, uti ne cupide emas neve opera tua parcas visere et ne satis habeas semel circumire. Quotiens ibis, totiens magis placebit quod bonum erit.*

4 Cato, *Agr.* 1.2–5.

5 Cato, *Agr.* 3.2: *Patrem familiae villam rusticam bene aedificatam habere expedit, cellam oleariam, vinariam, dolia multa, uti lubeat caritatem expectare: et rei et virtuti et gloriae erit.* On the importance of storage as a secure and profitable investment, see Mataix Ferrándiz (Chapter 12) in this volume (with earlier bibliography).

6 On Cicero's letters and his intensive engagement with urban and rural real estate transactions and investments, see the contributions by Koedijk (Chapter 7) and Pina Polo (Chapter 8), with earlier bibliographical references.

7 Plin. *Ep.* 1.24.1–2: *Tranquillus contubernalis meus vult emere agellum, quem venditare amicus tuus dicitur. 2 Rogo cures, quanti aequum est emat; ita enim delectabit emisse. Nam mala emptio semper ingrata, eo maxime quod exprobrare stultitiam domino videtur.*

8 Plin. *Ep.* 1.24.3–4. The expressions '*si modo arriserit pretium*' and '*tam salubriter emerit*' signal his determination to only accept a fair, and thus cheap, price for the property.

9 Plin. *Ep.* 3.19.1–4. On this famous letter and the theme of the expansion of estates, see Capogrossi Colognesi (Chapter 5) in this volume

10 On the management of risks and the perspective of the yield as the main criterion to justify the purchase, see Kehoe 1993, who describes Pliny's support for the tenants as a conservative strategy to manage the production of estates. For Pliny's concern about the rent of his estates and the capacity of the tenants to face bad vintages, see also *Ep.* 10.8. On Pliny's estates and their management, see Martin 1967; De Neeve 1990.

11 Plin. *Ep.* 6.19.1: *Scis tu accessisse pretium agris, praecipue suburbanis? Causa subitae caritatis res multis agitata sermonibus.*

12 Plin. *Ep.* 6.19.5: *Concursant ergo candidati; certatim quidquid venale audiunt emptitant, quoque sint plura venalia efficiunt* (transl. W. Melmoth).

13 Plin. *Ep.* 6.19.6: *Proinde si paenitet te Italicorum praediorum, hoc vendendi tempus tam hercule quam in provinciis comparandi, dum idem candidati illic vendunt ut hic emant. Vale.* (transl. W. Melmoth)

14 See Sirago 1958; Martin 1967; Lo Cascio 2000: 223–283. On the Veleia tablets as testimonies of developments in the conception and division of estates and immobile properties in Italy, see Capogrossi Colognesi (Chapter 5), this volume. The chapter by Dennis Kehoe (Chapter 4) also discusses this initiative and other alimentary foundations as long-term financial strategies based on landownership.

15 Hist. Aug., *Aur.* 11.8. On the connections between these government impositions and the archaeologically attested transformation of residential constructions and *villae* in Rome and the suburbs, see De Neeve 1985: 90–91; Morley 1996: 90–94 and Lo Cascio 2003.

16 See in particular the chapter by Rosillo-López (Chapter 2) on state interventionism.

17 On the inheritance and other taxes affecting immobile property, see the chapter by Rosillo-López (Chapter 2) in this volume (with further bibliography).

18 On inheritances as a source of wealth, see Corbier 1985. For the social and legal impact of succession laws and the practice of inheritance and legacies, see Watson 1971; Saller 1994.

19 Fabatus, in Pliny's words, mentions a hypothetical benefit of 900,000 sestertii for his 5/12 share, instead of the 700,000 that Pliny effectively obtained for the sale. This commentary is directly linked with another letter to Corellia herself, in which he refers to her insistence to pay to him 900,000 and not 700,000, as it would suit

better the corresponding twentieth part (*vicesima*) to be paid to the *publicani* (the inheritance tax), *Ep.* 7.14. On this case, see Sherwin-White 1966, 414–418.

20 On the economic mentalities and ideologies of ancient Romans, see Andreau, France and Pittia 2004.

21 See Kelly (Chapter 14), this volume.

22 On estate management and sales see Rathbone 1991 and Kehoe 1992. On the rental market in Roman Egypt see Rowlandson 1996.

23 Bagnall and Frier 1994. On the interactions between public authorities and private actors in letting agreements, see Kehoe 1995.

24 *P. Oxy.* XIII 2669 (AD 41–54). On both documents, see Gendy 1990: 188–193.

25 For instance, *P. Lond.* 1164, which includes several sales of houses and parts of houses among the transactions conducted through the Bank of Anoubion. Cf. Gendy 1990: 174–175. On the special status of Antinoopolis and its privileges, see Malouta 2009.

26 *SB VI 9636* (AD.136) is another example of a recommendation letter. This letter tells us that a veteran leased a house for two years in Karanis.

27 *P. Mich.* XI 620. On other documents related with this estate and on Titanianus, who held important equestrian offices under the Severans, including the post of *praefectus vigilum* in Rome, see Rathbone 1991: 56–58.

28 Payments in kind were in some cases an accepted alternative to cash.

29 *P. Strassb.*VI 569 (AD 162).

30 See Lerouxel 2016: 115–118.

31 The economic impact of the *bibliotheke enkteseon* has been extensively studied by Lerouxel 2015, 2016: 145–192; 2021. See also Kehoe (Chapter 4), this volume.

32 See Hobson 1983 and Lerouxel 2006.

33 An early example of an antichretic loan, *BGU IV 1115* (13 BC), shows a contract from Alexandria according to which the creditor, Theon, had the right to rent cheaper a room within a flat as a replacement for the interests owed to him by the debtor/lessor Aristonikos.

34 The concept of long-term investment and planning in connection with ideas of risk and security are the focus of Kehoe's chapter in this volume (Chapter 4).

35 Frier 1977, 1978, 1980; Garnsey 1976; Guilhembet 2006.

36 Van der Bergh 2003; Rosillo-López 2021b.

37 Pirson 1999; Priester 2002.

38 On the *villae* of the Ciceronian elite, see the classic contribution by Rawson 1976 and Frier 1978.

39 Carandini and Ricci 1985; Mielsch 1987; Lafon 2001; Marzano 2007.

40 Kehoe 1992 and Rowlandson 1996 on Roman Egypt; Erdkamp, Verboven and Zuiderhoek 2015 for the entire Roman world.

41 Van Oyen 2020.

42 On the sale of properties and Roman law, see Crook 1976. For the Republic: Watson 1968; Craver 2010. Principate: Dubouloz 2011 (see also Dubouloz 2016 on what constituted an *aedificium* in Roman law).

43 Dubouloz 2011. Regulations: Martin 1989; Saliou 1994.

44 Du Plessis 2006 and 2012; see also the double edited volume by Dari-Mattiaci and Kehoe 2020a, 2020b.

45 Capogrossi Colognesi 1969, 1976 and 1999; Kehoe 2007.

46 Lo Cascio 1997.

47 See Maiuro 2012 and the fundamental research by the ERC project Patrimonivm 2017–22, e.g. Dalla Rosa 2019.

48 Du Plessis, Ando and Tuori 2016; Dari-Mattiaci and Kehoe 2020a, 2020b (vols I and II).

49 Willems 2019. Rent control: Rosillo-López 2022.

50 See foremost Kehoe, Ratzan, and Yiftach 2015.

51 Rosillo-López and García Morcillo 2021, eds; Rosillo-López 2021.

52 Following a New Institutional Economics perspective, the notion of bounded rationality, which assumes the limitations of actors in the acquisition and use of knowledge, has been researched in relation to the modern property market (see De Bruin and Flint-Hartle 2003), and also tested in studies on Roman law and the rural economy, see Kehoe 2007; Frier and Kehoe 2007.

53 See Black, Brown, Diaz, Gibler, and Grissom 2003.

54 For a critical approach to valuation systems applied in the residential property market, see for instance Daly, Gronow, Jenkins, and F. Plimmer 2003. The challenges of property valuation are discussed by García Morcillo (Chapter 3), this volume.

55 See García Morcillo 2020 on the applicability of behavioural economics to the purchase of real estate in ancient Rome attested in Cicero's letters.

56 On loss aversion and anchoring in pricing and the behaviour of sellers and purchasers, see Genesove and Mayer 2001; Bokhari and Geltner 2011. On money illusion and housing, see Brunnermeier and Julliard 2008.

57 Salzman and Zwinkels 2017, with extensive bibliography.

58 Bell, Brooks, and Killick 2018.

59 Beijing: Raff, Wachter and Yan 2013. Toledo: Drelichman and González Agudo 2014. Amsterdam: Eichholtz, Straetmans and Theebe 2012. Milan: Barbot and Peroco 2019. Old Warsaw: Łozowski 2018. Edirne: Karagedikli and Tunçer 2021.

60 Desmond 2016.

61 Madden and Marcuse 2016.

62 Luc. *Char.* 20: οὐδὲν τῶν ἐνταῦθα σεμνῶν ἀΐδιόν ἐστιν, οὐδ' ἂν ἀπαγάγοι τις αὐτῶν τι σὺν αὑτῷ ἀποθανών, ἀλλ' ἀνάγκη τὸν μὲν γυμνὸν οἴχεσθαι, τὴν οἰκίαν δὲ καὶ τὸν ἀγρὸν καὶ τὸ χρυσίον ἀεὶ ἄλλων εἶναι καὶ μεταβάλλειν τοὺς δεσπότας (transl. Fowler, H. W. and F. G.). This research was financed by the project "El sector inmobiliario en el mundo romano: un análisis económico; s. II a.C.-s. II d.C." (HAR2016-76882-P), Ministerio de Ciencia, Innovación y Universidades, Spain.

References

Andreau, J., France, J., Pittia, S., eds. (2004) *Mentalités et choix économiques des romains.* Bordeaux: Ausonius.

Bagnall, R.S. and Frier, B.W. (1994) *The Demography of Roman Egypt.* Cambridge: Cambridge University Press.

Barbot, M., and Peroco, M. (2019) Does a Good Neighbour Have a Price?: Rental Prices and Residential Choices in 16th-17th Century Milan. In: E. Canepari, M. Crisci, eds. *Moving around in Town: Practices, Pathways and Contexts of Intra-Urban Mobility from 1600 to The Present Day.* Rome: Viella, 23–38.

Bell, A.R., Brooks, C. and Killick, H. (26 March, 2018) *The First Real Estate Bubble? Land Prices and Rents in Medieval England C. 1300–1500.* Available at SSRN: https://ssrn.com/abstract=3149574 or doi:10.2139/ssrn.3149574

Bergh, R. van der (2003) The Plight of the Poor Urban Tenant. *Revue internationale des droits de l'antiquité* 50, 443–478.

Black, R.T., Brown, M.G., Diaz, J., Gibler, K.M., and Grissom, T.V. (2003) Behavioral Research in Real Estate: A Search for the Boundaries. *Journal of Real Estate Practice and Education* 6. 1, 85–112.

Bokhari, S. and Geltner, D. (2011) Loss Aversion and Anchoring in Commercial Real Estate Pricing: Empirical Evidence and Price Index Implications. *Real Estate Economics* 39. 4, 635–670.

Brunnermeier, M.K. and Julliard, C. (2008) Money Illusion and Housing Frenzies. *Review of Financial Studies* 21. 1, 135–180.

Capogrossi Colognesi, L. (1969) *La struttura della proprietà e la formazione dei iura praediorum nell'età repubblicana*, vol 1. Milan: Giuffrè.

Capogrossi Colognesi, L. (1976) *La struttura della proprietà e la formazione dei iura praediorum nell'età repubblicana*, vol 2. Milan: Giuffrè.

Capogrossi Colognesi, L. (1999) *Proprietà e diritti reali: usi e tutela della proprietà fondiaria nel diritto romano*. Rome: Il Cigno Galileo Galilei.

Carandini, A. and Ricci, A. (1985) *Una villa schiavistica nell'Etruria Romana*. Modena: Panini.

Corbier, M. (1985) Idéologie et practique de l´héritage (Ier s. av. J.'C.). *Index* 13, 501–528.

Courrier, C. (2014) *La plèbe de Rome et sa culture (fin du IIe siècle av. J.-C. – fin du Ier siècle ap. J.-C.)*. Rome: École Française de Rome.

Craver, S.E (2010) Urban Real Estate in Late Republican Rome. *Memoirs of the American Academy in Rome* 55, 135–158.

Crook, J. (1976) Classical Roman Law and the Sale of Land. In: M.I. Finley, ed. *Studies in Roman Property*, Cambridge: Cambridge University Press, 71–83.

D'Arms, J.H. (1981) *Commerce and Social Standing in Ancient Rome*. Cambridge, MA: Harvard University Press.

Dalla Rosa, A. (2019) Imperial Properties and Civic Territories: Between Economic Interests and Internal Diplomacy. In: F. Luciani and E. Migliario, eds. *Boundaries of Territories and Peoples in Roman Italy and Beyond*. Bari: Edipuglia, 105–120.

Daly, J., Gronow, S., Jenkins, D., and Plimmer, F. (2003) Consumer Behaviour in the Valuation of Residential Property: A Comparative Study in the U.K., Ireland and Australia. *Property Management* 21. 5, 295–314.

Dari-Mattiaci, G., and Kehoe, D.P. (2020a) *Roman Law and Economics: Institutions and Organisations*, vol I, Oxford: Oxford University Press.

Dari-Mattiaci, G., and Kehoe, D.P. (2020b) *Roman Law and Economics: Exchange. Ownership, and Disputes*, vol. II, Oxford: Oxford University Press.

De Bruin, A. and Flint-Hartle, S. (2003) A Bounded Rationality Framework for Property Investment Behaviour. *Journal of Property Investment and Finance* 21, 271–284.

De Neeve, P.W. (1985) The Price of Agricultural Land in Roman Italy and the Problem of. Economic Rationalism. *Opus* 4, 77–109.

De Neeve, P.W. (1990) A Roman Landowner and his Estates: Pliny the Younger. *Athenaeum* 78, 363–402.

Desmond, M. (2016) *Evicted. Poverty and Profit in the American City*. New York: Crown Publishers.

Drelichman, M., González Agudo, D. (2014) Housing and the Cost of Living in Early Modern Toledo. *Explorations in Economic History* 54, 27–47.

Dubouloz, J. (2011) *La propriété immobilière à Rome et en Italie, Ier-Ve siècles*. Rome: École française de Rome.

Dubouloz, J. (2016) Définir ce qu'est un *aedificium* dans la jurisprudence romaine: enjeux théoriques et pratiques. In: R. Renaud, J. Beaucamp, eds. *Dire l'architecture dans l'Antiquité, Paris-Aix-en-Provence, Karthala-MMSH*. Paris: Maison méditerranéenne des sciences de l'homme, 321–341.

Du Plessis, P. (2006) Janus in the Roman Law of Urban Lease. *Historia* 55, 48–63.

Du Plessis, P. (2012) *Letting and Hiring in Roman Legal Thought: 27 BCE–284 CE*. Leiden: Brill.

Du Plessis, P., Ando, C., and Tuori, K. eds. (2016) *Oxford Handbook of Roman Law and Society*. Oxford: Oxford University Press.

Eichholtz, P., Straetmans, S. and Theebe, M. (2012) The Amsterdam Rent Index: The Housing Market and the Economy, 1550–1850. *Journal of Housing Economics* 21, 269–282.

Erdkamp, P., Verboven, K., and Zuiderhoek, A. eds. (2015) *Ownership and Exploitation of Land and natural Resources in the Roman World*. Oxford: Oxford University Press.

Finley, M.I., ed. (1976) *Studies in Roman Property*. Cambridge: Cambridge University Press.

Frier, B.W. (1977) The Rental Market in Early Imperial Rome. *The Journal of Roman Studies* 67, 27–37.

Frier, B.W. (1978) Cicero's Management of his Urban Properties. *Classical Journal* 74. 1, 1–6.

Frier, B.W. (1980) *Landlords and Tenants in Imperial Rome*. Princeton: Princeton University Press.

Frier, B.W. and Kehoe, D.P. (2007) Law and Economic Institutions. In: W. Scheidel, I. Morris, and R.P. Saller, eds. *Cambridge Economic History of the Greco-Roman World*, Cambridge: Cambridge University Press, 113–143.

García Morcillo, M. (2020) Mentality, Motivation and Economic Decision-Making in Ancient Rome: Cicero and Tullia's Shrine. *The Economic History Review* 73. 3, 623–643.

Garnsey, P. (1976) Urban Property Investment. In: M.I. Finley, ed. *Studies in Roman Property*, Cambridge: Cambridge University Press, 123–136.

Gendy, I.A. (1990) *Economic Aspects of Houses and Housing in Roman Egypt* (PhD thesis University College London).

Genesove, D. and Mayer, C.J. (2001) Loss Aversion and Seller Behavior: Evidence from the Housing Market. *The Quarterly Journal of Economics*, 116. 4, 1233–1260.

Guilhembet, J.-P. (2006) Acquérir, louer ou négocier des biens immobiliers de prestige à Rome à la fin de la République et aux premiers siècles de l'Empire. In: F. Lecocq, ed., *Sur la ville de Rome*. Caen: Maison de la recherche en sciences humaines de Caen, 91–197.

Grosdemouge, F. (2008) L'accession á la richesse chez Pétrone. In: A. Gonzales, J. Annequin, eds. *A La fin du statut servile? Affranchissement, libération, abolition*. Volume I, Besançon: Presses Universitaires de Franche-Compté, 241–250.

Hobson, D. (1983) Women as Property Owners in Roman Egypt. *TAPA* 113, 311–321.

Karagedikli, G., and Tunçer, A.C. (2021) House Prices in the Ottoman Empire: Evidence from Eighteenth-century Edirne. *The Economic History Review* 74. 1, 6–33.

Kehoe, D.P. (1992) *Management and Investment on Estates in Roman Egypt during the Early Empire*. Bonn: R. Habelt.

Kehoe, D.P. (1993) Investment in Estates By Upper-Class Landowners in Early Imperial Italy: The Case of Pliny the Younger. In: *De agricultura. In Memoriam Pieter Willem de Neeve*, Amsterdam: Gieben, 214–237.

Kehoe, D.P. (1995) Legal Institutions and the Bargaining Power of the Tenant in Roman Egypt. *APF* 41, 232–262.

Kehoe, D.P. (2007) *Law and the Rural Economy in the Roman Empire*. Ann Arbor: University of Michigan Press.

Kehoe, D.P., Ratzan, D., and Yiftach, U. (2015) *Law and Transaction Costs in the Ancient Economy*. Ann Arbor: University of Michigan Press.

Lafon, X. (2001) *Villa maritima. Recherches sur les villas littorales de l'Italie romaine*. Rome: École française de Rome.

Lerouxel, F. (2006) Les femmes sur le marché du crédit en Egypte romaine (30 avant J.-C.-284 après J.-C.): une approche néo-institutionnaliste. *Cahiers du centre de Recherches Historiques* 36, 121–136.
Lerouxel, F. (2015) The βιβλιοθήκη ἐγκτήσεων and Transaction Costs in the Credit Market of Roman Egypt (30 B.C.E. to ca. 170 C.E.). In: D. Kehoe, D. Ratzan, and U. Yiftach, eds. *Law and Transaction Costs in the Ancient Economy*. Ann Arbor: University of Michigan Press, 162–184.
Lerouxel, F. (2016) *Le marché du crédit dans le monde romain*. Rome: École française de Rome.
Lerouxel, F. (2021) Marriage and Asymmetric Information on the Real Estate Market in Roman Egypt. In: C. Rosillo-López and M. García Morcillo, eds. *Managing Information in the Roman Economy*. Cham: Palgrave Macmillan, 135–156.
Lo Cascio, E., ed. (1997) *Terre, propietari e contadini dell'Impero romano. Dall'affitto agrario al colonato tardoantico*. Rome: NIS.
Lo Cascio, E. (2000) *Il Princeps e il suo impero. Studi di storia amministrativa e finanziaria romana*. Bari: Edipuglia.
Lo Cascio, E. (2003) L'economia dell'Italia romana nella testimonianza di Plinio. In: L. Castagna and E. Lefèbre, eds. *Plinius der Jüngere und seine Zeit*. Munich: De Gruyter, 281–302.
Łozowski, P. (2018) The Social Structure of the Real Estate Market in Old Warsaw in the Years 1427–1527. *Economic History of Developing Regions* 33. 2, 147–182.
Madden, D. and Marcuse, P. ed. (2016) *In Defense of Housing. The Politics of Crisis*. London: Verso.
Maiuro, M. (2012) *Res Caesaris. Ricerche sulla proprietà imperiale nel Principato*. Bari: Edipuglia.
Malouta, M. (2009) Antinoite Citizenship under Hadrian and Antoninus Pius. A Prosopographical Study of the First Thirty Years of Antinoopolis. *The Bulletin of the American Society of Papyrologists* 46, 81–96.
Martin, R. (1967) Pline le Jeune et les problèmes économiques de son temps. *REA* 69, 62–97.
Martin, S.D. (1989) *The Roman Jurists and the Organization of Private Building in the Late Republic and Early Empire*. Brussels: Latomus.
Marzano, A. (2007) *Roman Villas in Central Italy: A Social and Economic History*. Leiden: Brill.
Mielsch, H. (1987) *Die römische Villa: Architektur und Lebensform*. Munich: Beck.
Morley, N. (1996) *Metropolis and Hinterland. The City of Rome and the Italian Economy 200 BC–AD 200*. Cambridge: Cambridge University Press.
Oyen, A. van, (2020) *The Socio-economics of Roman Storage*. New York: Cambridge University Press.
Pirson, F. (1999) *Mietwohnungen in Pompeji und Herkulaneum*. München: Pfeil.
Priester, S. (2002) *Ad summas tegulas. Untersuchungen zu vielgeschossigen Gebäudeblöcken mit Wohneinheiten und Insulae im kaiserzeitlichen Rom*. Rome: L'Erma di Bretschneider.
Raff, D., Wachter, S., and Yan, S. (2013) Real Estate Prices in Beijing, 1644 to 1840. *Explorations in Economic History* 50, 368–386.
Rathbone, D. (1991) *Economic Rationalism and Rural Society in Third Century A. D. Egypt. The Heroninos Archive and the Appianus Estate*. Cambridge: Cambridge University Press.
Rawson, E. (1976) The Ciceronian Aristocracy and Its Properties. In: M.I. Finley, ed. *Studies in Roman Property*. Cambridge: Cambridge University Press, 85–102.

Rosillo-López, C. (2021) Domum pestilentem vendo. Real Estate Market and Information Asymmetry in the Roman World. In: C. Rosillo-López and M. García Morcillo, eds. *Managing Information in the Roman Economy*. Cham: Palgrave MacMillan, 117–134.

Rosillo-López, C. (2021b) Destitute, homeless and (almost) invisible: urban poverty and the rental market in the Roman world. In: C. Courrier and J. C. Magalhães de Oliveira, eds. *Ancient History from Below. Subaltern Experiences and Actions in Context*, London: Routledge, 104–121.

Rosillo-López, C. (2022) Rent Control Measures in the 40s BCE: Housing Costs, Public Intervention and Inequality in the Roman World. In: N. Morley and M. Koedijk, eds., *Capital in Classical Antiquity*. Cham: Palgrave MacMillan, 175–204.

Rosillo-López, C., and García Morcillo, M. eds. (2021) *Managing Information in the Roman Economy*. Cham: Palgrave MacMillan.

Rowlandson, J. (1996) *Landowners and Tenants in Roman Egypt: The Social Relations of Agriculture in the Oxyrhynchite Nome*. Oxford: Oxford University Press.

Saliou, C. (1994) *Les lois des bâtiments: Voisinage et habitat urbain dans l'Empire romain*. Beyrouth: Presses de l'Ifpo.

Saller, R.P. (1994) *Patriarchy, Property, and Death in the Roman Family*. Cambridge: Cambridge University Press.

Salzman, D. and Zwinkels, R.C.J. (2017) Behavioral Real Estate. *Journal of Real Estate Literature* 25. 1, 77–106.

Sherwin-White, A.N. (1966) *The Letters of Pliny: A Historical and Social Commentary*. Oxford: Oxford University Press.

Sirago, V.A. (1958) *L'Italia agraria sotto Traiano*. Louvain: Bibliothèque de l'Université.

Veyne, P. (1961) Vie de Trimalchion. *Annales ESC* 16, 213–247.

Watson, A. (1968) *The Law of Property in the Later Roman Republic*. Oxford: Clarendon Press.

Watson, A. (1971) *The Law of Succession in the Later Roman Republic*. Oxford: Oxford University Press.

Willems, C. (2019) Urbanes Mietrecht? Der römische Wohnungsmarkt zwischen Preismechanismus und Intervention. *Zeitschrift der Savigny-Stiftung für Rechtsgeschichte: Romanistische Abteilung*, 136. 1, 233–270.

Part I

Concepts and Control

2 Government Intervention in Real Estate in the Roman World

Cristina Rosillo-López

Abstract

This chapter addresses the topic of how the Roman state, both under the Republic and the Principate, intervened within the real estate market. Even nowadays, its intervention remains a taboo topic in many countries, and many economists believe it will have negative consequences. However, the Great Recession of 2007 and beyond saw a change in many of these considerations; simultaneously, the last two years have seen the promulgation of measures in several countries that aimed to control rent increases. The time seems rife for a re-consideration of the role of the state through a historical perspective.

The Roman state passed laws limiting the heights of properties, controlling empty lots in the Roman cities, and preventing the crumbling of buildings. The leges *Tarentina, Ursonensis* and the *Senatusconsultum Hosidianum* established that a building could not be demolished if the lot would remain vacant. From the first century BCE onwards, a private person could denounce the construction or demolition of a building that could damage his or her own property (*operis novi nuntiatio*); this is demonstrated by legal sources (*Digest* 39.2.; *lex Rubria*, 20) as well as a papyrus dated from 121 CE with a practical example of this (*P. Fouad* 30). The state, under Caesar and Augustus, also modified the procedure of the census to turn it into a cadastre. Finally, what was the reaction of the Roman state in moments of crisis?

The study of state reactions and its adaptation to the evolution of the real estate market will provide us with an interesting view of the interrelation between public and private life.

***

Government intervention in real estate remains a taboo in numerous countries, while many economists believe that it has negative consequences, especially as regards the property market. As of the Great Recession of 2007, however, opinions in this respect have changed substantially, with several countries implementing measures aimed at controlling rent increases and property bubbles in recent years. So, the time seems ripe for reconsidering the role of governments from a historical perspective. Despite the fact that studies have been performed on specific interventions, it is a topic that has received little attention to date. For the specific case of ancient Rome, Rainer and Robinson have posited that building activities were

DOI: 10.4324/9781003187806-3

controlled by a mixture of legislation and jurisprudence, in short, by private law. They consider that this situation changed in the third century CE, when the government became more interventionist and enacted laws to control building.[1]

So as to gauge the extent to which the Roman government intervened in real estate, in this chapter it is contended that certain areas were monitored more closely than others and that, before the third century CE, special legislation was passed to deal with the specificities of real estate. Accordingly, the focus is placed on instances of government intervention in private real estate, specifically residential property, so as to determine whether intervention was exceptional or structural: (1) property taxation; (2) speculation; (3) expenditures by emperors; and (4) the extent to which jurists considered that the government had an interest in protecting real estate.

Property Taxation

Roman real estate was never taxed specifically. Nicolet suggested that for the Romans a tax on the annual income of individuals was unthinkable.[2] The *tributum* was based on a general assessment of the property and rank of citizens, not on their ownership of specific assets (such as real estate). Nonetheless, the Roman government had enough information for levying taxes: all the immovable assets owned by citizens were recorded in the *aestimatio censoria*.[3] During the Republic, taxation was clearly consistent with territorial expansion and the necessities of the government. In Roman history there was just one exception: the civil wars of the 40s BCE, during which a direct property tax was levied, since there was a need to fill the war chest.

The first instance of property taxation in Rome occurred at the beginning of 43 BCE, in the context of the conflict between Antonius and the Senate following the murder of Caesar. After Antonius had attempted to seize the province of Cisalpine Gaul by force, which had been officially assigned to Decimus Junius Brutus Albinus, the Senate, led by Cicero, outlawed him and dispatched the consuls Hirtius and Pansa, together with the young Octavian, to bring Antony to battle (which they subsequently did, defeating him at Mutina) in the spring of 43 BCE. Given the situation, the Senate levied new taxes in order to defray the costs of the war: "And since there was need of much money for the war, they all contributed the twenty-fifth part of the wealth they possessed and the senators also four obols for each roof tile of all the houses in the city that they either owned themselves or occupied as tenants."[4] Thus, all the senators had to pay ca. 10 asses for every roof tile, whose number had been previously used to determine the size of houses: the *lex Tarentina* (dated to between 89 and 52 BCE) established the requirements for becoming a decurion in the *municipium*, which included the ownership of a building roofed with no fewer than 1,500 tiles.[5] Cicero optimistically believed that 60 million sesterces could be collected through that tax (if three sesterces were charged for each roof tile), although some months later he claimed that the *inopia rei pecuniariae* was harsh, since the *boni viri* were reluctant to impose a *tributum* and the previous taxes had brought in enough money to pay the armies.[6]

The property tax based on the number of roof tiles was certainly an innovation. First, as had occurred with previous exceptional contributions, it targeted a certain group: only the buildings owned or rented by senators were affected. Second, the Senate broke new ground in this respect. The Roman government was aware of the properties owned by each citizen and their status (either rented or occupied by their owners), since such information was recorded in the census for both Rome and Italy.[7] However, as the previous census had been performed in 70–69, namely, 26 years before, the *aestimatio censoria* was frankly outdated.[8] And since no up-to-date information on real estate holdings was available, this begged the question of how to assess the amount of money that each senator should pay, with the Senate coming up with the idea of establishing roof tiles as a measure. Scuderi suggested that the tax was abusive because of the lack of an *aestimatio censoria*; on the contrary, I am of the mind that the Senate discovered a very accurate measure for remedying that lack of information.[9] In any case, the existence of an *aestimatio censoria* would not have really resolved this issue, since the tax was also imposed on the houses where senators lived as tenants and which, in the census, would appear under the name of their owners, not theirs. And this information was available because, in 46 BCE, Caesar created a register *vicatim per dominos insularum*, which would have helped to determine where senators lived.[10]

It was not only the Senate that was desperately looking for revenues at the beginning of 43 BCE, for some months after the adoption of the previous measures, the triumvirs established a second residential property tax.[11] According to Cassius Dio,

> in the first place, they levied upon all the houses, both in the city and in the rest of Italy, a tax which was the entire amount of the annual rent in the case of dwellings which people had leased, and half of that amount in the case of such as they occupied themselves, all based on the value of the domicile.[12]

Appian asserts that the triumvirs toyed with the idea of introducing taxes on sales and rents, while also mentioning an *eniautou phoron* for those whose property was worth over 400,000 sesterces.[13] Nicolet rejected a previous hypothesis that the taxes mentioned in Dio and in Appian were one and the same, holding that income tax was unheard of in ancient Rome.[14]

This second tax measure was different from that imposed on senators at the beginning of the year, for, on the one hand, it was introduced by the triumvirs, not by the Senate, and it does not seem to have been restricted to the senatorial elite. After analysing some of the tax measures of the triumvirs, Günther does not believe that they reflect a planned financial policy,[15] proposing instead that they were a sort of punishment meted out to the upper classes, especially senators and *equites*, who still felt equal to the triumvirs.[16]

By my reckoning, this fiscal policy is characteristic of the "économie tyrannique", as described by Nicolet, that is, a predatory system for raising as much money as the triumvirs needed to wage their wars and to implement their policies.[17] Taxing the poor is egalitarian, but does not bring in more resources. Second, it was not only restricted to the city of Rome, like the previous measure, but was also levied in Italy as a whole. Third, it was not ownership, but tenancy, that was being taxed. Cassius Dio mentions the value of a building as a proxy for the amount due, but where did that information come from? Again, the *aestimatio censoria* had not been updated, so the prices did not reflect the rental market of the mid-40s. A new assessment of the net worth of citizens was carried out in 42 BCE in the context of the war against Sextus Pompeius. As Cassius Dio mentions in passing, the taxes were self-assessed, with each citizen calculating the value of his own goods on which taxes were due:

> For since they were not ordered to contribute a stated amount according to the value of their possessions, but had the duty of assessing the value of their own goods, they were as a result liable to be accused of not having made a fair assessment and to lose in addition what they had left.[18]

How were taxes then assessed at the end of 43 BCE? Was the taxation on rents from 42 BCE onwards based on that assessment? These taxes were probably abolished after the war against Sextus Pompeius had ended or after the victory at the Battle of Actium, when Octavian injected money into the economy and distributed grain and sesterces to the people and the landowners.[19]

Property taxation was exceptional and regarded by the Romans as an intolerable burden. In 13 CE, Augustus, with the intention of making the citizenry less reluctant to pay the *vicesima hereditatium* of 6 CE, threatened to impose a property tax. After asking the Senate for proposals for other taxes, "he changed it to a levy upon fields and houses (ἐπί τε τοὺς ἀγροὺς καὶ ἐπὶ τὰς οἰκίας τὴν συντέλειαν ἤγαγε); and immediately, without stating how great it would be or in what way imposed, he sent men out everywhere to make a list of the property both of private individuals and of cities."[20] It was clearly a direct property tax.

These measures were never implemented since, according to Dio, they were used to persuade the citizenry to accept other kinds of taxation; *pace* Kienast, who suggested that Augustus planned to replace the *vicesima* with a *tributum*, but was forced to desist.[21] Regarding the logistics of a land and property tax, Brunt suggested that the information and the assessment could be related to the census of 13/14 CE, which would have provided the wherewithal to levy it.[22] The emperor Claudius clearly stated that one of the goals of the census was *ut publice notae sint facultates nostrae*.[23] The emperor Nero tried to enact a similar property tax law, after the revolt of Galba in 68 CE, ordering that all tenants *privatarum aedium atque insularum* should pay a year's rent to the *fiscus*, instead of to their landlords; he received many complaints from the people and earned their undying hatred for this and other similar measures.[24] Suetonius, for his part, describes measures of this kind as the mark of a tyrannical suzerain.

Evidence about property taxation in Roman Egypt is not conclusive. In his detailed survey of taxation in Egypt, Wallace concurred with Wilcken's interpretation, who understood the *(uper) enoikiou*, whose receipts have been preserved, as an income tax on rent, paid by landlords, rather than as a property tax per se. *P. Flor.* 1. 104 might point to a tax on buildings and vacant plots, but the evidence is still too fragmentary and uncertain.[25]

In sum, property taxation was a relatively brief measure, restricted to the conflictive years following the murder of Caesar and the period of the triumvirs. The fact that Augustus entertained the possibility of establishing such a tax once and for all, plus the fact that the citizenry considered it to be less acceptable than other types of indirect taxation, speaks volumes about the extent to which government intervention in real estate through taxation was unthinkable.

Real Estate and Speculation

Many properties were bought and sold in Rome for speculative purposes. In a lot of cases, buyers did not intend to live in them or rent them, but were more interested in the actual plot of land on which the building stood, either for demolishing it in order to reuse the building materials and/or to rebuild it anew. As early as in the first century BCE, the senator Marcus Licinius Crassus had made a name for himself for purchasing properties, which were being consumed, or had been destroyed, by fire, on the cheap, subsequently rebuilding them and making a hefty profit by letting them.[26]

The Roman government did not legislate on property speculation, but for more than 200 years it did indeed pass laws for controlling the demolition of buildings and the presence of ruins in the city. Davoine has compiled all the legal initiatives and jurisprudence on the demolition of buildings.[27] However, it is important to differentiate between *senatus consulta, leges*, and imperial *rescripta*, on the one hand, and jurisprudence, on the other. Even though the *lex citationum* (426 CE) established that the opinions of certain jurists (Ulpian, Paul, Gaius, Papinian and Modestinus) would be considered as law, prior to this, although they had been taken into account, they had not been enforceable as such.

Chronologically speaking, the first instance of government intervention appears in the *lex Tarentina*, dated to between 89 and 62 BCE. Although it is a municipal charter, many of its measures were also probably implemented in the city of Rome. The law forbade the demolition of any building if it was not replaced by one of the same quality: "No-one is to unroof or [demolish] or dismantle a building in the town which shall belong to that *municipium,* except one that he is about to restore in no worse state, except according to the opinion of the senate."[28] The penalties for breaking the law were harsh: a fine equal to the value of the building, plus the possibility of being prosecuted.

The *lex Ursonensis*, another municipal law dated to 44–43 BCE, also addressed the same issue – namely, a building *detegitus, demolitus, disturbatus* which was not going to be rebuilt – and established the same penalties; the only new proviso was that the *lex* required a quorum of 50 decurions for approving any exception to the rule.[29]

Finally, the *lex Flavia Malacitana* (dated to 82–84 CE) also dealt with the same legal concept (*detegitus, demolitus, disturbatus*), while including, as a novelty, a deadline of one year for the reconstruction of the building in question.[30] Crawford has suggested several reasons for the measure adopted in the *lex Tarentina*: the prevention of "speculative building of shoddy tenements, the dilapidation of the city centre or the diminution of the housing stock."[31] In any case, neither did this law, nor subsequent *leges*, specify the grounds for such a measure. In sum, the measures and penalties were consistent for 150 years, with heavy fines acting as a deterrent against derelict and dismantled buildings in the city.

In 47 CE, the *senatus consultum Hosidianum Vagellianum* prohibited buildings from being purposely left to run to ruin, in order that they could be demolished and rebuilt at a later date.[32] The fine was double the purchase price, that is, much harsher than in the municipal laws. Procchi has posited that the fine was established through an *actio popularis* that anybody could bring, which is not mentioned in the *senatus consultum*, but does appears in the municipal laws.[33] This *senatus consultum* mentioned specifically the grounds for the law: it addressed how speculation could become a problem, describing it as "this most cruel form of profiteering" (*cruentissimo genere negotiationis*). A few years later, in 56 CE, the *senatus consultum Volusianum Cornelianum* specified the application of the previous one to a specific case brought by Alliatoria Celsilla, the wife of the *clarissimus uir* Atilius Luperculus: the owner could certify that his property was *longa vetustas*, empty, or inhabited. Procchi has observed that the *senatus consultum Volusianum Cornelianum* actually broadened the scope of the *senatus consultum Hosidianum Vagellianum*, since the former did not even allow the owner of a building to demolish it, which the latter indeed permitted.[34]

In the following centuries, successive emperors endorsed such prohibitions. For his part, Vespasian legislated on the matter, although the details are unknown, while Hadrian placed a ban on the demolition of buildings for the purpose of obtaining cheap building materials that would then be transported to another city.[35] In a letter to the city of Stratonicea/Hadrianopolis, this emperor made a point of underscoring his policy against the demolition of buildings: "as for the house of Tib. Claudius Socrates which is in your city, let Socrates either repair it or sell it to one of the local inhabitants so that it does not collapse from age and neglect."[36] In 222 CE, Alexander Severus, for his part, banned the demolition of buildings *negotiandi causa*, as well as the extraction of their marble elements.[37]

There are differences of opinion on the existence of a *senatus consultum de aedificiis non diruendis* – that is, which forbade the demolition of buildings in Rome – with both Voigt and Garnsey in favour of its existence, and with Yavetz, Rainer, and Procchi against it.[38] Can the remnants of such a law be glimpsed in the *senatus consulta* and the few examples of imperial legislation that have come down to us? The evidence, to my mind, suggests an answer in the affirmative. Previous scholarship has considered that those first-century-CE *senatus consulta* were mainly concerned with the aesthetic character of a city's buildings and architecture. After analysing the use of the expression *aedificium negotiandi causa emere/vendere*, Procchi has linked it to the *dolus malus* intention of the seller.[39] In his opinion, the municipal laws were aimed at preventing the destruction of buildings, regardless of the intentions of their owners, or at simply conserving buildings on specific plots.[40] Either way, for Garnsey and Procchi there is no explicit condemnation of property speculation in the *senatus consulta*.[41]

In my view, the policy of the Roman government, both in the Republic and in the Principate, was consistent: there was a complete aversion and refusal to let buildings run to ruin in Rome and in provincial cities. At least one of the laws was absolutely clear on the grounds for such a decision: *negotiandi causa*, whether it was speculation involving plots of lands, marble, or building materials. They stressed that speculation could become a problem, describing it as "this most cruel form of profiteering" (*cruentissimo genere negotiationis*). Procchi observed that the *negotiandi causa* was an original aspect of the *senatus consulta*, since municipal laws did not include such provisions.[42] Modern scholars have drawn a distinction between laws that attempted to preserve the aesthetic value of a city and those aimed at curbing speculation.[43] This difference would seem to be a modern consideration, insofar as both aspects are not mutually exclusive, but reinforce each other.

Imperial Expenditures after Disasters

Fires and the collapse of buildings were common risks in ancient Roman cities.[44] The personal intervention of the emperors in the wake of natural disasters, especially fires, in Rome formed part of their self-image. In order to alleviate the losses, they handed out money to those whose properties had been affected, as a kind of evergetism, while also offering them the opportunity to show the citizenry the lengths to which they were willing to go to repair the damage. Suetonius considered such behaviour to be relevant enough to be included in his biographies, in which he mentions the handouts of Tiberius in 27 CE and Gaius in 35 CE.[45]

Disaster relief took the form of exceptional cash handouts to cities or individuals. The literary and epigraphic sources refer to four types of financial aid: monetary gifts, tax remissions (only after severe earthquakes), *bona caduca* (heirless property), and the appointment of one or more senators to oversee the reconstruction of damaged areas.[46] In order to qualify the intervention of the government in residential real estate, it is necessary to ponder on the procedures by which such financial aid was granted and its scope. Did inhabitants whose houses had been destroyed by fire give their names to government officials so that they could be identified? Did these handouts reach broad sections of the population or were they restricted to the socioeconomic elite, or even just to senators? Did the amount of money received depend on the size of the damaged building or was it a lump sum?

There are some indications as to the financial aid distributed by Tiberius after fires. Following the destruction of many houses and *insulae* in the fire on the Aventine Hill in 36 CE, according to Tacitus, Tiberius paid "the full value of the mansions and *insulae* destroyed. One hundred million sesterces were invested in this act of munificence, which came the more acceptable to the multitude that he was far from extravagant in building on his own behalf."[47] Regardless of the accuracy of the sum, since Cassius Dio offers a different figure, for once there is an indication of how property assessments were performed: the emperor selected four people, linked by marriage to the imperial family, who formed a board tasked with estimating the losses of each person.[48]

A similar procedure for assessing individual losses for determining the amount of compensation payable was employed after the Caelian Hill had been ravaged by fire in 27 CE; although Tacitus does not mention any board in that instance, it can be assumed to have existed.[49] McCoy has suggested that this procedure should be linked to Tiberius' frugality, which allowed him to compensate individuals "at a minimal cost to the state."[50] However that may be, caution should be taken when attributing such motivations, or even the procedure, exclusively to Tiberius, taking into account that there is no information on how Augustus or subsequent emperors distributed financial aid to individuals whose properties had been damaged or destroyed by fire.

After the great fire of 64 CE, Nero's policies and handouts were clearly aimed at rebuilding the city. Owing to the fact that he handed out money according to rank and resources, it was clearly a measure aimed at alleviating the losses of the rich and moneyed, in contrast with Tiberius' policy. These cash distributions came with a caveat: there was a deadline for rebuilding. Furthermore, he ordered that the affected plots be cleared of debris before being handed over to their owners.[51] Nero put into practice a new form of government intervention in residential real estate: in order to encourage reconstruction, he granted Roman citizenship to Latin citizens who built lavish houses in the city of Rome:

> Moreover, it was established in an edict published by Nero that if a Latin who had property worth two hundred thousand sesterces, or more, should build a house in the City of Rome on which he expended not less than half his estate, he should obtain the right of Roman citizenship.[52]

Obviously, this measure benefited a small number of people. Furthermore, it should be framed in the context of previous and later imperial measures that granted Roman citizenship to Latins who had built large ships and had transported grain to Rome for six years (during the reign of Claudius) and to Latin millers who had ground no fewer than 100 measures of grain each day in Rome during three years (Trajan).[53]

Nero's policy is reproduced nowadays by many governments, which grant citizenship to people who buy property worth over a certain (sizeable) amount of money through programmes called "Citizenship by Investment," a shortcut that has been informally nicknamed the Golden Visa.[54] For instance, the purchase of a house worth at least €350,000 in Malta makes the owner eligible for Maltese citizenship and, therefore, legal residence and the possibility to travel in the European Union. The European Commission has criticised such programmes for hindering the control of money laundering, tax evasion, and other corrupt practices.[55]

All previous measures were certainly aimed at property owners. In one of his epigrams, Martial criticises a certain Tongilianus, a clever man who, despite having lost a recently purchased house in a fire, had not suffered any substantial financial losses; quite the opposite, in fact, he had recovered ten times its price (*conlatum est deciens*), which makes the author suspect that he had set fire to his own house.[56] Had Tongilianus received that compensation as part of an imperial disaster relief programme? As to Tiberius' handouts, Velleius points out that such financial aid was not restricted to the elite, but reached all kinds of people.[57] Of course, if Velleius is to be believed, it can be assumed that people of modest means also received something. As regards the urban poor, however, they probably had few or no possessions at all to report to the board.

Juvenal is mordant about the inequality of such relief: if rich men lost their houses in a fire, collections were made for their relief, whereas humble people dwelling in *insulae* lost their meagre possessions and even ran the risk of becoming destitute: *nemo hospitio tectoque iuvabit*, no one offered them a roof over their heads or shelter.[58] No mention of imperial handouts is explicitly made, as Juvenal and Martial could not afford such liberties or to even suggest that the emperors had been cheated, but the intention behind Juvenal's remark is clear.

The suspicion of rich people provoking fires seems to be a *topos*, probably based on their financial capacity to compensate for any losses. Again according to Martial, only the rich received riches.[59] In contrast, there are few references to the construction of temporary shelters for those who had lost their homes in fires and who did not clearly belong to the elite. In the immediate aftermath of the great fire of 64 CE, Nero provided *subitaria aedificia* in the city, besides ensuring the food supply: "Still, as a relief to the homeless and fugitive populace, he opened the Campus Martius, the buildings of Agrippa, even his own gardens, and threw up a number of extemporized shelters to accommodate the helpless multitude."[60] Newbold estimated that at least 200,000 inhabitants were deprived of their lodgings and that many remained in those temporary shelters for years.[61]

In sum, imperial interventions in real estate following disasters were ad hoc policies aimed at mitigating the financial losses mainly of the elite and at displaying the generosity of the emperor in question. Tiberius' creation of a board to estimate such losses reflects a certain interest in making those handouts look less of a whim of a *princeps*.

Real Estate and the Interests of the *Res Publica*

The previous sections have dealt with how the government intervened in real estate in several ways. Jurisprudence and legislation created legal mechanisms for protecting property from third party damage. Private law was clearly aimed at safeguarding such conditions, even by modifying ordinary procedures, thus considering real estate as a category different from others, with its inherent concerns and problems. For instance, the jurist Celsus (beginning of the second century CE) pointed out specifically that, against the opinion of the jurist Proculus (mid-first century CE), in property transactions the seller and the buyer did not have full information or paid no attention to it, namely, that the real estate market was governed by asymmetric information and, thus, the law should reflect that concern.[62] Ulpian mentioned the need for *celeritas* (celerity) when addressing problems relating to real estate, especially in the case of *damnum infectum* (loss or damage threatened or anticipated but not yet sustained), since any delay could be prejudicial.[63]

Accordingly, in this section two sets of rules created to prevent damage caused by the collapse of buildings are examined – the *operis novi nuntiatio* (a protest or warning against [of] a new work) and the *damnum infectum* – and how such measures were justified in the interests of the government, the *res publica*.

In the *Digestum* there is a long section in which the academic lawyers tasked with compiling the question express their opinions on the following hypothetical case: a neighbour starts work on a new building that damages a neighbouring property or which prevents its owners from using it.[64] In such an event, Roman law included a complex procedure, with several steps, which highlights the importance attached to resolving this problem. The jurisprudence on these matters started at least with Labeo in the first century BCE, if not earlier.[65] First of all, the owner could resort to an *operis novi nuntiatio*, a protest grounded on the hypothetical damages that the new construction might cause. Jurists considered that the owner should be afforded every facility to lodge such a protest:

> It is not necessary that notice be served upon the owner himself, as it will be sufficient for it to be served on the premises and upon anyone who happens to be present, and this can even be done upon the workmen, or artisans who are performing the labor. And, generally speaking, notice to suspend operations can be served upon all those who are present in the name of the master, or upon the workmen themselves. Nor does it make any difference who he is, or what may be the rank of the person present at the time, for if the notice is served upon a slave, upon a woman, or a boy or a girl, it will be valid; as it is sufficient that service be made of the notice upon the premises in such a way that the owner can be informed of it.[66]

The *nuntiatio* was supposed to be served orally on the premises and, interestingly, upon anyone who happened to be present, regardless of their rank, gender, age, or socioeconomic status, which is quite exceptional. The intention behind this was, of course, to prevent the builder from hiding, thus hindering the efforts of the owner to serve the *nuntiatio*. Once it was served, the builder had to offer the praetor a warranty regarding the safety of works (*satisdatio de opera restituendo*). If he failed to do so, the plaintiff had the option of requesting an interdict (*interdictum ex operis novi nuntiatione*), by virtue of which the praetor could order the demolition of what had been built so far. In case of non-compliance, the builder could be prosecuted. After receiving the *nuntiatio*, the builder could have it annulled if he could show the praetor that the complaint was groundless.

On the other hand, the *damnum infectum* was a procedure that offered protection against loss or damage threatened or anticipated but not yet sustained, such as a derelict building that posed a risk to another property.[67] Considering that any delay could have negative consequences for the plaintiff, the praetor could delegate the matter to municipal magistrates to speed up the proceedings.[68] A number of magistrates could take action regarding buildings. The governor of a province could order the inspection of buildings and repairs to be carried out on them.[69] Robinson has pondered on the extent to which the jurisdiction of the praetor overlapped with that of other magistrates, such as those tasked with looking after the condition of the streets and even the *curatores operum publicorum*.[70] In my opinion, these possible overlaps were not avoided in Roman law because of the importance that the government attached to buildings. The enactment of special and specific measures in relation to real estate attests to its interest in this area, in which occasionally decisions had to be taken swiftly in order to avoid further damage.

Those laws and opinions of jurists were applied in real life. One of the Oxyrhynchus Papyri dating from 121 CE records the complaints lodged by two neighbours about an old house in the vicinity which, because of its derelict state, was in danger of collapsing onto their houses. They requested the intervention of local magistrates in order to prevent any potential damage.[71] In order to speed up the process, answering the need for *celeritas* in problems relating to real estate, as urged by Ulpian, it was not the praetor who dealt with such complaints, but municipal magistrates. The Roman government was not only aware of the nature of the problem, but was also willing to modify institutional procedures to guarantee and improve the protection of the citizenry against abuse or neglect.

How did jurists justify all these procedures? In the words of Ulpian, "The notice is served either for the purpose of protecting our rights to avert threatened injury, or to maintain the public welfare (*ius publicus*)."[72] Those rights had to be protected from impending danger (*damnum infectum*), either in a public or private place (*in publico vel in privato*), and upheld by laws and edicts of the emperors *quae ad modum aedificiorum facta sunt*.[73] Private law and jurists concurred that, as to the construction of a public building (*in publico*), any citizen could serve an *operis novi nuntiatio* and withdraw it.[74] The fact that such a possibility was not restricted to magistrates, for instance, but was also open to *omnes cives* reveals the importance that the Roman government attached to building and that it decided to involve all citizens in the surveillance of new constructions, thus creating a community of interests and of control. Paulus does not beat about the bush: "For it is to the interest of the *res publica* that the greatest number of persons possible should be permitted to protect their property."[75] The expression *ad defendendam suam causam* clearly stresses how far Roman law was prepared to go to defend property rights. Moatti has posited that the abstract concept of the *res publica*, which became an allegory, was developed as of the mid-first century BCE, making it visible; the interests of the *res publica*, as argued by Paul as a reason for protecting real estate, should be framed in that context.[76]

Conclusion

In this chapter, I have contended that, throughout its history, the Roman government made a point of upholding a set of laws and procedures that allowed for and promoted real estate as a financial and private sphere. Roman law recognised that the property market had special and specific needs, differing from those of other areas of law, and which the government had a special interest in protecting. The government passed laws aimed at limiting the height of building, controlling vacant lots and preventing buildings from running to ruin in Roman cities. From the first century BCE onwards, private citizens could report the construction or demolition of buildings that might damage their own property (*operis novi nuntiatio*). There are not only legal sources (*Digest* 39.2.; *lex Rubria*, 20), but also a papyrus dating from 121 CE setting out a practical case (*P. Fouad* 30), substantiating that the law was well known, if not enforced.

The government also modified the procedure for performing the census, under Caesar and Augustus, to turn it into a cadastre and to use it as an information source for property taxation. Finally, following natural disasters, the emperors provided those people whose properties had been damaged with relief and cash handouts. There were limits to such interventions. Throughout Roman history there were no controls on property prices, except for the exceptional measures adopted to establish a rent ceiling in Rome and Italy in the 40s BCE.[77] These regulations were not even repeated in Diocletian's Edict on Maximum Prices, neither for rents nor for sales. It has also been seen how exceptional a direct property tax was and how it could be used as a threat in order to persuade the citizenry to accept other taxes. There is no evidence of subsequent impositions.

In light of the foregoing and *pace* Rainer and Robinson, the notion of a non-interventional government which left all the control in the hands of private law should be discarded, at least for the period of the Late Republic and the Principate.

Notes

1 Rainer 1987; Robinson 1992: 35.
2 Nicolet 1976: 89–90.
3 Scuderi 1979: 343, 346, who highlighted that socioeconomic status was important in the case of voluntary contributions, like, for instance, those made *ex censu*

ordinibusque (Liv. 26.35.3) during the Second Punic War, whereas only senators were urged to make a contribution in 210 BCE (Liv. 26.36.2–12).

4 Cass. Dio 46–31.3: ἐπειδή τε πολλῶν χρημάτων ἐς τὸν πόλεμον ἐδέοντο, πάντες μὲν τὸ πέμπτον καὶ εἰκοστὸν τῆς ὑπαρχούσης σφίσιν οὐσίας ἐπέδωκαν, οἱ δὲ δὴ βουλευταὶ καὶ τέσσαρας ὀβολοὺς καθ' ἑκάστην κεραμίδα τῶν ἐν τῇ πόλει οἰκιῶν, ὅσας ἢ αὐτοὶ ἐκέκτηντο ἢ ἄλλων οὔσας ᾤκουν.

5 *Lex Tarentina*, l. 27–28: *is in o[pp]ido Tarentei aut intra eius muni[cipi] fineis aedificium quod non minu[s] (mille quingentis) tegularum tectum sit habeto* (Crawford 1996: 307). Crawford 1996: 310 bases his estimates on the most standard size of *tegula* in central Italy (0.65 m × 0.45 m).

6 The reintroduction of the tax: Cic. *Ep. Caes. Jun. Frag.* 5. The need for money and the reluctance to *tributum*: Cic. *Ad Brut.* 1.18.5: *maximus autem, nisi me forte fallit, in re publica nodus est inopia rei pecuniariae. Obdurescunt enim magis cotidie boni viri ad vocem tributi; quod ex centesima conlatum impudenti censu locupletium in duarum legionum praemiis omne consumitur.* Despite such reluctance, the *tributum* was finally reintroduced in 43 BCE (Cic. *Off.* 2.74; Phil. 2.37, 93).

7 As the *Tabula Heracleensis* shows (ll. 142–156; edition Crawford 1996).

8 Cass. Dio 43.14.4; Aug. *Res gestae 8* mentions a gap of 41 years between his *lustrum* (28 BCE) and the previous one.

9 Scuderi 1979: 349–350; see also García Morcillo 2020.

10 Suet. *Iul.* 41.5.

11 On the chronology of triumviral taxation, see Nicolet 1976: 89–90; Scuderi 1979: 367–368.

12 Cass. Dio 47.14.2: τοῦτο μὲν γὰρ ἐνοίκιον ἐνιαύσιον πασῶν τῶν τε ἐν τῷ ἄστει καὶ τῶν ἐν τῇ ἄλλῃ Ἰταλίᾳ οἰκιῶν, ὧν μὲν ἐμεμισθώκεσάν τινες, ὅλον, ὧν δὲ αὐτοὶ ᾤκουν, ἐξ ἡμισείας, πρὸς τὴν τῆς καταγωγῆς ἀξίαν ἐσέπραξαν.

13 App. *B Civ.* 4.5: ἤδη δέ τις καὶ διὰ κάλλος ἐπαύλεως καὶ οἰκίας προεγράφη.

14 Nicolet 1976: 90 (*pace* Jullian).

15 Günther 2016: 225.

16 Günther 2016.

17 Nicolet 1976: 87–98. The tax on the 1,400 richest women, against which Hortensia pleaded in the forum, formed part of the same extractive fiscal policy (App. *B Civ.* 4.31–34). On the new taxes, cf. Cass. Dio 47.14, 16; App. *B Civ.* 5.67. On how the triumvirs treated Italy as a province (including taxation and the extraction of resources) and the unrest that such a policy triggered in the late 40s and 30s, cf. Rosillo-López 2020.

18 Cass. Dio 47.16.5 (the text has been dated to 42 BCE, because Dio mentions the consuls of that year, Lepidus and Plancus).

19 Sextus Pompeius: Cass. Dio 49.15. Actium: Cass. Dio 51.20.45; Suet. *Aug.* 41; *RGDA* 15–16.

20 Cass. Dio 56.28.4–6. Swan 2004: 296 suggests that the precise details in Dio's narrative may have come from an annalistic account that he consulted.

21 Kienast 1982: 407 (cited in Swan 2004: 297). Fromentin and Bertrand 2014: 80 also argue that it was not a *tributum*, since the latter had already been established in early 43 BCE (even though it was cancelled when the war against Sextus Pompeius ended; Cass. Dio 49.15). Furthermore, Cassius Dio employs *phoroi* for *tributum* and *telé* for *vectigalia*, to wit, indirect taxes. Nicolet 1976: 96–97.

22 Brunt 1971: 83.

23 *ILS*, 212, l. 40.

24 Suet. *Ner.* 44.2: *Partem etiam census omnes ordines conferre iussit et insuper inquilinos privatarum aedium atque insularum pensionem annuam repraesentare fisco.* As to the complaints: Suet. *Ner.* 45. On the social impact of this measure, cf. Newbold 1974: 868.

25 Wallace 1938: 75–76; Mitteis and Wilcken 1912.

26 Plut. *Crass.* 2.5–6; Shatzman 1975: 375. According to Plutarch, Crassus had groups of slaves, masons, and architects whose job was to rebuild those houses.
27 Davoine 2016.
28 *Lex Tarentina* ll. 32–38 (ed. Crawford 1996): *Nei quis in oppido quod eius municipi e[r] it aedificium detegito neiue dem[olito] neiue disturbato, nisei quod non deterius restiturus erit, nisei d[e] s(enatus) s(ententia).*
29 *Lex Ursonensis* 75: *Ne quis in oppido coloniae Iuliae aedificium detegito neve demolito neve disturbato, nisi si praedes IIvirum arbitratu dederit se redaedificaturum, aut nisi decuriones decreverint, dum ne minus L adsint, cum ea res consulatur. Si quis adversus ea fecerit, quanti ea res erit, tantam pecuniam colonis coloniae Genetivae Iuliae dare damnas esto, eiusque pecuniae qui volet petitio persecutioque ex hac lege esto.*
30 *Lex Flavia Malacitana* 62 (ca. 82–84 CE): 62. *Ne quis aedificia, quae restiturus non erit, destruat. Ne quis in oppido municipii Flavii Malacitani quaeque ei oppido continentia aedificia erunt, aedificium detegito destruito demoliundumve curato, nisi de decurionum conscriptorumve sententia, cum maior pars eorum adfuerit, quod restituturus intra proximum annum non erit. Qui adversus ea fecerit, is quanti ea res erit, tantam pecuniam municipibus municipi Flavi Malacitani dare damnas esto, eiusque pecuniae deque ea pecunia municipi eius municipii, qui volet cuique per hanc legem licebit, actio petitio persecutio esto.*
31 Crawford 1996: 310.
32 *FIRA* I^2, 45. The date of the *senatus consultum* has been the subject of debate (either 44 or 47 CE), since it depends on the date of the consulship of Cn. Hosidius Geta, established in 47 CE by Buongiorno 2010.
33 Procchi 2001: 416. *Dig.* 47.23 on the *actiones populares.*
34 Procchi 2001: 418.
35 Vespasian: Procchi 2001: 428–430. Hadrian: SHA, *Hadr.* 18.2: *constituit inter cetera, ut in nulla civitate domus aliqua transferendae ad aliam urbem ullius materiae causa dirueretur.* Procchi 2001: 411, n. 1 with bibliography on the reuse of building materials; ibid: 424–425 on the thriving market for reused materials.
36 Oliver 1989, *Greek Constitutions*, No. 79, ll. 10–14; καὶ τὴν οἰκίαν Τιβ. Κλαυδίου Σωκράτους τὴν οὖσαν ἐν τῇ π[ό]λει ἢ ἐπισκευαζέτω Σωκράτης ἢ ἀποδό[σ]θω τινὶ τῶν ἐπιχωρίων ὡς μὴ χρόνῳ καὶ ἀμελίαι καταριφθείη. Martín 1982, *La documentación griega*, No. 22.
37 *Cod. Iust.* 8.10.2: *Imperator Alexander Severus. Negotiandi causa aedificia demoliri et marmora detrahere edicto divi Vespasiani et senatus consulto vetitum est. Ceterum de alia domo in aliam transferre quaedam licere exceptum est: sed nec dominis ita transferre licet, ut integris aedificiis depositis publicus deformetur adspectus* * *ALEX. A. DIOGENI.* **<A 222 PP. XI K. IAN. ALEXANDRO A. CONS.>*
38 Voigt 1903: 175; Garnsey 1976. *Pace* Yavetz 1958: 513; Rainer 1987: 31.
39 Procchi 2001: 419–422.
40 Procchi 2001: 418–419, n. 25.
41 Garnsey, 1976; Procchi 2001: 437, who on p. 422 has also suggested that not all revenues led to speculation (?), so a distinction should be drawn between those two categories. In my opinion, that difference is not supported by textual evidence.
42 Procchi 2001.
43 For instance, Murga Gener 1986: 10–11 (beauty and harmony), 35, with the goal of preserving the "unity" of a building, instead of dismantling it and reusing the materials (e.g. columns, marble, etc.) elsewhere.
44 Fires: Gell. 15.1. Collapses: Cic. *Att.* 14.9.1; 14.11.2.
45 Tiberius: Suet. *Tib.* 48.1–2; Tac. *Ann.* 4.64; 6.45; Cass. Dio 58.26.5. Gaius Suet. *Calig.* 16.3. On such fires, cf. McCoy 2014: 44–47.
46 McCoy 2014: 111–146.
47 Tac. *Ann.* 6.45.1: *quod damnum Caesar ad gloriam vertit exolutis domuum et insularum pretiis. Milies sestertium in munificentia conlocatum, tanto acceptius in vulgum, quanto*

modicus privatis aedificationibus ne publice quidem nisi duo opera struxit. Cass. Dio 58.26.5. Cf. McCoy 2014: 114–116.

48 Tac. *Ann.* 6.45.2: *sed aestimando cuiusque detrimento quattuor progeneri Caesaris, Cn. Domitius, Cassius Longinus, M. Vinicius, Rubellius Blandus delecti additusque nominatione consulum P. Petronius*. The men chosen to sit on this board were Gnaeus Domitius, Cassius Longinus, Marcus Vinicius and Rubellius Blandus, while the consuls appointed Publius Petronius as a fifth member.

49 Tac. *Ann.* 4.64.1: *tribuendo pecunias ex modo detrimenti*.

50 McCoy 2014: 115.

51 Tac. *Ann.* 15.43: *eas proticus Nero sua pecunia exstructurum purgatasque areas dominis traditurum pollicitus est*.

52 Gai. *Inst.* 1.33: *Praeterea a Nerone constitutum est, ut, si Latinus, qui patrimonium sestertium CC milium plurisve habebit, in urbe Roma domum aedificaverit, in quam non minus quam partem dimidiam patrimonii sui impenderit, ius Quiritium consequatur*. Tac. *Ann.* 15.43.

53 Gai. *Inst.* 1.32C; 1.34.

54 https://www.businessinsider.com/countries-where-you-can-buy-citizenship-residency-or-passport-2018-9?IR=T

55 Report of 2019: https://ec.europa.eu/info/sites/info/files/com_2019_12_final_report.pdf

56 Mart. 3.52. Cf. Garnsey 1976. Clever man: Mart. 12.88 (Tongilianus only has a nose, and nothing more). Cf. Moreno Soldevila, Marina Castillo and Fernández Valverde 2019: 593. Fusi 2006: 362 points out that Tongilianus had paid a low price for a house in Rome. My thanks go to Rosario Moreno Soldevila for her suggestions regarding this passage.

57 Vell. Pat. 2.130.

58 Juv. 3.190–223.

59 Mart. 5.82: *dantur opes nullis nunc nisi diuitibus*.

60 Tac. *Ann.* 15.39.2: *sed solacium populo exturbato ac profugo campum Martis ac monumenta Agrippae, hortos quin etiam suos patefacit et subitaria aedificia exstruxit, quae multitudinem inopem acciperent*.

61 On the social and economic consequences of the fire of 64 CE, cf. Newbold 1974.

62 *Dig.* 19.1.38.2 (*Cels. Dig. 8*). Cf. Hausmaninger 1991 on the controversies between Celsus and Proculus and p. 59 regarding this case; Rosillo-López 2021 on real estate and asymmetric information in Rome.

63 *Dig.* 39.2.1 (*Ulp. 1 ad ed.*): *Cum res damni infecti celeritatem desiderat et periculosa dilatio praetori videtur, si ex hac causa sibi iurisdictionem reservaret, magistratibus municipalibus delegandum hoc recte putavit*.

64 Ulpian considered that the definition of a new construction was that which involved changing the original shape of the property by adding or removing something: *Dig.* 39.1.11 (*Ulp. Edict. 52*). Most jurists agreed (although not without differences of opinion) that propping up an old building, for instance, did not give grounds for an *operis novi nuntiatio*, since no new structure had been erected: *Dig.* 39.1.13 (*Ulp. Edict. 52*).

65 *Dig.* 39.1.3.2 (*Ulp. Edict. 52*) (reference to Labeo).

66 *Dig.* 39.1.5.3 (*Ulp. Edict. 52*): *Nuntiari autem non utique domino oportet: sufficit enim in re praesenti nuntiari ei, qui in re praesenti fuerit, usque adeo, ut etiam fabris vel opificibus, qui eo loci operantur, opus novum nuntiari possit. Et generaliter ei nuntiari opus novum potest, qui in re praesenti fuit domini operisve nomine, neque refert, quis sit iste vel cuius condicionis qui in re praesenti fuit: nam et si servo nuntietur vel mulieri vel puero vel puellae, tenet nuntiatio: sufficit enim in re praesenti operis novi nuntiationem factam sic, ut domino possit renuntiari*.

67 *Dig.* 39.2.2 (*Gai, prov. ed.*).

68 *Dig.* 39.2.1 (*Ulp. 1 ad ed.*).

69 *Dig.* 1.18.7 (*Ulp. 3 opin.*).

70 Robinson 1992: 33.

71 *P. Fouad* 30 (one of the plaintiffs was a woman named Tasionis alias Dionysia); Crook 1967: 166–167. On women as property owners in Roman Egypt, cf. Hobson 1983.
72 *Dig.* 39.1.1.16 (*Ulp. Edict. 52): Nuntiatio fit aut iuris nostri conservandi causa aut damni depellendi aut publici iuris tuendi gratia.*
73 *Dig.* 39.1.17 (*Ulp. Edict.* 52); also ibid, 19.
74 *Dig.* 39.1.3.4 (*Ulp. Edict.* 52).
75 *Dig.* 39.1.4 (Paul. Edict. 48): *Nam rei publicae interest quam plurimos ad defendendam suam causam admittere.*
76 On the evolution of the concept of *res publica*, cf. Moatti 2018.
77 On rent control, cf. Rosillo-López 2022. This research was financed by the project "El sector inmobiliario en el mundo romano: un análisis económico; s. II a.C.-s. II d.C." (HAR2016-76882-P), Ministerio de Ciencia, Innovación y Universidades, Spain.

References

Brunt, P.A. (1971) *Italian Manpower 225 B.C.-A.D. 14.* Oxford: Clarendon Press.

Crawford, M.H. (ed.) (1996) *Roman Statutes.* London: Institute of Classical Studies.

Crook, J. (1967) *Law and Life of Rome.* Ithaca NY: Cornell University Press.

Davoine, C. (2016) Le vocabulaire des ruines dans le droit romain. In: R. Robert, ed. *Dire l'architecture dans l'antiquité.* Aix-en-Provence: Karthala, 305–320.

Fromentin, V. and Bertrand, E. (2014) *Dion Cassius, Histoire romaine, livre 47.* Paris: Belles Lettres.

Fusi, A. (2006) *M. Valerii Martialis Epigrammaton liber tertius.* Hildesheim: Olms.

García Morcillo, M. (2020) Hasta infinita? Financial Strategies in the Triumviral Period. In: F. Pina Polo, ed. *The Triumviral Period: Civil War, Political Crisis and Socioeconomic Transformations.* Zaragoza: Prensas Universitarias de Zaragoza, 379–400.

Garnsey, P. (1976) Urban Property Investment. In: M.I. Finley, ed. *Studies in Roman Property.* Cambridge: Cambridge University Press, 123–136.

Günther, S. (2016) Financing the Civil Wars – The Case of Duties and Taxes. *Marburger Beiträge zur Antiken Handels-, Wirtschafts- und Sozialgeschichte* 33, 213–227.

Hobson, D. (1983) Women as Property Owners in Roman Egypt. *TAPA* CXIII, 311–321.

Kienast, D. (1982) *Augustus. Princeps und Monarch.* Darmstadt: Wissenschaftliche Buchgesellschaft.

Martín, F. (1982) *La documentación griega de la cancillería del emperador Adriano.* Pamplona: Universidad de Navarra.

McCoy, M.T. (2014) *The Responses of the Roman Imperial Government to Natural Disasters 29 BCE-180 CE.* PhD. University of Arkansas, Fayetteville.

Mitteis, L. and Wilcken, U. (1912) *Grundzüge und Chrestomathie der Papyruskunde.* Leipzig: B.G. Teubner.

Moatti, C. (2018) *Res publica. Histoire romaine de la chose publique.* Paris: Fayard.

Moreno Soldevila, R., Marina Castillo, A. and Fernández Valverde, J. (2019) *A Prosopography to Martial's Epigrams.* Berlin: De Gruyter.

Murga Gener, J.L. (1986) *El edificio como unidad en la jurisprudencia romana y en la lex.* Seville: Publicaciones de la Universidad.

Newbold, R.F. (1974) Some Social and Economic Consequences of the AD 64 Fire at Rome. *Latomus* 33, 858–869.

Nicolet, C. (1976) *Tributum. Recherches sur la fiscalité directe sous la République romaine.* Bonn: Rudolf Habelt.

Nicolet, C. (1987) La Table d'Heraclée et les origines du cadastre romain. In: *L'Urbs, espace urbain et histoire (Ier siècle av. J.-C.-IIIe siècle apr. J.-C.)*. Rome: École Française de Rome, 1–25.

Oliver, J.H. (1989) *Greek Constitutions of Early Roman Emperors from Inscriptions and Papyri*. Independence Square: Philadelphia American Philological Society.

Procchi, F. (2001) Si quis negotiandi causa emisset quod aedificium… : prime considerazioni su intenti negoziali e speculazione edilizia nel principato. *Labeo* 47. 3, 411–438.

Rainer, J.M. (1987) Zum senatusconsultum Hosidianum. *Tijdschrift voor Rechtsgeschiedenis* 55, 31–38.

Robinson, O.F. (1992) *Ancient Rome: City Planning and Administration*. London: Routledge.

Rosillo-López, C. (2020) The Socio-Political Experience of the Italians during the Triumviral Period. In: F. Pina Polo, ed. *The Triumviral Period: Civil War, Political Crisis and Socioeconomic Transformations*. Zaragoza: Prensas Universitarias de Zaragoza, 353–378.

Rosillo-López, C. (2021) Domum pestilentem vendo: Real Estate Market and Information Asymmetry in the Roman World. In: C. Rosillo López, M. García Morcillo, eds. *Managing Information in the Roman Economy*. Cham: Palgrave MacMillan, 117–134.

Rosillo-López, C. (2022) Rent Control Measures in the 40s BCE: Housing Costs, Public Intervention and Inequality in the Roman World. In: N. Morley, M. Koedijk, eds. *Capital in Classical Antiquity*. Cham: Palgrave MacMillan, 175-204.

Scuderi, R. (1979) Problemi fiscali a Roma in età triumvirale. *Clio* 15. 3, 341–368.

Shatzman, I. (1975) *Senatorial wealth and Roman Politics*. Brussels: Latomus.

Swan, P.M. (2004) *The Augustan Succession: An Historical Commentary on Cassius Dio's Roman History, Books 55–56 (9 B.C.-A.D. 14)*. New York: Oxford University Press.

Voigt, M. (1903) *Die römische Baugesetze*. Teubner.

Wallace, S. Le R. (1938) *Taxation in Egypt from Augustus to Diocletian*. Princeton: Princeton University Press.

Yavetz, Z. (1958) The Living Conditions of the Urban Plebs in Republican Rome. *Latomus* 17, 500–517.

3 Beyond Price

Constructions of Value and the Real Estate Market in Ancient Rome

Marta García Morcillo

Abstract

What do prices and judgements of value tell us about the economic mentalities and behaviour of ancient Romans? Value is a polysemic concept that essentially helps articulate and classify individual and collective choices, preferences, beliefs, and emotions. In matters concerning economic appraisals and pecuniary considerations, ancient Romans used a large variety of expressions that revealed different notions of value, but also a deep understanding of their function within and outside market relationships, including the effect on estimations of institutional constrains, and of the complex scaffolding of social norms and ethical expectations. This contribution analyses value creation in the specific context of the real estate market. The chapter discusses what ancient evidence and discourses about appraisals and pricing can tell us about the intrinsic characteristics of immovable assets, their status as favourite objectives of economic investments, their exposure to risk and uncertainty, and their heterogeneous nature as goods that could not be replaced by identical properties. Sales and other types of transfers of properties and usufruct, judicial estimations and reasoning aiming to resolve conflicts of property rights ultimately reveal to us a sophisticated, intellectual engagement with the construction of conventions and criteria of value that aimed to legitimate costs and prices.

★★★

Introduction

Price is a form of economic value that is expressed in monetary terms. Value is a more elusive concept that can also reflect individual choices, preferences, beliefs, and emotions, and which may arise as the outcome of negotiation and of collective and normative conventions. The Latin term *pretium*, which can be translated as price, value, or cost, exemplifies the dynamism of the concept. In his *De Lingua Latina* (*On the Latin Language*), Varro defines *pretium* as "what is fixed for the purpose of purchase or of evaluation." The second part of the definition is more controversial, as it proposes an erroneous etymology for the word: "it is named from the experts (*periti*), because these alone can set a price correctly."[1] In truth, *pretium* derived from *compenso* (to weigh, balance, compensate), and thus dated

DOI: 10.4324/9781003187806-4

back to the idea of the transfer or compensation for an equivalent that defines monetary payments. Beyond this confusion, Varro's mistaken connection between *pretium* and *peritus* ultimately reveals a mentality rooted in the belief that the existence of a true price could only be interpreted and set by those who were in possession of qualified experience and knowledge. This epistemological approach to value finds reinforcement in Seneca's moral reasoning, informed by Stoicism: "only the saviour knows exactly the value at which something should be appraised."[2] Without that knowledge: "the unwise (*stultus*), even if he holds good intentions, either pays less than what he owes, or pays it at the wrong time or place."[3] On an abstract level, Seneca states that the truth can only be contemplated by the soul (*animus*) who is an expert (*peritus*) at determining the value of things (*pretia rebus inponens*), not according to opinion but to nature.[4] Seneca's saviour is thus someone who holds and applies in his judgements a moral notion of knowledge informed by natural law. This philosophical reasoning presupposes the existence of a true, indisputable price that can only be properly interpreted by those in possession of the *peritus animus*. In essence, both Varro and Seneca situated the figure of the "expert" as a kind of solution for the uncertainty that affected price and value formation. The shaping of the *peritus* as the perfect valuer is thus predominantly an ideal response to the absence of stable and reliable comparative information on which valuation could be anchored, a problem that especially affected markets and transactions of non-standard goods. On a practical level, private valuers and public arbitrators had to face real situations that required collectively accepted conventions and solutions to different and contested views on value, such as those emerging from property rights transfers and conflicts.

These initial considerations, which contrast an ideal notion of value with a more realistic and empiric approach to it, guide the direction of the present contribution. This chapter investigates the complex processes that shaped conventions of value of immovable properties in ancient Rome. This was a market characterised by the irregularity of transactions, volatile prices, exposure to multiple risks, and the incommensurability of assets. While these factors are also defining traits of real estate markets in other historical periods, including the present day, the use, possession, and transfer of immovable properties in ancient Rome played a distinguishing, fundamental role in the construction of the social, economic, and legal status of individuals. The transfer and division of real estate represented a particular challenge for legislators, given its central function in the structure of the census, in legacies, inheritances, and donations, as well as in property rights conflicts, which were very frequently attested throughout the social strata, as were transfers linked to the credit market. The use of immovables as security for loans, as well as indebtedness as a regular strategy to finance the purchase of an estate, were very common in Roman society. Seneca's moral letters come once again to our aid to capture the impact of the problem of insolvency, even among landlords: "His estates are wide, but his debts are large." "He has a fine house, but he has built it on borrowed capital."[5] This picture of the apparently volatile wealth of a proprietor, who was in fact bankrupt, made updated valuations and the function of valuers central to public debates about the use, limits and legitimacy of normative decisions concerning the real worth of properties. As I will attempt to show throughout this chapter, the different notions of value of immovable goods articulated a great diversity of socioeconomic ideas about individual and collective interests, aspirations and identities. I am particularly interested in identifying and understanding the social and psychological mechanisms that led to conventions of value of real estate in Roman society.

Theories of Value and the Real Estate Market

The topic of price formation in Greco-Roman antiquity has been the focus of some scholarly attention in the last years, particularly in connection to the question of state interventionism in the free market and the impact of public regulations, specifically those affecting standard products.[6] There is a certain consensus among scholars concerning the idea that prices were only limited or regulated by the Roman state in exceptional moments of crises, and that it was the dynamics of supply and demand which fundamentally led to price setting.[7] Yet, as formulated by Varro and Seneca, beyond the rather abstract concept of the rules of the market, we also need to take into account the impact of social forces as triggering factors that shape both value and price.

The conflict and interaction between price and value, and its applicability to immovable assets in particular, remains a rather understudied subject, despite its centrality in Roman moral and legal thought, as well as in early-modern and modern economic theory.[8] The debate about value has gained renewed interest in sociological research that critically questions the still influential weight of Neoclassical economics and the marginalist theory in contemporary economic studies.[9] In a nutshell, marginalists advocate for the merging of price and value. This theory conveys the principle that price is merely the outcome of the market forces that are shaped by supply and demand, which balance themselves until they reach what is called the equilibrium price.[10] The main sociological criticism of this objectivist model is that it ignores the impact of subjective views and social forces on the shaping of prices and notions of price. The paradox of the marginalist theory is that, in essence, it projects equilibrium price as a regulative – and thus ideal – concept, not as a real price.[11] Actors can hold very different ideas of worth and ideal prices, and these can influence transactions and real prices. Ultimately, economic value rather expresses the price a thing *ought* to be sold at.[12] This idea depicts value as having a double normative nature, both as the outcome of subjective and ethical notions of what should be a just price, and as the result of empiric valuations that are also shaped by social norms.[13] The lack of clarity about the nature of valuation, the function of valuers, and the very concept of market value lies at the core of recent critical studies that question the models of assessment applied in modern real estate markets before and after the sub-prime mortgage crisis of 2007. While the capacity to generate revenues dominated – and to a large degree continues to dominate – this profitable market, the criteria and parameters that measured this factor have been criticised for not being backed by empirical data. The very essential idea of a self-regulated market governed by the law of supply and demand applied to the modern paradigm has thus proved to be ineffective.[14]

Behavioural studies on modern real estate markets emphasise the cognitive limitations and deficiencies of the models of information often used by appraisers and property experts, which tend to impose predictable prices onto a highly volatile sector, while ignoring factors such as high transaction costs, the non-financial perspectives of consumers, the changing notions of subjective value, and the heterogeneity of assets, which are typical traits of residential properties.[15] These issues are not new. The impact of opacity and irregular systems of information on the transfer and valuation of real estate was a major preoccupation for Roman moralists and legislators, who tried to compensate frequent abuses and unfair disadvantages by exercising control over such practices and over sellers.[16] An important consideration that is applicable to both ancient and modern markets is that any price (market, personal, real, or projected) is the outcome of valuation, and that valuation expresses a decision by one or more actors that can lead to agreements and collective conventions. Thus, neither price nor value can exist independently of the actors and social norms that condition their decisions and behaviour.

Modern considerations of the fair or ideal price find enlightening echoes in ancient thought, and particularly in Aristotle.[17] They also take us back to Seneca's ethical conception of *pretium*. The ancient author unrolls his argument concerning the interconnections, but also the conflicts between subjective estimations, price, and real value. A telling example highlighted by Seneca is the common misunderstanding of value as a form of price, and the frequent judgement of a thing not according to what it is, but to what it costs (*non quale sit quidque, sed quanti*).[18] In *De Beneficiis*, we encounter typical circumstances in which what is paid underrepresents the real value of what is acquired, as in the case, for instance, of the services paid for a physician and for a teacher.[19] An important consideration here is that, in Seneca's view, value cannot reflect a market price, even if this price is the outcome of an agreement between seller and buyer.[20] The reason for this is that the buyer purchases the thing not at its own value but at the price agreed by the seller, while the latter will believe that the thing is "worth more than what it costs" (*pluris est quam venit*), even if it could not have been sold for more (*sed pluris venire non potuit*). Crucially to Seneca, the price of a thing is circumstantial (*pretium autem rei cuisque pro tempore est*),[21] as it is determined not by its utility and effectiveness (*non ex usu effectuve*), but by custom and the market (*sed ex consuetudine et annona aestimetur*).[22] Circumstantial need or demand is also a fundamental factor that can raise economic estimations, as – using Seneca's examples – when someone tries to find lodging in the wilderness, a shelter in rain, a warm bath, or a fire in cold weather. Without that need, the price of these services lowers substantially.[23] A further practical example concerning the frequent asymmetry between price/cost and value is the case of the cheap fixed rate (*pretium*) of the worker who secures a teetering house, and who, with incredible skill, manages to keep erect an *insula* that is cracking at the bottom.[24] This instance reveals how immovable goods were – both from an economic and a personal perspective – typically valued very highly by those who owned, possessed, and used them, yet also how they were subject to frequent risks that could devaluate them. I will return to this point below.

Ultimately, Seneca defends that the value of any kind of benefit depends on the will of whoever judges it, the *animus iudicis*.[25] By placing the *peritus* as the only judge that can rightly estimate the worth of things, Seneca completes the picture of true value as a virtuous idea towards which actors should aspire. Ultimately, in order to take the right, informed decision and control their own impulses, in Seneca's view it is indispensable that actors are able to categorise and estimate everything (*aestimata habere omnia*) and know the real value of things (*pretia rerum*).[26] All in all, Seneca's deep reasoning on the idealisation of value offers a rich testimony on the multifactual and interpretative nature of price, but also on the weight of social normative conventions in the shaping of fair valuations that guide the actor's decisions.

When thinking about the circumstantial nature of prices as discussed by Seneca, it is also important to scrutinise the different categories of products, services, and market frameworks in which transactions and valuations took place. Pliny the Elder's *Natural History* provides a useful, comparative glimpse into the price variations of pigments in different places and years, which were (in the author's view) the outcome of the shipping costs, as well as the intermediation of traders and dealers who dominated the market.[27] Subsequently, the final price of paintings, which depended entirely on the supply and price variations of the primary materials, would also have experienced variations. Similarly, Pliny refers to the case of aromatic products, which were sold in exclusive marketplaces such as the Seplasia, in Capua, for very high prices. The solution proposed by the author to prevent abusive practices by traders was the publication of a list of the usual prices of these products in Rome, which could be issued as a scale of value for sellers and purchasers.[28] The setting of scales of value based on historical prices to reduce opacity and transaction costs is a mechanism that can potentially work for standard products, such as those shaping the Plinian anecdotes. However, these mechanisms become less effective and much more complex to calculate when such goods (e.g. pigments) are appraised as essential parts or components of art works or decorations that improve the quality – and thus raise the value – of a house.

"In how many ways have we raised the prices of objects!"[29] Pliny's assertion brings forth a moral theory of value that he applies specifically to the art market. The author connects the lowering in the quality of individual objects with the massive demand and ignorant behaviour of consumers as the main reason for the inflationary prices of artworks: "and surprisingly, while the prices of works have grown *ad infinitum*, the reputation of craftmanship has vanished."[30] The relevance of knowledge and the behaviour of actors as a fundamental factor of price formation in the market of singular objects also appears prominently in Cicero's written Speech against Verres. In order to demonstrate that three famous statues by Praxiteles, Myron, and Polyclitus had been the subject of an illegal appropriation – masked as a cheap sale – by the rapacious Verres, Cicero invites his imaginary audience to consider how different the valuation of such items would work in reality. The orator distinguishes between the appraisal of experts (*studiosi*), the price normally paid for the statues (*quanti uenire soleant*), and the price that they could reach if they were sold openly and freely (*quanti haec ipsa, si palam libereque venirent, venire possent*), comparing these with Verres' own very low estimation (*denique ipse Verres quanti aestimet*).[31] Assuming that his audience has a familiarity with the art market and the estimated price of such works, Cicero shares the high price of a similar piece at an apparently real past auction, and assumes that in this kind of market, it is desire (*cupiditas*) that bounds the price (*aestimatio*).[32]

Cicero's elaborated discourse about customary price formation in the art market delineates a socially informed communication system in which the uncertainties about value are compensated by a collective discussion, comparison, and sanctioning of price by experts, actors, and audience. In contrast to the markets for standard products, such as that of pigments described by Pliny above, this system meets the definition of a status market, a structure of exchange that lacks a value scale that is independent of the one shaped by the participants themselves, including the opinion of experts, and in which, beyond the artwork itself, the actual object being traded is the very position of the actors within this social framework.[33]

The differentiated social and economic functions of real estate assets – both in pre- and modern societies – include traits from both standard and status markets. Some criteria, such as location, size, the quality and transaction costs of the materials, techniques and labour employed, productivity of buildings and facilities, featured as relevant pieces of information to appraise immobile properties in ancient Rome. Others, such as political instability, war, natural disasters, and the speculative practices that impacted upon landed property and buildings, were – as they are today – factors that greatly contributed to the volatility of prices in the sector. Finally, as in the art market – and equally challenging to measure and appraise – there were criteria such as the personal interest conferred upon a house or an estate, the changing dynamics of demand, the interdependence with other markets, the history of the building, and the social identity of its possessors. While Seneca's ideal of true value traces an aspiration that is impossible to achieve in real valuations that are expressed in monetary terms, his notion of personal value, as well as the authority conferred upon the expert appraiser, featured strongly in legal literature and were central and challenging factors in transactions and conflicts affecting the property rights of immobile goods.

Despite the absence of an exact term equivalent to modern value, Romans used a large variety of expressions that reflected highly nuanced, and complementary, distinctions of the perspectives and contextualisation of economic valuations. Considering the instances discussed above, *quanti aestimet* or *mea est, quanti est, venire soleat* and *venire posset* captured ideas such as projected individual appraisals, real prices, frequent prices, and potential transfer prices. Such distinctions were fundamental in complex matters involving legal estimations. Take, for instance, a text by the jurist Ulpian concerning monetary condemnations, which offers a refined explanation of the equivalence between the monetary value of a property (*quanti res est*) and "the extent of anyone's interest in keeping possession" (*quanti uniuscuiusque interest possessionem retinere*). Against the opinion of the earlier jurist Servius, who upheld that the appraisal of a possession should equal its worth (*existimantis tanti possessionem aestimandam, quanti ipsa res est*), Ulpian clarifies that "the price of a thing is far from being that of its possession, which is quite a different thing" (*longe enim aliud est rei pretium, aliud possessionis*).[34] Two considerations appear from Ulpian's words. On the one hand, the author differentiates the price that a property could achieve at any given moment or transaction from the value that the possessor confers upon it. This rather abstract idea is, for practical purposes, here simply reduced to the interest in keeping the *res*, which should be considered when calculating any kind of penalties or compensations. On the other hand, disregarding the price – whether past or via valuation by the appraiser – as a valid scale for the calculation for compensations implicitly recognises its volatility, and thus unreliability, as a measure of value. This argument meets Seneca's *pretium pro tempore*, the circumstantial nature of price, that particularly concerned incommensurable goods, and the changing and subjective notions of value generally attached to immobile assets.[35]

Changing Value(s) and Notions of Price Formation of Real Estate

The moral and legal considerations on price formation unpacked in the previous section show the Romans' awareness of the multiple factors that determined economic valuation. In this section, I would like to deepen the analysis of the Romans' understanding of the fluctuation of real estate prices and the notion of the changing value of immovables. The transformation of such properties, in the form of structural or aesthetic improvements, damage, or destruction, as well as changes affecting its location and neighbourhood, use, occupation, and ownership, or simply the passage of time, directly impacted on their value and valuation. In Seneca's moral scrutiny of benefits, time becomes a fundamental factor for measuring not only the altruistic liberality of gift-makers and friends, but also to appraise certain categories of gifts over others. This is the case with a productive estate that, due to its fertility, can contribute to lowering the price of grain in times of famine.[36] Beyond this idealised notion of utilitarian immovables, urban houses and productive buildings and estates stood at the centre of social and economic investments and strategies. Despite the irregularity of price behaviour, the uncertainty and risks that characterised the sector, real estate, and particularly landed property that shaped the *res familiaris*, were perceived as the most secure and valuable type of wealth.[37] Prices of sumptuous villas in the city of Rome could illustrate narratives of excessive expenditures, inflationary markets, and luxurious behaviour, but also their fundamental role in the construction of elite identity.[38] Despite price irregularity, the indisputable high esteem of immovable properties explains why they were alluded to as a scale of value for moral comparatives with other categories of items – movable unique objects – which were often sold at exaggerated, and socially questionable prices.[39] At the opposite pole, devaluations provoked by monetary fluctuations and insolvency, but also by political conflicts, such as proscriptions and confiscations, triggered discussions about the asymmetric relationship between price and value.[40]

The difficulty of establishing price comparatives for real estate, even in similar locations and of similar size, has to do with not only the incommensurable nature of immovables, but also with the typical problem of hidden information – such as defects – not declared by owners and sellers. This irregularity is discussed in Cicero's moral treatise *On Duties* (*De Officiis*) as a form of behaviour that seeks advantage and profit at the expense of honesty and transparency.[41] The responsibility of sellers to publicly declare any defects – visible or invisible – of a house, a slave, cattle, and other types of fungible goods, is the focus of particular attention and regulation in the legal sources.[42] The requirement to inspect, test, and – in the case of fungible products such as wine – quantify and taste the commodity to guarantee the control of quality and the fair conditions of transfer was a fundamental mechanism to combat uncertainty, but also an essential criterium for price settlement and comparison.[43] The jurist Gaius makes it clear that the personal criteria of fair estimation by the seller and the purchaser alone cannot lead to contract agreement without a clearly defined and transparent weighing, measuring, or counting of the thing.[44] Similar rules were applied to productive estates.[45] An inspection of the land and a comparison of the quality and quantity of the yearly harvest was certainly a valid reference – although not the only criterion – to determine the price of properties.[46] In his *De Re Rustica*, Varro admits that along with such criteria as aesthetics, the productivity (*utilitas*) of an estate significantly impacted on its value – despite intrinsic risks in all calculations of profit regarding land – while also making it more vendable.[47] The author offers a very suggestive insight into the not always straightforward relationship between the value of a property and its revenues.[48] When it comes to estimating the value of a *fundus*, criteria such as past sales or even a present fair estimation could be considered highly useful when future expectation of profit or contextual factors were also included in such judgements.[49] In a commentary on legacies and the *Lex Julia et Papia* (9 CE), the jurist Terentius Clemens explains one of these situations: a person is bequeathed a farm (*fundus*) worth a hundred (hypothetical figure) on condition that the heir receives a hundred. Sometimes, adds Clements, it would be more profitable to keep the estate in the expectation of acquiring neighbouring farms, even for more than their correct value (*iusta aestimatio*).[50] The addition of new buildings, and the improvement of houses by means of decorative elements such as wall paintings, but also movable objects such as statues, and their impact on value was given careful consideration by the jurists.[51] From a different perspective, the poet Martial exposes the moral incongruities of a seller who declared his willingness to sell a house, even for less than what he paid for it, while in reality he increased the apparent value of the house with ostentatious decoration in order to ask four times its former price.[52] A frequent circumstance that led to the depreciation of immovable properties were sales following pledges as the result of unpaid debts. Any damages or changes, such as the cutting down of trees or the demolishing of buildings while the property was in the hands of the creditor, had to be deducted from the indebtedness.[53] The endemic, and historically recurrent, problem of speculators of valuable estates, urban or rural, and their methods of depreciating and inflating prices is discussed in a commentary by the third-century CE jurist Paul to a *Senatus Consultum*. The measure forbade the destruction of any domus or villa in order to make a profit from its acquisition (*quo plus sibi adquireretur*) and prevented buying or selling with the same business purpose (*neve quis negotiandi causa eorum quid emeret venderetve*), with the penalty being double the price paid for the property.[54] Another typical practice that was sanctioned by the state were auctions of confiscated properties put up for sale by the public treasury that concluded with incredulously cheap prices. These held a suspicion of bidders colluding, usually with the former owner.[55]

One of the most restrictively regulated types of property transfers were those undertaken between spouses. In the case of the dowry, the concerns of legislators specifically addressed whether the objects of such transfers, movable or immovable, could end up unfairly impoverishing or enriching one of the parties. A decree by Emperor Alexander Severus (227 CE) specified that if a property were legally appraised in advance, the husband would obtain its ownership, but would also be the debtor of its value. Without the valuation, and in case of divorce, the husband would have to restore the property, but not the money.[56] Particularly important in the sources is the requirement to avoid speculative practices with goods that could change their economic worth over time, as was the case with the offspring of slaves, cattle, and estates. For this reason, it was recommended, although not compulsory, to appraise such properties before the dowry contract was agreed.[57] In the case of land given as a dowry without valuation, any profit or loss fell upon the wife, not the husband, even if he was the owner of the property.[58]

The persistent discussion of matters concerning the value of productive estates in Roman sources in many ways reflects the complex nature of these kinds of assets, their double – and paradoxical – existence as incommensurable, and thus unique goods, but also as assets generating standard products. These revenues featured as useful proxies for private and judicial appraisals of these properties.

Cicero's letters provide a fertile corpus of materials on the Romans' engagement with real estate transactions and the multiple factors that shaped value and price formation.[59] The letters offer a phenomenological approach to the valuation of immovables, in which the orator and other members of the late-republican elite frequently participated.[60] They also offer a unique glimpse into the economic mentalities, judgements, and the process of decision-making that conditioned the financial strategies of the Roman upper classes.[61] Information about pricing and price-setting in his correspondence is particularly rich in the case of Tullia's shrine: Cicero's complex and arduous search for a suitable property in the Roman suburbs to build a temple in memory of his deceased daughter (45 BCE).[62] The similar characteristics and references to the price of villas potentially for sale in this area are discussed and compared by Cicero in several letters.[63] Particularly interesting is the possibility to observe Cicero's own evaluations and comparisons between his limited financial capabilities, the high prices set by the sellers, and his own estimation of these properties, which are highly influenced by emotional and non-economic motivations.[64] Cicero's firm desire to acquire the Hortus Scapulanus, a garden property located in the Transtiberim and auctioned off by the heirs, triggered a series of strategies to gather cash and obtain direct information on the true condition of the villa, and the maximum bid that the sale could reach.[65] Complementary to this information, Cicero also compared the possible prospective price of the Scapulan property with that of another, larger property sold for a very high price in the same area before the war. The orator noticed, however, that prices had dropped significantly since then (*omnia scilicet nunc minoris*).[66] This relevant case study helps us reveal the interconnection between personal notions of value, evaluations based on the processing of empiric information, and information based on the price fluctuations of similar, albeit not entirely equal, items.

To conclude this section, I would like to examine another relevant real-estate sale from Cicero's letters. In March 49 BCE, at the beginning of the civil war, Cicero reported to his friend Atticus about an attractive property from an inheritance offered for sale in Lanuvium, about 32 kms southeast of Rome. In the epistle, Cicero expressed his hope, provided the Republic would continue, that one of his friends would purchase the property, even if he admitted to not having considered his best friend Atticus as a buyer. The text continues with an allusion to Atticus' experience in the field: "I know that you used to search for 'how much per year' and 'how much per land'; and I have seen your account-books, not only in Rome, but also in Delos."[67] Cicero's words paint Atticus as an expert in the prices and costs of productive estates, which prompts us to consider that the Lanuvium property may not have been on his radar given its proximity to Rome and subsequent high price. The following part of the letter reinforces this interpretation, but also explains why Cicero still hoped that his friend might be interested in the *hortulus* (farm): "Anyhow, nice as it is, I don't think it's worth as much as it was reckoned to be in Marcellinus' consulship (56 BCE)."[68] We know that, at that time, Cicero was searching for a possible replacement for his Tusculum property, which had suffered substantial damage during his exile, and required expensive rebuilding.

Returning to the letter, we learn that the orator had offered 500,000 sesterces for the estate, an offer that was rejected by the owner. However, the situation had changed after the escalation of the political conflict, when debt and a lack of monetary liquidity became more general problems. Cicero reflected upon this in the letter: "But I imagine all these things have dropped in value because of the money shortage (*caritas nummorum*). It will suit me best, or rather us, if you buy it."[69] His final words on the topic not only echo (or rather anticipate) the drop in prices of the Scapulan episode, but also express concern about the uncertain future of the charming property – its possible destruction or confiscation – due to the outbreak of the civil war.[70]

Cicero's considerations about the changing value of the Lanuvian property lead us to a richer understanding of the functioning of the market from the perspective of the late Republican *nobiles*. The case provides evidence about the importance of monetary circulation for the stability of prices, as well as the direct impact of other external risks such as the political and military uncertainty on the behaviour of purchasers. The prospect of losing a property due to confiscation following political proscriptions is very present throughout the letter.

In a nutshell, both Ciceronian episodes concerning the sale of urban and rural estates show different notions of value, including personal interest, as well as the importance of practical knowledge and proxies in the search for a fair estimation. A common element within the texts seen above, and also from the legal literature, is the actors' acknowledgement of the importance of the political context and of time – e.g. the notion of change with the passage of time – as a fundamental factor in creating the criteria of value. In the next section, I will specifically look at the role of appraisers and formal appraisals in the formation of social conventions of value.

In Search of the *verum pretium*: A Radiography of Property Appraisals

The problem of the lack of reliable parameters for appraising property, and the questionable efficiency of valuers in the modern real estate market is, as we have seen, largely associated with the uncertainty and price irregularity attached to this very special commodity. Similar preoccupations about valuations related to the citizen's census, or aimed at solving conflicts of property rights and transfers, permeate throughout Roman legal literature.[71] Classical and Post-Classical Roman law show a particular sensibility towards different notions of value, which reveal sophisticated attempts to translate and transform the abstract into workable concepts that could be expressed in monetary terms. Judicial appraisals are the best documented systems of property valuation in ancient Rome. The intervention of a judge or magistrate to resolve different kinds of conflicts of property rights, as well as to fix fines and compensations to the affected party, features a rich diversity of legal cases that contrasts with the almost total absence of information about private, informal appraisals that did not end up in court. Judicial valuations also faced the epistemic and social challenge of being accepted as an indisputable true value, the *verum pretium*, without overlooking other types of individual and subjective notions of value, including the highly personal *pretium* or *aestimatio affectionis*.[72] Seneca's idealised figure of the *peritus* as a moral authority and proper interpreter of the value of things was a mirror to the *iudex*, and both were somehow modelled after the *vir bonus*. In Cato the Elder's *De Agricultura*, we meet an early version of this respected and honest member of the community, who was chosen by the parties to act as an impartial arbitrator in private transfers, such as lease agreements and sale contracts.[73] This consensus authority, who guided the actors and resolved conflicts of property rights, helps us to understand the indispensability of this figure both in court and in society.

Formal *aestimationes*, conducted, supervised, or sanctioned by a judge or magistrate, enjoyed the reputation of being a reliable system to fix the value of things. In a chapter from the *Digest* devoted to the meaning of expressions (*De verborum significatione*), the jurist Ulpian clarifies that the popular expressions "*quanti ea res erit*" (whatever it will be worth) and "*quanti eam rem esse paret*" (whatever it appears to be worth) do not actually refer to the appraisal or interest of any of the parties, but rather to the *vera aestimatio* of the property.[74] This "true estimation" expresses the idea of an indisputable valuation that does not (or should not) depend on subjective and personal considerations, and should be sanctioned or directly conducted by a legitimate authority. This procedure was for instance followed for things given in deposit, or loaned for their use but not returned. In those cases, explains Gaius, the judge sentenced the offender of the fraud to pay a monetary equivalent of the value of the tangible property, which could consist of an estate, a slave, a garment, gold, or silver.[75]

A scrutiny of property valuations linked to the application of the *Lex Falcidia* (41–40 BCE) offers a productive framework of analysis for the application of the *vera aestimatio* and the underlying notions of value attached to it. The *Lex Falcidia* was a *plebiscitum* that obliged testators to leave at least one fourth of their wealth to their heirs, to prevent the dissipation of family fortunes into legacies that would break natural succession lines. The so-called Falcidian quarter remained in place throughout all antiquity, and has persisted in several civil legislations through to the modern age.[76] One of the reasons for the longevity of this law was its effective protection against the abuse of legacies, but also the particular interest of the state in its correct application, given the fact that inheritances – a very common type of transfer in ancient Rome – were subject to a 5 per cent tax (the *vicesima hereditatium*).[77] Formal valuations of testamentary properties were thus necessary to avoid legacies that could exceed three quarters of the total worth of the testator's wealth. The calculation was based on the worth of the property left at the moment of the death of the testator, after any eventual debts or obligations had been discounted. In the *Digest*'s chapter dedicated to the *Lex Falcidia*, Ulpian clarifies that the estimation of the value of assets should be made according to their true worth (*In Falcidia aestimatio pretii rerum ex veritate facienda est*).[78]

Yet, what exactly was this true value or price on which the calculations for the division of legacies and inheritances should be based? The same Ulpian, in a commentary on the *Lex Julia et Papia*, points out that the assets from the deceased's estate (*corpora*) should be valued at their true worth (*secundum rei veritatem aestimanda erunt*), which means according to the price fixed presently (*hoc est secundum praesens pretium*), and not according to a nominal or formal valuation (*nec quicquam eorum formali pretio aestimandum esse*).[79] The differentiation between true and formal valuation and the prioritisation of the first implicitly reveals that the fixing of the *verum pretium* should not be based on abstract, arbitrary decisions that overlook the dynamics of the current market and the specificities of the property under appraisal. Two passages by Javolenus in the same chapter discuss different notions of value considered in transfers of property affected under the Falcidian law. Appraisals under oath (*ius iurandum in litem*) by the claimant for a legacy were not accepted for such calculations of value. Instead, only the true value of the property was considered (*quanti re vera id fuit quod petitum est*).[80] The author unpacks a more complex situation in which the heir ends up purchasing a *fundus* from a legacy of the deceased for an inflated price that surpassed its real value (*emit multo pluris, quam quanti erat*). The overpayment had implications on the shares of the legatees to the estate. Javolenus concludes that even if the heir claimed that the wish of the deceased forced him to pay more than the real value for the *fundus* (*quod ex voluntate defuncti pluris emerit fundum, quam quanti erat*), he was not entitled to claim a share from the legatees, because he had acted negligently and could instead have opted for a *vera aestimatio*.[81] The passage does not reveal what should be the basis for the *vera aestimatio*, although it suggests, as with Ulpian's texts above, that the "true appraisal" was understood as a fair market value, e.g. a price that would be accepted as a *praesens pretium*, even if this valuation did not necessarily match the actual price paid for the property in the transaction.

What should then be the criteria informing the 'true value' of things? Paul, in his own observations on the *Lex Julia et Papia*, adds relevant considerations on the matter: "The prices of things (*pretia rerum*) are achieved not by the interest or utility of individuals (*non ex affectu nec utilitate singulorum*), but by their communal usefulness (*sed communiter*)."[82] Implicit is the recognition of a convention of value shaped by a process that goes beyond any personal interest. The special relationship developed between a master and certain kinds of slaves exemplifies in the passage how personal affections and subjective considerations could differ from other types of valuation. External factors such as the place or time are also mentioned by the author as determining variations in value (*Nonnullam tamen pretio varietatem loca temporaque adferunt*). The example provided by Paul to illustrate these variations is that of oil, which "will not be equally valued in Rome and in Hispania nor given the same assessment in periods of lasting scarcity as when there are crops." The author adds that "in the latter case, prices are not determined by vicissitudes and chance events."[83] The relatively predictable factors determining the price setting of a standard commodity such as oil, however, were not entirely the same as those shaping the valuation of slaves, particularly domestic. This reasoning can be also applied to real estate, in which, as we have seen above, the irregularity of transactions, the incommensurability of assets, and the impact of multiple environmental, social, and political factors made it very difficult to set comparative scales of value, especially in the case of residential properties.

In the chapter dedicated to the *Lex Aquilia* in the *Digest*, we find a verbatim repetition of the expression, attributed to the earlier jurist Sextus Pedius, concerning communally determined prices (*communiter*), in contrast to those influenced by personal affections or interests.[84] The different criteria applied in the valuation of properties illustrate Paul's discussion about the specific problem of the calculation of damages affecting slaves, particularly in cases in which the plaintiff had personal feelings or interests.[85] How to set an economic value for the harm, intentional or not, caused by the killing of a slave who was also a natural son of the claimant? This extreme example prompts us to consider the challenge of setting a fair valuation for property that was unique or irreplaceable. The third chapter of the *Lex Aquilia* was applicable to the wrongful damage of any kind of properties, apart from slaves or cattle. How was the *pretium ex utilitate communiter* considered and applied in the law for compensation of damages that affected real estate? This Republican law, which was expanded and enriched during the Principate, specified that those responsible for the wrongful burning, breaking, or spoiling of a property should pay the owner a monetary amount equivalent to the cost of the damage or *damnum* (*quanti ea res erit*).[86] Several texts seem to indicate that the amount to be paid by the condemned may have been calculated according to the highest cost of the loss or damage within the previous year, or in the preceding 30 days.[87] A short temporal window for the calculation of the cost of the damage – instead of the value of the entire property – as the basis for the condemnation makes more sense if we assume that the law included not only frequently marketed movable things such as slaves, cattle, and the produce from a harvest, but also immovable properties, whose transfers and prices were much more irregular and unpredictable.[88]

The legal evidence for the procedure offers some relevant information about the decision-making process for the fixing of these penalties. The second century jurist Gaius explains that in his time, the praetor permitted the plaintiff to estimate the damage (*iniuria*), yet a judge ultimately decided whether the condemned party should pay that amount or a lesser one. In the case of an atrocious injury, the praetor personally intervened to fix the amount of the damage, the quantity to be paid, and the security (*vadimonium*) to be handed in by the defendant. Even if the judge could decide to lower the amount, Gaius tells us that he tended to respect the authority of the praetor.[89]

A comparison with the famous episode of the damages caused by Clodius to Cicero's properties following the exile of the orator (57 BCE) can shed some light on the challenges of such estimations, particularly when different kinds of interests collided. In a letter to Atticus, Cicero provides details about the appraisal, which was decided by the Consuls after consulting with his advisers (*de consili sententia*).[90] They estimated a compensation of 2,000,000 sesterces for the rebuilding of his heavily damaged *domus* on the Palatine, while his other properties, the Tusculan and the Formian villas were – in the orator's view – valued very ungenerously (*valde illiberaliter*), for 500,000 and 250,000, respectively. These appraisals were, according to Cicero, heavily criticised, both by the upper and the lower classes (*quae aestimatio non modo vehementer ab optimo quoque sed etiam a plebe reprehenditur*). The reason behind this controversial decision was in Cicero's opinion clearly political: the suspicion that his enemies did not want him to return to the public stage. Yet the official version was that Cicero himself had, out of modesty, decided to accept the compensation instead of pushing his claim more firmly. At the discursive level, Cicero here constructs the argument that the *aestimatio* was unfair, the evidence for which was that a large number of people across social strata perceived that the compensation figures were below the real value of these properties. Leaving aside any speculative exercise of price and value comparison with other equivalent properties in that period, and the clear political motivation of the episode, the relevant point for the purpose of my analysis is the perception that judicial valuations needed a certain collective and social consensus, beyond the authority of magistrates and judges, and that they should also consider the plaintiff's own interest in the matter. The lack of a general convention in this case moved thus the arbitrary decision of the judges away from what the jurists Pedius and Paul would much later call the principle *ex utilitate communiter.*

In late antique legislations we find some interesting mechanisms and adjustments aimed at solving conflicts of valuations in difficult cases of damaged and lost properties dominated by uncertainty. An imperial rescript by Zeno dated to 477 CE discusses the application of a double system of appraisal.[91] While the judge should conduct an assessment (*taxatio*) that also took into consideration the character and type of business of whoever suffered the act of violence (*pro personarum atque negotii qualitate*), the plaintiff should set by oath a general *aestimatio* of the property lost, yet without surpassing the upper limit of the estimate fixed by the judge. The text suggests that the lack of value scale for the goods lost justified that the judge used, among other criteria, the reputation of the plaintiff to determine his own appraisal of the property. This adjusted system of valuation, including social information, emerged as an attempt to compensate for the problem of uncertainty due to the lack of proxies of value and the subjectivity of the affected party (the *pretium affectionis*).

Legislators were aware that the problem of uncertainty and asymmetric information could also affect the judging authority who, in the end, also embodied the very trustworthiness of the system. In this regard, a Constitution by Justinian (530 CE) imposed a reform that specifically aimed to reduce the endless doubts and the prolixity or verbosity that had affected judicial decisions on property damages in the past.[92] In cases in which the value of the property was known, thanks to sales, leases, and other contracts, Justinian stipulated that the interests to pay should not exceed double the value of the property (*quod hoc interest dupli quantitatem minime excedere*). In cases of uncertain value, the judges should carefully calculate the actual amount of damage to be compensated (*quod re vera inducitur damnum, hoc reddatur*). The constitution specified that such calculations should avoid any machinations and immoderate perversions leading to inextricable circles (*non ex quibusdam machinationibus et immodicis perversionibus in circuitus inextricabiles redigatur*). Above all, they should prevent calculations without restrictions that become impossible to apply (*ne, dum in infinitum computatio reducitur, pro sua impossibilitate cadat*).[93] Instead, the judges were urged to impose penalties with proper moderation, according to the laws. The aim of the reform was an appeal to clarity, moderation, and the end of the *antiqua prolixitas* that complicated the valuation procedure and could potentially open the door to manipulation and corruption.

These attempts to regulate the law of damages, but also to guide and monitor the behaviour of the judging authority, suggest a crisis of credibility of arbitrators and a need to, as much as possible, back fair valuation with established and observable conventions. As discussed above, these were easier to apply in the appraisal of productive estates. This was the case with sales of landed property for the benefit of the imperial Fiscus in which, according to the third-century jurist Callistratus, honesty (*fides*) and carefulness (*diligentia*) were expected from the fiscal procurator when he fixed the fair prices (*iusta pretia*). These were to be established not on the basis of a past sale, but from an updated appraisal (*ex praesenti aestimatione constitui*).[94] The valuation of the property thus also considered the variability of prices according to good and bad harvests.[95]

A useful comparative study of a very well-documented corpus of building estimations in early-modern Milan can shed some light on an appraisal system that bore some similarities to the Roman one.[96] The collegiate Milan engineers, who for centuries acted as appraisers of properties, constructed their reputation through a perceived image of efficiency in the successful application of a systematic methodology of valuation based on an empirical process, even if this process inevitably also included subjective – and thus potentially questionable – criteria. The incomparable nature of the assets examined by these appraisers made it impossible – as was the case in ancient Rome – to follow strict rules or apply a single method of assessment. The inevitable uncertainty and high transaction costs of this market were thus compensated by the accepted conventions of value-setting that resulted from a combination of objective and subjective criteria. When the perception of fairness of the process was weak, as in the case of the *antiqua prolixitas* of valuers faced by Justinian, the entire system was called into question.

Conclusion

The specific characteristics of immovable goods as incommensurable assets situates valuation at the centre of economic thinking. This singularity challenges not only the very idea of value as a synonym of market price, but also as an abstract notion that is independent of the valuer. However, the very limited explanations about the process and method of valuation in the legal sources should not lead us to assume, as neoclassical economists often do, that value is a kind of self-sufficient entity waiting to be discovered and interpreted. This chapter has attempted to show how the rich and heterogeneous notions of value related to real estate in ancient Rome primarily reflected an understanding of its complex application in real situations and decisions affecting property rights. The *verum pretium* of the legal literature expressed nothing but a communal convention, the *pretium communiter*, which aspired to go beyond arbitrary decisions of judges that did per se not meet a generally accepted status of fairness and fair price. With some exceptions, the lack of sufficient proxies to back valuations turned the idealised *peritus* of Varro and Seneca into real social actors that tried to react to uncertainties and deficiencies by introducing normative procedures that strengthened trust in the system, while also aspiring to meet social conventions. Behind apparently elusive notions such as *utilitas* and *pretium affectionis*, we discover a rich variety of personal perceptions of value that legislators tried to define and concretise under the umbrella of the interest of the parties. Overall, these texts encapsulated a deep understanding of value as a socially – and constantly – negotiated judgement that ultimately shaped the dynamic function and position of individuals in relation to collective beliefs, norms, and institutions.

Notes

1 Varro *Ling.* 5.177: *Pretium, quod emptionis aestimationisve causa constituitur, dictum a peritis, quod hi soli facere possunt recte id* (transl. R.G. Kent, LCL).
2 Sen. *Epist.* 81.8: *Uni sapienti notum est, quanti res quaeque taxanda sit.*
3 Sen. *Epist.* 81.8: *Nam ille, de quo loquebar modo, stultus etiam si bonae voluntatis est, aut minus quam debet aut alio quam debet tempore aut quo non debet loco reddit* (transl. R.M. Gummere, slightly changed). This principle informs not only economic but also social relationships.
4 Sen. *Epist.* 66.6: *Animus intuens vera, peritus fugiendorum ac petendorum, non ex opinione, sed ex natura pretia rebus inponens.*
5 Sen. *Epist.* 87.6: *Late possidet, sed multum debet; habet domum formosam, sed alienis nummis paratam* (transl. R.M. Gummere).
6 On price formation, see notably Andreau, Briant, and Descat 1997; Rathbone and von Reden 2015; Kroops 2016; Lo Cascio 2018; 2020; Chankowski 2020.
7 Kroops 2016, and Lo Cascio 2018; 2020, on price formation and the role of the state.
8 The notion of the just price from Aristotle to the twenty-first century has recently been studied in Chankowski, Lenoble, and Maucourant 2020. This contribution persuasively shows the importance of approaching this topic from a social, cultural and long-term perspective.
9 See the critical postulates by Orléan 2014; Elder-Vass 2019.
10 On Walras and the Marginalists' notion of equilibrium price, see Mirowski 1991, and criticism by Orléan (2014). A partial alternative to marginalist price theory is proposed by post-Keynesians, who argue that prices are not adjusted constantly in response to market forces, or determined by marginal costs of production, but instead set by producers in advance of trade. These ideas, however, only apply to certain types of markets.
11 Elder-Vass 2019: 189.
12 As convincingly defined by Elder-Vass, who highlights that this expression essentially denotes an ethical claim, 2019: 1485–1490.
13 Such subjective valuations are also embedded in and influenced by social norms, see Aspers and Beckert 2011.

14 See Mooya 2009.
15 Salzman and Zwinkels 2017 (with earlier bibliography).
16 On transactions costs and information asymmetries in the Roman real estate market, see Rosillo-López 2021, and her chapter on state intervention in this volume (Chapter 2).
17 Aristotle draws upon the differentiation between the value and the price of an object, e.g. *Eth. Nic.* 4.2.18–19. On fair, market, normal, and other notions of price in the ancient Greek economy, see Chankowski 2020 (with discussion of earlier scholarship).
18 Sen. *Epist.* 115.10.
19 Sen. *Ben.* 6.15.1–2: *Adversus hoc respondetur quaedam pluris esse, quam emuntur.* 6.15.3: *Quaedam, pluris sunt, quam venierunt.*
20 Sen. *Ben.* 6.15.4: *Primum quid interest, quanti sint, cum de pretio inter ementem vendentemque convenerit?*
21 Sen. *Ben.* 6.15.4.
22 Sen. *Ben.* 6.15.5.
23 Sen. *Ben.* 6.15.7: *Quanti aestimas in solitudine hospitium, in imbre tectum, in frigore balneum aut ignem? Scio tamen, quanti ista consecuturus deversorium subeam!*
24 Sen. *Ben.* 6.15.7: *Quantum nobis praestat, qui labentem domum suscipit et agentem ex imo rimas insulam incredibili arte suspendit! Certo tamen et levi pretio fultura conducitur.*
25 Sen. *Ben.* 3.12.2: *Proinde ista [beneficia] maiora aut minora erunt, prout fuerit iudex aut huc aut illo inclinatus animo.*
26 Sen. *Epist.* 89.14–15.
27 Plin. *NH.* 33.164.
28 Plin. *NH.* 9.138. Similarly, he mentions the very high prices for dye products, which were conditioned by their seasonal harvest.
29 Plin. *NH.* 33.4: *Heu prodiga ingenia, quot modis auximus pretia rerum!*
30 Plin. *NH.* 34.5: *Mirumque, cum ad infinitum operum pretia creverint, auctoritas artis extincta est.*
31 Cic. *Verr.* 2.4.13.
32 Cic. *Verr.* 2.4.14.
33 I am following Patrik Aspers' definition of status markets. In contrast, standard markets are characterised by the existence of scales of value that orientate the pricing of the products, see Aspers 2009.
34 *Dig.* 43.17.3.11 (*Ulp. 69 ed.*).
35 On the interest of the plaintiff in other legal sources, see Matthews 1921: 235. Besides *utilitas*, this idea is encapsulated by expressions such as *quanti mea interest, quanti res est, quanti* (or *id quod*) *alicuius interest*, etc. E.g. *Dig.* 19.1.1.pr. (*Ulp. Sab. 28*): *Id quod interest, hoc est quod rem habere interest emptoris.*
36 Sen. *Ben.* 3.8.2–3.
37 Also from a sentimental and sometimes highly idealised point of view, cf. Treggiari 1979. On land as a long-term financial resource, see Kehoe, this volume (Chapter 4).
38 See Craver 2010 and Dubouloz 2011 for social and legal issues regarding urban properties in the Republic and Imperial period, respectively.
39 Cicero narrates, for instance, the story of a curious metal object, a self-cooker (*authepsa*), which was auctioned by the influential freedman of Sulla, Chrysogonus, at a price equivalent to a *fundus*, Cic. *S. Rosc.* 133. An epigram of Martial criticises the extravagant Quintus for purchasing items at exaggerated prices, including a golden chariot for the price of a farm, and a mule for the value of a house, 3.62.
40 See for instance the famous case of the properties of the exiled Milo (52 BCE) auctioned for a devaluated price, which became an opportunity for purchasers, Cic. *Att.* 5.8.2–3; *Fam.* 8.3.2; *Ascon. tog. Cand. in Mil.* 54.20–21; García Morcillo 2021: 74–75.

41 Cic. *Off.* 3.55. On this case, which is framed as a Stoic dialogue between the philosophers Antipater and Diogenes, and the issue of information asymmetry and adverse selection in the relationship between sellers and purchasers, landlords and tenants, see Rosillo-López 2021.

42 This is the case with the Edict of the Curule Aediles extensively covered in *Dig.* 21.1. A recent scrutiny of the Aediles' Edict in relation to the problem of adverse selection is provided by Lavan 2021 (with earlier bibliography). Book 18.1 from the *Digest* discusses further the responsibilities and risks of vendors.

43 On the importance of tasting the product to avoid risk and validate the sale, see Cato. *Agr.* 148; and *Dig.* 18.1.34.5 (*Paul. Ed. 33); Dig.* 18.1.35.5 (*Gaius, Prov. Edict 10); Dig.* 18.6.1 (*Ulp. Sab. 28*). The risk management of wine and the legal responsibilities of the parties involved in its commercialisation have been studied by Jakab 2009; see also Ruffing 2013.

44 *Dig.* 18.1.35.1 (*Gaius, Prov. Edict 10*).

45 *Dig.* 18.1.40 (*Paul, Epit. Dig. Alben. 4*).

46 According to Columella, the improvement of the product cultivated on the land not only led to a profitable surplus, but also increased the value of the property, 3.3.10–13. On the evidence for land valuation, see also Duncan-Jones 1965: 224–226.

47 Varro, *RR.* 1.4.2–3.

48 Varro, *RR.* 3.2.7–18. The author mentions, for instance, villas with fishponds, which are expensive to maintain, but also very profitable to sell, *RR* 3.17.3.

49 See Kehoe in this volume (Chapter 4).

50 *Dig.* 31.1.54 (*Terent. Clem. Lex Iulia et Papia 13*).

51 *Dig.* 6.1.23; 8.3.6; 17.1.16 (*Ulp. Edict. 31*); See also Coll. 3.2.15. Paul discusses the case of accessory mobile objects that are worth more than the houses that contain them, *Dig.* 18.1.34 (*Paul. Edict. 33*).

52 Mart. 12.66.

53 This is very clearly stated in an imperial decree from 242 CE, *CI* 4.24.6.

54 *Dig.* 18.1.52 (*Paul. Edict 54*). In another passage, Paul clarifies that in the case of a building destroyed by fire with no fault on the side of the vendor, the valuation should be applied to the site, which will nonetheless be transferred to the purchaser, *Dig.* 18.4 (*Paul. Quaest.* 16). On legal issues linked to urban properties, see Dubouloz 2011. The economic strategies followed by urban real estate speculators and predatory investors, along with their traces in textual and material evidence, are analysed by Maschek (Chapter 11, this volume), whilst Rosillo-López (Chapter 2, this volume) evaluates the state's responses to this problem.

55 See for instance, *Cod. Iust.* 10.1.3. On this practice and its difficult detection, see García Morcillo 2021.

56 *Cod. Iust.* 5.12.5

57 The texts insist on the importance of the moment of the valuation, *Dig.* 23.4.29 (*Scaev. Resp. 2); Dig.* 24.1.7 (*Ulp. Sab. 31*), as well as how movable and immovable properties are treated differently, *Cod. Iust.* 5.12.31.2 (AD 530).

58 *Dig.* 23.3 (*Ulp. 10 Sab.*).

59 On economic business and monetary transactions in the Ciceronian correspondence, see extensively Ioannatou 2006.

60 On Cicero's interest in the real-estate market, see Shatzman 1975; Rawson 1976; Garnsey 1976; Frier 1978; Wiseman 1987; Narducci 1985; Rauh 1989; Treggiari 1999; Wallace-Hadrill 2008; Craver 2010; Rosillo-López 2021.

61 See Andreau 2004.

62 The complex financial credit and cash operations in this episode are analysed by Benöhr 1986 and Rauh 1989. On the relevance of mentalities, motivations, and psychological bias in this case, see García Morcillo 2020a. On the use of information, agency and financial intermediation in this lengthy episode, see Rosillo-López 2021 and Koedijk in this volume (Chapter 7).

63 Cic. *Att.* 12.23.3; 12.31.1.
64 Cic. *Att.* 12.31.2–3. While still considering different property and financial options, Cicero confesses to Atticus to be a buyer motivated by desire (*qui emere cupiat*), eagerness (*cupiditas*), and grief (*dolor*).
65 A detailed inspection of the *horti* permitted Cicero to evaluate its current state and build an informed strategy for the bidding, Cic. *Att.* 13.1.3; 13.29.1.
66 Cic. *Att.* 13.31.4.
67 Cic. *Att.* 9.9.4 (Formiae, 17 March 49): *Sciebam enim te quoto anno et quantum in solo solere quaerere, neque solum Romae sed etiam Deli tuum digamma [*diagramma] videram.* I am largely following the translation by J. Bayet, in the Collection Budé edition (CUF, 1964), who proposes that the *digamma* of the text, the Greek letter from the Ionic alphabet lost in the Classical period, yet still in use in the numeric system, would have been originally read as *diagramma*, a term employed to refer to accounts books, yet no longer used in that sense in the medieval period when the manuscript was copied, as is convincingly explained by Bruneau 1988. As a contrast, D.R. Shackleton Bailey, in the edition of the Loeb Classical Library (1999), assumes *digamma* as a valid term and translates it as "mark": "I did not think, being aware that you generally want to know about price-yield ratio and immovables and having seen your mark (?) in Delos as well as in Rome."
68 Cic. *Att.* 9.9.4 (transl. D.R. Shackleton Bailey, LCL): *verum tamen ego illud, quamquam est bellum, minoris aestimo quam aestimabatur Marcellino consule.*
69 Cic. *Att.* 9.9.4 (transl. D.R. Shackleton Bailey, LCL): Cic. *Att.* 9.9.4 (Formiae, 17 March 49): *Cum ego istos hortulos propter domum antiquam tum habebam iucundiores mihi fore putabam et minore impensa quam si Tusculanum refecissem. volui HS q. egi per †predum†, ille daret tanti, cum haberet venale. noluit. sed nunc omnia ista iacere puto propter nummorum caritatem. mihi quidem erit aptissimum, vel nobis potius, si tu emeris.*
70 Cic. *Att.* 9.9.4 (Formiae, 17 March 49): *Valde est venustum. quamquam mihi ista omnia iam addicta vastitati videntur.*
71 The judicial valuations that populate the legal sources have received some scholarly attention, see Matthews 1921; Kroops 2016. On the challenges of the Roman census, see Wiseman 1969; Nicolet 1976; 2000; Balbo 2018; Maiuro 2018; and Rosillo-López (Chapter 2, this volume). Valuations of property also issued public solutions to financial crises. This seems to have been the case with a law passed by Caesar in 49 BCE, which allowed the transfer of land assessed at pre-war prices (before they dropped) to creditors, Caes. *Civ.* 3.1.2; Cic. *Fam.* 13.8.2; cf. Verboven 2003: 51–53.
72 On the complex legal reception of the notion of *affectio* and the *aestimatio affectionis*, see Kindler 2012.
73 Cat. *Agr.* 144; 148–149. The playwright Terentius confirms that by the second century BCE the parties in property rights conflicts used to choose an arbitrator to help them resolve disputes such as property boundaries, *Heaut.* 498–501.
74 *Dig.* 50.16.179 (*Ulp. 51 Sab.): Inter haec verba "quanti ea res erit" vel "quanti eam rem esse paret" nihil interest: in utraque enim clausula placet veram rei aestimationem fieri.* See also, very similarly, *Dig.* 50.16.193 (*Ulp. 38 Ed.): Haec verba "quanti eam rem paret esse" non ad quod interest, sed ad rei aestimationem referuntur.*
75 Gaius, *Inst.* 4.48: 48: *Omnium autem formularum, quae condemnationem habent, ad pecuniariam aestimationem condemnatio concepta est. itaque et si corpus aliquod petamus, uelut fundum, hominem, uestem, aurum, argentum, iudex non ipsam rem condemnat eum, cum quo actum est, sicut olim fieri solebat, sed aestimata re pecuniam eum condemnat.*
76 On the institutional developments that led to the introduction of the *Lex Falcidia*, see García Morcillo 2020b.
77 On the *vicesima hereditatium*, see Günther 2005.
78 *Dig.* 35.2.42 (*Ulp. 14 Ed*).
79 *Dig.* 35.2.62 (*Ulp. 1 Iul. et Pap.*).

80 *Dig.* 35.2.60 (*Iavolenus 14 ex cass.*).
81 *Dig.* 35.2.61 (*Iavolenus 4 epist.*).
82 *Dig.* 35.2.63.pr (*Lex Iulia et Papia lib. 2*).
83 *Dig.* 35.2.63.2. 1–2 (*Paul. 2 l. Iul. et Pap.*). Transl. Watson.
84 *Dig.* 9.2.33pr (*Plautius 2): Sextus quoque pedius ait pretia rerum non ex affectione nec utilitate singulorum, sed communiter fungi.* On the *Lex Aquilia* and its application since the middle Republic, see Daube 1936; Corbino 2008; du Plessis 2019.
85 *Dig.* 9.2.33pr (*Plautius 2*).
86 *Dig.* 9.2.27.5 (*Ulp. 18 Ed.*).
87 *Dig.* 9.2.2pr (*Gaius prov. Ed. 7*); 9.2.29. 8 (*Ulp. 18 ad Ed.*); Gaius, *Inst.* 3.218: *Hoc tamen capite non quanti in eo anno, sed quanti in diebus XXX proxumis ea res fuerit, damnatur is, qui damnum dederit.*
88 On the calculation of value as *damnum*, see Daube 1948; Valditara 1995; du Plessis 2019,
89 Gaius, *Inst.* 3.224.
90 Cic. *Att.* 4.2.5.
91 *Cod. Iust.* 8.4.9 (477 CE).
92 *Cod. Iust.* 7.47.1 pr (531 CE): *Cum pro eo quod interest dubitationes antiquae in infinitum productae sunt, melius nobis visum est huiusmodi prolixitatem prout possibile est in angustum coartare.*
93 *Cod Iust.* 7.47.1.1–2.
94 The information declared in the censuses, even if it was supposed to be highly detailed and include a valuation of the property, had a relative value, as it could be outdated, *Dig.* 50.15.4 (*Ulp. Cens. 3*).
95 *Dig.* 49.14.3.5 (*Callistratus 3 d. i. fisci.*).
96 See the enlightening research by Barbot 2015, whom I follow here.

References

Andreau, J. (2004) Sur les choix économiques des notables romains. In: J. Andreau, J. France, and S. Pittia, eds. *Mentalités et choix économiques des Romains*. Bordeaux: Ausonius, 71–85.

Andreau, J., Briant, P., and Descat, R., eds. (1997) *Économie antique: prix et formation des prix dans les économies antiques*. Saint-Bertrand-de-Comminges: Musée archéologique départemental de Saint-Bertrand-de-Comminges.

Aspers, P. (2009) Knowledge and Valuation in Markets. *Theory and Society* 38, 111–131.

Aspers, P. and Beckert, J. (2011) Value in Markets. In: P. Aspers and J. Beckert, eds. *The Worth of Goods: Valuation and Pricing in the Economy*. Oxford: Oxford University Press, 1–38.

Balbo, M. (2018) I censori nel II secolo a. C. tra ideologia ed economia. In: M. Valerani, ed. *Valore delle cose e valore delle persone dall'antichità all'età moderna*. Rome: Viella, 169–188.

Barbot, M. (2015) The Justness of *Aestimatio* and the Justice of Transactions: Defining Real Estate Values in Early Modern Milan. In: B. de Munck and D. Lyna, eds. *Concepts of Value in European Material Culture, 1500–1900*. Farnham: Routledge, 133–149.

Benöhr, H.-P. (1986) Das *Faberianum negotium*—Schuldenbereinigung zur Zeit Ciceros. *Zeitschrift der SavignyStiftung fur Rechtsgeschichte, RA* 103, 275–320.

Bruneau, P. (1988) Deliaca VII. *Bulletin de Correspondance Hellénique* 112. 2, 569–582.

Chankowski, V. (2020) Juste prix, prix libres et prix fixés dans les cités du monde grec antique: histoire d'un malentendu. In: V. Chankowski, C. Lenoble, and J. Maucourant, eds. *Les infortunes du juste prix: Marchés, justice sociale et bien commun de l'Antiquité à nos jours*. Lormont: Le Bord de l'Eau, 25–68.

Chankowski, V., Lenoble, C., and Maucourant, J., eds. (2020) *Les infortunes du juste prix: Marchés, justice sociale et bien commun de l'Antiquité à nos jours*. Lormont: Le Bord de l'Eau.

Corbino, A. (2008) *Il danno qualificato e la lex Aquilia*, 2nd ed. Padova: Cedam.

Craver, S.E. (2010) Urban Real Estate in Late Republican Rome. *Memoirs of the American Academy in Rome* 55, 135–158.

Daube, D. (1936) On the Third Chapter of the *lex Aquilia*. *Law Quarterly Review* 52, 253–268.

Daube, D. (1948) On the Use of the Term Damnum. In: *Studi in Onore di Siro Solazzi nel Cinquantesimo Anniversario del Suo Insegnamento Universitario, 1899–1948*. Naples: Jovene, 93–156.

Dubouloz, J. (2011) *La propriété immobilière à Rome et en Italie, Ier-Ve siècles. Organisation et transmission des praedia urbana*. Rome: École Française de Rome.

Duncan-Jones, R. (1965) An Epigraphic Survey of Costs in Roman Italy. *Papers of the British School at Rome* 33, 189–306.

Elder-Vass, D. (2019) No Price without Value: Towards a Theory of Value and Price. *Cambridge Journal of Economics* 43, 1485–1498.

Frier, B.W. (1978) Cicero's Management of His Urban Properties. *Classical Journal* 74, 1–6.

García Morcillo, M. (2020a) Mentality, Motivation and Economic Decision-Making in Ancient Rome: Cicero and Tullia's Shrine. *The Economic History Review* 73. 3, 623–643.

García Morcillo, M. (2020b) Hasta infinita? Financial Strategies in the Triumviral Period. In: F. Pina Polo, ed. *The Triumviral Period: Civil War, Political Crisis and Socioeconomic Transformations*. Seville: Zaragoza, 379–397.

García Morcillo, M. (2021) Managing Uncertainty and Asymmetric Information in Roman Auctions. In: C. Rosillo-López and M. García Morcillo, eds. *Managing Information in the Roman Economy*. Cham: Palgrave-Macmillan, 61–88.

Garnsey, P. (1976) Urban Property Investment. In: M.I. Finley, ed. *Studies of Roman Property*. Cambridge: Cambridge University Press, 123–136.

Günther, S. (2005) Die Einführung der römischen Erbschaftssteuer (vicesima hereditatium). *Münstersche Beiträge zur Antiken Handelsgeschichte* 24. 1, 1–30.

Ioannatou, M. (2006) *Affaires d'argent dans la correspondance de Cicéron. L'aristocratie sénatoriale face à ses dettes*. Paris: De Boccard.

Jakab, É. (2009) *Risikomanagement beim Weinkauf. Periculum und Praxis im Imperium Romanum*. München: C.H. Beck.

Kindler, M. (2012) *Affectionis aestimatio. Vom Ursprung des Affektionsinteresses im römischen Recht und seiner Rezeption*. Berlin: Duncker & Humblot.

Kroops, E. (2016) Price Setting and Other Attempts to Control the Economy. In: C. Ando, P. du Plessis, and K. Tuori, eds. *Oxford Handbook of Roman Law and Society*, Oxford: Oxford University Press, 609–620.

Lavan, M. (2021) Asymmetric Information and Adverse Selection in the Roman Slave Market: The Limits of Legal Remedy. In: C. Rosillo-López and M. García Morcillo, eds. *Managing Information in the Roman Economy*. Cham: Palgrave-Macmillan, 179–202.

Lo Cascio, E. (2018) Market Regulation and Transaction Costs in the Roman Empire. In: A. Bowman and A. Wilson, eds. *Trade, Commerce and the State in the Roman World*, Oxford: Oxford University Press, 117–132.

Lo Cascio, E. (2020) Setting the Rules of the Game. The Market and Its Working in the Roman Empire. In: G. Dari-Mattiaci and D.P. Kehoe, eds. *Roman Law and Economics: Institutions and Organisations* I, Oxford: Oxford University Press, 111–136.

Maiuro, M. (2018) Patrimonio, reddito e censo in due momenti di età repubblicana. In: M. Valerani, ed. *Valore delle cose e valore delle persone dall'antichità all'età moderna*. Rome: Viella, 153–167.

Matthews, N. (1921) The Valuation of property in the Roman Law. *Harvard Law Review* 34, 229–259.

Mirowski, P. (1991) The When, the How and the Why of Mathematical Expression in the History of Economics Analysis. *The Journal of Economic Perspectives* 5. 1, 145–157.

Mooya, M.M. (2009) Market Value without a Market: Perspectives from Transaction Cost Theory. *Urban Studies* 46.3, 687–701.

Narducci, E. (1985) Valori aristocratici e mentalità acquisitiva nel pensiero di Cicerone. *Index* 13, 93–125.

Nicolet, C. (1976) Le cens sénatorial sous la République et sous Auguste. *The Journal of Roman Studies* 66, 20–38.

Nicolet, C. (2000) *Censeurs et publicains. Économie et fiscalité dans la Rome antique*. Paris: Fayard.

Orléan, A. (2014) *The Empire of Value: A New Foundation for Economics*. Cambridge MA: MIT Press.

Plessis, P. du, ed. (2019) *Wrongful Damage of Property in Roman Law*. Edinburgh: Edinburgh University Press.

Rathbone, D. and von Reden, S. (2015) Mediterranean Grain Prices in Classical Antiquity. In: R.J. van der Spek, B. van Leeuwen, and J.L. Zanden, eds. *A History of Market Performance. From Ancient Babylonia to the Modern World*. London and New York: Routledge, 149–235.

Rauh, N.K. (1989) Finance and Estate Sales in Republican Rome. *Aevum* 63, 45–76.

Rawson, E. (1976) The Ciceronian Aristocracy and Its Properties. In: M.I. Finley, ed. *Studies in Roman Property*. Cambridge: Cambridge University Press, 85–102.

Rosillo-López, C. (2021) Domum pestilentem vendo: Real Estate Market and Information Asymmetry in the Roman World. In: C. Rosillo-López and M. García Morcillo, eds. *Managing Information in the Roman Economy*. Cham: Palgrave-Macmillan, 117–134.

Ruffing, K. (2013) Auctions and Markets in the Roman Empire. In: M. Frass, ed. *Kauf, Konsum und Märkte. Wirtschaftswelten im Fokus: Von der römischen Antike bis zur Gegenwart*. Wiesbaden: Harrassowitz, 213–228.

Salzman, D. and Zwinkels, R.C.J. (2017) Behavioral Real Estate. *Journal of Real Estate Literature* 25. 1, 77–106.

Shackleton Bailey, D.R. (1996) Tullia's Fane (Appendix 3). In: D.R. Shackleton Bailey, *Cicero's Letters to Atticus*, vol. V, books XI–XIII, Cambridge: Cambridge University Press, 404–413.

Shatzman, I. (1975) *Senatorial wealth and Roman politics*. Brussels: Latomus.

Treggiari, S. (1979) Sentiment and Property: Some Roman Attitudes. In: A. Parel and Th. Flanagan, eds. *Theories of Property. Aristotle to the Present*. Waterloo ON: Wilfrid Laurier University Press, 53–85.

Treggiari, S. (1999) The Upper-class House as Symbol and Focus of Emotion in Cicero. *Journal of Roman Archaeology* 12, 33–56.

Valditara, G. (1995) *Dall'aestimatio rei all'id quod interest: Evoluzione del criterio di stima del danno aquiliano*. Pavia: G. Iuculano.

Verboven, K. (2003) 54–44 BCE: Financial or Monetary Crisis? In: E. Lo Cascio, ed. *Credito e moneta nel mondo Romano. Atti degli Incontri capresi di storia dell'economia antica.* Bari: Edipuglia, 49–68.

Wallace-Hadrill, A. (2008) *Rome's Cultural Revolution.* Cambridge: Cambridge University Press.

Wiseman, T.P. (1969) The Census in the First Century B.C. *The Journal of Roman Studies* 59. 1–2, 59–75.

Wiseman, T.P. (1987) Conspicui postes tectaque digna deo: The Public Image of Aristocratic and Imperial Houses in the Late Republic and Early Empire. In: *L'urbs. Espace urbain et histoire (Ier siecle av. J.-C–IIIe siècle ap. J.-C).* Actes du colloque internationale organisé par le CNRS et l'ÉFR (Rome, 8–12 May 1985), Rome: École Française de Rome, 393–413.

Part II

Land, Property, and Law

4 Land and Securing the Future in the Roman Empire

Dennis Kehoe

Abstract

In this chapter, I examine the ways in which important constituencies in the Roman Empire, including the Roman imperial government, private property owners, and civic benefactors, used land as an economic resource to achieve their most important goals. In an economy that largely revolved around agriculture, land represented the most important source of wealth for most Roman property owners, while taxes from land and rents from imperial properties provided the bulk of revenues for the imperial government. Thus it is to be expected that long-term financial planning would revolve around land. I examine this situation more deeply by analysing the way in which economic actors used land to achieve specific financial goals and the factors that limited their ability to do so.

To consider the Roman administration, its efforts to maintain the viability of town councils as an institution of government in the empire depended on ensuring that decurions were protected against the possibility of losing their land, and accordingly it adopted a series of policies, including prohibiting the alienation of land belonging to key social groups and, in late antiquity, defining the assets of decurions as being held in a kind of corporate trust by the local council. To secure benefactions, such as alimentary foundations in cities in Italy and the provinces, the imperial government and private benefactors found various ways to tie the expenditures for their programmes to income generated from land. However, there were limits to the capacity of land to support long-term financial goals. Although it was common for borrowers to use their land as security in credit arrangements, the evidence for loans secured by land from papyri in Egypt suggests that such loans were mostly short-term, and most often to meet immediate financial needs. Thus it seems unlikely that land could have often been leveraged to fund long-term investment in potentially productive business arrangements. An analysis of the ways in which land factored into long-term financial planning helps us to better understand the nature of the Roman economy and the limits on its capacity to grow.

***

In his extraordinary paper, "Did the Romans Have a Future?", published in the *Journal of Roman Studies* in 2019, Brent Shaw explores the limited capacity that the Romans had, at least in comparison with a modern society, to engage in

DOI: 10.4324/9781003187806-6

long-term economic planning.[1] The reasons for this are complex, stemming from a tendency to think of the future primarily in the short term as something linked directly with present events or even the past (Shaw, p. 3). One of the arguments that Shaw makes in support of his understanding of Romans' conception of the future can be seen in the Roman system of credit: private individuals seldom took advantage of their wealth in land by using it as security for long-term loans for productive purposes, while the imperial government, in contrast to early-modern states, never leveraged its own extensive holdings in property to secure credit to meet emergency expenses. When fiscal emergencies did arise, for example, during the military crises in the 160s under the emperor Marcus Aurelius, the Romans followed what was for them a common strategy in responding to such situations, that is, raising funds by selling off furnishings and other luxury items from the imperial palace (SHA *Marc.* 17.4–5, 21.9).[2] Recourse to such sales makes some sense, since in the Roman world savings often consisted of stored wealth, especially precious metals.[3] But selling off stored wealth is at best a short-term solution, and probably an inadequate one in most situations. The Roman government did take out loans to meet emergencies in the Republic. For example in the year 210 BCE during a crisis in the Second Punic War, when money was scarce for maintaining the fleet, senators, at the urging of the consul M. Valerius Laevinus, offered funds to meet the financial emergency, as did members of the other orders (Livy 26.35–66); these funds were to be paid back later in three instalments.[4] This emergency loan was exceptional, and, as Shaw points out, at no time during the principate did the imperial government leverage its immense holdings in land to secure credit. Private property owners might borrow funds when they faced financial emergencies of their own, but they rarely if ever used their land as a resource for long-term credit. As François Lerouxel (2016) demonstrates in his careful study of the credit market in Roman Egypt, even the loans taken by relatively wealthy people against the security of their land were always short term in nature, with a repayment period of no more than several years. In Shaw's view, the Romans' incapacity to engage in strategic long-term economic planning stems at least in part from their perception of the future.

Shaw's analysis invites closer consideration of the ways in which economic actors in the Roman Empire, including the imperial government, civic benefactors, and other private property owners, planned their finances. In an economy that largely revolved around agriculture, land represented the most important source of wealth for most Roman property owners, while taxes from land and rents from imperial properties provided the bulk of revenues for the imperial government. Thus it is to be expected that any long-term financial planning that characterised the Roman economy would revolve around land. As I will argue, the strategies that the Roman administration and private property owners developed to leverage their land were adaptations to the constraints imposed by a predominantly agrarian economy with limited growth beyond what could be accounted for by population increase. At the same time, these strategies affected the market for agricultural land and other forms of real estate.

Credit Institutions

We can gain some perspectives on the constraints on economic planning in the Roman world by considering the nature of Roman credit institutions. On the one hand, as Peter Temin and William Harris argue, the Roman Empire had sophisticated credit institutions, ones that, in their understanding, were comparable to those of early modern Europe.[5] The importance of credit to the Roman economy can be seen in the ways in which Roman law developed to facilitate credit arrangements. To cite one key aspect of this, Roman law developed a sophisticated system of secured credit, which gave creditors security against the risk of default on the part of the debtor. It also allowed debtors to make use of the property that they pledged as collateral for loans so as to produce income that would help them to pay off their debts, while reserving the possibility of using the land as collateral in other secured loans, including ones that would help them to pay off existing obligations.[6] Indeed, the archive of the Sulpicii, which documents the work of a specialised group of money lenders at Puteoli in the first century CE, demonstrates the complex and sophisticated arrangements to provide credit in one of the Roman Empire's most important commercial hubs.[7] Upper-class Roman landowners, such as Pliny the Younger (*Ep*. 3.19.5–6), regularly supplemented the income that they gained from their estates by lending money out at interest, and in this effort they were supported by a substantial network of intermediaries who helped to connect borrowers with property owners with money to lend.[8] In Rome, at least, banks run by *argentarii* played some role in providing credit, but much credit also came from individual lenders.[9] In Egypt, as Lerouxel observes, the numerous banks documented there functioned chiefly to facilitate payments, and did not play a direct role in arranging credit. But they do seem to have served as clearinghouses for information, where borrowers could be brought together with potential lenders.[10]

In view of the sophistication of the legal infrastructure supporting credit in the Roman world, it can be reasonably be asked, as Shaw and other historians have, why the Roman imperial government never resorted to long-term credit arrangements to meet the kinds of financial emergencies that the emperors Marcus Aurelius and later Pertinax faced or to finance potentially lucrative wars, in the ways that monarchs in early-modern Europe did. As Raymond Goldsmith points out in his survey of early-modern economies, the Florentine Republic in the fifteenth century regularly resorted to loans, often compulsory, to finance its frequent wars. Somewhat later, England under Elizabeth I also borrowed occasionally from private sources to finance the government.[11] In Florence, the claims against the Republic arising from loans were freely tradable among citizens of the Republic, but generally at a fraction of their nominal value, and the payment of interest on these loans was by no means reliable. In later societies, with larger banks capable of bringing together immense capital, it became more common for monarchies to borrow from private lenders to finance wars.

The lack of borrowing on the part of the Roman government, however, does not indicate the existence of a severe constraint on its scope for action in comparison with early-modern states. Rather, the Roman emperor could generally draw on a much larger resource base than could his early-modern counterparts. Taxation accounted for at most 10 per cent of the empire's GDP (gross domestic product), with the bulk of this representing tax and other imposts that were paid to the imperial government, while local communities collected some taxes of their own.[12] In addition, the Roman emperor controlled a vast system of lands, quarries, and mines throughout the empire, which provided an important supplement to the revenues coming from taxation. In Goldsmith's estimate, by contrast, in Elizabethan England, the Crown controlled about 5 per cent of the land, and the Church a comparable amount. The Queen's revenues were likely to have been less than 2 per cent of GDP, and, with all other imposts taken into account, overall tax revenue might have been in the order of 5 per cent of GDP.[13] As Marco Maiuro points out in his discussion of imperial property in Italy, the ownership of considerable resources in land was an important element of the emperor's power. Not only did this land provide the emperor with significant revenues, but it also provided a store of wealth with which he could amply reward supporters.[14]

It seems clear that the emperor's control over such land was a matter of some concern to the Roman elite. Thus Dio (52.28.3–4) has Maecenas, when debating with Agrippa over the best way to manage the empire, urge Augustus to sell all but the most useful imperial properties, and to use the proceeds from such sales to finance private farmers. This measure, Maecenas argues, would restore tax revenues. In a similar vein, the agrarian reform that Herodian (2.4.6) attributes to Pertinax involved turning over all vacant property in Italy and the provinces to individual cultivators, who would have a ten-year tax immunity and full rights of ownership. These proposed measures, arising from contemporary concerns about perceived revenue shortfalls, represented solutions that would diminish the emperor's control of land. From another perspective, however, the emperor became owner of much land that had formerly been the property of wealthy senators and equestrians, regularly passing to his control through bequest or confiscation. Even if most of this property, as Maiuro argues, was sold off, the emperors retained lands that were in strategically important locations or that formed a critical mass that could be managed efficiently by the Fiscus.

The Fiscus' long-term control over substantial tracts of farmland throughout the empire thus gave it a strategic financial reserve that better enabled it to meet continuing expenses such as the food distributions in Rome and supporting the Roman military, as well as to meet sudden and unforeseen financial emergencies. In the Roman Empire, it is difficult to see how the Roman government could have raised substantial sums of money from private lenders. To the contrary, it was more likely that the Fiscus was the only entity in the Roman world that disposed over cash reserves substantial enough to underwrite the kinds of projects for which governments in later societies had to borrow.

The deep pockets of the Fiscus can be clearly seen in the financial crisis in 33 CE when, as discussed by Tacitus (*Ann.* 6.16–17), the emperor intervened with infusions of cash to stabilise prices for land. The crisis resulted when creditors called in loans to comply with the Caesarian law as revised by the senate that two-thirds of senators' wealth had to be invested in Italian land. But this situation led to a glut of property on the market, falling prices, and a shortage of cash, as debtors sold property to be able to pay off their loans. The emperor made 100 million sesterces available, lending it without interest for three years if the borrower pledged twice the value in land, a measure that helped to stabilise prices and the credit market.[15] The point is that the emperor disposed of substantial reserves of cash that it was able to invest. In addition, the emperor controlled the mines that produced silver and gold. Of course, at certain times, such as during the principate of Commodus and especially under Septimius Severus, the extent of imperial property expanded greatly as a result of confiscations from political enemies of the emperor.

In retaining control of imperial estates and other properties, the Fiscus could exercise greater control over how these properties were exploited, as it did in maintaining a system of small-scale cultivation by tenants as documented in North Africa, Asia Minor, and Egypt. By leasing its land out to small-scale cultivators, the Fiscus received much higher revenues, often in specific crops, than it would have by following the alternatives suggested by Dio and Herodian of returning the land to private ownership. Imperial ownership of such land displaced private "rentiers," and allowed the revenues imperial estates produced to be directed toward public goods rather than to the private consumption of wealthy landowners. The key to the imperial government's interests was to maintain the productive capacity of its resources in lands, which explains why, when there were conflicts between middlemen collecting the rent of the imperial tenants, as in North Africa in the second century, or between nearby towns and imperial estates over the services of tenants, as in Asia Minor in the same period, the imperial administration consistently intervened to protect the tenure rights of its tenants.[16]

Land was the most important financial resource for both the imperial government and for private landowners because of its capacity to provide stable revenues. Using land as collateral to raise funds, even for productive purposes, ran the risk of losing access to such income. When property owners pledged their land to secure credit, this was in all likelihood a step taken when there was no alternative to meet a financial obligation, such as by drawing on existing savings, or cutting back on anticipated spending. Pliny the Younger seems to be thinking in this way when, after he has forgiven the substantial debt that his relative Calvina's father had owed him so that she might take up her inheritance, he attributes his ability to afford such acts of generosity to his frugality, which makes up for the uncertain revenues from his lands (*Ep.* 2.4.3).[17] Financial difficulties might compel a person to use land as collateral to secure credit, but property owners seem to have been unwilling to commit their land for the long term to secure credit. One indication of this is that, outside of the imperial alimentary foundations to be discussed shortly, there is little evidence that landowners used land to leverage long-term loans. The Roman law of secured credit would make this possible with various types of security involving the owner's remaining in possession of any land pledged as security for a long-term loan and so retaining the ability to raise the funds to pay off the loan.[18] But the lack of firms that would remain in business for the long term and thus be able to manage such loans would have made it difficult to obtain long-term credit. Although it was clearly common for landowners to borrow against the security of their land, such loans were commonly for the short term, a period of several years, and they apparently were to meet short-term financial needs rather than to provide long-term credit for business operations. The best evidence for the nature of private loans involving land as security comes from Roman Egypt. As François Lerouxel argues, the development of the "archive of acquisitions," or βιβλιοθήκη ἐγτήσεων, under the Flavian emperors allowed potential creditors to know more precisely about the status of land that borrowers might put up for security – whether land was subject to existing liens, held by either the imperial government or private individuals – and so facilitated using land as security to obtain credit.[19] But the loans that Lerouxel documents in the period after the establishment of this registry were generally for a limited number of years and involved relatively modest sums of money.

In one exception to this, at least in terms of the size of the loan, a certain C. Iulius Ptolemaios, a former eutheniarch and eventually councillor in Alexandria, made a substantial loan to one Apollonianos, son of Dionysios, from Oxyrhynchus (*PSI* XIII 1328, Oxyrhynchus, 201 CE). The loan was for two talents of silver, to be repaid within a year, at 10 per cent annual interest.[20] To secure the loans, the borrower had pledged considerable property, including a one-third share of a vineyard (ἀμπελικὸν κτῆμα) comprising 13 3/16 arouras, with a variety of associated resources, such as date-palms, an orchard, a reed bed, a set of buildings (*epoikion*) that housed storing and pressing equipment, irrigation equipment, and one-third shares of two other parcels of land, consisting of a bit more than sixteen and ten arouras, respectively (ll. 36–51). Unfortunately, the borrower was unable to repay the loan, which was originally contracted in 194, and the document that provides a description of the loan represents an application on the part of the lender to proceed against the pledged property. This loan appears to have been taken out to meet an immediate financial need. To be sure, one cannot draw conclusions from a single example about the full range of purposes for which land might be pledged, but the loan in this document does not seem to be different from most other loans secured with land as security.

Land and Foundations

But if loans against land were not a means of funding long-term purposes, land still represented a resource to accomplish such efforts, and analysing how land was used for long-term financial planning helps us to understand better the nature of the Roman economy and the limits on its capacity to grow. The imperial government disposed over more resources than even the very richest members of the Roman elite, and, more important, it had many more means to enforce the provision of revenues to support public goods than any private individual could have. We can see how the Roman government applied its enforcement capabilities to plan for the long term by considering how it used land to fund its alimentary foundations. The imperial alimentary foundations, beginning apparently in the reigns of Nerva and Trajan, involved using money belonging to the Fiscus to set up funds to defray the costs of feeding children in many cities in Italy. Private benefactors, including Pliny the Younger, as we will see, established comparable programmes in Italy and the provinces.[21] The imperial alimentary foundations in Italy represent an effort of the imperial Fiscus to invest its immense cash reserves to support a significant public good. In the best known of the imperial alimentary foundations, that at Veleia in northern Italy under Nerva and Trajan, subscribing landowners pledged properties whose assessed value exceeded a minimum threshold, and they received loans from the Fiscus representing approximately one-twelfth of the value of the property pledged. The landowners were then required to pay 5 per cent interest on these loans in perpetuity. In effect, the funding for the alimentary programs was an effort to impose a tax while making the burden shouldered by participating landowners as light as possible. Presumably, the imperial programmes at Veleia and elsewhere in Italy were organised at the local level to promote greater oversight by the local community and to foster the long-term viability of the programmes. The subscribing landowners were likely to have been more welcoming of the loans if, as Elio Lo Cascio argues (2000), the Fiscus also intended to use the loans to provide a stimulus to agriculture in the towns concerned. Participating landowners would welcome the infusion of cash if it they invested it in improving their farms and thereby increasing their productivity. Such a consideration, however, would apply only to the initial subscribers, and not to the future owners of the land pledged to the foundations, who would remain obligated to make the payments. Once the land was pledged, its owners would always be obligated to pay the 5 per cent interest to the town's fund to support each new generation of children. By restricting the amounts of the loan to a fraction of the pledged land's appraised value, the Fiscus kept the charge that any particular landowner would have to pay relatively low, certainly lower than the taxes that landowners in the provinces generally had to pay for their land. But it is also important to analyse the mechanism that the imperial administration pursued to finance this programme in light of the limited institutions that would support long-term financing in the Roman world.

Private benefactors did not have the same options at their disposal as the imperial government did, but they also used land to adapt to the constraints imposed by ancient economic conditions to secure the future. To take the most generous of the documented private foundations, in Sicca Veneria in Africa in the 160s (*ILS* 6818, *CIL* VIII 6141), the equestrian Licinius Paprianus set aside 1.3 million sesterces, a sum that was to produce an annual income of HS 65,000, a return of 5 per cent, to fund monthly allowances for 300 boys and HS 10/ month, and 300 girls at HS 8/ month. In this case, it is apparent that the benefactor made a calculation about how much money he could donate and what a reasonable level of support for individual children would be. Having done this, his priority was to maintain the same number of recipients year after year, and so he spelled out the process by which new children would be recruited to replace those who grew up or died. Children who were citizens of the town had priority, and if they did not provide sufficient numbers, resident aliens, *incolae*, were to be recruited. Like many, but by no means all private benefactors, he left it up to the town to lend the money at interest and to use the proceeds to fund the programme.[22] In effect, Papirianus imposed on the town the duty of managing his endowment and supervising the alimentary programme, and it is uncertain whether his confidence in the ability of the town to carry out this task was well placed. In setting up his own alimentary foundation for his hometown of Comum, Pliny the Younger had little confidence in the ability of his town either to lend out a cash donation or to manage land donated to the town (*Ep.* 7.18.2). Instead, Pliny sought to use privately owned land as a means for securing his alimentary foundation for the future. Accordingly, he temporarily assigned some portion of a much larger estate that he owned to the town's ownership, and the town imposed an annual charge, or *vectigal*, of HS 30,000, representing a 6 per cent return on the HS 500,000 that Pliny was nominally donating. He then received the land back from the town, with the burden of providing the funds for the foundation falling on any future owner of the estate. Pliny believed that this would be a successful financing scheme because the yearly payment would only represent a fraction of the estate's overall income and so would not deter potential future owners. Even so, the estate's value, conventionally calculated as a function of the annual income it furnished, would be reduced considerably.

It is impossible to known how long the programmes of Pliny or of Papirianus endured, but we can see the success of the imperial programmes paradoxically in a report about problems they had encountered: in 193, the emperor Pertinax endeavoured to solve problems arising from unpaid arrears in the imperial programmes (SHA *Pert.* 9.3).[23] This report indicates that, whatever problems might have arisen with the imperial alimentary programmes, they were still functioning about a century after they were first established. The Roman administration thus successfully anchored a vital long-term programme in the capacity of land to generate income.

Land and Roman Estate Planning

Perhaps the clearest picture of how upper-class Romans envisioned agricultural property as providing financial security emerges from their estate planning. We can trace such planning in the extant wills in which Roman property owners made dispositions to support loved ones and other close connections. But we can gain a broader view of land as a resource by considering the evidence of the ways in which the Roman legal authorities, both the classical jurists whose writings are preserved in the Digest of Justinian, and the Roman chancery in responding to petitions, addressed legal issues connected with bequests of land and other resources. One particularly useful legal discussion is the Roman legal authorities' regulation of a particular type of bequest that seems to have been essential to Roman estate planning, namely, the legacy of a *fundus cum instrumento*, that is, the legacy of an estate with the equipment that was essential for its operations.[24] In defining what might be included in such a legacy, the jurists were concerned to balance to the interests of the testator and the beneficiary of the legacy, or legatee, on the one hand, and the testator's heirs, on the other. The testator is understood to have desired to provide the legatee with an agricultural property that would provide a certain level of income, whereas the heirs had an interest in surrendering as little as possible to the legatee and so would want to retain whatever property did not contribute directly to the estate's income.

To resolve these issues, the jurists conceived of the *fundus cum instrumento* as providing an income through the production of a crop, and so they included in the legacy only equipment, livestock, and slaves that played a role in actually producing, storing, and transporting of the crop, whatever type of estate might be at issue, whether one with the conventional range of crops including grain, wine, and olive oil, or one dedicated to livestock raising or other more specialised forms of agriculture (*Dig.* 33.7.8 pr.-14 (*Ulp. 20 ad Sab.*)). In other words, the legacy of a *fundus cum instrumento* included, in Ulpian's formulation, everything without which the estate could not be cultivated (*Dig.* 33.7.12 pr. (*20 ad Sab.*)). Clearly, this definition of the *fundus cum instrumento* simplified reality to some extent, since estates were also the sites at which property owners or their subordinates carried out significant business, including money lending and other forms of commerce, that were not directly connected with agriculture. However, account books and stores of money associated with such activities were excluded from a legacy of the *fundus cum instrumento*. The point was to develop an objective way to interpret the intentions of the testator (who was obviously in no position to respond to questions about what he or she had in mind) by establishing a general and unambiguous understanding of what such a legacy would entail. Such a methodology, ideally, would help to minimise the disputes between legatees and heirs.

This conception of an agricultural property as the pre-eminent resource from which an income could be achieved, and whose income came from the production of a crop, underlies the economic planning of both private individuals and the Roman government. We can see the basic assumptions guiding the jurists when they interpreted testamentary dispositions of land in a text of the early third-century jurist Papinian, who considered the legacy of land without its usufruct to be of little value to the legatee, since the income generated from the land is what gave such a legacy its value (*Dig.* 31.66.6 (*17 quaest.*)):

> in the legacy of a farm if the usufruct belongs to someone else, it is no less to be sought from the heir: the usufruct, even if it consists of a right, rather than a share, nevertheless contains the emolument of a piece of property.[25]

In another text, Papinian argues that it could not be consistent with the intentions of a testator that the heir retain the right of enjoyment of a farm that has been bequeathed in a legacy (*Dig.* 31.76.2 (*7 resp.*)).[26] The point here is that a legacy of a farm had one particular purpose, to provide its recipient with an immediate income to be derived from the production of a crop, rather than, say, vesting the beneficiary of the legacy with the possibility of having full ownership rights over a farm while another person, in these cases the heir, should enjoy the income from the farm.

Trusts Involving Lands

To turn now to private estate planning, individual Romans pursued much the same strategy when they established trust to provide loved ones or other dependents with stable incomes. For example, the second-century jurist Scaevola discusses an elaborate legacy for a freedman whom the testator wanted to be supported for his entire lifetime. Accordingly, the testator bequeathed to the freedman one-fiftieth of the revenues from a set of properties, *praedia*, including those gained from rents from tenants and the sale of crops (*Dig.* 33.1.21 pr. (*22 dig.*)).[27] In this case, the legal question concerned what the freedman's claim would be if the heirs sold the properties in question. In Scaevola's interpretation, even if the heirs had in some manner compromised the planning of the testator, they would still be obligated to provide the share of the revenues specified in the will, rather than interest on one-fiftieth of the sale price of the properties. One can imagine that there might be plausible reasons for the heirs to sell the properties they inherited, such as simply an effort to divide the estate or, in a more extreme case, to raise funds to pay off inherited debts. But the planning that this testator is envisioned as undertaking involved taking a small cut from the revenues that his heirs would otherwise receive. The difference between the disposition in this case and Pliny's method of funding his alimentary programme is that the obligation to provide for the freedman would fall on the heirs or their successors, rather than on the eventual owners of the property in question. In another case, Scaevola discusses a legacy to a freedman of a *fundus* carrying a notional income of 60 with the proviso that the legatee provide an annual income of 10 to another woman (Pamphila, presumably a freedwoman); here, in Scaevola's interpretation, even if, as a result of the restrictions on legacies imposed by the *lex Falcidia*, the freedman's legacy had to be reduced, the trustee would still be entitled to her full income (*Dig.* 33.1.21.1 (*22 dig.*)).[28]

The scenarios considered by Scaevola suggest how property owners saw designating specific properties to provide a set income as the surest way to plan for the future. Similarly, Paul (*Dig.* 31.77.4 (*14 resp.*)) discusses a complicated situation in which a father of five children emancipated them all and conferred most of his property on one son. In his will, the father bequeathed through a legacy two properties that he had retained to this same son and included a trust that the son provide an income to a brother and sister from the properties he had already received. The legal point in this case concerns the application of the *lex Falcidia* (by which the heirs had to receive at least one-fourth of the estate), since the trusts apparently would substantially reduce the value of the inheritance. But Paul, citing a ruling by the emperor Alexander Severus, enforced the trust because of the disproportionate share of the family's property that the favoured son had already received. Another way to use land to guarantee the payment of a trust was, as discussed in a response by Papinian, to pledge a specific farm to assure the legacy of annual payments to freedmen (*Dig.* 33.1.9 (*7 resp.*)). To be sure, plans to use agricultural properties as reliable sources of income were not guaranteed to succeed; as with a tutor's management of an orphan's property, the obligation to pay off inherited debts trumped any consideration of protecting the ownership of property. Scaevola addresses this specific issue in a case in which he prioritises paying off inherited debts over fulfilling a trust; in this case a son could pledge or even sell inherited properties to pay off debts despite a trust imposed by his father to preserve them for his children and other relatives (*Dig.* 32.38 pr. (*19 dig.*)).

The possibility of selling inherited properties despite a trust indicates the jurists' assumption that land could readily be liquidated, even if doing so might be highly disadvantageous for the recipient of the land. Accordingly, Scaevola would allow the tutor of an underage pupil to sell a *fundus* whose income, or *reditus*, the father had bequeathed to his wife, and then to pay to the wife the annual income that the father had received from leasing the land out (*Dig.* 33.2.38 (*3 resp.*)). Indeed, in yet another case discussed by Scaevola (*Dig.* 33.2.32.7 (*15 dig.*)), a mother, in her efforts to provide an annual income for her son, imposed a trust on her heirs either to provide this payment directly or to purchase properties (*praedia*) sufficient to produce this income and to assign the usufruct over them to her son.[29] The testator in this will was operating on the assumption that there was a functioning market for real estate, an assumption shared by testators who imposed on their heirs the obligation to purchase a particular property and give it to the legatee. To be sure, the heirs could fulfil such a trust by providing the legatee the appraised value of the property in question. The purchase price of agricultural property, at least in the understanding of the Roman jurists, was a direct function of the annual income that it produced, which itself was often the rent for which it was leased out.[30]

Testators had to restrict the level of income from the land that the heir or legatee would be required to pay to fulfil a trust, so that the ultimate owner, whether the benefactor's heirs or some other party, would be able to afford what the benefactor wanted. This strategy of requiring an heir or legatee to use some portion of the income of inherited land to provide for a third party fulfilled two goals at once, namely, to pass on income-producing agricultural property to someone who would hold it for the long term, while also leveraging that property to provide income for other purposes. With a limited range of ways to invest large amounts of money safely in the Roman world, property owners often found that the surest way to provide income for a long-term purpose was to set aside discrete lands as a resource, and then, to the extent possible, to make sure that the land would be available by taking steps such as imposing a trust on heirs or legatees not to alienate it.

Bequests of Land to Support Towns

Despite Pliny's reservations about donating property to Comum to fund his alimentary programme, it seems clear that Roman property owners frequently bequeathed land to their hometowns to fund a wide range of purposes. For instance, Scaevola examines a codicil to a will in which a person from Syria bequeathed to his hometown all the properties he owned in the province, with all of their flocks, crops, slaves, stored crops, and equipment (*Dig.* 32.101 pr. (*16 dig.*)).[31] In Egypt, a certain Aurelius Horion, an equestrian from Oxyrhynchus, was praised by the emperors Septimius Severus and Caracalla for setting a private estate at the disposal of his town, the revenues from which were to offset the costs of liturgies to be performed by his fellow townsmen (*P. Oxy.* IV 705, 202 CE).[32] The main issue faced by benefactors and the jurists in dealing with such cases did not involve whether the land could be counted on to provide the revenues that the town would need, but whether the town used the funds for the purposes envisioned by the benefactor, and the recourse of the benefactor's heirs if it failed to do so.[33] For example, Scaevola addresses a conflict between heirs to a benefactor and the town on which to which the benefactor had bequeathed properties with a trust that the revenue from them be used to fund games every year (*Dig.* 33.2.17 (*3 resp.*)). The town failed for four consecutive years to put on the games, and the question was whether the town had to restore to the heirs the revenues that it had realised in those four years or re-direct them to another purpose arising from the same legacy. Scaevola's decision was that fruits that had been turned over to the town during the four years were to be restored to the heirs so that what the town had not spent in accordance with the will of the benefactor could be used for other obligations arising from his will.[34]

In such disputes, Roman legal procedure and jurisprudence tended to favour the interests of towns. The state required the magistrates of a town to enforce the payment of legacies, and if they failed to do so, they would be financially liable (*Dig.* 50.1.38.2 (*Papir. 2 const.*)). But enforcing the actual performance of the testator's desires was quite another matter. The praetor might enforce performance by requiring the legatee, i.e. the town, to provide a *cautio* before taking the legacy. But once the town received the money or property left to it, the only party with a capacity to sue the town was the heir or heirs. However, the heir's interest in suing the town was not to enforce the condition in the will, but to reclaim the legacy when the beneficiary failed to perform as the testator expected. For example, Scaevola discusses a case in which a testator left a legacy of money to a town, under the condition that the town put on games in alternate years (*Dig.* 33.1.21.3 (*22. dig.*)).[35] In Scaevola's ruling, the heirs could reclaim the money that the provincial governor had assigned to the town if the town failed to put on the games. The governor did not have the capacity to compel the town to put on the games, and the heirs had the only legal remedy (cf. *Dig.* 33.1.7 (*Pomp. 8 ad Quint. Muc.*)). In the similar case of Scaevola discussed above in which a man left a town a legacy of land to fund annual games (*Dig.* 33.2.17 (*3 resp.*)), the only solution for the town's failure to carry out the benefactor's wishes was to restore the wasted money to the heirs. There was no remedy that involved the town's being compelled to carry out the benefactor's wishes. However, the Roman government did show some flexibility in how towns used money as the emperor became more directly involved in the issue. Oversight of bequests to towns passed from the senate to the emperor. Thus, the second-century jurist Valens cites a rescript by Antoninus Pius that required the permission of the emperor to use money bequeathed to a town for a purpose other than the one desired by the testator (*Dig.* 50.8.6 (*2 fideic.*)); cf. *Dig.* 50.8.1 (*Ulp. 10 disput.*).[36] According to Valens, the town could, if the money had been designated for games or spectacles in a way forbidden by the senate, use it for a purpose particularly needed for the town, with the donor's name inscribed.[37] By Ulpian's time, apparently, there was less flexibility in how a town could use a bequest, since he states that it was not permitted to convert to other uses money that had been bequeathed to a town for a specific purpose (*Dig.* 50.8.1 (*Ulp. 10 disput.*)). Callistratus quotes a rescript of Antoninus Pius that money left to a town to build buildings could, if the town had enough buildings, be used "for the maintenance of existing buildings" (*Dig.* 50.10.7 pr. (*Call. 2 cognit.*)).[38]

Legal Policies to Protect Landownership

One of the basic policies pursued by the Roman imperial government in administering the empire was to promote and protect the private ownership of land.[39] The Roman system of governing the empire depended on maintained town councils, composed of landowners with sufficient resources to shoulder the expenses of important liturgical services, especially those connected with the collection of taxes. To the extent possible, Roman legal and administrative policies were designed to protect the economic security of this class of landowners. We can see such a policy in the Roman legal authorities' treatment of the institution of tutorship in the late principate.[40] Tutorship was a basic institution in Roman society, since all fatherless children, or pupils, were required to have guardians or tutors manage their property until they reached the age of puberty. Thereafter, many people were assisted in the management of their property by curators until they reached full majority at the age of 25, and in the late principate the advisability of minors' having a curator for significant financial transactions increasingly became a requirement.[41] In this period, it seems highly likely that the imperial government became concerned with closely regulating tutors out of a concern to make sure that local town councils would continue to have a pool of people with sufficient property to guarantee their increasingly crucial performance of liturgies, particularly those connected with the collection of taxes.[42] The Roman administration privileged land over all other forms of wealth as a resource for the social class on whose continued viability the governing of the Roman Empire depended, and accordingly it required tutors not to allow any surplus finds that a pupil had to sit idle. Instead, whenever possible, Roman legal policy required the tutor to invest available funds in land, and only when it was impossible to do this, either because the pupil did not have sufficient funds to buy land, or there was no land available, were tutors required to turn to the other form of investing generally available to upper-class Romans, namely, lending the pupil's money out at interest.[43]

The Roman administration's understanding of the finances of the curial class in the Roman Empire can be readily seen in the legislation that the emperor Septimius Severus had the senate pass in 195 CE, the *Oratio Severi*, which prohibited tutors from alienating land belonging to pupils. The only exception to this was to pay off inherited debt, and even to take this step tutors had to obtain a decree from the praetor or the provincial governor. The Severan legislation was quickly applied to curators managing the property of minors. In implementing this policy, the Septimius Severus and the jurists of his time, notably Ulpian and Paul, simplified reality by overlooking other potential types of investment, such as in commerce or even in urban real estate, but in doing so they adapted a broadly shared understanding of financial security in fashioning a legal policy designed to protect the empire's social order.[44] In late antiquity, the imperial government continued to apply the restrictions on managing the property of pupils, and it intervened more explicitly in protecting the financial resources of decurions by restricting their capacity to alienate their own property. The Roman administration went so far as to give town councils a legal claim on land belonging to decurions, so that, if a decurion defaulted on his obligations, or even died without suitable heirs, his land could be claimed by the council. The late imperial administration in effect defined the assets of decurions as held in a kind of corporate trust by the local council.[45]

Conclusion

In a society in which the few options for investing wealth to produce stable returns and commercial enterprises generally had a fleeting existence, it would make sense for property owners to leverage land to secure the financial future for themselves, their dependents, and the causes in which they believed. The strategies that the Roman administration and private property owners developed to use their land represented adaptations to the basic constraints imposed by the economy, and perhaps the adequacy of the solutions for their own interests explains why Roman society was slow to develop the kinds of financial institutions to which governments turned in early-modern Europe. A property owner looking out for the future would have little choice: besides investing wealth in land, the major option for most people would be to store wealth in precious metals and art, something that the emperors implicitly did when mounting expenses compelled them to sell off furnishings from imperial palaces, as Shaw (2019) discusses. But by far the most important means to secure a long-term financial goal was to tie it to the ownership of land, or at least to revenues that could be derived from specific lands. This brief summary suggests how, in an economy with limited options for investing wealth and minimal economic growth from one year to the next, land represented the most important financial resource for securing the future. At the same time, the strategies the private landowners and the imperial government adopted to exploit their land are likely to have affected the market for agricultural land and other forms of real estate. As valuable as real estate might be to the individual owner, the steps contemplated by the jurists when developing legal rules for institutions as varied as the bequest of property, tutorship, not to mention dowry, presuppose that there was an active market for land, one in which land could be freely bought and sold, with its price representing a function of its expected annual income.

Notes

1 Shaw 2019. My chapter here has developed from the response that Prof. Shaw invited me to give as one of the respondents to his paper "Did the Romans Have a Future?", which he presented as the Michael I. Rostovtzeff lecturer for the Department of Classics at Yale University in November 2017. I am grateful to Prof. Shaw for including me in this event.
2 See Shaw 2019: 3 and n. 13.
3 See most recently Hollander 2007.
4 For difficulties in the repayment, see Livy 31.13; with Briscoe 1973: 91–92, and Shaw 2019: 4 n. 14. Roman *publicani* might also, in effect, provide credit to the state when fulfilling public contracts by allowing the state to defer payment, as also happened during the Second Punic War. See Livy 23.48.10–49.4, with Malmendier 2002: 28–29.
5 For a broad discussion of financial intermediation in the Roman world, see Temin 2013: 157–189, as well as Harris 2006.
6 For discussion of secured credit in the Roman world, see Verhagen 2020.
7 On the Sulpicii, see especially Camodeca 1999; Lerouxel 2016: 193–244; and Andreau in this volume (Chapter 6).
8 Verboven 2008.
9 For bankers in Rome, see Andreau 2020.
10 See Lerouxel 2016: 85–86, 113–143.
11 Goldsmith 1987: 167–168, 194–195.
12 Lo Cascio 2007: 622–627 discusses plausible estimates of the Roman imperial government's tax revenues, with the maximum being 10 per cent GDP; see also Scheidel and Friesen 2009: 68 and n. 26.
13 Goldsmith 1987.
14 Maiuro 2012: 11.
15 See Elliott 2015, and 2020: 90–96, as well as Maiuro 2012: 114–117.
16 See Kehoe 2007: 53–91; 2013: 41–42.
17 Pliny, *Ep.* 2.4.3: *Sunt quidem omnino nobis modicae facultates, dignitas sumpuosa, reditus propter condicionem agellorum nescio minor an incertior; sed quod cessat ex reditu, frugalitate*

suppletur, ex qua velut fonte liberalitas nostra decurrit. [We have altogether modest resources, an expensive social rank, and an income either reduced or more uncertain on account of the condition of our small fields; but what is lacking from income is supplied by frugality, from which, as if from a spring, our generosity flows.]

18 See Verhagen 2020.

19 Lerouxel 2015; 2016: 93–144.

20 *PSI* XIII 1328.33–36: ἀργυρίου ταλάντων δύο κεφαλαίου τόκου/ πεντωβωλειου (*) ἀργυρικοῦ ἑκάστης μνᾶς κατὰ μῆνα ἀπὸ/ τοῦ ἑξῆς μηνὸς Μεσορή, εἰς ἀπόδοσιν τῶν μὲν τόκω(ν)/ [ἐντὸς μ]ηνῶν δώδεκα, τοῦ δὲ κεφαλαίου τῷ ἑξῆς γ (ἔτει) … [Two talents of silver as principal with five-obol interest for each mina every month starting in the next month of Mesore, until the repayment of the funds with interest within twelve months, with the principal in the following third year.]

21 For the foundations, see especially Duncan-Jones 1982: 288–319, as well as Lo Cascio 2000.

22 For the methods of funding such programmes, see Kehoe 1997: 78–88.

23 For discussion see Lo Cascio 2000.

24 On the legacy of the *fundus cum instrumento*, see Kehoe 1997: 113–123, and earlier Steinwenter 1942.

25 Pap. *Dig.* 31.66.6: *Fundo legato si usus fructus alienus sit, nihilo minus petendus est ab herede: usus fructus enim etsi in iure, non in parte consistit, emolumentum tamen rei continet.*

26 Pap. *Dig.* 31.76.2: *Dominus herede fructuario scripto fundum sub condicione legavit. voluntatis ratio non patitur, ut heres ex causa fructus emolumentum retineat* … [An owner conditionally bequeathed a farm over which his designated heir held a usufruct. It was responded that the understanding of the (testator's) intention does not allow that the heir should retain the emolument on the basis of his right to the fruits.]

27 Scaev. *Dig.* 33.1.21 pr.: *Liberto suo ita legavit: "praestari volo Philoni, usque dum vivet, quinquagesimam* (*quinquagesimas*, Mommsen) *omnis reditus, quae* (*de*, Mommsen) *praediis a colonis vel emptoribus fructus ex consuetudine domus meae praestantur." heredes praedia vendiderunt, ex quorum reditu quinquagesima relicta est: quaesitum est, an pretii usurae, quae ex consuetudine in provincia praestarentur, quinquagesima debeatur. respondit reditus dumtaxat quinquagesimas legatas, licet praedia vendita sunt* (*an pretii quinquagesima debeatur usuraeque, quae … praetarentur, licet praedia vendita sunt. respondit reditus … legata*, Mommsen). [A person made a legacy to his freedman in this way: "I want a fiftieth of all the revenue that is provided from (my) properties by tenants or the purchasers of the crop in accordance with the custom of my household to be provided to Philo as long as he will live." The heirs sold the properties from whose revenue the fiftieth part was bequeathed; the question was raised whether a fiftieth of the interest on the price that is customarily furnished in the province is owed. The response was that fiftieths of the revenue were bequeathed, even if the properties have been sold.]

28 Scaev. *Dig.* 33.1.21.1: *A liberto, cui fundum legaverat ferentem annua sexaginta, per fideicommissum dederat Pamphilae annua dena: quaesitum est, si lex Falcidia liberto legatum minuerit, an Pamphilae quoque annuum fideicommissum minutum videatur, cum ex reditu legata sint, qui largitur, etiamsi Falcidia partem dimidiam fundi abstulerit, annuam Pamphilae praestationem. Respondit secundum ea quae proponerentur non videri minutum, nisi si alia mens testatoris probaretur* (the last clause is suspected of interpolation). [A testator had given to Pamphila through a trust an annual income of 10 to be paid by a freedman to whom he had bequeathed in a legacy a farm carrying an income of 60; the question was raised whether, if the Falcidian law reduced the legacy for the freedman, the annual trust for Pamphila should also be deemed as reduced, since the legacies have been made from the revenue that bestows the annual provision on Pamphila, even if the Falcidian law has taken away half of the farm. He responded

that according to what is stated it does not seem to be diminished, unless a different intention on the part of the testator should be proved.] For discussion, see Kehoe 1997: 89–90.

29 Scaev. *Dig.* 33.2.32.7: *Heredis instituti fidei commisit filio suo annua decem praestare aut ea praedia emere et adsignare, ut usum fructum haberet, reditum efficientia annua decem: filius fundos sibi ab herede secundum matris voluntatem traditos locavit: et quaesitum est, defuncto eo reliqua colonorum utrumne ad heredem filii fructuarii an vero ad heredem Seiae testatricis pertineant. Respondit nihil proponi, cur ad heredem Seiae pertineant.* [(Seia) imposed a trust on her heir to provide an annual income of ten to her son or to purchase those properties producing an annual income of ten and assign them, so that he have the usufruct; the son leased out the farms handed over to him by the heir in accordance with the wishes of the mother. The question was raised whether, when the son died, the arrears of the tenants would belong to the heir of the son who held the usufruct or to the heir of the testator Seia. He responded that no reason in mentioned why they should belong to the heir of Seia.]

30 Cf. Jul. *Dig.* 30.92 pr. (*39 dig.*), in which a co-heir, to pay off inherited debt, purchases from his fellow-heirs a *fundus* left to another person through a trust: *excusso pretio secundum reditum eius fundi* [establishing the price in accordance with the income of that farm]. I discuss this text in Kehoe 1997: 111.

31 Scaev. *Dig.* 32.101 pr.: *Qui habebat in provincia, ex qua oriundus erat, propria praedia et alia pignori sibi data ob debita, codicillis ita scripsit:* "τῇ γλυκυτάτῃ μου πατρίδι βούλομαι εἰς τὰ μέρη αὐτῆς δοθῆναι (καὶ Μο.) ἀφορίζω αὐτῃ χωρία πάντα, ὅσα ἐν Συρίᾳ κέκτημαι, σὺν πᾶσιν τοῖς ἐνοῦσιν βοσκήμασιν δούλοις καρποῖς ἀποθέτοις κατασκευαῖς πάσαις." [A person who had in the province from which he had originated properties of his own and others given to him as pledges for debts, wrote in a codicil as follows: "I want to be given to my dearest hometown in accordance with its shares and I impart to it all of the lands as many as I possess in Syria, with all their accompanying flocks, slaves, crops, stores, and equipment."]

32 On Aurelius Horion, see Kehoe 1997: 86; his donations also paid for games to celebrate the conclusion of the Jewish rebellion under Trajan decades earlier.

33 See Johnston 1985.

34 Scaev. *Dig.* 33.2.17: *Quidam praedia rei publicae legavit, de quorum reditu quotannis ludos edi voluit, et adiecit: "Quae legata peto, decuriones, et rogo, ne in aliam speciem aut alios usus convertere velitis." Res publica per quadriennium continuum ludos non edidit: quaero, an reditus, quos quadriennio res publica percepit, heredibus restituere debeat vel compensare in aliam speciem legati ex eodem testamento. Respondit et invitis heredibus possessione adprehensa perceptos fructus restituendos esse et non erogatum secundum defuncti voluntatem in alia quae deberentur compensari.* [Someone bequeathed in a legacy to a town properties from whose revenue he wanted annual games to be staged, and he added "I seek, decurions, and I ask that you not wish to convert these legacies into another purpose or other uses." The town did not stage games for a four-year period; I ask whether the town ought to restore to the heirs the revenues that it received in the four-year period, or by way of compensation to pay them for another purpose arising from a legacy from the same will. He responded that the fruits garnered when possession was taken hold of against the will of the heirs must be restored and that what was not spent in accordance with the will of the deceased be paid to cover other purposes that were owed.]. On this case, see Johnston 1985: 119–120.

35 Johnston 1985: 118–119.

36 Valens *Dig.* 50.8.6: *Legatam municipio pecuniam in aliam rem quam defunctus voluit convertere citra principis auctoritatem non licet.* [It is not permitted to convert money that was bequeathed to a municipality into another purpose other than the one that the deceased wished without the authority of the emperor.] See Johnston 1985: 120–121.

37 Ibid.: *Sed municipio pecuniam legatam, ut ex reditu eius venatio aut spectacula edantur, senatus in eas causas erogare vetuit: et pecuniam eo legatam in id, quod maxime necessarium*

municipibus videatur, conferre permittitur, ut in eo munificentia eius qui legavit inscriptione notetur. [The senate has forbidden that money bequeathed in a legacy so that from its income either a wild-beast hunt or games be staged be spent for these purposes; and it is permitted that spend money bequeathed for this reason on what would be deemed particularly necessary by the townspeople, such that the munificence of the one who made the bequest be noted on an inscription on it.]

38 Johnston 1985: 123. Cf. Paul. Sent. book 1 (*Dig.* 50.8.7.1): *Nisi ad opus novum pecunia specialiter legata sit vetera ex hac reficienda sunt.* [Unless the money has been bequeathed specifically for a new work old ones should be repaired with it.]

39 See Kehoe 2016; Jördens 2016.

40 Kehoe 1997: 22–76; 2018; Saller 1994: 181–191.

41 Cervenca 1979.

42 For fuller discussion of this point, see Kehoe 2018.

43 In Paul. (*2 sent.) Dig.* 23.3.71.1, the situations in which the dowry can be returned to the wife while the marriage continues include purchasing a suitable *fundus: Manente matrimonio non perditurae uxori ob has causas dos reddi potest: ut sese suosque alat, ut fundum idoneum emat, ut in exilium vel in insulam relegato parenti praestet alimonia, aut ut egentem virum fratrem sororemve sustineat.* [While the marriage is enduring the dowry can be returned to the wife who is not going to lose it for these reasons: that she feed herself and her family, that she buy a suitable farm, that she provide support for a parent sent into exile or relegated to an island, or that she support an impoverished husband, brother, or sister.]

44 A point discussed further in Kehoe 1997.

45 See Kehoe 2022.

References

Andreau, J. (2020) Banking, Money-Lending, and Elite Financial Life in Rome. In: G. Dari-Mattiacci and D.P. Kehoe, eds. *Roman Law and Economics*. Oxford: Oxford University Press vol. II, 81–111.

Briscoe, J. (1973) *A Commentary on Livy Books XXXI-XXXIII*. Oxford: The Clarendon Press.

Camodeca, G. (1999) *Tabulae Pompeianae Sulpiciorum, edizione critica dell'archivio dei Sulpicii*. 2 vols. Vetera: Ricerche di storia epigrafia e antichità 12. Rome: Quasar.

Cervenca, G. (1979) Studi sulla 'cura minorum', 3. L'estensione ai minori del regime dell'Oratio Severi. *Bulletino dell'istituto di diritto romano* 21, 41–94.

Duncan-Jones, R.P. (1982) *The Economy of the Roman Empire: Quantitative Studies*, 2nd ed. Cambridge: Cambridge University Press.

Elliott, C. (2015) The Crisis of A.D. 33: Past and Present. *Journal of Ancient History* 3. 2, 267–281.

Elliott, C. (2020) *Economic Theory and the Roman Monetary Economy*. Cambridge: Cambridge University Press.

Goldsmith, R.W. (1987) *Pre-modern Financial Systems: A Historical Comparative Study*. Cambridge: Cambridge University Press.

Harris, W.V. (2006) A Revisionist View of Money. *Journal of Roman Studies* 96, 1–24.

Hollander, D. (2007) *Money in the Late Roman Republic*. Leiden: Brill.

Johnston, D. (1985) Munificence and *Municipia*: Bequests to Rome in Classical Roman Law. *Journal of Roman Studies* 75, 101–125.

Jördens, A. (2016) Possession and Provincial Practice. In P.J. du Plessis, C. Ando, and K. Tuori, eds. *The Oxford Handbook of Roman Law and Society*, Oxford: Oxford University Press, 553–565.

Kehoe, D.P. (1997) *Investment, Profit, and Tenancy: The Jurists and the Roman Agrarian Economy*. Ann Arbor: The University of Michigan Press.

Kehoe, D.P. (2007) *Law and the Rural Economy in the Roman Empire*. Ann Arbor: University of Michigan Press.

Kehoe, D.P. (2013) The State and Production in the Roman Agrarian Economy. In: A. Bowman and A. Wilson eds. *The Agricultural Economy: Production and Consumption*, Oxford: Oxford University Press, 33–53.

Kehoe, D.P. (2016) Tenure of Land and Agricultural Regulation. In P.J. du Plessis, C. Ando, and K. Tuori, eds. *Oxford Handbook for Roman Law and Society*. Oxford: Oxford University Press, 646–659.

Kehoe, D.P. (2018) Agency, Tutorship, and the Protection of Pupils in Roman Law. In: D. Mantovani, ed. *Diritto romano e economia. Due modi di pensare e organizzare il mondo (nei primi tre secoli dell'Impero)*. Pavia: Pavia University Press, 375–396.

Kehoe, D.P. (2022) Private Property Rights and Public Claims on Land in the Roman Empire. In: K. Verboven and P. Erdkamp, eds., *Law and Economic Performance in the Roman World*, Leiden: Brill, 25–46.

Lerouxel, F. (2015) The βιβλιοθήκη ἐγκτήσεων and Transaction Costs in the Credit Market of Roman Egypt (30 B.C.E. to ca. 170 C.E.). In: D.P. Kehoe, D.M. Ratzan, and Y. Firanko, eds. *Law and Transaction Costs in the Ancient Economy*. Ann Arbor: University of Michigan Press, 162–184.

Lerouxel, F. (2016) *Le marché du crédit dans le monde romain (Égypte et Campanie)*, Bibliothèque des Écoles françaises d'Athènes et de Rome 374. Rome: École française de Rome.

Lo Cascio, E. (2000) Gli alimenta e la "politica economica" di Pertinace. In: *Il princeps e il suo impero, Il princeps e il suo impero: Studi di storia amministrativa e finanziaria romana*. Bari: Edipuglia, 293–311.

Lo Cascio, E. (2007) The State and the Economy. In: W. Scheidel, I. Morris, and R. Saller, eds. *The Cambridge Economic History of the Greco-Roman World*. Cambridge: Cambridge University Press, 619–647.

Maiuro, M. (2012) *Res Caesaris: Ricerche sulla proprietà imperiale nel Principato*. Bari: Edipuglia.

Malmendier, U. (2002) *Societas Publicanorum: Staatliche Wirtschaftsaktivitäten in den Händen privater Unternehmer*. Köln-Weimar-Wien: Böhlau.

Saller, R.P. (1994) *Patriarchy, Property and Death in the Roman Family*. Cambridge: Cambridge University Press.

Scheidel, W. and S.J. Friesen (2009) The Size of the Economy and the Distribution of Income in the Roman Empire. *Journal of Roman Studies* 99, 61–91.

Shaw, B.D. (2019) Did the Romans Have a Future? *Journal of Roman Studies* 109, 1–26.

Steinwenter, A. (1942) Fundus cum instrumento: Eine agrar- und rechtsgeschichtliche Studie. *SAWW* (Phil.-hist. Kl.) 221. 1.

Temin, P. (2013) *The Roman Market Economy*. Princeton: Princeton University Press.

Verboven, K. (2008) Faeneratores, Negotiatores and Financial Intermediaries in the Roman World (Late Republic and Early Empire). In: K. Verboven, K. Vandorpe, and V. Chankowski, eds. *Pistoi dia tèn technèn: Bankers, Loans and Archives in the Ancient World, Studies in Honour of Raymond Bogaert*, Studia Hellenistica 44. Leuven: Peeters, 211–229.

Verhagen, H.L.E. (2020) Secured Transaction in Classical Roman Law. In G. Dari-Mattiacci and D.P. Kehoe, eds. *Roman Law and Economics*. Oxford: Oxford University Press vol. II, 113–156.

5 *Praedia agris meis vicina atque etiam inserta venalia sunt*

A Reflection on the Modalities and Effects of the Circulation of Agrarian Properties between the Late Republic and the Principate

Luigi Capogrossi Colognesi

Abstract

This contribution aims to investigate how legal sources discuss the strategy, followed by large-estate proprietors, of expanding their domains through accumulative mechanisms, rather than through the substantial modification of their existing production structures. For this reason, these texts tend to consider various estate units of the same owner as separate entities, even in cases where land units are adjacent to each other. The autonomous management of various properties is also confirmed by the particular emphasis that Roman jurists placed on internal distributions within larger estates, as well as on the single *partes fundi*.

The lack of transformation into larger land units of the majority of single *fundi* probably facilitated the quantity and speed of land estate circulation. A relevant piece of evidence of this phenomenon is provided by the Tablet of Veleia, in which many *fundi* are mentioned under more than one name. This information has been interpreted as the trace of a property transfer between holders of different *nomina* (not necessarily as the result of acquisitions *inter vivos*, although this may be the most likely explanation). It is even more interesting that this text mentions several estates which have the same name yet belong to different owners. In this case, it is plausible to interpret that a unique *fundus* was later divided among several owners, either as the result of an inheritance or following the sale of a *pars fundi*, as in the instances so often mentioned by jurists. Although we cannot obtain any statistically certain information from these testimonies, we can certainly gain evidence of practices closely attached to the maximisation of estate productivity under given conditions, as well as to the commercial enhancement of land properties. This internal disarrangement of large estate units seemed to be more accentuated whenever new pieces of land were added to the unit and continued to be enlarged.

***

DOI: 10.4324/9781003187806-7

The Organisation of Landed Property

The reader might recognise in my title an excerpt from the well-known letter by Pliny the Younger in which he discusses the risks and advantages of purchasing a large landed estate bordering his own.[1] As he himself admits, he was motivated to make this new purchase by the gratification of *pulchritudo iungendi*, a sentiment widely shared among wealthy landowners in late Republican and early imperial Roman Italy. In this chapter I will focus on a few specific aspects of the many land acquisitions that took place in Italy during the last two centuries of the Republic, and on some of the effects they had on the organisation of landed estates in the imperial age.

It is well known that the Roman aristocracy of the late Republic, but also of the early Empire, bought and sold substantial landed properties with relative ease. In the many references to such activity that we encounter in ancient authors, particular attention is often paid to the economic gain or loss arising from these transfers. It is possible, however, to suspect that, at least in some cases, less strictly pecuniary considerations might also have weighed on the purchases and sales mentioned in the ancient texts – such as a desire to show off one's wealth and power. In typical "nouveau riche" fashion, they would buy, flaunt their purchase for a time, and then resell it: much as one would now do with a quickly outmoded luxury car or yacht. This is what I would call the "culture of display", which is clearly evident in certain passages of Cicero's correspondence, as well as in many passages of Varro's *De re rustica*. But that is not the point I would like to entertain here; it has been thoroughly discussed ever since the early studies by E. Rawson and J.H. D'Arms.[2]

I would instead like to consider here what we might call "minor exchanges" – those involving just portions of the large estates that had come into being in the last century of the Republic. Many references, both in legal texts and in literary and epigraphic sources, well into the imperial age, attest to a particular conception of the landed estate, identified either with the late-republican *villa* – the country residence of the rich city owner, including the agricultural land attached to it – or the *fundus*, now much larger than the *agellus* of two or seven *iugera* belonging to the small landholders or peasants of the early republican age. These *fundi* appear in turn conceived as a set of *partes*, themselves often the result of progressive acquisitions of neighbouring parcels of land, combined to form larger units. But – and this is the main point – their unification remained rather precarious, since the *domini* held the old and new *partes* of the *fundus* as separate or separable entities, which could be managed independently. These characteristics are, in my view, valuable evidence, not only of the mechanisms underlying the construction of the model of the large aristocratic *villa* and its extensions of land, but also of its internal organisation and its remarkable organisational elasticity. And there is more: precisely these aspects must have contributed to a much more varied and, I would say, "piecemeal" system of land circulation, by comparison with a simple transfer of properties as they had grown over time and in accordance with the choices made by their *domini*.

This is the starting point of my analysis, which aims to clarify what specific factors determined, in actual practice, how the Romans organised the system of their landed properties, investigating its historical roots, on the one hand, and its economic and administrative implications, on the other.

The Complexities of the *fundus* System

Some characteristics of this organisational system can be clearly discerned from the kinds of questions that Roman jurists addressed when discussing actual cases involving both the transfer of individual *fundi* and the potential rights that other owners might have had over them, as in predial servitude; where, of course, the material reference to the legal object at stake, the *fundus*, is central – *fundus* was a key word in the law but also in agricultural practice. It indicates land defined as a unit, not only from a material standpoint – land set apart from the surrounding territory in accordance with land-surveying techniques – but also and above all land exploited as a unit by its owner, with its own productive organisation: the "*fundus* as economic unit."[3]

Now, what interests us here is the fact that, according to many passages in the Roman jurists, this unitary identity is not lost even if the parcel of land is bought by the owner of an adjoining *fundus*. In theory, a single right – the *dominium ex iure Quiritium* – would encompass both *fundi* as a single entity, making it impossible, at least from a legal standpoint, to distinguish the previously owned land from that acquired *ex novo*. But, in practice, this is not the case, since the Roman jurists all appear inclined to consider the two *fundi* as distinct objects, although attributed in property to the same holder – like any other two *res mancipi* that do not transmute into a single entity just because they are owned by the same person.

In the *Corpus iuris* we find many instances of this persisting autonomy of two neighbouring properties belonging to the same owner, starting with two well-known texts probably attributable to a point in Servius, and reported by Paul, in *Dig.* 8.3.29 (2, *epit. Alf., dig.): qui duo praedia confinia habuerat, superiorem fundum vendiderat…*, and in *Dig.* 8.3.30 (*Paul. epit. Dig. Alf. l. 4*), where the fact that the *duo praedia* owned by the same holder were adjoining, can be deduced from the reported evidence.[4] The same situation recurs, at the height of the principate, in Javolenus Priscus (but perhaps already in Labeo) with another reference, in *Dig* 33.7.4 (*ex* l. 2 *post. Lab*), to *qui duos fundos contiguos habeat.* To this we should add the interesting statement by Salvius Julianus reported in *Dig* 8.3.31 (2 *ex Minicio*), which also seems to echo the previous generation's ideas.[5] Finally, the entire passage of Paul reported in *Dig.* 10.1.12 (*ex* l. 3 *resp.*) deals in an exemplary way with the separateness of the two contiguous *fundi* belonging to the same owner and the importance of the existing boundary markers between them.[6]

But above all, we should bear in mind the evidence given us by one of the most detailed sources about the organisation of land tenure in Italy during the imperial age. I am referring to the Table of Veleia, which lists numerous landed properties in the two *municipia* of Placentia and Veleia that were pledged as security for loans made by the imperial administration to its owners. It was, as is well known, a mechanism designed by Trajan for allocating the fixed sums from the repayments of these loans to the sustenance of young orphans in need.

The statistically significant number of properties mentioned in the Table gives us a very interesting insight into the ways the various *fundi* were identified, first of all through their owner's name – '*fundus Sempronianus* or *Calvinianus*', for example – combined with the name of the *municipium* and the rural district (the *pagus*) where each was located. Finally, this topographical identification appears to have been supplemented by the mention of the names of the two neighbouring *fundi*. As I have pointed out in previous studies, it is remarkable how the varied names of these agrarian properties preserve the memory, not only of their former owners, but also of changes in ownership and of the ways the properties were recombined, as a result of the break-up of some larger properties, but also the merging of smaller units with new and larger ones.

We might thus encounter a *fundum Cornelianum Collaterianum Flaccellianum cum colonia Munatiana Arteficia, parte dimidia, et coloniam Vettianam Cornelianam pro parte quarta* (1.32), or, in the plural, the *fundos Terentianos et Malapacios* (1.54). But we also come across two *fundos Antonianum et Cornelianum* (1.65), each named in the singular, or, in the plural, the *fundos II Albonianos Vibullianos… et fundos Antonianos II* (1.68), and the *fundos Virianos Calidianos Salvianos duos* (1.78).[7]

Since the early twentieth century, scholars have been well aware that the nomenclature of the *fundi* in the Table was of great importance for understanding the history of this area, both before and after its conquest by the Romans.[8] The multiple names used for a single *fundus* provided clear evidence of the successive integration of several parcels of land, each bearing the gentile name of its owner; and these names remained, even after the lots had been joined together. But our information goes much further, since we also encounter a single gentile name used to designate two properties kept separate but owned by a single holder (as in the legal texts just mentioned). Even more interesting are the two examples at the end of my list, because they reveal a more complex history: here we have evidence of earlier land accretions forming a larger *fundus*; this was then divided into two autonomous parts, but the multiple designations of the original smaller units remained.

The Table of Veleia, however, grants us yet more insights and raises new interpretative difficulties, as for example, in the case of a *fundum Munatianum Ancharianum cum fund(is) Paspidiano et Rosiano et Mariano et Aconiano et Tarquitiano cum casis in Carracino et silvis sagatis et loco agri Nasulliani* (4.41.44); where, as Criniti rightly observed, we see a constellation of *fundi* – with their individual designations – almost certainly covering a vast area, with its woods and houses, that encompassed several *pagi* and two different *municipia*.[9] Of course, all these lands belonged to a single *dominus*, T. Volumnius Epaphroditus, and were worth a substantial amount, valued in the mortgage table at 250,000 sestertii.

If multiple names often converge to designate a single *fundus*, generally signalling its derivation from a set of smaller landholdings progressively acquired by the same owner and obviously bordering each other, more interesting are other situations evoked in the Veleia inscription. I am referring especially to the use of the same *nomen gentilicium* to designate different *fundi* that might be located at some distance from each other. This is the case, for example, of the *Fundum Manlianum Hostilianum* (1.11), and the *Fundum Manlianum Stracianum Calpurnianum* (1.14), located in the same *pagus* as Veleia, and that were combined into one mortgage by their owner, M. Virius Nepos. This suggests the likelihood that an original Manlian *fundus* was split into two parts, later recombined into the new units listed in the text considered here.

Even more complex is the history of land ownership evoked by a group of *fundi* bearing the gentile name *Aurelianus*, an important *gens* whose presence in the area is attested by an Aurelia Exorata, mentioned in the Table of Veleia.[10] A certain Gaius Vibius mortgaged his *fundos Aurelianos Vettianos* (4.93) and *fundos Aurelianos Betutianos* (4.98), both in the *pagus Bagiennius,* in the Veleia area. But, in the same area, although in two other districts – the first two in the *pagus Ambitrebius* and the third in the *pagus Moninas* – other *fundi* are attested in which the gentile name Aurelianus appears: a *fundus Quintiacus Aurelianus* (1.2), a *fundus Aurelianus* (7.48), and finally a *fundus Aurelianus Virtinaus Cornelianus* (4.34). It is highly unlikely that all references to the gentile name *Aurelianus* reflect the existence of an original single large estate owned by an individual belonging to this family. What is more likely is that the recurrence of this name for several *fundi,* that were reorganised following the absorption of other lands, testifies to the existence of substantial landholdings in that region owned by a single or a few members of the same family and *gens.*

Rethinking Property Tenure and Agricultural Production

I have chosen these examples because they demonstrate quite clearly the complex nomenclature the Romans employed to designate their landed properties. It is a system that gives us important clues about their histories, but it certainly does not allow us to make broad generalisations. What it does allow us to do, however, as I have variously and repeatedly insisted in my research, is to identify certain common patterns in the way the great landowners and Italo-Roman oligarchy conceived and directed their agrarian investments, clearly a privileged form of property, at least from an ideological standpoint and as the foundation of their social pre-eminence.[11]

These examples are just a few among the many that show how mid-size and larger Roman rural properties, after the Punic War, were created through a complex process of assembling and reassembling plots of land, mostly involving the acquisition of smaller parcels.[12] But, above all, the enduring memory of the earlier configuration of those *fundi* that were absorbed into different and generally larger units is important confirmation of what I have long maintained was a distinctive aspect of Italian agriculture between the end of the republic and the principate. And that is: changes in the ownership structure of a property that had greatly expanded did not necessarily or always lead to equally substantial changes to its system of agricultural production.

Since the mid-1980s, I have been emphasising the peculiar nature of the quantitative growth of late-republican landed estates; this is because I do not believe that such growth automatically entailed a parallel growth and transformation of farming practices.[13] When one *fundus* was added to another, this did not necessarily affect how each was managed. It is no accident that Weber should have found the same kind of structural rigidity in the Roman artisanal production of urban artefacts, where there was no trend towards the formation of large-scale enterprises.[14] All the more reason, then, to avoid confusing the existence of great agrarian properties with the advent of "large-scale farming." In other words, the diversity in the management of small and medium-sized properties does not disappear with their absorption into a much larger estate. The accumulation of multiple properties in the hands of a single owner did not necessarily result in radical changes to the production specialisations of the pre-existing smaller lots. The diversity that characterised the smaller landholdings – where the wheat-planted *agellum* coexisted with row crops and wooded areas, but also with the small vineyard of a few *iugera* and the grove of olive trees, as well as with the vegetable garden – was altered only to a very limited extent by the new owner. But this point I believe has now gained widespread acceptance among agricultural history specialists.

Throughout these years I have explored two further aspects connected to these agrarian transformations in Roman Italy: the first concerns the cautiousness that landowners displayed with respect to any technical and organisational innovations that would have allowed an absolute increase in agricultural production; they paid close attention to cost–benefit ratios, in a market that was expanding only to a limited extent.[15] The second relates to the diversified character of the agrarian landscape itself, where there was a multiplicity of integrated micro-systems of production and consumption, linked to the presence of hundreds of consumption centres. Many of these were distant from the waterways, which were the primary means of circulation of foodstuffs, especially the least valuable or those heavier to transport, such as grain;[16] therefore, local needs had to be supplied almost wholly from the surrounding countryside. And this, in turn, speaks to the greater complexity of the late-republican agrarian system, compared with the simplified models derived from the slave villa that were widely used in the 1970s and 1980s to paint a uniform picture of the economic features of late-republican Italo-Roman agriculture.[17] In fact, it was precisely its complexity that gave the system the elasticity it needed to survive the decrease in maritime exports that started during the principate.

The Economic Impact of the Transformation of Estates

The last point I would like to address relates to some economic consequences of the premises outlined so far. As we have seen, larger estates were generally organised as an aggregate of smaller production units that remained relatively autonomous, not so much in terms of overall management and control, but as concerns their internal production arrangements. This is clearly reflected in the legal sources, where there are repeated references to several neighbouring *fundi* belonging to the same owner, but considered as separate entities, together with an insistence on the operational autonomy of the various *partes fundi*.[18] And, in turn, this explains why it continued to be so easy for an individual owner to sell only one *pars fundi* or a single *fundus* that adjoined his other agrarian properties, but was only relatively integrated with them. Because, I repeat, the joining up of multiple parcels of land did not greatly alter the agrarian landscape of central Italy, not least because of the constraints that the terrain, mostly hilly, and always unevenly developed, imposed on landowners.[19] These constraints were particularly severe, for we must never forget that agriculture at this time relied almost exclusively on the power provided by man and animals; the use of wind power or *aqua profluens* was confined to very marginal activities and thus would have been insufficient for effecting major changes at will, or on a large scale, and, above all, for rendering such technological interventions economically viable.

But precisely this missing, or only limited, structural transformation of production is what accounts for the ease with which properties could be dismembered and reassembled, with the consequent circulation of the same *fundi* that appears to persist over time. This, together with the demographic fragility of the Roman aristocracy, both in the late-republican era and later, prevented land ownership, as a mechanism of social advancement and distinction, from translating into that enduring connection to the land, destined to last for centuries, which was experienced by other European societies in more recent times.

And, moreover, do we not find confirmation of my argument in that magnificent example of the conduct of large estate owners that is Pliny the Younger's well-known letter, *ep.*, 3.19? Now, it must be admitted that one of the reasons for Pliny's purchase of the large property next to his own was the possibility of achieving some cost-cutting in the management of the whole, by extending the administrative governance of his property over the new land as well: this was the usual apparatus of *actores, prosecutores* and the *vilicus* or the *vilici* already in charge of such management, as well as the permanent structures used by the *dominus* – the *pars urbana* of the *villa.*[20] However, if we then look at the work done in the fields and the varied layout of the crops – the organisation of production, in short – we discover that they are associated with a system of leaseholds and share-cropping that presupposes precisely what I have been emphasising here: the fragmentation of the large estate into a multitude of relatively autonomous production units.

Notes

1 Plin. *Ep.* 3.19.1–2 "An estate is offered to be sold which lies contiguous to mine, and indeed is intermixed with it" (transl. W.M.L. Hutchinson).
2 D'Arms 1970; Rawson 1976.
3 Ulpian, in *Dig.* 50.16.60 pr. (69 *ad ed.*). See De Neeve 1984.
4 On this, see Capogrossi Colognesi 1966.
5 See Capogrossi Colognesi 1996: 312 nt. 12.
6 In this regard, see also *Dig.* 39.3.17.3 (*Paul.* 15 *ad Plaut.*), and *Dig.* 8.4.7.1 (*Paul.* 5 *ad Sab.*), which even discusses the existence of *tria praedia* belonging to the same *dominus*. Particularly interesting are also the texts by Cervidius Scaevola; they attest an

intricate reality of successions and wills that reveal the frequency of the decomposition of *fundi* into their *partes*; see foremost *Dig.* 31.88.4 (*Scaev., 3 resp.*) and Dig. 32.4 pr. (*Scaev., 22 dig.*).

7 *CIL* 11.11.47.

8 See De Pachtère 1920; and foremost Sereni 1955: 314–316, and n. 19, in which the names of the *fundi* are connected to Ligurian and Gaulish *gentes*.

9 From Piacenza and from Veleia: cf. text and translation by Criniti 2003: 209. As regards the possible extension of the properties, what is striking is the relatively modest value of their inscription, 50,000 sestertii.

10 Scopelliti 2003: 154.

11 Cf. Capogrossi Colognesi 1981 (also in 2010: 131–141); 1982 (also in 2010: 169–197).

12 This is what in general we read in the ancient writers, from Appian to Plutarch, with reference to the *pulchritudo iungendi* of the great landowners (Plin. *Ep.* 3.19.1, see n. 1). They were considered in these writings as the main reason for the disappearance of the small peasant-farmers, who had been the foundation of military power in the golden age of the Republic.

13 Capogrossi Colognesi 1982, and 2012: 139–160.

14 Weber 1909 (and in 1976: 354–455; 1981: 342–343; 2006: 711–712). See also Capogrossi Colognesi 2000: 332–333. Weber's analysis highlights in particular the absence of a capitalistic development in ancient artisan activity, although this diagnosis also concerns the agrarian economy.

15 Capogrossi Colognesi 2012: 178–184.

16 It has been calculated that there were almost 400 Italic towns and villages by the end of the Republic. This is an enormous figure for this period.

17 Capogrossi Colognesi 2012: 31–56.

18 Capogrossi Colognesi 2014.

19 This does not mean that the original crop configurations were strictly preserved; far from it. Fallow land might be replaced by a *pomarium*, and next to it deep ploughing might prepare the land for a new vineyard. But the point on which I always insist is that the new owner's changes almost never led to the alteration of the agrarian landscape in favour of those extensive systems of uniform crops or "plantations" which are instead described in many recent studies.

20 This point is made very clear in Plin. *Ep.* 3.19.2–3.

References

Capogrossi Colognesi, L. (1966) *La struttura delle servitù d'acqua in diritto romano*. Milan: Giuffrè.

Capogrossi Colognesi, L. (1981) Alcuni aspetti dell'organizzazione fondiaria romana nella tarda repubblica e nel principato. *Klio* 63, 347–357.

Capogrossi Colognesi, L., ed. (1982) *L'agricoltura romana. Guida storica e critica*. Bari: Laterza.

Capogrossi Colognesi, L. (1996) *Ai margini della proprietà fondiaria* (2nd edn). Rome: La Sapienza.

Capogrossi Colognesi, L. (2000) *Max Weber e le economie del mondo antico*. Bari: Laterza.

Capogrossi Colognesi, L. (2010) *Scritti scelti*, vol. I. Rome: Jovene.

Capogrossi Colognesi, L. (2012) *Padroni e contadini nell'Italia repubblicana*. Rome: "L'Erma" di Bretschneider.

Capogrossi Colognesi, L. (2014) I vari tipi di complessità nella società agraria repubblicana. In C. Apicella, M.L. Haack, Lerouxel, F., eds. *Les affaires de Monsieur Andreau. Économie et société du monde romain*, Bordeaux: Ausonius, 67–76.

Criniti, N., ed. (2003) *Ager Veleias. Tradizione, società e territorio sull'Appennino Piacentino (con nuova edizione e traduzione della Tabula Alimentaria di Veleia)*. Parma: La Pilotta Editrice.

D'Arms, J.H. (1970) *Romans on the Bay of Naples. A Social and Cultural Study of the Villas and their Owners from 150 BC to AD 400*. Cambridge MA: Harvard University Press.

De Neeve, P.W. (1984) Funds as an Economic Unity. *Revue d'histoire du droit* 52, 3–19.

De Pachtère, F.G. (1920) *La Table Hypothécaire de Veleia. Etude sur la propriété foncière dans l'Appennin de Plaisance*. Paris: E. de Boccard.

Rawson, E. (1976) The Ciceronian Aristocracy and Its Properties. In: M. Finley (ed.), *Studies in Roman Property*. Cambridge: Cambridge University Press, 85–102.

Scopelliti, C. (2003) "Veleiates cognomine Vetti Regiates...": Storia e onomastica nel Veleiate. In N. Criniti, ed. *Ager Veleias. Tradizione, società e territorio sull'Appennino Piacentino (con nuova edizione e traduzione della Tabula Alimentaria di Veleia)*. Parma: La Pilotta Editrice, 185–268.

Sereni, E. (1955) *Comunità rurali nell'Italia antica*. Rome: Edizione Rinascita.

Weber, M. (1909) Agrarverhältnisse im Altertum. In: *Handwörterbuch der Staatswissenschaften*[3], I, Jena: Gustav Fischer, 52–188.

Weber, M. (1976) *The Agrarian Sociology of Ancient Civilizations*. London: Verso Books.

Weber, M. (1981) *Storia economica e sociale dell'antichità*. Rome: Editori Riuniti.

Weber, M. (2006) *Max Weber Gesamtausgabe* (MWG). I/6 (edited by H. Baier, G. Hübinger, M.R. Lepsius, W.J. Mommsen, W. Schluchter, and J. Winckelmann). Tübingen: Mohr Siebeck.

6 The Real Estate Market in the Campanian Wax-Tablets

Jean Andreau

Abstract

This chapter investigates the economic information concerning land estates and properties documented in the three corpora of Vesuvian tablets (Pompeii, Herculaneum, and Puteoli (the Murecine tablets)) dated to the first century CE. Although monetary loans and financial practices dominate in the *tabulae* of Pompeii and Murecine, issues regarding real estate and land are also present in these documents. These are particularly relevant in the tablets found in Herculaneum, to which G. Camodeca dedicated a volume in 2017. Urban properties are less predominant than productive land estates in these tablets. Two main observations can be extracted from this material: first, that the sale of land was not uncommon in the Herculaneum tablets (e.g. the sale of the *fundus* Licinianus (TH^2 A10; – 295 000 HS)); and second that auction sales are also well attested, particularly in Pompeii and Puteoli. These were held in towns in which weekly markets (*nundinae*) took place. *Nundinae* certainly contributed to the formation of the market price. I will analyse these materials and activities, paying particular attention to aspects of land management that are less known from other sources, such as the sale of the harvest of the *fundus* and the sale undertaken by the co-owner of a *fundus*.

***

This contribution evaluates the transfers and the management of land and immovable properties recorded in the Campanian Wax-Tablets and dated to the middle of the first century AD.

The tablets fall into three groups. First, there are the 153 tablets of the banker (the *argentarius* or *coactor argentarius*) Lucius Caecilius Jucundus, found at Pompeii in the nineteenth century, which were published by Karl Zangemeister in Supplement 1 of *CIL* IV. Following this, we have the tablets referred to as "of Murecine" or "of the Sulpicii," found in 1959 in a building close to the river port of Pompeii, but which concern the business affairs carried out at Puteoli. The tablets of Murecine were read and studied by Giuseppe Camodeca, who published two volumes on them, in 1992 and 1999. They comprise 127 tablets. Finally, there are the tablets found in eight different houses in Herculaneum during the 1930s. These Herculaneum tablets, first published by Giovanni Pugliese Carrattelli and Vincenzo Arangio Ruiz, have been re-examined, published and studied for more than

DOI: 10.4324/9781003187806-8

20 years by Camodeca. They form a group of about 160 tablets. Camodeca wrote a number of articles about them, as well as a book, published in 2017, but he has not yet studied all of them with the same precision and detail.[1] The research that he did complete concerning the Murecine tablets, and later the Herculaneum tablets (or at least a large part of the latter group), means that we now have authorised editions for most tablets of the Vesuvian cities. All these tablets must be dated before 79 CE, of course, and almost all date back to the second or third quarter of the first century CE.

As I have recently written, these tablets conform to a very specific category of documents.[2] They provide a type of information that cannot be found in literary texts or in inscriptions on stone. Fundamentally, they concern economic affairs in which legal matters are clearly (or almost clearly) defined. Yet they do not supply information about the social context in which these operations took place, nor do they inform about the aims of the protagonists named in the tablets.

The tablets of Lucius Caecilius Jucundus and those of the Sulpicii concern, above all, commercial and financial operations: loans of money with guarantees, loan repayment, auction sales in connection with loans, etc. Accordingly, we only find in the Sulpicii archive a single tablet that is explicitly connected to the rental of gardens (*horti*), while in the tablets of Jucundus there is only one reference to the rental of land and the sale of movable objects from an estate. By contrast, several persons who have been identified as the owners of documents found in Herculaneum were mainly engaged with rural properties and agricultural land. So, the Herculaneum tablets supply substantially more information on matters linked with real estate and property management, in particular rural properties rather than specifically buildings. However, we can assume that, even if they are not mentioned, it is extremely likely that in a fair number of cases such properties also contained permanent buildings.

The first part of this chapter, which is also the shortest, will be devoted to the renting of land, buildings, or houses. In the second part, I will analyse the references to auctions, which are far more numerous than the rental agreements, particularly in the tablets of Jucundus and the Sulpicii. The discussion will include the Herculanean tablet *TH*^{2} 4, which focuses on a certain *fundus blandianus*. This *fundus* belonged to two landlords, one of whom decided to sell the property to the other, Q. Junius Theophilus, even if no document attesting the sale survives. The former owner, A. Tetteius Severus, was authorised to take part of the harvest, equipment, slaves, and cattle that were still entitled to him as co-proprietor of the *fundus* (*et res mancipia et pecora*). He held the right to seize these and auction them as he desired. The third part of the chapter will be devoted to land and property transactions aside from auctions. Specifically, I will analyse the tablet *TH*^{2} D 12, which attests to the sale of the entirety of the harvest from the *fundus cadianus* to another *fundus* in Herculaneum.

★

Rentals are hardly to be found in the three groups of tablets from the cities of Vesuvius, a fact which may seem surprising. The Herculaneum tablets that

Camodeca has already analysed in his volume show no cases of rental of property, unless I am mistaken. As for the tablets of Lucius Caecilius Jucundus, they concern a piece of land that belongs to the city, the *fundus audianus*. This *fundus* is to be rented, but it is not the usual agricultural tenancy. The rental is "*in avitum et patritum*," that is, exceptional guarantees are made to the one who takes over the *fundus*. The rental payment, in this case, is 6,000 sesterces a year. If this sum is regularly paid, the city cannot get out of the contract. The renter can even mortgage the land, and his rights over it can be bequeathed to his heirs, or even to a third party.[3]

Finally, among the Murecine tablets, *TPSulp*. 47 states that one Titus Hordeonius Barba rented several *horti*, which undoubtedly were located near the town of Puteoli. We know almost nothing about these *horti*, but in all probability they had something to do with horticulture.[4] For these "gardens," whose owner we do not know, T. Hordeonius Barba had to pay a rent of 24,000 sesterces a year.

None of the series of tablets is complete. We do not have all the documents of the *argentarius* L. Caecilius Jucundus from Pompeii, nor of the Sulpicii from Puteoli. It probably lacks a substantial number of documents. This is also the case for the *tabulae* from Herculaneum. The fact that only one case of rental of private land is preserved (*TPSulp*. 47) could be due to how they were classified by the landowner, or simply the result of risk. In general, it is important to distinguish between the rental of urban apartments, which was probably quite common, particularly in a big city like Rome,[5] and the rental of land to farmers or sharecroppers (*coloni*), who had to pay fees (in money or kind) to the landlord. These land tenancies were probably less frequent at the beginning of the Principate, and in Italy in general, than in later periods and in the provinces. In those regions that are best known to us in the Augustan period during the first century CE – Campania and Latium – the most typical system of land exploitation is direct management by the dominus or by his slaves, under the direction of a *vilicus*.[6]

⋆

When I studied the tablets of L. Caecilius Jucundus, about 50 years ago, between 1968 and 1973, the bibliography on auctions was very thin. The only serious works were those of Mario Talamanca (1954) and G. Thielmann (1961), both focused on the juridical aspects of the matter. The further I proceeded with my study, the more convinced I became of the importance of auctions. In fact, a large number of the tablets from L. Caecilius Jucundus concern sales by auction. In my study of the tablets, I emphasised the presence of auctions, but since there was no good social and economic study of auctions at that time, I also tended to minimise their role. I treated them as a merely local phenomenon, partly involving peasants, something a little ethnographic, taking place alongside local periodic markets (called *nundinae* in Latin). A good illustration of this attitude may be found in the first of the two articles I wrote concerning the chronology of the *nundinae* in Pompeii and in the region of the Gulf of Naples: "Pompeii: Auctions, Fairs and Markets."[7]

My article concerned the problem of the frequency of the *nundinae*. Certain authors have written unequivocally that the *nundinae*, in Campania in the middle of the first century AD, still took place every eight full days. Others consider, to the contrary, that the *nundinae* were weekly.[8] But, in some way, these matters have been largely considered as mere mysteries of erudition, lacking any great historical or economic significance, and not the substance of a real debate.

Today, to the contrary, we see clearly from Camodeca's publication of the Murecine tablets that, during the second and third quarters of the first century AD, the *nundinae* of the cities of Vesuvius no longer took place every eight days, but had fallen into a week-by-week schedule according to the planetary 7-day system.[9] This alteration of the schedule of the *nundinae* raises a number of problems: when did this change take place? Why do Latin texts not mention it? Was it an official change, or something that just happened? Must we think in terms of 56-day cycles, in order to conciliate the 8-day and 7-day periods, as G. Tibiletti and more recently A. Storchi Marino have suggested?[10] These questions are far from being resolved. But the fact that the 7-day week was such an influential pattern in Tyrrhenian central Italy shows the influence exerted by the cultural worlds of the eastern Mediterranean, especially by means of maritime transportation and commerce.

At any rate, auctions have now been much better studied, and are better known. Marta García Morcillo wrote an important book and several articles about them.[11] François Lerouxel was also very interested in them, particularly in regard to "real" guarantees of the loans.[12] And we know, with certainty, that in Campania, in the towns of the *nundinae*, auctions took place the same day that the *nundinae* were held.

Auctions appear very frequently on the tablets of L. Caecilius Jucundus. In his edition of the Jucundus' archive (*CIL* IV, Suppl. 1), K. Zangemeister concludes that from the 153 tablets that have come to us, 138 are connected with auctions. In my book about the archive, I have followed Zangemeister's conclusions.[13] However, some tablets are in such a lacunary state that it is impossible to know what kind of activities they refer to. In any case, it is certain that the majority of the documents are receipts of auctions. However, only one of them appears to concern, indirectly, the sale of a building: tablet 23.[14] In reality, it is the sale of *res impositiciae* that is recorded. This expression designates objects that are indispensable to the equipment of a residence (or any location), but which can be detached from a building and therefore taken away. It is therefore practically certain that the sale described in tablet 23 was preceded by another sale, that of the building itself. Was the sale of the building, which left no trace, carried out at an auction, like the auction in which the *res impositiciae* of tablet 23 were sold? We do not know.

Among the Murecine tablets, a dozen documents are also connected with auctions.[15] But only one of them concerns the sale of *fundi* by auction, *TPSulp*. 88. This document concerns the announcement of a sale of at least three *fundi*, which had been handed in as security (*fiducia*) of an unpaid loan (*mutuum*). The tablet, dated to 11 May, AD 53, is lacunary. One of the *fundi* is named Pompeianus, and another most probably Publilianus, while the name of a third *fundus* is unknown, as is that of the debtor.

Auctions appear less frequently in the tablets of Herculaneum. A remarkable exception is *TH*^{2} 4, which concerns the production and the *instrumentum* of the *fundus blandianus*. This farm was at one point the property of two men: Aulus Tetteius Severus, who had served as *duovir* of the city some years before the tablet was made,[16] and Quintus Iunius Theophilus, until the moment when Tetteius Severus deeded his part over to him. In respect of this new state of affairs, Theophilus, who was thenceforth the sole owner of the *fundus*, wrote a chirograph, *TH*^{2} 4, on 2 September, 60 CE. This tablet is one of those found at Herculaneum during the 1930s. This document enumerates the rights that Tetteius Severus will continue to enjoy as regards the *fundus*, though he will no longer be an owner, in accordance with the agreements made between the two: he can take possession of the harvest produced by his former part of the *fundus*; he can store his wine in a cellar belonging to the farm, at least until the next ides of August; he can continue to command the use of the *instrumentum fundi*, that is, *et res et mancipia et pecora* (his property, his slaves, and his various farm animals) – unless he wants to sell all of this at auction. The tablet concludes with a stipulation. It is Tetteius Severus, the former owner, who stipulates, and it is Quintus Iunius Theophilus who becomes responsible for acting in accordance with it (*spondere*).

This tablet was discovered in March 1932, and has been the subject of research by V. Arangio Ruiz and E. Lepore.[17] Maria Vittoria Bramante wrote a fairly long article about it.[18] After presenting the document, she studies its vocabulary (particularly the verbs that express the actions available to Tetteius Severus upon taking possession of what still belongs to him). Following this, she asks, from a legal point of view, about the nature of the association that existed between the two owners, before Tetteius Severus renounced his part. The nature of this association is not clear. Maria Vittoria Bramante believes that it was perhaps a contract to arrange a company to do business, a *societas unius rei*, for the purpose of operating the *fundus*. Within this company, the two owners may not have provided the same things: Iunius Theophilus seems to have provided the land, while Tetteius Severus would have provided his expertise, and that of his own workers and his slaves. I am not quite convinced by this hypothesis by Maria Vittoria Bramante, however. Nor am I convinced by the explanation given by Ettore Lepore. This author had an exceptional talent for linking a document to a tradition of research and to a historiographical problem. He saw in this tablet an indication of a movement toward the concentration of farmland. While this is an interesting interpretation, it is easily contested because the two men, prior to this, were co-owners, and an agreement was made between them, such that the *fundus blandianus* would become the property of only one, without there being any violence in the matter. And this is the source of the originality I claim for it: in my opinion, it shows us an example of a farm (*fundus*) owned by two people, until one of them (Tetteius Severus) voluntarily gives up ownership for reasons we do not know, leaving the entire property to his former partner, Quintus Iunius Theophilus.

Auctions happen frequently, which is an important point in economic terms, because they play a significant role in price-setting.[19] In Roman Italy, commodities and slaves were very probably sold by auction more often than were land and houses, but houses and rural properties were sold by auctions all the same. When rural properties or houses were used as guarantees or pledges (for instance for a loan), they may often have been sold by auction. If they were part of an inheritance that had to be divided, they may have been sold by auction as well.[20]

★

Now we turn to the transactions that take place without an auction. What do the tablets from Campania allow us to conclude about such transactions involving land or buildings? On this point, the three groups of tablets are not all equally rich in information. As I already noted at the beginning of this chapter, from this perspective the tablets of Herculaneum are richer than the two other groups of tablets, and provide several examples of the purchase and sale of agricultural land, or *fundi*. In truth, it is not possible to say how many examples there are. Seven *fundi* are recorded in the index published by Camodeca in 2017. But this book is only the first volume in his publication of the tablets, and it is not clear how much he still has to publish.

Tablet *TH*^{2} A10 is a good example of the real estate transactions that are attested in the Herculaneum tablets. It concerns a man named Lucius Cominius Primus, a person of no more than middle rank, likely a freedman or the descendant of one, who moved to Herculaneum from Naples. It is a chirograph from P. Comicius Severus, dated 12 June, 64 AD, and shows that Comicius Severus sold to Cominius Primus an agricultural estate of considerable value, the *fundus Linisianus*, for the price of 295,000 sesterces (*TH*^{2} A10).[21] If we assume an annual revenue of 6 per cent, as G. Camodeca does, the property yielded about 18,000 sesterces a year. At 2,000 or 3,000 sesterces for every *iugerum* (0.25 ha), the parcel could have comprised about 30 hectares, although it could also have been smaller. Cominius Primus paid for the land in several instalments: on 12 June, AD 64, the date of one of the chirographs that has been preserved, the largest part of the amount was paid by the purchaser, but not the full amount. Was there an auction? Most probably not. Nothing indicates that an auction was present in this case. If there was a farm, buildings used in agriculture, or living quarters connected with this parcel of land, tablet *TH*^{2} A10 does not indicate them.

Camodeca underlines that the fundus' name is certainly *lisinianus*, even if we do not know any gentil name Lisinius.[22] Should we suppose that this was just a mistake, and the person who wrote the document misplaced the consonant "n" and "s" in the word? This is not implausible.

An important question to consider regards the source of the money that Lucius Cominius Primus used for his purchase. Camodeca thinks that the money could have come from the sale of other properties, or from borrowed money. In fact, we know that in the years 66, 69–71, Cominius Primus was in debt, and the money he borrowed had been loaned to him by two persons belonging to the Senatorial order. On these dates, Cominius Primus owed 10,000 sesterces to Cnaeus Sentius Saturninus, the ordinary consul for 41. In addition, he owed 60,000 sesterces to Ulpia Plotina, who owned land located near that owned by Cominius Primus, but who did not reside at Herculaneum. Ulpia Plotina was very probably the paternal aunt of the future Emperor Trajan.[23] Camodeca has formulated the hypothesis that these senatorial owners reinvested money earned through the sale of crops, loaning the money to small and medium-sized agricultural operators from cities close to their own property.[24] This is an attractive hypothesis, and quite plausible as well.

Two other tablets (*TH*^{2} 40 and *TH*^{2} A11), dating from 62 and 64, testify to the existence of business dealings between the seller and buyer that I speak of, P. Comicius Severus and L. Cominius Primus[25]; one of these two tablets is very probably linked to the sale of the *fundus linisianus*. Another chirograph dating from the early 60s bears witness to another real estate transaction, concerning the *fundus comicianus alficianus*.[26]

In addition to these transactions, Camodeca mentions two other pieces of land, which were worth about 70,000 sesterces each. He adds that we know of at least five *fundi* that were sold in Herculaneum between the early 50s and the early 60s, valued at a total of around 500,000 sesterces. All in all, we know the names of about ten *fundi* at Herculaneum, as well as the names of their owners.

For that period, between the Julio-Claudians and Vespasian, one may therefore say that, at Herculaneum, the market for the sale of agricultural land and land for stock-raising was relatively active. It is certainly impossible to quantify this, and in all probability it was a partly local market phenomenon: partly, but not exclusively or entirely, local, since we have seen that in this vicinity several landowners belonged to the highest levels of Roman society, for example Cnaeus Sentius Saturninus, the ordinary consul for 41, and Ulpia Plotina. The situation was probably comparable in Pompeii and the other neighbouring cities; but on this subject, the sale of land, we only have additional data for Herculaneum.

In addition, I would like to discuss another tablet from Herculaneum, which concerns an unknown operation and did not involve an auction. The tablet *TH*^{2} D 12 was written in Nola, and is dated 16 October in the year 40 or 41. It concerned a stipulation regarding the sale of the harvest from a farm called *fundus cadianus*, for the price of 1800 sesterces, which had to be paid by the calends of March at the latest.[27] The one making the stipulation was Nico, a slave owned by the farm's owner, Herennia Tertia; the purchaser of the crop was a man named Lucius Annius Agathemer. Judging by the dates involved (mid-October, 1 March) and the crops known to have been widely grown in the region, Camodeca thinks the crop may have been grapes, and compares this tablet of Herculaneum to *Letter* 8.2 by Pliny the Younger.[28]

I am not at all opposed to the notion that the crop involved should be mostly or even entirely made up of a grape harvest. However, I would like to make two observations regarding the letter of Pliny and the Herculaneum tablet. First, Pliny's letter is not necessarily explained with reference to the sale of the standing crop. André Tchernia has even tried to show, I believe successfully, that the sale of grape harvest in letter 8.2 is not a sale of the standing crop (*pendente vindemia*).[29] Further, it does not appear certain to me that in the case of the *fundus cadianus* the crop was sold standing. My second observation concerns the originality of this tablet. If we compare the tablet with Pliny the Younger's letter 8.2, we do not do justice to that originality. The tablet tells us that it is neither wine nor grapes that is being sold, but the entire harvest of the *fundus*. The text is clear: *ob fructum fundi cadiani venditum*. Whether or not grapes constituted the bulk of this harvest, it seems plausible that other productions were included. Pliny, in his letter, only speaks of a grape harvest.

⋆

All in all, we see how these tablets from the cities around Vesuvius, most of all Herculaneum, give us interesting insights into land sales, but also new information about the sale of entire harvests and the management of certain kinds of real estate by co-owners.

In closing, I would like to insist on two important ideas discussed above. The first concerns the existence of a land market that was not necessarily only local. On account of the quantity and the subject of the preserved tablets, the number of transactions (and of the managerial practices concerning *fundi*) is remarkable, even aside from the use of auctions as the chosen method for the transfers. Even more remarkable is the fact that some of these transactions involved members of the senatorial elite.

The second idea that I would like to underline regards the system chosen for the economic exploitation of land. In accordance with the information provided in the tablets, but also considering the absence of other information, the most visible method of land management in this region and during this period was the direct administration and use by the landowner or through a *vilicus*, rather than the leasing out of the property. For instance, in the two tablets TH^2 D 12 and TH^2 4, which I have studied, there is no trace of tenant farmers, nor of renting. This complete absence is certainly significant. If there were tenants, it would have been difficult not to mention them.

Notes

1 Camodeca, 1992 and 1999; Camodeca 2017.
2 Andreau 2020: 418–419.
3 Andreau 1974: 62–67.
4 See especially Camodeca 2003: 95.
5 See especially Frier 1977 and 1980.
6 See Capogrossi Colognesi 2012 and 2015; Kehoe 2007; Launaro 2011 and Lo Cascio 2004.
7 Andreau 1976.
8 I myself had put forward this idea, but without seriously reflecting on it (Andreau 1974: 80: "Le marché de Pompéi se tenait le samedi" = "The market at Pompeii

was held on Saturday"). A.K. Michels also favoured this notion, which made it seem much more plausible (Michels 1967: 89 and 192).

9 Camodeca 1999: 185 and 194–198.

10 Storchi Marino 2000.

11 García Morcillo 2005 and 2008.

12 Lerouxel 2016.

13 Andreau 1974.

14 Andreau 1974: 106–107 and 326–328; García Morcillo 2005: 113.

15 *TPSulp*. 81 and 83–93. Camodeca considers that *TPSulp*. 82 concerns an auction, but I do not think so; on this question regarding *TPSulp.82*, see Verboven 2003.

16 Camodeca 2017: 302. I would like to sincerely thank my friend L. Capogrossi Colognesi for the valuable information and suggestions regarding tablet *TH*[2] 4.

17 Lepore 1955.

18 See Camodeca 2017: 299–303; Bramante 2014.

19 Lerouxel 2016: 259–267 and 281–287.

20 On the inheritances that had to be divided, see *Dig*. 10.2.

21 Camodeca 2012: 114–123; Camodeca 2017: 271–279.

22 Camodeca 2012: 120, and n. 11; Camodeca 2017: 274, n. 8.

23 Camodeca 1993: 115–119 and 135; Camodeca 2017: 274.

24 Camodeca 2012: 121–122; Camodeca 2017: 275.

25 Camodeca 2012: 123–130; Camodeca 2017: 280–285.

26 Camodeca 2012: 130–133; Camodeca 2017: 285–288.

27 See Camodeca 1999: 537–540 and Camodeca 2017: 295–298. Concerning this tablet, see also Verboven 2017: 375–376 and n. 79.

28 The letter starts as follows, *Ep* 8.2: *Alii in praedia sua proficiscuntur, ut locupletiores revertantur, ego, ut pauperior. Vendideram vindemias certatim negotiatoribus ementibus. Invitabat pretium, et quod tunc et quod fore videbatur. Spes fefellit.* ("Other people visit their estates in order to recruit their purses; whilst I go to mine only to return to much the poorer. I had sold my vintage to the merchants, who were eager to purchase it, encouraged by the price it then bore, and what it was probable it would rise to; however they were disappointed in their expectations.") (Transl. W. Melmoth 1963, LCL.)

29 See Tchernia 2000: 202–205 and 2016: 142–147 (his interpretation was not considered by Camodeca).

References

Andreau, J. (1974) *Les Affaires de Monsieur Jucundus*. Rome: Collection de l'École Française de Rome.

Andreau, J. (1976) Pompéi: enchères, foires et marchés. *Bulletin de la Société Nationale des Antiquaires de France*, 104–127.

Andreau, J. (2020) Capital and Investment in the Campanian Tablets. In: P. Erdkamp, K. Verboven, and A. Zuiderhoek, eds., *Capital, Investment and Innovation in the Roman World*, Oxford: Oxford University Press, 417–435.

Bramante, M.V. (2014) TH4 e la prassi romano-campana 'de re rustica. *Index* 42, 141–163.

Camodeca, G. (1992) *L'Archivio puteolano dei Sulpicii*, I. Naples: Eugenio Jovene.

Camodeca, G. (1993) Per una riedizione delle Tabulae Herculanenses, I. *Cronache ercolanesi* 23, 109–119.

Camodeca, G. (1999) *Tabulae Pompeianae Sulpiciorum, Edizione critica dell'archivio puteolano dei Sulpicii*, 2 vol. Rome: Quasar.

Camodeca, G. (2003) Il Credito negli archivi campani: il caso di Puteoli e di Herculanum. In: E. Lo Cascio, ed., *Credito e moneta nel mondo romano*. Bari: Edipuglia, 69–98.

Camodeca, G. (2012) Riedizione delle Tabulae Herculanenses: gli affari fondiari di L. Cominius Primus con P. Cominius Severus. *Oebalus* 7, 113–141.

Camodeca, G. (2017) *Tabulae Herculanenses, Edizione e commento.* Rome: Quasar.

Capogrossi Colognesi, L. (2012) *Padroni e contadini nell'Italia republicana.* Rome: "L'Erma" di Bretschneider.

Capogrossi Colognesi, L. (2015) Appunti per una storia dell'economia agraria romana. In: V. Di Cataldo, V. Meli and R. Pennisi, eds., *Impresa e mercato, Studi dedicati a Mario Libertini*, III, Milan: Giuffré, 1693–1713.

Frier, B.W. (1977) The Rental Market in Early Imperial Rome. *Journal of Roman Studies* 67, 27–37.

Frier, B.W. (1980) *Landlords and Tenants in Imperial Rome.* Princeton: Princeton University Press, 1980.

García Morcillo, M. (2005) *Las ventas por subasta en el mundo romano: La esfera privada.* Barcelona: Publicacions de la Universitat de Barcelona.

García Morcillo, M. (2008) Staging Power and Authority at Roman Auctions. *Ancient Society* 38, 185–213.

Kehoe, D. P. (2007) The Early Roman Empire: Production. In: W. Scheidel, I. Morris, and R. Saller (eds.), *The Cambridge Economic History of the Greco-Roman World.* Cambridge: Cambridge University Press, 543–569.

Launaro, A. (2011) *Peasants and Slaves, The Rural Population of Roman Italy (200 BC to AD 100).* Cambridge: Cambridge University Press.

Lepore, E. (1955) Sul carattere economico-sociale di Ercolano. *Parola del Passato* 10, 423–439.

Lerouxel, F. (2016) *Le Marché du Crédit dans le monde romain.* Rome: École Française de Rome.

Lo Cascio, E., ed. (2000) *Mercati permanenti e mercati periodici nel mondo romano, Atti degli Incointri capresi di storia dell'economia romana (Capri, 13–15 ottobre 1997).* Bari: Edipuglia.

Lo Cascio, E. (2004) The Economy of Roman Italy According to the Younger Pliny. In: A. Gallina Zevi and J.H. Humphrey (eds.), *Ostia, Cicero, Gamala, Feasts, and the Economy. Papers in memory of John H. D'Arms* (JRA Suppl. Series 57). Portsmouth RI: Journal of Roman Archaeology, 127–135.

Michels, A.K. (1967) *The Calendar of the Roman Republic.* Princeton, Princeton University Press.

Storchi Marino, A. (2000) Reti interregionali integrate e circuiti di mercato periodico negli *indices nundinarii* del Lazio e della Campania. In: E. Lo Cascio, ed., *Mercati permanenti e mercati periodici nel mondo romano.* Bari: Edipuglia, 93–130.

Talamanca, M. (1954) *Contributi allo studio delle vendite all'asta nel mondo classico.* Rome: Accademia Nazionale Dei Lincei.

Tchernia, A. (2000) La Vente du vin. In: E. Lo Cascio, ed., *Mercati permanenti e mercati periodici nel mondo romano.* Bari: Edipuglia, 199–209.

Tchernia, A. (2016) *The Romans and Trade.* Oxford: Oxford University Press.

Thielmann, G. (1961) *Die römische Privatauktion. Zugleich ein Beitrag zum römischen Bankierrecht.* Berlin: Duncker & Humblot.

Verboven, K. (2003) The *Sulpicii* from *Puteoli, argentarii* or *faeneratores*? In: P. Defosse, ed., *Hommages à Carl Deroux, vol. III, Histoire et archéologie, Droit.* Brussels: Latomus, 429–445.

Verboven, K. (2017) Currency and Credit in the Bay of Naples in the First Century AD. In: M. Flohr and A. Wilson, eds, *The Economy of Pompeii.* Oxford: Oxford University Press, 363–386.

Part III

Social Status, Forms of Investment, and the Roman Elite

7 Understanding the Roman Real Estate Market

A Case Study of Information Constraints and Behaviour

Max Koedijk

Abstract

Finley once implied that the absence of real estate agents in the ancient world prevented a property market from emerging (Finley 1999, p. 118). He based this conclusion on the implicit assumption that the role of estate agents is crucial to the functioning of the property market. The role of real estate agent revolves largely around the collection and dissemination of information, which buyers use to make their decisions. The absence of estate agents would therefore imply an information problem. However, if the Roman world lacked such institutions but nevertheless managed to transfer property freely and frequently, it seems that they found a way around this problem.

Although far from perfect, Cicero's writings offer us the most detailed insight into property in the late Republic. Consequently, we can use his letters to discern the practicalities of buying property. My chapter will run through the entire process, from finding a property to making an offer, as a case study of property exchange. Specifically, the focus will lie on Cicero's extended search for a suburban property on which to build a shrine to his daughter. I will argue that the information problem created by the absence of estate agents was overcome in part by social relations that may have usurped many of the functions of estate agents and which consequently played a major role in how properties were found, how the price was determined, where the money came from, and how the quality was assessed. However, even if many of an estate agent's functions could be otherwise fulfilled, this does not mean that the Roman property market operated along the same lines as markets with estate agents (such as modern markets) do. Our evidence suggests that the Romans faced much higher levels of uncertainty, which affected the efficiency of the market and their rate of success. The Romans may have approached property from a different starting point and followed a different order from that which modern buyers are likely familiar with. In short, the buying process can give us insight into the social networks and associated norms in the Roman world, as well as the effects of information constraints on the decision-making process.

***

In the modern world, the process of buying property normally follows four consecutive steps: 1) people work out their budget, 2) they consult publicly available

DOI: 10.4324/9781003187806-10

listings to find properties for sale, 3) they inspect property, and 4) then make a bid. But this process is underpinned by an availability of information that the modern mind might never even think about. We might simply assume its existence and carry this assumption with us when we look at the Roman real estate market. This is arguably evident when we look at the two most influential accounts on the Roman real estate market: that of Moses Finley and that of Peter Temin.[1] To start, it is important to recognise that neither Finley nor Temin had any real interest in understanding how the Roman market functioned; both were primarily focused on the question of whether a "market" for property existed. Both focused on the structures of the market or the absence thereof and assumed behaviour based on these. Neither made much of an effort to empirically demonstrate that the behaviour they assumed was actually practised.

Finley, discussing the property market as part of his broader enquiry into economic behaviour, concluded that in the absence of calculated rational investment, "there was neither a recognizable real-property market nor a profession of estate agent or realtor."[2] Temin, in contrast, focused primarily on potential indicators for a functioning market of land, particularly the fluctuating of price. Their respective disbelief and belief in the existence of economic rationality leads to different assumptions about behaviour. Temin assumes economic rationality and therefore concludes that fluctuations in price were "the result of market exchanges, that is, *purchasers rushing to buy land that was offered cheaply* and thinking long about buying expensive land."[3] Consequently, Temin concludes that "the market for land in the Roman Empire worked approximately like the land market today."[4] Finley, on the other hand, suggests that instead of a "market" operating under the conditions of economic rationality, there existed a system of exchange that was largely opportunistic: "the normal purchase of land in antiquity … was windfall purchase (which is not to say that windfalls were rare)."[5] Windfall property is defined as "*visibly cheap* or dear" and, as such, does not require any calculation other than general rules of thumb.[6]

It is not my intention to discuss Finley's and Temin's arguments in detail, but I want to focus instead on some of the implications of their arguments. I have emphasised part of Finley's and Temin's arguments in the previous paragraph. We can see that both scholars imply buyers were able to recognise "cheap" property and gravitated towards it.[7] This in turn implies the availability of accurate price information, without which no decisions based on price can be made. Both also imply that comparison was made between "cheap" and "dear/ expensive," which requires the existence and availability of information for multiple properties. Moreover, this information must have been available at the start of the purchasing process because otherwise purchasers could not have differentiated between properties in the way modern buyers do. However, neither author establishes that this information actually existed.

Finley got closest to questioning this information availability when he included in his argument the absence of professional real estate agents.[8] However, he did not expand on this somewhat throwaway remark and appears to have failed to fully grasp its implications. Finley was absolutely correct that aside from some rare, highly specialised roles, there were no professionals dealing with the exchange of property.[9] There are no indications that real estate agents, in our modern conception of the role, existed in the Roman Republic.[10] This is a crucial point with major implications. A key component of modern estate agencies is the creation, collection, collation, and dissemination of information. At the click of a button or leafing through a magazine, we can see exactly which properties are for sale, how much a property is valued at, how much it has sold for in the past, and we can get the same information again for every single comparable property. We can find accurate information about a property and even get an impression of what it looks like, all from the comfort of our own homes. In contrast, in the Roman Republic there was no comparable shared record of third-party assessed value. There were no central records of historical price that might easily be consulted. This lack of information creates at the very least the *possibility* that the Republican property market operated in a fundamentally different way than the property markets we are more familiar with.

In the remainder of this chapter, I shall explore this possibility through a case study. I shall focus on Cicero's search for a suburban property on which to build a shrine for his recently deceased daughter, taking place over the course of several months in 45 BC.[11] As with any case study, there are certain caveats to keep in mind. This case study is based on Cicero's extensive letters to his friend Atticus, which provide the most detailed account of the property buying process from the Republican period. But, sadly, *most* detailed does not equal detailed. As always, we possess only one side of the conversation, which more often than not contains vague references rather than detailed information. Further, Cicero and Atticus meet on a few occasions, which creates further gaps in our evidence. The search commences days before the civil war concluded and it seems this war had depressed the price of land, or at least so Cicero assumed.[12] Since Cicero's daughter had died – the reason for the search – Cicero was grieving, and this could have affected his actions, but maybe only insofar that he displayed a perhaps unusual fervour to get a property and in the fact that he had little to no interest in the productive capabilities of any of these estates.[13] Finally, it should be noted that Cicero was unsuccessful in his search, so we cannot comment on any steps beyond the making of a bid. Regardless of circumstances, the information constraints Cicero faced were common and I see no reason to suspect his actions were particularly unusual, or at any rate not so unusual that we should dismiss him as an outlier. With regards to the questions at hand, I therefore believe this case study should give a good indication of the realities of the late Republican property market more generally.

Cicero's Search for a Suburban Estate

In his search, Cicero considered a total of twelve properties of which eight were pursued to some extent, by which I mean that they were mentioned in more than one letter.[14] It is on these eight that I shall focus my attention. The preferred location was the suburban area of Rome because Cicero wanted the shrine to be in the public way.[15] Chronologically, the search was conducted between 17 March and 9 July 45 BC. Listing the eight pursued properties chronologically (Table 7.1) gives some indication of the information flows at play:

Table 7.1 The eight main properties under consideration in Cicero's search for a sub-urban estate

Date	*Properties under consideration, ranked in order of preference*
17 March	**Drusus'** = Lamia's = Cassius'
18 March	**Drusus'** = Silius' = Lamia's
19 March	Silius', **Drusus'** = Lamia's, Cotta's
25 March	Silius', **Drusus', Damasippus'**, Cotta's
26 March	Silius', **Drusus', Damasippus'**
30 March	**Drusus'**
2 May	**Drusus'***
3 May	Scapula's, **Drusus'**
7 May	Scapula's, Clodia's, **Drusus'**
11 May	Scapula's, Clodia's, Silius', **Drusus'**, Cusinius and Trebonius', (Tusculum)
14 May	Scapula's, Clodia's, **Drusus'**, (Tusculum)
21 May	**Scapula's**, Clodia's
28 May (?)	**Scapula's**
5 June	**Scapula's**, Silius' (?)
10 June	**Scapula's**

* Some other property or properties had been excluded in the interim – most likely Damasippus'.

The significance of the bolded names can be ignored for now. The first thing to note is that the process essentially consists of two stages that both conform to the same pattern. We see an initial phase of information gathering followed by the creation of a preference hierarchy. The options are then further explored and narrowed down. In the list the equal sign is used to indicate that the properties are not yet assigned a place in the hierarchy. How exactly this information comes to Cicero is unfortunately partially obscured from us. The pattern we can observe seems consistent with network-based information gathering, in the sense that a request for information is sent out and information comes in over time. This information is initially vague and is clarified over time, as other sources report in or follow-ups are arranged. Let's look at a couple of cases to see how this actually shows up in Cicero's letters to Atticus.

The Drusus Property

In the case of the Drusus property, Cicero appears to learn about its availability from an unknown source on 17 March.[16] Two days later, Atticus reports a previous bid on the property to Cicero who had already received the information from another source, perhaps the same source as before.[17] Eight days pass before any progress is made. Cicero is advised by Sicca, who is working on a different property for him, to write to a man called Egnatius for information about the Drusus property.[18] After two days, Egnatius has reported the asking price to Atticus, who reports it to Cicero; Egnatius also contacts Cicero directly.[19] Thereafter, Atticus is charged with following up on the Drusus matter, but going through Egnatius since, as Cicero puts it, "it is easiest to negotiate through him."[20]

The Silius Property

This case is a little more complicated. On 18 March Cicero either receives information from an unknown source or infers from personal knowledge that Silius' property might be for sale.[21] The following day, Cicero asks Atticus to have a word with Silius while also giving a commission to Sicca, who therefore makes an appointment with Silius.[22] Two days later, Sicca reports back directly to Cicero and to Atticus, who then informs Cicero as well. Cicero notes that the terms are agreeable, which suggests that Sicca has negotiated on his behalf. Atticus is tasked with arranging the financing.[23] When Cicero and Sicca meet three days after, Cicero expects more information, but it turns out Sicca has already relayed all he knows in the letter.[24] Atticus is then to meet Silius, and returns with information contradictory to Sicca's. Following the meeting with Silius, Atticus expects the deal to fall through, assuming that a) Silius simply will not sell and b) "that he will want more than our figure."[25] "Our figure" may here refer to the terms Sicca reported back, but this is not clear. Sicca still thinks Silius will sell, but in the following days Atticus is proven correct as Silius refuses to sell. It is at this stage that Cicero reveals he has never actually visited the property in question and the question of how much he values it at first comes up. He tells Atticus he knows the villa is old and relatively small but has a good plantation.[26] This information must have come to him from a source unknown to us. The fact that he relates it to Atticus suggest that Atticus also had not actually visited the property they were trying to purchase.

When we look at the eight properties together (Table 7.2), it quickly becomes apparent that the Drusus and Silius cases were not exceptions to the rule.

Table 7.2 reveals several lines of inquiry to explore further. The first and most obvious thing to note is that there is not a single case in which it was clear from day one that both a) a property was for sale and b) what the asking price was. The case that comes closest is the interesting case of Damasippus, who split up his estate into parcels he put up for sale for fixed prices.[27] In that case, a prospective buyer *could* have known both availability and asking price at the start but it is notable that Cicero did not know the latter. Since information was spread via networking, corruption and loss of information were inevitable. Therefore, Cicero does not know what the prices are, even though he knows that there are fixed prices in this case; an effort still had to be made to acquire this information. Further, Damasippus' case is far more likely to be the exception than the rule; it is the only clear-cut case known to us of a fixed price being advertised and evidence both from this

Table 7.2 Comparison of the eight properties

	Information and actions mentioned (in days since the property was first identified)				
	Confirmed to be available	*Asking price known*	*Inspection of the property*	*Bid made*	*Valuation*
Drusus	0	12	-	-	2
Lamia	-	-	-	-	-
Silius	3*	3*	-	3	-
Cotta	-	-	-	-	-
Damasippus	1	?**	-	-	-
Scapula	~16	-	22	-	8/24/29***
Clodia	-	-	16		9
Cusinius and Trebonius	-	-	-	-	-

*Cicero reports "terms" after 3 days but negotiations evidently continued, and after 10 days there was still uncertainty about Silius' asking price and willingness to sell; after 12 days Silius had changed his mind about selling the property at all.

** Damasippus had apparently divided his property into plots that he offered for fixed prices, but Cicero did not know what the prices were. He must have found out at some point but we do not know when.

*** After 8 days Cicero has some idea about the value of the property but we do not know what this is based on. After 24 days, he seems to attempt a valuation of the property by comparing it with another sale in the area that had taken place some years earlier. However, after 29 days a letter reads, with apparent reference to the Scapula estate: "we shall see about the valuation when we start negotiating." *de aestimatione … cum agere coeperimus.*

case study and other instances suggests that valuation negotiation was normally the way to figure out the price of a property.

The Damasippus case is also interesting because it was positively identified as being for sale one day after it was first mentioned in the letters. It is certainly possible that this is just a quirk of the letters – Cicero may have simply neglected to mention it on day one. On the other hand, it is also possible that Cicero heard it might be available and only got confirmation that it was for sale a day later. Out of the eight properties Cicero pursued, only three were ever publicly advertised for sale (Drusus', Damasippus', Scapula's). Out of these three, the Scapula property was not for sale when Cicero identified it; the heirs of the property were planning to auction it off privately between themselves.[28] It required extensive efforts by Cicero and Atticus to open the auction up to the public so that Cicero might bid.[29] Going back to the chronology in Table 7.1, when we look at the properties that were publicly advertised at each juncture – highlighted in bold – we see that Cicero mostly pursued properties that were not formally advertised for sale and that he spent several weeks primarily pursuing properties that were not officially for sale. In all, with six out of eight properties, Cicero and Atticus expended resources without any certainty that the object they pursued could actually be obtained.

The impact of the absence of professional real estate agents, or rather of centralised records, is clearly visible here. Cicero could not simply choose from a list of available properties; consequently, in many cases, the availability of the property remains in doubt throughout the entire process. The Silius case demonstrates this well. Cicero assumed Silius might be willing to sell his estate because he did not use it. Consequently, Sicca and then Atticus probe his willingness to sell and Sicca appears to get at least a rough indication of the sum that would be required for Silius to part with his property. However, later in the process Silius simply changes his mind, preferring to retain the property for his son.[30]

This availability issue – the absence of formal lists of sale – also has significant implications for the issue of price. As we can see from Table 7.2, there was not one property where Cicero knew the asking price on day one. If a property was not formally for sale, discovering the price became part of the negotiation process. However, as the Drusus case shows, even if a property was advertised for sale, this did not mean that the price was advertised as well.[31] In the table I have distinguished between the asking price and the valuation of the property. This is essentially the distinction between what the seller and buyer think the property is worth, respectively. Valuation is another of those key functions of modern real estate agents: they act as third parties who use commonly agreed upon methodologies to establish the actual value of a property as objectively and accurately as possible. In the modern world, both seller and buyer normally agree that this third-party valuation offers the best indicator of value, and price therefore normally closely follows valuation and there is at least broadly an agreement that this price is "fair" and "accurate." The importance of this becomes evident when we look at the Roman situation, where in the absence of estate agents no comparable shared record of third-party valuations existed.

In the late Republic, buyer and seller performed their own valuations. Cicero references several methods one might use to estimate the value of a property. When trying to estimate the value of the Scapula estate, Cicero tries to extrapolate from a previous sale by noting that C. Albanius had bought, several years earlier, 1000 *iugera* very close to the Scapula estate for HS 11,500,000.[32] But such a method relies on price stability, which was not always the case. So Cicero immediately after notes "of course everything has dropped now."[33] As an additional influence on the price he notes "the factor of anxiety to buy, in which except for Otho I think I shall have no rival."[34] Otho, one of the co-heirs of the Scapula property, may however have used a different method for his valuation: Cicero remarks in a later letter that "as you say, we shall see about the valuation when we start negotiating, though his [Otho's] letter says nothing except about the acreage."[35] This suggests Cicero had asked Otho for a valuation of the estate, and the latter used productive capability as a proxy; consequently, Cicero suspects the valuation is not accurate.

When discussing the valuation of the Drusus estate, Cicero acknowledged that extrapolating from the yield of the land was a common method of estimating value, but clearly eschews this method in this search because the productive capability of the land was not important to him at this point: "these places are to be valued in terms of my present need rather than by any ordinary reckoning."[36] One obvious issue with such a method of valuating is that it only attempts to establish the value of the productive parts of the estate; any non-productive buildings or functions would not contribute to yield and their value could therefore not be deduced from yield. This is another way in which differences in valuations could occur. Table 7.2 reveals another pertinent point here: it seems that valuations were taking place before a property was visited. Cicero even put in a bid for the Silius property without ever having visited it.[37] He relied on information he received from Atticus and once or twice sends Atticus to inspect a place in his stead but not once during this search does Cicero personally inspect the object he pursues.[38] This may have been of great significance given the likely difficultly of valuating something subjective that cannot easily be reduced to numbers – i.e. living quarters or a place for your daughter's shrine. It is easy to imagine how someone living in a property might reach a very different conclusion about it from someone who has never seen it, which could easily lead to vastly different valuations. The lack of comparable information on price and the lack of agreement about the method of valuation, or rather the inability of such methods to produce very narrow bands of valuations, inevitably lead to broad ranges in valuations, which leaves open the possibility that different individuals – like buyer and seller – might have had vastly different ideas about what a property was worth.

I have now established two crucial points: first, that price information was not normally available to a buyer at the start of the process and, second, that each party carried out their own valuations using methodologies that could not reliably produce very narrow bands of valuations. This means that it was realistically impossible for a buyer to shop based on a price comparison. The price information for each property would have to be extracted at the cost of time and resources. Even *if* a buyer went to the trouble of valuating each property he was considering – and the evidence suggests this would not have been the case – this set of valuations would still not be of much use in making comparisons based on price, because each seller would have his own valuation of his property. We see this play out in the Drusus case, where Drusus is very eager to sell but he demands what Cicero considered to be an exorbitant amount of money. This leads to the inescapable conclusion that people could not normally, as Temin puts it, "rush to buy land that was offered cheaply" because nobody could tell which land was "cheap."

Finley's position is a lot vaguer than Temin's but is undermined by the same problem. In the system he envisions, people utilise windfalls to pursue "visibly cheap" property. But what does "visibly cheap" mean? In the absence of price information one might imagine that simple heuristics would be used to tell "cheap" from "dear." Might an owner eager to sell indicate the possibility of a good bargain – a "visibly cheap" property? Drusus shows that was at the very least not always true – Cicero seems to consider him to offer the worst value for money despite his eagerness to sell.[39] How then would "visibly cheap" property be identified? We might think of a few more possibilities – a house on fire, a farm flooded, an owner on the brink of bankruptcy – but while such cases do of course exist and might indeed have offered a bargain, they hardly characterise the system or the normal state of affairs.[40] Nor would these heuristics necessarily have been reliable. There is at least one case where a senator sold a villa estate, the buildings of which had burned down and the fields of which were left in a poor condition, but nevertheless extracted from his purchasers 1.5 times the, apparently already exorbitant, price he had originally paid for the estate when it was still in good condition.[41]

The issue of price is further complicated by the issue of affordability. We, modern day readers, may be disinclined to attach much weight to this issue because we know beforehand what our budget is. This is due to the fact that a bank will normally provide us with the whole sum, minus our cash deposit. What this means is that in our minds the issues of "price" and "affordability" are likely very closely related. In today's market, minor wrangling aside, a property is either within our budget – and therefore affordable – or it is outside our budget – and therefore unaffordable. The situation in the Republic, however, was noticeably different. With the more expensive properties, at least, we see signs that "price" and "affordability" become separate issues. Paradoxically, a more expensive property could, in some cases, actually be more affordable than a lower priced alternative. The more costly the purchase, the more significant this issue becomes.

In the late Republic, banks were far too small to take on financing of properties like the ones Cicero pursues.[42] These properties had to be privately financed, from one's own means and those of one's friends.[43] Yet the buyer was not the only part of the equation; the willingness of the seller to facilitate the sale by extending credit or accepting property in return was also of crucial importance.[44] Cicero understood this. When evaluating his finances at the start of the search, he writes that "without any sales and with payment of interest to the vendor for no more than one year I can gain my object."[45] He initially expected that "Silius ... will be the easiest to hold off with interest payments,"[46] but a later letter reveals that Silius instead wanted one of Cicero's properties as partial payment (*aestimatio*).[47] Silius apparently would have wanted one of Cicero's productive estates, which Cicero was not willing to part with and talk therefore returns to trying to get Silius to accept credit.[48] The deal later fell through, though it is not clear if the credit issue had anything to do with it.[49] The point is that the financing of these purchases could be very complex and might rely in part on the willingness of the seller to accept alternative arrangements.[50] This creates a clear distinction between "price" and "affordability," which in turn makes it more difficult to shop based on price.

Given these problems, the idea that "the market for land in the Roman Empire worked approximately like the land market today" is not tenable, at least for the Republican period.[51] However, this is certainly not to say that Finley was correct in asserting that there was no recognisable property market.[52] It may have operated in a way that is foreign to us, but it is clear that a structured system of exchange existed in the late Republic. Whether one actually wants to call this a "market" or not is, in my view, largely a question of semantics.[53]

What more then can this case study tell us about the functioning of the Republican real estate market? It should be clear by now that Roman buyers did not identify properties based on either availability or price. Certainly, the cases from Cicero suggest that the properties considered all *might* have been available but remember that half of them turned out not to be. Instead of availability and price, Cicero's primary driver in this search was suitability. The question of whether a property was suitable for his purposes took precedence over all others. One consequence of this is that Cicero considered properties that varied very widely in price. The letters contain some information from which we can very roughly deduce the range of prices. At the start of the search Cicero estimated that he could gain his objective without making sales and without recovering a major debt owed to him by Faberius.[54] He does not relay how much money he has in mind but we might deduce that from information in later letters. About the Silius property, Cicero writes:

> Where then is the cash to come from? Well, you will squeeze HS 600,000 out of Hermogenes, especially as the money will be needed; and I see I have HS 600,000 in hand. For the remainder we mustn't mind paying interest to Silius until we pay cash with what comes from Faberius or some debtor of Faberius.[55]

The Faberius debt was huge, probably (far) larger than the debt owed by Hermogenes.[56] Since Cicero expects to repay "the remainder" of the sum offered to Silius by recouping this debt we should assume that "the remainder" was a very substantial sum as well. The Silius property was therefore worth in excess of HS 1.2 million but possibly closer to, or even more than, HS 2 million.

If we assume that Atticus indeed "squeezed HS 600,000" out of Hermogenes, Cicero would have had some HS 1.2 million in cash after this point.[57] There is throughout the letters no indication that Cicero could not afford the Drusus property, which may suggest that it fell within this initial sum of HS 1.2 million.[58] Cotta's property is described as having very little ground and was therefore probably significantly cheaper.[59] The Clodia estate, on the other hand, would have cost in excess of HS 1.2 million: Cicero writes he is confident he could get her property on a cash down basis, but only "because Dolabella's debt now seems well on the way to settlement."[60] The size of Dolabella's debt is unknown but may have been significant; it was a (partial) repayment of the dowry Cicero had paid to him. In any case, it is clear that, since the recovery of this debt is included, the Clodia property must have been worth (well) in excess of HS 1.2 million.

From the same letter, we learn that Clodia's property was "much less valuable" than that of Scapula. Even with the incoming money from Dolabella, Cicero acknowledged that the Scapula estate was well beyond his means. Only the recovery of the substantial Faberius debt would put him in with a shot of being able to afford it: "if you [Atticus] clear up Faberius, let us buy even at a high price; otherwise we can't, even at a low one."[61] The Scapula estate was therefore the most expensive of all and was clearly well beyond Cicero's initial estimates, almost certainly well in excess of HS 2 million. The differences in price between the various estates under consideration were clearly substantial. Also note that at least the Clodia and Scapula estates, but possibly Silius' as well, fell (well) outside Cicero's initial budgetary estimates. Again, this emphasises the differences between the Republican and modern markets: Cicero, in contrast to modern buyers, does not start with a budget and look for properties in his price range but rather cobbles his budget together on the fly, consistently choosing to gamble that budgetary issues can be overcome, rather than pursuing safer, more affordable options. This is because suitability is the primary motivator.

But there are significant risks attached to such an approach. If we glance back at Table 7.1, we see that from early May onwards, Cicero's top choices – Scapula's and Clodia's – are properties that were not necessarily within his reach. As we just saw, he gambled on being able to afford Scapula's and, although Clodia's was much cheaper, Cicero took a different gamble here: on whether it was available. If a property was not formally for sale there was no easily accessible point of contact who might supply information and facilitate the process. If one wanted to know if a property was available when it was not advertised for sale the owner had to be contacted. This meant that, if the owner could not be reached, no reliable information could be gathered. This is a problem that plagued Cicero in his search. In three out of eight cases (Lamia; Clodia; Trebonius and Cusinius) the owner of the estate was unavailable.[62]

The consequences of such absence play out most clearly in the Clodia case. Right from the start, on 7 May, Cicero does not think her property is for sale.[63] On 10 May Atticus seems to have persuaded Cicero that Clodia's place might be available. Cicero asks Atticus if he knows where Clodia is or when she will return to Rome. He still thinks she will not sell.[64] In the following week, Cicero sells himself on Clodia's place, noting that he is inclining more and more to make it the top priority. However, there has still not been any contact. He asks Atticus again when Clodia will be back in Rome but also asks him to estimate how much her estate would cost.[65] Another week passes and now Atticus is doubtful about their prospects; they still do not know when Clodia will be back nor do they know if her place is actually for sale.[66] Another week later, on 27 May, Cicero is hopeful that he could buy from Clodia on a cash basis.[67] After this, all mention of Clodia's estate disappears from the correspondence. There is nothing to suggest that Cicero or Atticus had been able to contact Clodia at any point before the 27th and it is certainly tempting to speculate that shortly after the 27th contact was made and Clodia sold them nothing but a resounding "no." But consider the resources spent on what even Cicero considered to be a folly. Some 20 days passed between the first and last letter. Atticus spent at least some of his time in that period trying to track down a woman, valuating her estate, and arranging Cicero's finances in a fruitless chase all because they did not know if the property was for sale and had no way of finding out without contacting the owner. Nevertheless, Cicero gave priority to this property and simply gambled on it being available.

Our case study throws up a couple of other points of interest. Through Atticus' pursuit of Clodia we can segue into another apparent point where the Roman market diverges from modern markets: intermediaries. It will be clear by now that Cicero is not actually doing any of the legwork. Atticus takes care of virtually everything on Cicero's behalf. However, in several cases Cicero prefers to work through someone else, normally in addition to Atticus (Table 7.3). The question is why these people were engaged: what did they offer that Atticus could not?

In one case, the answer is straightforward: Chrysippus was almost certainly a trusted builder, brought in for his technical expertise.[68] Sicca and Egnatius, however, seem to have been brought in due to their personal ties with the owners. The relationship between Egnatius and Drusus is obscured from us; our only hint is Cicero's claim that "it is easiest to negotiate through him."[69] One possibility is that Drusus appointed Egnatius as a sort of point of contact, through whom enquires for his estate would pass. Another possibility is that Egnatius was a social relation of Drusus' which might have offered some sort of advantage. This latter option was certainly why Cicero initially engaged Sicca: "because he is on friendly terms with L. Cotta."[70] Sicca's relationship with Silius is not revealed to us but was likely also friendly.[71] It is curious that Cicero and Atticus were willing to contact some owners directly but not others. This could be read as indicating they had established ties with some of the owners – and could therefore contact them directly – and did not know others – and therefore had to use a go-between.

We may further speculate on why social ties could be beneficial. One explanation is that those familiar with a person had more chance of gaining access to them and were therefore more likely to be able to extract useful information. Another possible reason presents itself elsewhere in Cicero's letters:

Table 7.3 Cicero's property search intermediaries

Property	*Intermediaries*
Drusus	Atticus + Egnatius
Lamia	Atticus
Silius	Sicca + Atticus
Cotta	Sicca
Cusinius and Trebonius	Atticus
Damasippus	Atticus
Clodia	Atticus
Scapula	Atticus + Chrysippus

> When Philotimus [Cicero's freedman] told me that he could buy that lodge from Canuleius for HS 50,000 and that the price would be even less if I approached Vettienus, I did so, asking him to get it reduced if he could. He promised, then wrote to me the other day that he had bought the place for HS 30,000.[72]

In this case, Vettienus could evidently get a much better price than Cicero's freedman could. The reason is unclear but it seems highly likely that Vettienus had a prior relationship with this Canuleius and that he was somehow able to leverage that relationship in order to get better terms. Cicero may well have had the same thing in mind when he engaged Sicca and Egnatius to aid him in his business. In the Scapula case, Cicero also implies at several points that Otho, as heir to the estate, may have enjoyed some kind of advantage at the auction but it is unclear what this advantage might be.[73] Nevertheless, it is another hint that social ties might play a role. If social ties could (significantly) alter the terms of an agreement, this creates a further area where information uncertainty existed. There may have been social obligations on the part the seller which came into effect depending on who approached him; this in turn means that even in those cases where an asking price was certain, i.e. publicly advertised, the possibility that the right social connections could alter this price made it (a little) uncertain.

The final point that stands out from this case study again relates to the absence of real estate agents. Another function of estate agents is to provide information on rules, regulations, and laws both existing and pending. This information was less easily available in the Republic, and so we see that Cicero's quest is impeded several times by unexpected regulatory constraints. On 2 May, Cicero realises that an area they had been looking at was unsuitable for his purposes because in that area "a fine has to be paid on a monument equal to the excess of the expenditure over the legal maximum, whatever that is."[74] This is a problem for Cicero because "I should not wish what I put up to be called by any other name except a shrine."[75] Consequently, he decides that "if that is what we want, I am afraid we cannot get it without changing the locality."[76] Unfortunately, this letter is preceded by a month-long gap in the letters, so we do not know exactly which property or area this involved. It was not the Drusus property, which continued to be an option in the following days, but it may have been Damasippus' plots of land, which were an option before the gap but are not mentioned again after. Similarly, Cicero got caught out by an announcement that Rome was to be enlarged. This expansion was to absorb the Scapula estate Cicero was pursuing, thereby throwing months of work into disarray.[77] Cicero gives up the search after this.[78] Here again we see that information problems are Cicero's undoing, forcing him to abandon two options.

Conclusion

In the pursuit of greater narratives, the question of how the Roman real estate market actually functioned has hitherto been largely ignored. In this chapter I have attempted to show that a careful exploration of the property market calls into question the grand narratives in which individuals act on price information that is assumed to exist. This opens the door to a more nuanced understanding of the historically unique system of exchange we usually refer to as "the Roman real estate market." But there is a great deal left to study; this case study is only a small start but I hope it offers something for my fellow historians to build on.

I opened this chapter by noting that modern buyers normally follow four consecutive steps in the property market. The discussion above, and a glance at Table 7.2, should make it clear that the Roman buyer was not systematic like this. I can only very broadly establish a pattern in Cicero's behaviour, which I'll contrast with the modern equivalent (Table 7.4).

First, Cicero selected properties based solely on their potential suitability without much consideration of – or knowledge of – what such properties would actually cost. The next step was to ascertain the availability of the property – whether it was actually for sale. Third, an attempt was made to establish the asking price and/or to value the property. Fourth, terms were negotiated. The question of affordability comes into play here. This phase may also include a formal bid. Note that an inspection of the property does not seem to have been any kind of priority. A further thing to note is the apparent differences in rigidity between these two schemes. In the modern day, virtually all buyers conform to the steps in the order they are presented here. From Cicero's dealings, however, we see a distinct lack of systematic behaviour; the order of the steps appears to have been far more flexible in the Republic. Steps could be tackled in a different order or might even be skipped completely, as Table 7.2 above clearly shows.

Based on this case study's exploration of this system of exchange, it seems fair to conclude that – in comparison with modern real estate markets – the Roman market was characterised by a high degree of inefficiency, stemming largely, but not entirely, from various information problems. We have seen that, in the absence of professional real estate agents, information was scarce, uncertain, and unreliable. It generally took days and weeks to gather even the most basic information, like whether or not a property was for sale. Yet even

Table 7.4 Comparison of the modern buying process with that of the Roman Republic

Modern day	*Roman Republic*
1. People work out their budget.	1. Identify suitable properties.
2. Consult public listing of available properties for those within said budget.	2. Establish if the owner is willing to sell.
3. Inspect the property.	3. Determine the asking price and/or value.
4. Make a bid.	4. Negotiate terms and make a bid.
	? Inspect the property.

the information that could be gathered was not always reliable and was certainly subject to change; this was most clear in the Silius case, where Sicca and Atticus came to diametrically opposed conclusions about Silius' willingness to sell after meeting him in the span of a few days. Silius, of course, ultimately lost interest in selling and this points us to another major opening for inefficiency: trying to persuade an owner to sell by simply making a bid is a hazardous enterprise. They may at any time decide that your bid is not interesting enough, as Cicero found out.

The dearth of comparable information on price and the lack of agreement about the method of valuation, or rather the inability of such methods to produce very narrow bands of valuations, lead to broad ranges in valuation which leaves open the possibility that different individuals – like buyer and seller – might have had vastly different ideas about what a property was worth. In some cases these differences would be irreconcilable, like it was with Drusus and Cicero. The absence of records of available properties also has significant implications. For example, do we imagine that the eight properties Cicero pursued were the only possible options? It seems unlikely. The suburbs of Rome were dotted with hundreds of villas, and at least dozens of these would have been "in the public way," which was Cicero's primary criterium. But only those properties that one knows about could actually be pursued. Cicero was therefore effectively forced to pursue properties that were possibly not for sale at all because he lacked the means to identify more options. His information was essentially limited to what his personal network and possibly the networks of his friends possessed in personal knowledge or could pick up via hearsay. This should alert us to the serious limitations on personal networks to replace the information provision of professional real estate agents.

Taken altogether, we see a system in which buyers had to expend considerable resources while uncertainty always loomed in the background. A purchase could flounder at any moment for any number of reasons. Yet there was little choice but to press ahead; so Cicero and Atticus kept pursuing properties even when they thought they were *probably* not for sale. The end result, however, is that a four-month long intensive property hunt yielded no results whatsoever.

Notes

1 See Finley 1999; Temin 2012; 2001. See also Finley 1976a. The various chapters in Finley 1976b make some allusions to the question of whether "a market" existed but make no effort to explore how such a market would have worked. Rawson 1976 and Treggiari 1979 both discuss aspects of Roman attitudes towards property. Treggiari focuses on sentimentality and its possible influence on the willingness to sell, while Rawson takes the opposite view on this issue while also discussing property and its exchange more generally, based on Cicero's letters. Rawson concludes in favour of a lively exchange while Treggiari takes a more negative view. However, even they do not actually define what they think "a market" is nor do they try to study exchange behaviour systematically. Frier 1980 and 1977 should be acknowledged here as being highly influential on the study of the Roman rental market, but of limited relevance here because they do not deal with exchange.

2 Finley 1999: 118.
3 Temin 2001: 179. My emphasis.
4 Temin 2012: 139. Cf. Temin 2012: 44: "[i]f Duncan-Jones [1994] is right that wealthy Romans made an economic decision about the assets in which to hold their wealth, they must have considered the price of these assets," which implies the availability of information.
5 Finley 1999: 119.
6 Finley 1999: 120. My emphasis.
7 Finley's position does not explicitly state that buyers would gravitate towards "cheap" property but I think this logically follows. If buyers can separate "cheap" from "dear" and look to make opportunistic purchases, which is what windfall purchases are, they would logically try to buy the "cheap" options while avoiding the "dear."
8 Finley 1999: 118. He further noted that the Greek language, despite lending itself to the creation of compound nouns, does not possess words for "land-seller," "house-seller," "property-seller," or "broker." "And the same holds true for Latin," he notes. On 118–119 he further seems to suggest that "small-town gossip" was the major (and only?) source about the availability of property.
9 There were some professionals dealing with land and property. For example, the *praediator* dealt with matters related to land acquired by the state as *praedium*, which is to say, land given as surety by a guarantor with respect to a transaction between the state and a third private party. See Berger 1953: 642. Cf. p. 754. It is in this capacity that we come across a *praediator* in Cicero's letters. See Cic. *Att.* 12.14.2 and 12.17. *Praediatores* also appear to have acted as legal experts in their area. Cic. *Balb.* 45. Cf. Val. Max. 8.12.1. This *praediator* was most likely the father of A. Cascellius, a jurist from Cicero's day. The father appears to have enjoyed some fame in the 90s. See Mommsen 1880: 114, n. 3 and Frier 1985: 152, n. 57. Suet. *Claud.* 9 mentions a *lex praediatoria* but it is unknown what this entailed. The services of the auctioneer had some overlap with the services of modern-day estate agents. E.g. in the facilitation of sale and the provision of some information. On auctioneers in the Roman world see Rauh 1989a. More generally, the services of an estate agent were largely undertaken by friends, family, clients, or slaves. Information gathering, surveying, bidding and some legal aspects were all at least sometimes taken care of in this way. E.g. Cic. *Att.* 1.6.1, 4.8, 12.23.3, 13.8 are all examples of information about property being sought, requested or shared on behalf of another. *Dig.* 18.1.18.1 (Pomp. 9 *ad Sab.)* shows that the boundaries of an estate were indicated by one of the seller's slaves. In Cic. *Fam.* 9.15.3–5 Cicero asks his friend Papirius Paetus to survey a property with a group of builders. Bidding on another's behalf is evidenced in e.g. Cic. *Att.* 9.9.4, 11.13.4, 12.25, 14.31.4. At times this clearly extended into the power to negotiate and buy and sell on another's behalf. E.g. Cic. *Fam.* 14.6., *Q. Fr.* 3.1.3, *Att.* 5.5.3. Cic. *Att.* 13.50.2, 15.26.4 shows some legal aspects. Cic. *Dom.* 116 shows that the purchase might even be completed in its entirety by a third-party. There is nothing to suggest that this was not legal, but Cicero certainly indicates that it was morally wrong in the specific case he refers to. However, some crucial key tasks of the modern-day estate agent are missing from the list above, namely valuation, price record-keeping and advertising.
10 Crook 1976: 77 gives further reasons to believe estate agents were absent. He lists several cases from the *Digest* involving peculiar errors whereby, for example, A thinks they are buying property X while B thinks they are selling property Y, errors in measurement of acreage, or the sale of sacred land as private land. Crook concludes: "It all sounds very careless, and implies pretty certainly the absence of professional land agents, who would presumably have obviated such errors." Cf. p.72.
11 Shackleton Bailey 1966: 404–413 provides an excellent technical discussion of this saga and the source material. Englert 2017 discusses the shrine with a focus on

Cicero's motivations and grief and some broader background. Rauh 1989b: 60–74, esp. 60–69 discusses Cicero's search for a property as part of his discussion on financing estate sales. See also Benöhr 2013, who focuses in particular on Cicero's extensive efforts to recover a debt from Faberius. García Morcillo 2020 applies ideas from behavioural economics to the case, stressing Cicero's emotional and psychological state and its effects on decision-making.

12 Cic. *Att.* 13.31.4: After talking about the price of a property sold years earlier, Cicero notes "of course everything has dropped now." *omnia scilicet nunc minoris.* See Verboven 1997 for broader context and discussion of possible price movements in this period. All translations of Cicero's letters to Atticus are taken from Shackleton Bailey's translation.

13 Cicero's primary criterium appears to have been location, as I discuss further below. Cicero's letters to Atticus make it abundantly clear that Cicero felt morally and emotionally obligated to buy a property for this shrine; he writes: "I consider myself as virtually bound by a vow and pledge." *iam quasi voto quodam et promisso me teneri puto.* Cic. *Att.* 12.18.1. He reiterates this belief in three further letters. Cf. *Att.* 12.23.3, 12.38a.2, 12.43.3–4. See Englert 2017 for a discussion of Cicero's motivations and goals in more detail, with specific regard for his grief as a driving factor.

14 See Appendix 1 below for a list of all properties with source references. Tusculum is mentioned thrice, but I do not include it in the list of eight because a) it almost certainly refers to Cicero's own property and b) it was never mentioned as anything but a last fallback option.

15 Cf. Cic. *Att.* 12.12.1, 12.37.2.

16 Cic. *Att.* 12.21.2.

17 Cic. *Att.* 12.23.3; Cicero may in fact have informed Atticus, since he writes "I think I mentioned it in my letter yesterday." *ut opinor, heri ad te scripseram.*

18 Cic. *Att.* 12.30.

19 Cic. *Att.* 12.31.1–2.

20 Cic. *Att.* 12.31.2. *commodissime enim per eum agi potest.*

21 Cic. *Att.* 12.22.3.

22 Cic. *Att.* 12.23.3.

23 Cic. *Att.* 12.25.

24 Cic. *Att.* 12.28.1. Cf. *Att.* 12.26, 12.27.1

25 Cic. *Att.* 12.33.1, 12.30. *de Sili voluntate vendendi et de eo quanti, tu vereri videris, primum ne nolit, deinde ne tanti.*

26 Cic. *Att.* 12.31.1–2.

27 Cic. *Att.* 12.33.1. Cf. *Att.* 12.29.2.

28 Cic. *Att.* 12.38a.2.

29 For Cicero's attempts to ensure an open auction See *Att.* 12.40.4, 13.26.1, 12.47.1, 12.49.3, 12.51.2, 12.5a, 13.3.1, 13.33.2, 13.5.1–2, 13.7.

30 Cic. *Att.* 12.22.3, 12.23.3, 12.25, 12.26, 12.27.1, 12.29, 12.33.1, 12.30.1, 12.31, 12.34.3, 12.39.2, 12.44.2, 12.41.3. Three later letters make vague references to a Silius, but it is not clear if it is the same Silius as before and it is unclear if the mentions relate to Silius' property or to something else. See Cic. *Att.* 12.52.2, 13.5.1–2, 13.7.1.

31 On 17 March Cicero is certain that Drusus' property was for sale. *Att.* 12.21.2; Cf. 12.22.3. On 19 March, *Att.* 12.23.3, he heard about a previous bid on the estate, but Drusus' asking price is not known to Cicero until 29 March. See Cic. *Att.* 12.31.1–2.

32 Cic. *Att.* 13.31.4. Cf. *Att.* 12.23.3 where a previous bid is mentioned in relation to the Drusus estate.

33 Cic. *Att.* 13.31.4. *omnia scilicet nunc minoris.*

34 Cic. *Att.* 13.31.4.

35 Cic. *Att.* 13.33.2.

36 Cic. *Att.* 12.31.1–2.

37 Cic. *Att.* 12.31.1: "You ask me what limit I fix, and how much higher I rate this property [Silius'] than that of Drusus. I have never visited it." *quaeris a me quod summum pretium constituam et quantum anteire istos hortos Drusi. accessi numquam.*

38 Atticus certainly visited the Scapula estate and probably that of Clodia as well. See Cic. *Att.* 13.1.3, 13.28.1, 13.29.1. The last of these letters also reveals that Chrysippus, almost certainly a trusted builder, had also sent Cicero a report on the Scapula estate.

39 None of the other properties Cicero pursued could in any way be construed as being "visibly cheap."

40 Finley 1999: 119 cites "derelict land, going at a bargain because of neglect, war devastation or someone's bad lack" as one form of "visibly cheap" windfall property, while confiscated land, like *ager publicus*, is cited as a second option and "land extorted from peasants through usurious loans, illegal seizure or 'patronage'" makes up a third form. These are heuristics that are asserted to be reliable indicators of a low price. But this tells us nothing about the prevalence, reliability, and accessibility of this information. Importantly, Finley also does not back these assertions up with evidence. There is, for example, no proof that derelict or devastated land would automatically be cheap, as the case cited at the end of the paragraph attests to. M. Licinius Crassus is famous for buying up burning buildings at very low prices, but there is nothing to suggest that this was common behaviour. In fact, Crassus is consistently depicted as an outlier of morally dubious character for precisely this behaviour. Plut. *Crass.* 2.4. Frier 1980: 33–34. rightly notes that Plutarch's statement that Crassus came to own most of Rome in this way is almost certainly exaggeration. These "fire sales" likely made up a relatively small, though not insignificant, part of Crassus' overall portfolio, not least because the crew of 500 slaves he is said to have used to salvage burning buildings would have been insufficient as firemen for all of Rome, even if they had been intended to have that role (which seems unlikely).

41 Cic. *Tull.* 14.

42 Professional banks went into decline in the first century and the space they left was filled by what Jean Andreau has termed "aristocratic financiers." Which is not to say that banking disappeared; rather it seems banking was reduced in scale and catered to people lower down the scale while the aristocracy provided credit to itself. See Kay 2016: 235–265. On aristocratic financiers see Andreau 1978. "Elite financiers" in Andreau 1999: 9–29, 140 and *passim.*

43 So Cicero says, right at the start of the process, that the search for the suburban property must "be backed with all my available resources and those of others who I know will not fail me." *omnibus meis eorumque quos scio mihi non defuturos facultatibus (sed potero meis) enitendum mihi est.* Cic. *Att.* 12.22.3. See Verboven 2002 on the moral and social obligations of friends to help each other.

44 Rauh 1989b discusses the financing of estate sales in more detail, with some reference to the properties discussed in this case study.

45 Cic. *Att.* 12.22.3.

46 Cic. *Att.* 12.22.3.

47 Cic. *Att.* 12.25.

48 "For the remainder we mustn't mind paying interest to Silius until we pay cash with what comes from Faberius [a debtor of Cicero's] or some debtor of Faberius." *reliquae pecuniae vel usuram Silio pendemus, dum a Faberio vel [cum] aliquo qui Faberio debet repraesentabimus.* Cic. *Att.* 12.25.

49 Credit was certainly not the reason Silius gave Cicero but that does not necessarily mean it played no part: "Sicca was surprised to hear of Silius' change of mind. For my part it surprises me more that, since he gave his son as a reason." *Silium mutasse*

sententiam Sicca mirabatur. equidem magis miror quod, cum in filium causam conferret. Cic. *Att.* 12.31.1.

50 A further complication was that a seller could change his mind at any point. E.g. Cic. *Att.* 12.31.1: "you [Atticus] say you think he [Silius] will sell if we throw in an extra item, one which he turned down after having himself previously agreed to take it." *ais te putare, si addiderimus aliud, a quo refugit cum ab ipso id fuerit destinatum, venditurum*.

51 Temin 2012: 139.

52 Finley 1999: 118.

53 I tend to use market as shorthand for "system of exchange," a term I have adopted from Biggart and Delbridge 2004, who argue against a universality of "market behaviour" and instead suggest that exchange behaviour can be helpfully categorised using four distinct typologies of exchange.

54 Cic. *Att.* 12.21.2. Cf. *Att.* 12.22.3. On the Faberius debt see Rauh 1989b: 62–68; Rollinger 2009: 154–160; Benöhr 2013.

55 Cic. *Att.* 12.25. Given the precise sum mentioned and the language used, it seems exceedingly likely to me, following Benöhr 2013: 268, n. 58, that Hermogenes was a debtor of Cicero's, rather than a friend or a moneylender.

56 Cicero and Atticus spend a lot of time trying to recoup this debt. It is first mentioned in March but is not (partially) recouped until June. See Cic. *Att.* 12.21.2, 12.25, 12.29, 12.31.1–2, 12.40.4, 12.47.1–2, 13.27.2, 13.28.1, 13.29.1, 12.2a.1, 13.31.1, 13.30.1, 13.32.1, 13.33.1–2.

57 Though on 29 March the Hermogenes debt had not yet been settled: "Hermogenes too can be of great help to us in making cash payment." *magno etiam adiumento nobis Hermogenes potest esse in repraesentando*. *Att.* 12.31.1–2.

58 See Cic. *Att.* 12.23.3, 12.33.1, 12.31.1–2, 12.37.2, 12.38a.2, 12.41.3, 12.44.2, 13.26.1.

59 Cic. *Att.* 12.23.3. Cf. *Att.* 12.27.1.

60 Cic. *Att.* 13.29.1.

61 Cic. *Att.* 13.29.1.

62 Lamia: Cic. *Att.* 12.22.3; Cusinius and Trebonius: *Att.* 12.43.3; Clodia: *Att.* 12.38a.2, 12.42.1–2, 12.47.1–2, 12.52.2.

63 Cic. *Att.* 12.38a.2.

64 Cic. *Att.* 12.42.1–2.

65 Cic. *Att.* 12.47.1–2.

66 Cic. *Att.* 12.52.2

67 Cic. *Att.* 13.29.1.

68 Cic. *Att.* 13.29.1.

69 Cic. *Att.* 12.31.1–2. Cf. *Att.* 12.30.

Cic. *Att.* 12.23.3.

71 See Cic. *Att.* 12.23.3, 12.25, 12.26, 12.27.1, 12.28.1, 12.30, 12.31.1–2.

72 Cic. *Att.* 10.5.3.

73 Cic. *Att.* 12.47.1–2: "but it's a big thing and it's hard to compete with a rich man, eager to buy and an heir to the estate." *sed et magna res est et difficile certamen cum cupido, cum locuplete, cum herede*. Cf. *Att.* 12.43.3. One conceivable advantage is that a co-heir might have had better ties to the other heirs than an outsider would and may consequently have possessed better information about the estate and the desires of the other heirs than other bidders would have. García Morcillo 2020: 637 speculates that Otho may even have colluded with the other heirs to engage in shill-bidding in order to drive up the price for Cicero. Cf. García Morcillo 2021: 80.

74 Cic. *Att.* 12.35. *numquam mihi venit in mentem, quo plus insumptum in monimentum esset quam nescio quid quod lege conceditur, tantundem populo dandum esse*. Cf. *Att.* 12.36.1.

75 Cic. *Att.* 12.35. *nollem illud ullo nomine nisi fani appellari*.

76 Cic. *Att.* 12.35. *quod si volumus, vereor ne adsequi non possimus nisi mutato loco.*

77 Cf. Cic. *Att.* 13.20.1 and 13.33a.1. In the end, Caesar was murdered before the law could be passed, but the expectation that it would pass was sufficient to put Cicero off pursuing the property further. On information asymmetries in the real estate market, see Rosillo-López 2021, esp. 127–128 on the Scapula case.

78 All mention of it disappears from the correspondence. We hear of the shrine only once more: a year later, in July 44, Cicero speaks of income that "had been put aside for that shrine." *quodque ex istis fructuosis rebus receptum est, id ego ad illud fanum sepositum putabam.* Cic. *Att.* 15.15.4. It is implied that the money should still be available, and therefore that the shrine was never built. It is not clear why he gave up, but Englert has recently suggested that it was a conscious, philosophical decision on Cicero's part as he worked through his grief and relieved himself of the obligation he had put upon himself to build the shrine (Englert 2017). Shackleton Bailey 1966: 11 suggests the acquisition of Cluvius' suburban estate at Puteoli shortly after this episode may have helped console Cicero after his disappointment.

Appendix 1

Table A.1 List of all properties considered by Cicero with full references

Property	*Mentioned in Cic. Att.*
An estate between Antium and Circeii	12.19.1
The Isle of Arpinum	12.12.1
Drusus'	12.21.2, 12.22.3, 12.23.3, 12.25.2, 12.33.1, 12.33.1, 12.30.1, 12.31, 12.37.2, 12.38a.2, 12.39.2, 12.44.2, 12.41.3
Lamia's	12.21.2, 12.22.3, 12.29
Cassius'	12.21.2
Silius'	12.22.3, 12.23.3, 12.25, 12.26, 12.27.1, 12.29, 12.33.1, 12.30.1, 12.31, 12.34.3, 12.39.2, 12.44.2, 12.41.3, 12.52.2, 13.5.1–2, 13.7.1
Cotta's	12.23.3, 12.27.1, 12.29.2
Damasippus'	12.29.2, 12.33.1
Scapula's	12.36.1, 12.37.2, 12.38a.2, 12.40.4, 12.42.1–2, 12.41.3, 12.43.3,12.44.2, 13.26.1, 12.47.1–2, 12.49.2, 12.51.2', 12.52.2, 13.27.2, 13.1.3, 13.28.1, 13.29.1, 13.31.4, 12.5a, 13.3.1, 13.33.1–2, 13.5.1–2, 13.7.1, 13.12.4, 13.33a.1
"Tusculum"	12.37.2, 13.26.1, 12.44.2,
Trebonius and Cusinius'	12.38a.2, 12.43.3, 12.41.3
Clodia's	12.38a.2, 12.40.4, 12.42.1–2, 12.41.3, 12.43.3,12.44.2, 13.26.1, 12.47.1–2, 12.52.2, 13.29.1

References

Andreau, J. (1978) Financiers de l'aristocratie à la fin de la republique. In: E. Frézouls, ed. *Le dernier siècle de la République romaine et l'époque augustéene*. Strasbourg: AECR, 47–62.

Andreau, J. (1999) *Banking and Business in the Roman World*. Cambridge: Cambridge University Press.

Benöhr, H.-P. (2013) VI. Das Faberianum *negotium* – Schuldenbereinigung zur Zeit Ciceros. *Zeitschrift Der Savigny-Stiftung Für Rechtsgeschichte: Romanistische Abteilung* 103, 275–320.

Berger, A. (1953) Encyclopedic Dictionary of Roman Law. *Transactions of the American Philosophical Society* 43, 333–809.

Biggart, N.W. and Delbridge, R. (2004) Systems of Exchange. *Academy of Management Review* 29, 28–49.

Crook, J. (1976) Classical Roman Law and the Sale of Land. In: M.I. Finley, ed. *Studies in Roman Property*. Cambridge: Cambridge University Press, 71–83.

Duncan-Jones, R. (1994) *Money and Government in the Roman Empire*. Cambridge: Cambridge University Press.

Englert, W. (2017) Fanum and Philosophy: Cicero and the Death of Tullia. *Ciceroniana On Line* 1, 41–66.

Finley, M.I. (1976a) Introduction. In: M.I. Finley, ed. *Studies in Roman Property*. Cambridge: Cambridge University Press, 1–6.

Finley, M.I. (1976b) (ed.) *Studies in Roman Property*. Cambridge: Cambridge University Press.

Finley, M.I. (1999) *The Ancient Economy*, updated ed. Berkeley: University of California Press.

Frier, B.W. (1977) The Rental Market in Early Imperial Rome. *Journal of Roman Studies* 67, 27–37.

Frier, B.W. (1980) *Landlords and Tenants in Imperial Rome*. Princeton: Princeton University Press.

Frier, B.W. (1985) *The Rise of the Roman Jurists – Studies in Cicero's "Pro Caecina"*. Princeton: Princeton University Press.

García Morcillo, M. (2020) Mentality, Motivation, and Economic Decision-Making in Ancient Rome: Cicero and Tullia's Shrine. *Economic History Review* 73, 623–643.

García Morcillo, M. (2021) Managing Uncertainty and Asymmetric Information in Roman Auctions. In: C. Rosillo-López and M. García Morcillo eds. *Managing Information in the Roman Economy*. New York: Palgrave MacMillan, 61–88.

Kay, P. (2016) *Rome's Economic Revolution*. Oxford: Oxford University Press.

Mommsen, T. (1880) Die Litteraturbriefe des Horaz. *Hermes* 15, 103–115.

Rauh, N.K. (1989a) Auctioneers and the Roman Economy. *Historia: Zeitschrift Für Alte Geschichte* 38, 451–471.

Rauh, N.K. (1989b) Finance and Estate Sales in Republican Rome. *Aevum* 63, 45–76.

Rawson, E. (1976) The Ciceronian Aristocracy and its Properties. In: M.I. Finley, ed. *Studies in Roman Property*. Cambridge: Cambridge University Press, 85–102.

Rollinger, C. (2009) Solvendi Sunt Nummi. *Die Schuldenkultur Der Späten Römischen Republic Im Spiegel Der Schriften Ciceros*. Berlin: Verlag Antike.

Rosillo-López, C. (2021) Domum pestilentem vendo: Real Estate Market and Information Asymmetry in the Roman World. In: C. Rosillo-López and M. García Morcillo, eds. *Managing Information in the Roman Economy*. London: Palgrave MacMillan, 117–134.

Shackleton Bailey, D. R. (1966) *Cicero: Letters to Atticus, Vol. 5 (Books XI - XIII)*. Cambridge, MA: Harvard University Press.

Temin, P. (2001) A Market Economy in the Early Roman Empire. *Journal of Roman Studies* 91, 169–181.

Temin, P. (2012) *The Roman Market Economy*. Princeton: Princeton University Press.

Treggiari, S. (1979) Sentiment and Property: Some Roman Attitudes. In: A. Parel and T. Flanagan, eds. *Theories of Property: Aristotle to the Present*. Waterloo: Calgary Institute for the Humanities, 53–88.

Verboven, K. (1997) Caritas Nummorum. Deflation in the Late Roman Republic? *Münstersche Beiträge Zur Antiken Handelsgeschichte* 16, 40–78.

Verboven, K. (2002) *The Economy of Friends: Economic Aspects of Amicitia and Patronage in the Late Republic*. Brussels: Latomus.

8 *Ocelli Italiae*

Senatorial *villae* as Information Hubs

Francisco Pina Polo

Abstract

The *villae* that both Cicero and other members of the Roman elite possessed in various regions of Italy were first and foremost sources of income for their owners. However, like their *domus* in Rome, these *villae* were also a significant instrument of prestige and self-representation. The social life in the *villae* also fulfilled a substantial "political" function. This chapter takes a snapshot of a short yet intensive period, between April and July of 44 BCE, when Cicero spent most of his time outside Rome, going from one of his estates in Latium and Campania to another. Then, as now, interpersonal relationships played a fundamental role in politics, and so it was always significant to hold face-to-face meetings. To upper-class Romans it was important to participate in this temporary community by spending at least a few days in each of those places. This resulted in constant invitations to each other's homes. Such meetings allowed for the exchange of first-hand information, but also for attempts to directly and indirectly influence a certain trend of opinion. The aim was to become updated about the political situation from different perspectives and to anticipate future movements of both allies and adversaries. As interrelated networks of exclusive communication, upper-class *villae* contributed thus to the shaping of information as a particularly precious commodity.

***

Although the accumulation of money and movable goods did play its role in Rome society, wealth, as in all pre-modern societies, predominantly resided in acquisition of real estate. While there were different ways of obtaining wealth (bequests, commercial activities, booty, agricultural income, etc.), there generally was a close connection between power and wealth: wealth opened up the path to power, and power facilitated the creation of a network of influence and personal relationships that, in turn, became a source of further affluence. Wealth and power, then, went hand in hand, mutually supporting each other in Republican politics and society more broadly.[1]

Cicero provides a particularly illustrative example of this trend since we can follow in some detail when and how he accumulated various properties throughout his life. One clearly sees that most of them were obtained, by various means, after he had held the consulship in 63. This cannot be chalked up

DOI: 10.4324/9781003187806-11

to chance. In the case of other prominent politicians of the time, however, we cannot draw such a detailed picture and can only extract general facts about their wealth and, in some particular cases, the lands that they owned throughout different regions of Italy. Depending on each politician's profile and undertakings (e.g. whether inclined towards the military or focused on the law in Rome), sources of income would vary. However, there is a constant feature in each case: gathering riches was intimately linked with holding magistracies and being a member of the senate.[2]

Though only beginning with a relatively modest patrimony, by the end of his life Cicero had turned himself into a wealthy landowner with many assets. The most important part of his holdings consisted of the estates he owned outside Rome. Cicero acquired various properties on arable land throughout Latium and Campania: Tusculum, Formiae, Alba, Antium, Astura, Frusino, Cumae, Pompeii, and Puteoli. In order to facilitate access to his estates, he also acquired a series of inns (*deversoria*) along the main roads linking Rome with the Latium and Campania, thus building a genuine network of private lodgings. Those located on the *via Appia* in Lanuvium, Minturnae, and Sinuessa served as stopping points during his trips to his properties in Campania. His quarters in Anagnia were located between Rome and Arpinum, and his residence in Aquinum fell between this city and the Thyrrenian coast. In total, Cicero became the owner of at least 15 properties outside Rome.[3]

Cicero loved his *villae*, which he affectionately referred to as the *ocelli Italiae* at the end of his life.[4] He used them whenever possible as a refuge in the countryside or by the sea. He spared no effort or money to furnish them with comforts and deck them with high-quality wall paintings, Greek statues, and artwork.[5] In some cases he even created a private library,[6] a real luxury at the time that he could use when writing some of his works of rhetoric and philosophy far from Rome. The *villae* were, therefore, places of leisure and recreation. Nevertheless, we cannot forget that many of them were above all an investment aimed at generating future wealth, since they were not simply places for rest but also operating farms located in some of the most fertile and populated areas of Italy whose products were subsequently sold.[7]

The *villae* spread across Italy that both Cicero and the other members of the Roman elite possessed were therefore first and foremost sources of income for their owners. However, like their *domus* in Rome,[8] these *villae* were also important tools for representing one's prestige and status, and the number and the calibre of one's visitors reflected one's social prestige.[9] The very idea of a vacation outside the city in one's own home was itself a luxury that showcased the social pre-eminence of those who could enjoy it. And naturally, like a *domus* in Rome,[10] the place where a *villa* was located was far from irrelevant: leaving aside the question of economic productivity, what really counted was being visible and perceived as part of the political and social aristocracy, just like in the *Urbs*. It is therefore logical that a large portion of the senatorial and, more generally, aristocratic *villae* of which we know were concentrated in Latium (especially in Tusculum and along the coastal areas of Formiae-Minturnae) and Campania, particularly in the coastal area on the Bay of Naples, between Cumae and Pompeii (most notably in the barely 25 km stretch between Cumae and Neapolis in places like Baiae[11] and Puteoli), as the classic works of D'Arms and Shatzman have demonstrated.[12] Not only were the views, landscape, and comfort of the *villae* important: the decisive point was having eminent neighbours with whom, in particular during certain months of the year, it was possible to forge deep social bonds, almost as if the holidaymaker lived in a miniature Rome.[13]

This intense social life also contained an inevitable and substantial political component, given that most of the participants were senators who keenly followed the goings-on in Rome from afar, with news coming in from the city and rumours circulating in response.[14] It is precisely this "political" aspect of the senatorial *villae* that attracts me here. In order to discuss this issue, I have chosen to limit myself to a short timeframe, the four months between April and July of the year 44, a period during which Cicero spent most of his time outside Rome, hopping from one of his estates in Latium and Campania to another. Our main source of information is obviously the orator's correspondence with Atticus and, to a lesser extent, with others. Some of the relevant questions analysed in the following pages are: how and what kind of information did Cicero receive while staying at his *villae*? Which people did he see and how did he interact with them? How did owning such properties facilitate the flow of information? What was discussed? Ultimately, one might ask to what extent Cicero and the other senators were able to follow events unfolding in the *Urbs* reliably and to what extent they were able to influence those very events from a distance.

It is evident that the means by which Cicero – and in all likelihood other senators as well – obtained information from Rome was mainly through letters. Cicero often reveals his anxiety about receiving letters that were needed to stay informed, especially at those particular moments when important events were expected to unfold in Rome. Between April and July 44, we know of some 60 letters sent by Cicero to Atticus, that is, an average of one letter every other day, although sometimes the exchange was daily. Accordingly, we are not wrong to speak of the constant daily movement of private couriers around Italy who were employed to deliver the letters, sometimes as an assignment from people whom they did not serve directly. Depending on the distance to be covered, delivery times would vary, but the data provided by Cicero show that letters reached their destination in a reasonable time, even when the recipient was constantly jumping from one *villa* to another. Cicero's correspondence also shows that it was a very common practice to forward copies of received letters to other recipients, since it was quite usual for Cicero to send Atticus a copy of a letter he had received or sent and, presumably, vice versa.

As usual, the correspondence would contain a mix of private information and discussions of the political situation; furthermore, the letters that have been preserved show that they were sometimes accompanied by other documents, such as edicts or speeches delivered in Rome (both in a *contio* and Senate). Thus, Cicero receives Brutus' so-called *contio Capitolina*, whose author was waiting for Cicero's corrections before publication[15]; the laudatory speech about Caesar that was delivered towards the middle of April by someone whose name Cicero does not mention[16]; the one by Dolabella at the end of April[17]; the *horribilis contio* by L. Antonius, which Cicero contrasts with the *praeclara* one penned by Dolabella, at the beginning of May[18]; Octavian's first speech before the people in early May, which the orator anxiously awaited and he undoubtedly finally received.[19] Cicero also knew Ser. Sulpicius Rufus' *oratio* in the Senate, which he received in Pompeii in early May.[20] In one of his letters to Atticus, Cicero mentions an edict issued by Brutus and Cassius, of which he approves.[21] Finally, after Dolabella had nominated Cicero to be his legate on 3 June, Cicero receives the official communication a few days later in one of his *villae* in Latium.[22]

The list of known names of the authors and recipients of Cicero's letters in the four months under examination provides some very interesting information about which politicians were his main interlocutors. As would be expected, correspondence with Brutus and Cassius is frequent both when he is in Campania and in Latium, particularly with the former, with whom the orator tries to maintain a patronising relationship. Both were for Cicero the main leaders of the "tyrannicides," but they were also serving praetors, and therefore it was essential to be aware of their intentions and also to try to steer their actions. Letters to and from Dolabella are also well attested, given his double status as *consul suffectus* in 44 and as Cicero's ex-son-in-law. During the four months that followed Caesar's assassination, Cicero had a fluid relationship with Hirtius and Pansa. As in the cases of Dolabella, Brutus, and Cassius, Cicero clearly sought to influence Hirtius and Pansa politically, this time because it should not be forgotten that both were consuls designate for 43.

But Cicero did not limit his correspondence to those who had or were going to play a prominent institutional role, nor did he only communicate with those with whom he saw eye to eye on political matters; instead, he was also in touch with non-magistrates and political adversaries. Thus, he exchanges letters with M. Antonius, the other consul of the year, and with his brother L. Antonius, tribune of the plebs in 44, even though Cicero abhorred them both. He corresponds with Q. Fufius Calenus, a Caesarian who had been consul in 47 and who was to be, in 43, one of Cicero's great adversaries in the Senate. He also maintained a regular epistolary relationship with Balbus and Oppius. Although they did not occupy any magistracy, both had been very close to Caesar during his government and after his assassination remained extremely influential in Rome and, crucially, had coveted access to first-hand political information. Cicero's relationship with L. Iulius Caesar is also interesting. Cousin of the dictator, on whose side he had actively fought during the civil war, L. Iulius Caesar had been an active Caesarian, but after the Ides of March he took on a conciliatory role in trying to avoid the outbreak of a new civil war. Cicero also corresponded with Theophanes of Mytilene, someone who had been very close to Pompey, though in 44 had no major political role to play. The issues addressed in his letters seem to have been of a private nature.

As can be seen, Cicero was in touch with a bunch of big players: whether magistrates in office (the consuls M. Antonius and Dolabella, the praetors Brutus and Cassius, the tribune of the plebs L. Antonius, the prefects to assign land to veterans Plotius Plancus, Ateius Capito, and Cupiennius), magistrates designate for 43 (consuls Hirtius and Pansa, praetor Plotius Plancus), consulars with a Caesarian background (Fufius Calenus and L. Iulius Caesar), or otherwise influential Caesarians (Balbus and Oppius). In short, we can see that the exchange of letters was a good way to stay up to date about what was going on in Rome and to learn what some of those who were wielding political power at the time thought.

As we have seen before, most of the *villae* should not be taken as merely places of leisure, but as centres of economic activity. Even so, they still were places of leisure and rest for their owner. The life that Cicero led on these estates was certainly more relaxed than life back in Rome, with fewer commitments and obligations, which allowed him to dedicate a good part of his time to writing. Nevertheless, as in Rome social relations continued to play an essential part of his daily activities.[23] It is unlikely that during those weeks of "vacation," in an atmosphere that allowed for the relaxation of habits, aristocrats would have maintained customs like the regular morning *salutatio*, because it would have been difficult for their *clientes* and inferiors to follow them to their estates.[24] However, it was common to receive visits, especially in the morning, from local people, somehow mirroring the *salutatio* of the *Urbs*.[25] In exchange, visits and invitations to lunch or dinner at the home of someone were quite frequent.[26] In the politically convoluted and tumultuous context of the spring and summer of 44, it is easy to see how these conversations and the visits themselves often veered towards the political.

As his correspondence shows, Cicero spent the months following Caesar's assassination away from Rome (his first letter to Atticus outside the city is dated to 7 April). In the first half of April he visited (or simply spent the night at) some of his estates in Latium (Tusculum, Lanuvium, Astura, Fundi, Formiae, and Sinuessa) and then divided the second half of the month and the first half of May between his *villae* in Campania (Puteoli, Cumae, and Pompeii). Cicero's behaviour may have been partly influenced by a desire to get away from a Rome that was wracked by turmoil and disarray in the wake of the dictator's death, but being away was by no means exceptional. The senate interrupted its sessions during April and May (the *discessus senatus*), and in those two months it was common for a veritable exodus of senators, and aristocrats more broadly, to leave Rome and flock to their estates.[27] In fact, in the second half of May Cicero gradually approached Rome following an itinerary that was largely the opposite of that of April: Puteoli, Sinuessa, Arpinum, and finally Tusculum, only 20 km from the *Urbs*. The reason is that a session of the Senate had been called for 1 June, which Cicero thought about attending, though he ultimately decided against it. This explains why Cicero, instead of returning to Rome as he usually would have done, returned in June–July to his estates in Latium and Campania (Antium, Astura, Tusculum, Arpinum, Formiae, Puteoli, and Pompeii), during which time he was constantly debating whether he should leave Italy and flee for Greece.

Therefore, during the months when Cicero was absent from Rome, especially in April and May, he could expect to meet other senators and members of the social elite near his *villae* (particularly in Campania), since they too were enjoying some time at their estates. And this did indeed happen.[28]

When Cicero left Rome at the beginning of April, he first went to the house of his friend C. Matius Calvena. Calvena was a Caesarian who remained faithful to the memory of Caesar after his death and who later would closely collaborate with Octavian. It is precisely because of his Caesarian status that Cicero was interested in knowing his opinion on the political situation.[29] On his way to the Campanian coast, at his estate in Formiae (actually located between Formiae and Caieta), Cicero met L. Aemilius Paullus (consul in 50) on 14 April, who filled him in on the so-called "false Marius" and the political situation in Rome.[30] Once in Puteoli, social events intensified dramatically. Already in his first letter from this destination, Cicero states that many people had come to the area (*turba magna est*) and that there would be even more people in the following weeks.[31] Naturally, when Cicero speaks of a *turba* he is referring to members of the Roman social elite, which is the group that interested him.[32] He adds that two consuls designate (i.e. Hirtius and Pansa) also had *villae* in Puteoli.[33] Immediately conversations multiplied and opinions and information began flowing. It is implicitly evident that Cicero had already met with Hirtius and Pansa, but also Balbus, who was in Puteoli too,[34] and with whom Cicero says they spent a lot of time.[35] Balbus, Hirtius, and Pansa became frequent interlocutors of Cicero's during his stay in Campania,[36] and the two consuls designate would even be his pupils of rhetoric, a good occasion for Cicero to exercise influence over them,[37] although Hirtius also enjoyed a close relationship with Balbus (*vivit habitatque cum Balbo*).[38]

It was not long before Octavian made his appearance on the scene. Once he had become the slain dictator's heir, the young Caesar rushed back from Greece, though he importantly stopped in Campania before going to Rome, where he knew he could meet with many senators and influential people. Accordingly, his presence there was a kind of social occasion at which he could orchestrate his upcoming political appearance.[39] Octavian arrived in Neapolis on 18 April. Balbus went to meet him the next morning, and that same day Balbus visited Cicero at his estate in Cumae, to which he had moved from nearby Puteoli.[40] Balbus passed on to Cicero important information that would later become decisive: Octavian was going to accept Caesar's legacy. Three days later, on 21 April, Cicero returned to his villa in Puteoli and from there informed Atticus that Octavian was in the house of his stepfather L. Marcius Philippus (consul in 56), very close to Cicero's.[41] According to Cicero, the young Caesar was totally devoted to him.[42] Finally, Cicero and Octavian met at the former's house in Puteoli, as he tells Atticus in a letter dated to 22 April. Philippus must have accompanied Octavian during his visit. Cicero seems surprised that his relatives and friends call him Caesar, his new official name, but he claims that Philippus did not and so Cicero likewise opted not to do so.[43]

As with his correspondence, Cicero was also willing to meet with people with different political views. Cicero had exchanged letters with Marcus Antonius in the second half of April concerning the return of the condemned Sextus Cloelius to Rome. The letters from both sides, whose texts are preserved, provide good examples of diplomacy, but also of hypocrisy.[44] Days later, Cicero shows his disposition (in a letter from 3 May) to have a meeting with Antonius, to talk about the Buthrotum matter, which occupied and worried Cicero and Atticus during the whole spring and summer. Cicero was obviously thinking of Antonius coming to the coast, but was under the impression he would not and would only go to Capua.[45] Finally, Cicero was unable to see Antonius, although the latter did go to Misenum on the coast. But, at that time, Cicero was in Pompeii and heard about Antonius' presence too late.[46] Cicero was only in Pompeii for a few days before returning to Puteoli (perhaps because his social life was not so intense there),[47] even though – if not because – he lived with Pansa in Pompeii.[48] On 10 May Cicero travelled by boat from his *villa* in Pompeii to the house of M. Licinius Lucullus, son of the consul of 74, on the island of Nesis, located at the entrance to the Bay of Naples. From there he left for Puteoli the next day.[49]

The Puteoli estate is undoubtedly where Cicero spent the longest time during these spring months.[50] The choice was influenced by the fact that many aristocrats had houses in the area of Cumae–Puteoli–Baiae, which considerably extended the possibilities of socialising with others and, above all, of keeping up on the news and rumours.[51] The spring concentration of senators and well-to-do people in that little Rome made the area a much more interesting hotspot in terms of information than the estates in Latium, despite their being located much closer to the *Urbs*. Additionally, Puteoli was an important seaport, and through the port came news and rumours from Rome and all over the Mediterranean. Cicero himself would make that reflection months later: in a letter sent in November from Arpinum, Cicero tells Atticus that he has absolutely nothing to write to him; in contrast, while in Puteoli where he had spent the end of October and the beginning of November, every day he learned something new about Octavian as well as many things (sometimes false) about Antonius.[52]

When Cicero spent a week in Puteoli, Balbus went to see him the very day he arrived (11 May). Balbus provided Cicero with information about Antonius' plans, who wanted to get the veterans to sanction Caesar's measures and to commit themselves to their implementation.[53] Cicero was planning to visit Hirtius at his home the next day. In fact, during his stay in Puteoli, it seems that the two men met daily, partly because of the lessons in declamation that Cicero gave Hirtius, but also because, as he confesses to Atticus, he intended to win the consul designate for 43 over to the side of the *optimates*.[54] Two days later, it was Cicero who had invited Hirtius to dinner at his house. This close relationship between the two men may at first come as a surprise, because they had very different views, particularly on Caesar and on his political significance. Cicero summarises Hirtius' (and those who think like him) opinion about Caesar: an illustrious man (*vir clarissimus*) has been murdered; his death has constituted a great disturbance for the *res publica*; his clemency backfired and led him to death.[55] Cicero and Hirtius still met once more, on 16 May, just before Hirtius left to join the other consul designate, Pansa, at his house in Neapolis.[56]

This happened on the eve of Cicero's departure for his estates in Latium. A session of the Senate had been called for 1 June, which would mark the resumption of senatorial activities. Cicero had doubts about whether he should attend,[57] but he had to approach Rome just in case. On 17 May, Cicero began his journey back from his beloved Campanian estates, passing via Cumae to greet Pilia, Atticus' wife, and Sinuessa before arriving in Arpinum, from whence he would move on to Tusculum a few days later. The epistolary exchange from Arpinum was just as active and sustained as in other estates in Latium and Campania, but certainly Arpinum was not a place where many senators owned properties nor of course was it a popular vacation destination: Cicero was therefore deprived of the daily encounters he enjoyed in Campania. In the end, Cicero opted to not go to Rome, nor did he attend the sessions of the Senate on 1 and 5 June. During those days he remained at his house in Tusculum, practically at the gates of the *Urbs*, constantly informed thanks to Atticus' letters about what was happening there.[58] There is no news in the letters preserved from those days about any personal meetings with politically significant individuals.[59]

From that moment and over the following weeks, Cicero began a slow journey to some of his *villae* in Latium and Campania (Antium, Astura, Tusculum, Arpinum, Formiae, Puteoli, and Pompeii), which was similar to the one carried out in April–May. Around 7 June Cicero visited Brutus in Antium. This proved to be a well-attended meeting, since Servilia, Tertula, and Portia (respectively the mother, half-sister, and wife of Brutus), as well as the senator Marcus Favonius, also attended. A little later Cassius joined the conversation, which revolved around what the two praetors ought to do. Cicero relates the details of the discussion, in which Servilia also intervened, and how he finally persuaded Brutus not to go to Rome to preside over the games he was organising.[60] A couple of days later Cicero saw Philippus, Octavian's stepfather, in Astura. According to Cicero, Philippus did not believe that the young heir to Caesar could be trusted, and he himself doubted that much hope could be placed in him, given his age, reputation, and education. The most important thing, however, was to separate him from Antonius.[61] Around 14 June, M. Valerius Messalla Corvinus visited Cicero in Astura, on his return from Greece, where he had completed his education. The conversation focused on Marcus, Cicero's son, about whom Messalla spoke in glowing terms.[62]

From Astura, Cicero moved on to Tusculum, where he spent the second half of June. In his letters from those days, Cicero debates whether or not to leave Italy and from which port he would depart (Brundisium, Puteoli, or Hydruntum). He also ponders when he would return to Italy, preferring 1 January 43, the date on which Hirtius and Pansa were to enter the consulship. Cicero craves, above all else, the acquiescence of Atticus, who has even gone to see him in Tusculum (and later in Arpinum in early July).[63] He receives, however, different opinions from many people who visited him in his *villa*, although he does not mention any names.[64] From Tusculum Cicero went to Arpinum, where he met his nephew Quintus.[65] Quintus then followed his uncle to Puteoli and spent a few days with him.[66]

Cicero embarked for Greece from his Pompeian estate on 17 July,[67] on a journey he cut short a month later to return to Pompeii and then Rome.[68] He spent the previous days in Puteoli, without stopping in Formiae.[69] It is clear that July was not high season in Puteoli, so neither there nor in the surrounding area was it to be expected to find so many prominent people as one would in April–May. Cicero arrived at his estate in Puteoli on 7 July, and the next day, with his nephew Quintus in tow, he saw Brutus on the nearby island of Nesis, where Brutus was living in the house of his relative M. Licinius Lucullus.[70] Cicero spoke with Brutus about the possibility of travelling to Greece together, but it does not seem that this prospect was overly attractive to Brutus.[71] On his return the same day to Puteoli, Cicero saw Cn. Lucceius, a person close to Brutus, who made him understand that Brutus was hesitant about his departure for the eastern Mediterranean, hoping that something would happen in Rome.[72] On 10 July, L. Scribonius Libo, father-in-law to Sextus Pompeius and later consul in 34, arrived in Puteoli.[73] Scribonius brought important news about Pompeius, including the copy of a letter to the consuls that Cicero read before suggesting that it also be addressed to praetors, tribunes of the plebs and Senate.[74] In his last letter from Puteoli, dated to 11 July, Cicero informs Atticus that Cassius had arrived in the area with his small fleet, although they did not meet. When Cicero started his journey from Pompeii on 17 July, Brutus was still on Nesis and Cassius was at his *villa* in Neapolis.[75] In fact, Brutus was still in the area when Cicero returned to Pompeii and went to see him at Velia on 17 August.[76] Cicero eventually travelled to Rome and returned to his political activity in the Senate with the delivery of his first speech against Antonius, the first *Philippica*: Cicero's pilgrimage between his Italian *villae* was over and his fight against Antonius had begun.

The Ides of March 44 ushered in a period of uncertainty in Rome that led to civil strife, the Triumvirate, and finally a change of regime with the installation of the Principate. There can be no doubt that Caesar's assassination was a political bomb that shook Roman society. We know all that as historians. However, the majority of the senators behaved as they would have done in any other year: just two weeks after the assassination, the Senate interrupted its sessions to begin the usual spring break, and senators dispersed throughout Italy to enjoy their vacations at their *villae*. Were they indifferent to politics and to what might happen in Rome? Not at all. Cicero, who visited virtually all his estates in Latium and Campania between April and July, is a good example of this.

Far from Rome, the great challenge was access to reliable and quick information. The main means of getting this was the regular sending of letters that members of the Roman elite exchanged with each other with surprising frequency and promptness, bearing in mind that, in the absence of a public postal system, the organisation of such an exchange was left entirely to the individuals involved. As we can see from Cicero's correspondence, which was certainly not exceptional, letters from different individuals arrived at his *villae* every day, wherever he was, even on his way from one estate to another. Consequently, an important part of his daily routine was also devoted to writing letters, most frequently to Atticus, but of course also to other recipients. The letters contained both private and public information, news, fake-news, rumours and gossip, speeches delivered in Rome, documents such as bills and edicts, and even copies of letters from third parties. In short, it can be said that a senator could stay reasonably well informed even when far from the *Urbs*.

But then, as it is the case now, interpersonal relationships played a fundamental role in politics, and so it was always important to have face-to-face conversations so as to talk and discuss issues in person.[77] Was this possible when not only Cicero but many other senators were outside of Rome living on their estates, scattered in different parts of Italy? The Ciceronian correspondence shows that during their stay at their *villae* senators did maintain a very active social life, mainly because many of their neighbours were also prominent players in Roman politics. In certain areas one can speak of a real concentration of well-to-do people, in particular in the area around the Bay of Naples, where Puteoli occupied a pre-eminent place as a seaport where news and rumours would arrive. As in Rome, it was important to see and be seen, to have a presence not only (and not so much) in the local community, but above all among the temporary community of upper-class Romans who spent some time in those places. In that respect, a house in the country or by the sea, like the *domus* in the *Urbs*, had a special meaning: it conferred visibility and prestige. This had its translation in constant visits and invitations to each other's homes. Such meetings allowed for first-hand information, but also for an exchange of views and for attempts to influence directly (or indirectly) certain opinions.

In this regard, it is very interesting to note that senators actively sought to get in touch with individuals with different political ideas and positions. The aim was to be aware of the political situation from different perspectives and to anticipate future actions of allies and adversaries alike. Cicero always showed a keen interest in the plans of Brutus and Cassius, but he also wanted to know what Lucius and Marcus Antonius (with whom Cicero tried to meet without success), Dolabella and Octavian (whom Cicero met in Campania before he went to Rome) thought and were going to do. Cicero exchanged letters and met with magistrates in office in 44 and with magistrates designate for 43 of various political stripes. The consuls designate Hirtius and Pansa were his main interlocutors during his stay in their Campanian *villae*, where Cicero did not hide his desire to influence them. But in May Hirtius remained a resolute Caesarian and still spoke of Caesar as a *vir clarissimus*, which in no way prevented Cicero from keeping in touch with him. Cicero's third great interlocutor was Balbus, another prominent and very influential Caesarian, with whom he maintained a fluid epistolary and face-to-face relationship (to a lesser extent the same goes for Oppius). They are not the only Caesarians with whom Cicero communicated: there is also Q. Fufius Calenus, L. Iulius Caesar, and C. Matius Calvena. Obviously, the same can be said from the opposite perspective: the declared Caesarians were interested in knowing the opinion of a resolute anti-Caesarian like Cicero. In some cases, communication with certain persons allowed Cicero to access information about third parties. Thus, L. Marcius Philippus provided him with news about Octavian, and L. Scribonius Libo did the same about Sextus Pompeius.

In short, it can be said that senators, far from living within an ideological bubble, pragmatically reached out to others when forming their political networks, in which friendship undoubtedly played a prominent role, even trumping ideological differences. Like the *domus* at Rome, the *villae* that so many aristocrats possessed in Latium and Campania were meeting points and information hubs for senators (to a greater or lesser extent depending on the area), who exchanged opinions and information, but also were places where it was possible to negotiate with both potential allies and political rivals, strike agreements, indirectly influence decision-making, etc.

However, we must never lose sight of the fact that the institutions where the political decisions were made were in Rome. Cicero tried to pull strings from his *villae* in April–May during the break of the Senate's activity; however, when he refused to attend the Senate sessions in June, he was left without any real possibility of influencing the decision-making process. Still living in his *villae* during June–July, Cicero continued to see and communicate with significant figures, but the magistrates in office and the vast majority of senators were then in Rome, taking decisions, and Octavian was pulling strings as well. Only when Cicero decided to return to Rome (he arrived in the city on 31 August, after his aborted trip to Greece) and got back to the activity in the Senate could he again exercise any real political leadership.

Notes

1 Pina Polo 2016: 177.
2 Pina Polo 2016: 176. This does not mean, of course, that those who were not involved in politics or were not senators could not become rich through their other business ventures, as is clearly demonstrated by Cicero's great friend, Atticus.
3 Pina Polo 2016: 171.
4 Cic. *Att.* 16.6.2. Elsewhere he refers to "his modest estates, beautifully built and pleasantly located" (Cic. *Att.* 16.3.4).
5 Cic. *Att.* 1.6.2; 1.10.3.
6 Cic. *Att.* 4.4a.1; 4.8.2.
7 See in general Marzano 2007; Marzano and Métraux 2018.
8 See Saller 1984; Wiseman 1987; Rilinger 1997; Hales 2000; 2003; Beck 2009. Cf. Hölkeskamp 2004: 102: "the prominent senator had to be publicly visible in the Forum, in the Curia, and in the lawcourts but also – in other functions – in his representative house, which, as a physical and social space, provided an equally important stage for the permanent assertion of his status and influence."
9 On the prestige of receiving many visitors, see Cicero, who states: "the house of a distinguished man, in which numerous guests must be received, care must be taken to have it spacious" (Cic. *off.* 1.139). In a similar vein, Vitruvius (6.5.2) recommends that men of rank who, by reason of their offices and magistracies, had political and social obligations

to their fellow citizens, should maintain homes with "spacious atriums and peristyles ... appropriate to their dignity." Cf. Hales 2000: 44: "The house that was constantly invaded by outsiders was a statement of the owner's high standing .... It was just as important to know the house as the man, the two were inseparable." It was also a gesture of distinction to lend someone a *villa*. Cicero leaves the house of Cumae with satisfaction for Atticus' wife, Pilia, while he goes to Pompeii via Puteoli (Cic. *Att.* 14.15.3; cf. 14.16.1; 14.17.1; 14.19.6). On different occasions he writes to Atticus that he would like Brutus to stay for a while in his *villa* in Astura, while he is in Campania (Cic. *Att.* 14.15.3; 14.19.5; 15.3.2: Brutus eventually stayed at Cicero's house in Astura).

10 If there was a particularly noble or fancy quarter, it was surely the Palatine, on whose hill the houses of many distinguished families presided over the forum: while certainly not all the aristocracy lived on the Palatine, everyone who lived on the Palatine was an aristocrat (Shatzman 1975: 22–23). Proximity to public spaces was a sign of social prestige: "it is safe to assert that in Cicero's days at least fifty, if no more, families of the senatorial elite settled in the dense public space around the Forum, Comitium, and Capitol" (Beck 2009: 374).

11 D'Arms 1970: "Baiae was Rome's first resort."

12 D'Arms 1970; Shatzman 1975: 29–33, with his main conclusion: "most consulars, *nobiles* and patricians owned property in Latium and Campania." Nonetheless, it is necessary to remain cautious, because most information comes from Cicero, who speaks above all of those around him and who were of interest to him; furthermore, estates located in other regions of Italy attracted less attention. Cf. Lafon 2001. Strabo claims in relation to the concentration of *villae* in the Bay of Naples: "The whole is dotted by the cities we have described, by villas and cultivated fields so close together that to the eye they appear but one city" (Str. 5.4.8). See Annalisa Marzano's chapter in this volume (Chapter 9).

13 That is exactly the expression used by Cicero when in May 51 he proudly tells Atticus that there were so many people (of significance) in the area that his *villa* at Cumae was a kind of small Rome: *habuimus in Cumano quasi pusillam Romam. Tanta erat in his locis multitudo* (Cic. *Att.* 5.2.2). Cf. Wallace-Hadrill 1994: 5: "the villa was also a focus of hospitality," and "the social life of the city was in many ways transported to the countryside in the wake of the peregrinating rich."

14 As soon as Cicero arrived in Tusculum from Rome on 9 April 44, the masons working on his *villa* brought back from the *Urbs* a rumour, no doubt false, that all the grain was being stored in the house of Antonius (Cic. *Att.* 14.3.1).

15 Cic. *Att.* 15.1A.2. Cf. Plut. *Brut.* 18.10.

16 Cic. *Att.* 14.11.1 (letter of 21 April received perhaps in Puteoli).

17 Cic. *Att.* 14.17A.7 (letter of 3 May received in Pompeii).

18 Cic. *Att.* 14.20.2 and 4 (letter of 11 May received in Puteoli). In a later letter Cicero claims not to know the details of a speech made by L. Antonius, because nothing is written (Cic. *Att.* 15.2.2). If it is the same *contio*, it is not clear that the text of Antonius' *horribilis contio* reached Cicero.

19 Cic. *Att.* 14.20.5; 14.21.4; 15.2.3.

20 Cic. *Att.* 14.19.4.

21 Cic. *Att.* 14.20.4. Cf. *Att.* 16.7.1: while sailing back to Pompeii, in Rhegium Cicero reads the text of an edict issued in August by Cassius and Brutus.

22 Cic. *Att.* 15.11.4.

23 Hales 2003: 34: she makes a clear distinction between the *domus* in Rome as a place for public and socio-political obligations, and the rural *villa* as a place for luxury, leisure, and rest. The distinction is broadly acceptable, but there were also social obligations in the *villa* and there was also an active political life there.

24 On the *salutatio*, see Goldbeck 2010.

25 Goldbeck 2010: 88. Cicero sometimes speaks proudly of how beloved he is to the people of the place where he is, who come enthusiastically to talk to him,

particularly about the political situation (Cic. *Att.* 14.6.2). In a later letter to Dolabella, written in May from Pompeii, Cicero states that he receives many visits from his friends staying in nearby towns (Cic. *Att.* 14.17A.1).

26 Invitations to eat at someone's house were almost daily (D'Arms 1970: 59: "a proprietor seems rarely to have dined alone"). Cf. Stein-Hölkeskamp 2005: 221–223.

27 In a letter of May 45, Cicero summarises this practice: "If anyone asks why I am not in Rome, it is because it is a time of vacation. And why I am not in those of my little estates that are suitable for these dates: because it is difficult for me to bear such crowds" (Cic. *Att.* 12.40.3). Cf. Cic. *Fam.* 3.9.4; *Att.* 14.5.2.

28 Sometimes a stay in one's *villa* could be disturbed by excessive or annoying visits, as Cicero complains to Atticus in a letter sent from Formiae in April 59 (Cic. *Att.* 2.14.2).

29 Cic. *Att.* 14.1; 14.2. Cicero maintained his friendship with Calvena, with whom he had an epistolary exchange in October 44 (Cic. *Fam.* 11.27; 11.28).

30 Cic. *Att.* 14.7.1; 14.8.1. Cf. 14.6.1.

31 Cic. *Att.* 14.9.2.

32 Cicero makes this clear in the aforementioned letter to Dolabella from Pompeii, in which he tells Dolabella that he sees a lot of people every day, because many *optimi viri* come to the area (*in haec loca*) for health reasons (Cic. *Att.* 14.17A.1). In another letter he describes his *villae* in Cumae and Puteoli as adorable, but at the same time almost to be shunned because of the crowd of visitors (Cic. *Att.* 14.16.1).

33 Shatzman 1975: 344 and 437. Hirtius possibly had a house in Cumae, and Vibius Pansa in Cumae, Neapolis, and perhaps Pompeii. Cf. D'Arms 1970: 173 and 190.

34 Shatzman 1975: 330: Balbus had *villae* at Puteoli, Neapolis, and Cumae.

35 Cic. *Att.* 14.9.3.

36 Cicero calls them "the choir" of Baiae (Cic. *Att.* 14.8.1). In a letter from 46, Cicero shows his pride in maintaining a close relationship with these three Caesarians (*Caesaris familiares*) (*Fam.* 6.12.2). It becomes clear in various letters (*Fam.* 9.19.1; 9.17.1; 6.8.1) that Balbus (and also Oppius) is one of Cicero's main sources of information.

37 Cicero claims that he has been forced to give them lessons in rhetoric, so that they do not even leave him any time to rest by the sea (Cic. *Att.* 14.12.2). Cf. Cic. *Att.* 14.11.2; 14.19.2; *Fam.* 9.16.7 (year 46).

38 Cic. *Att.* 14.20.4. D'Arms 1970: 169: although Hirtius also owned a *villa* in the area, it seems clear that he spent some time as a guest at Balbus'.

39 Cicero shows great interest in Octavian's arrival in Italy (Cic. *Att.* 14.5.3; cf. 14.6.1).

40 Cic. *Att.* 14.10.3.

41 D'Arms 1970: 181–182; Shatzman 1975: 384.

42 Cic. *Att.* 14.11.2. Cicero's guest that day was P. Cornelius Lentulus Spinther, son of the consul in 57, who planned to leave the next day. Cicero does not report his conversation with Lentulus Spinther.

43 Cic. *Att.* 14.12.2. Cicero wrote this letter while eating at Vestorius' house.

44 Cic. *Att.* 14.13.6; 14.13A; 14.13B.

45 Cic. *Att.* 14.17.2; 14.17A.3. Cf. D'Arms 1970: 176.

46 Cic. *Att.* 14.20.2; 15.1.2.

47 D'Arms 1970: 189.

48 Cic. *Att.* 14.20.4.

49 Cic. *Att.* 14.20.1.

50 A factor in favour of this *villa* could have been its novelty, since he had inherited it from Cluvius in 45 (Cic. *Att.* 14.9.1).

51 D'Arms 1970: 54: "more than forty Romans, among them the most prominent political personalities of the Ciceronian age, can be shown to have owned villas or private houses along the Campanian coast."

52 Cic. *Att.* 16.14.1. Cf. D'Arms 1970: 190. Cicero says something similar about Lanuvium, where he really just passes by (Cic. *Att.* 14.4.1, 9 April).

53 Cic. *Att.* 14.21.2. Cicero had written this letter in Vestorius' house at dessert time (*secunda mensa apud Vestorium*).
54 Cic. *Att.* 14.21.4.
55 Cic. *Att.* 14.22.1.
56 Cic. *Att.* 15.1.3.
57 Cic. *Att.* 14.22.2.
58 Cicero tells Atticus that he has sent Tiro and many others so that Atticus can give each person letters individually, as things unfold; that way, Cicero would have detailed and up-to-date briefings on what was happening (Cic. *Att.* 15.8.1).
59 It should be noted that many senators, unlike Cicero, were certainly in Rome. In a letter written by Hirtius to Cicero it is clear that Hirtius had been in the city, but that, perhaps already on 2 June, he decided to leave for his estate in Tusculum (Cic. *Att.* 15.6.2). Perhaps Cicero was counting on meeting Balbus personally in Tusculum before the senatorial session on 1 June, but in a letter of 27 or 28 May Cicero tells Tiro that Balbus has suffered a stroke and that he cannot speak (Cic. *Fam.* 16.23.1–2).
60 Cic. *Att.* 15.11.1–2. Cf. 15.12.1. In the following days, during his stay in Astura, Cicero showed interest in meeting Brutus again, but it does not seem that this encounter took place (Cic. *Att.* 15.16A; 15.17.1).
61 Cic. *Att.* 15.12.2.
62 Cic. *Att.* 15.17.2.
63 Cic. *Att.* 15.14.2 (Tusculum); 15.27.2 (Arpinum).
64 Cic. *Att.* 15.25. Publius Silius visited him in Tusculum to discuss a legal issue, not a political one (Cic. *Fam.* 7.21; cf. *Att.* 15.23; 15.24).
65 Cic. *Att.* 15.27.3.
66 Cic. *Att.* 15.29.2; 16.5.2.
67 Cic. *Att.* 16.3.6.
68 Cic. *Att.* 16.7.1.
69 Cic. *Att.* 15.29.3: Cicero dines at his house with people from Formiae.
70 D'Arms 1970: 176; 178–179; Shatzman 1975: 380 n. 642.
71 Cic. *Att.* 16.1.1; 16.5.2–3; 16.4.1; 16.2.3.
72 Cic. *Att.* 16.5.3. Cf. D'Arms 1970: 179.
73 D'Arms 1970: 185.
74 Cic. *Att.* 16.4.1–2. Previous rumours about Sex. Pompeius in *Att.* 15.21.3.
75 Cic. *Att.* 16.3.6.
76 Cic. *Att.* 16.7.5.
77 See Rosillo-López 2022.

Appendix: People (in Addition to Atticus) with Whom We Know that Cicero Maintained Correspondence from His *villae* in April–July 44. Those who sent letters to Cicero are in Italics.

- *M. Antonius* (by 22 April, received in Puteoli): *Att.* 14.13.6. Cicero sent a copy to Atticus (*Att.* 14.13A).
- M. Antonius (26 April, sent from Puteoli): *Att.* 14.13B. Cicero sent a copy to Atticus.
- M. Iunius Brutus (3 May, sent from Pompeii): *Att.* 14.17.4. Cicero sent a copy to Atticus.
- C. Cassius Longinus (3 May, sent from Pompeii): *Att.* 14.17.4; *Fam.* 12.1. Cicero sent a copy to Atticus.

- P. Cornelius Dolabella (3 May, sent from Pompeii): *Att.* 14.17.4; *Fam.* 9.4. Cicero sent a copy to Atticus.
- *M. Antonius* (by 8 May, received in Pompeii): *Att.* 14.19.2.
- P. Cornelius Dolabella (by 8 May, sent from Pompeii): *Att.* 14.19.4.
- M. Iunius Brutus (by 11 May, sent from Puteoli): *Att.* 14.20.4.
- C. Cassius Longinus (by 11 May, sent from Puteoli): *Att.* 14.20.4.
- *P. Cornelius Dolabella* (11 May, received in Puteoli): *Att.* 14.21.1. It is a response to the letter from 3 May.
- *Q. Fufius Calenus* (24 May, received in Arpinum): *Att.* 15.4.1.
- M. Iunius Brutus (25 May, sent from Arpinum): *Att.* 15.4A. Cicero announces to Atticus his intention to write to Brutus.
- P. Cornelius Dolabella (25 May, brought from Arpinum by Tiro): *Att.* 15.4A.
- *L. Iulius Caesar* (by 25 May, received in Arpinum): *Att.* 15.4A.
- *M. Iunius Brutus* (25 May, received in Arpinum): *Att.* 15.5.1.
- *C. Cassius Longinus* (25 May, received in Arpinum): *Att.* 15.5.1. Cicero sent a copy to Atticus.
- *Oppius*? (25 May, received in Arpinum): *Att.* 15.5.2.
- *L. Cornelius Balbus* (25 May, received in Arpinum): *Att.* 15.5.2.
- *A. Hirtius* (25 May, received in Arpinum, sent from Tusculum): *Att.* 15.5.2.
- *M. Terentius Varro* (25 May, received in Arpinum): *Att.* 15.5.3. Varro includes a copy of a letter that someone sent to him, whose name has been erased.
- A. Pompeius Bithynicus (27–28 May, sent from Tusculum): *Att.* 6.17. Cf. *Fam.* 16.23.1.
- Tiro (27–28 May, sent from Tusculum): *Fam.* 16.23.1.
- *L. Cornelius Balbus* (before 31 May, two letters received in Tusculum): *Att.* 15.8.1. One of these letters could be the one mentioned by Cicero to Tiro (*Fam.* 16.23.1), in which Balbus told him he had had a stroke.
- *A. Hirtius* (31 May, received in Tusculum): *Att.* 15.8.1.
- M. Antonius (31 May, sent from Tusculum): *Att.* 15.8.1. Since access to Antonius was complicated, Cicero sent the letter to P. Volumnius Eutrapelus, who would get it to him.
- *Greceius* (31 May, received in Tusculum): *Att.* 15.8.2.
- *M. Iunius Brutus* (by 2 June, received in Tusculum): *Att.* 15.6.1.
- *C. Cassius Longinus* (by 2 June, received in Tusculum): *Att.* 15.6.1.
- A. Hirtius (before 2 June, sent from Tusculum): *Att.* 15.6.1.
- *A. Hirtius* (by 2 June, received in Tusculum): *Att.* 15.6.2. Cicero sent a copy to Atticus.
- *L. Cornelius Balbus* (2 June, received in Tusculum): *Att.* 15.6.4; 15.9.1.
- *M. Iunius Brutus* (by 5 June, received in Tusculum; Brutus was in Antium at the moment): *Att.* 15.10.1.
- P. Cornelius Dolabella (by 10 June, possibly sent from Astura (or Antium): *Att.* 15.12.1.
- *L. Antonius* (by 10 June, received in Astura or Antium): *Att.* 15.12.2.

- *Theophanes of Mytilene* (mid-June, received in Tusculum): *Att.* 15.19.1.
- *Statius* (Q. Cicero's freedman) (mid-June, received in Tusculum): *Att.* 15.19.2.
- C. Vibius Pansa (23–24 June, sent from Tusculum): *Att.* 15.23. Cicero promises to send his correspondence with Pansa to Atticus.
- M. Iunius Brutus (23–24 June, sent from Tusculum): *Att.* 15.23. The letter did not reach Brutus, who had already left according to Servilia (*Att.* 15.24).
- *P. Cornelius Dolabella* (16 June, received in Tusculum): *Att.* 15.14.1. Cicero sent a copy to Atticus.
- C. Trebatius Testa (second half of June, sent from Tusculum): *Fam.* 7.21.
- P. Cornelius Dolabella (before 28 June, sent from Tusculum): *Att.* 15.14.1–2. Cicero sent a copy to Atticus.
- *M. Iunius Brutus* (30 June, received in Anagnia on the road from Tusculum to Arpinum): *Att.* 15.26.1.
- M. Iunius Brutus (1 July, sent from Anagnia or already from Arpinum): *Att.* 15.26.1. Cicero sent a copy to Atticus (*Att.* 15.26.2; 15.28).
- C. Oppius (1 July, sent from Arpinum): *Fam.* 11.29.
- P. Sestius (2 July, sent from Arpinum): *Att.* 15.27.1.
- L. Plotius Plancus (4–5 July, sent from Arpinum): *Att.* 16.16.1. Cicero sent a copy to Atticus (*Att.* 16.16A).
- *M. Iunius Brutus* (6 July, received in Formiae): *Att.* 15.29.1. Cicero sent a copy to Atticus.
- L. Plotius Plancus (10–11 July, sent from Puteoli): *Att.* 16.16B (cf. 16.2.5).
- C. Oppius (10–11 July, sent from Puteoli): *Att.* 16.2.5.
- C. Ateius Capito (10–11 July, sent from Puteoli): *Att.* 16.16C.
- C. Cupiennius (10–11 July, sent from Puteoli): *Att.* 16.16D.
- L. Plotius Plancus (mid-July, sent from Pompeii): *Att.* 16.16E.
- C. Ateius Capito (mid-July, sent from Pompeii): *Att.* 16.16F.
- L. Cornelius Balbus (mid-July, sent from Pompeii): *Att.* 16.3.5.

References

Beck, H. (2009) From Poplicola to Augustus: Senatorial Houses in Roman Political Culture. *Phoenix* 63, 361–387.

D'Arms, J.H. (1970) *Romans on the Bay of Naples*. Cambridge: Cambridge University Press.

Goldbeck, F. (2010) *Salutationes. Die Morgenbegrüßungen in Rom in der Republik und der frühen Kaiserzeit*. Berlin: Akademie Verlag.

Hales, S. (2000) At Home with Cicero. *Greece & Rome* 47, 44–55.

Hales, S. (2003) *The Roman House and Social Identity*. Cambridge: Cambridge University Press.

Hölkeskamp, K.-J. (2004) Under Roman Roofs: Family, House, and Household. In: H. I. Flower, ed. *The Cambridge Companion to the Roman Republic*. Cambridge: Cambridge University Press, 101–126.

Lafon, X. (2001) *Villa maritima. Recherches sur les villas littorales de l'Italie romaine*. Rome: École française de Rome.

Marzano, A. (2007) *Roman Villas in Central Italy. A Social and Economic History*. Leiden-Boston: Brill.

Marzano, A. and Métraux, G.P. (eds.) (2018) *The Roman Villa in the Mediterranean Basin: Late Republic to Late Antiquity*. Cambridge: Cambridge University Press.

Pina Polo, F. (2016) Cupiditas Pecuniae: Wealth and Power in Cicero. In: H. Beck, M. Jehne and J. Serrati, eds. *Money and Power in the Roman Republic*. Brussels: Latomus, 165–177.

Rilinger, R. (1997) Domus und res publica. Die politisch-soziale Bedeutung der aristokratischen "Hauses" in der späten römischen Republik. *Historische Zeitschrift Beihefte* 23, *Zwischen "Haus" und "Staat." Antike Höfe im Vergleich*, 73–90.

Rosillo-López, C. (2022) *Political Conversations in Late Republican Rome*. Oxford: Oxford University Press.

Saller, R.P. (1984) Familia, domus, and the Roman Conception of the Family. *Phoenix* 38, 336–355.

Shatzman, I. (1975) *Senatorial Wealth and Roman Politics*. Brussels: Latomus.

Stein-Hölkeskamp, E. (2005) *Das römische Gastmahl. Eine Kulturgeschichte*. Munich: Beck.

Wallace-Hadrill, A. (1994) *Houses and Society in Pompeii and Herculaneum*. Princeton: Princeton University Press.

Wiseman, T.P. (1987) Conspicui postes tectaque digna deo: the Public Image of Aristocratic and Imperial Houses in the late Republic and early Empire. In: *L'Urbs: espace urbain et histoire (Ier siècle av. J.-C. - IIIe siècle ap. J.-C.). Actes du colloque international de Rome (8–12 mai 1985)*. Rome: École française de Rome, 393–413.

9 A Luxury Maritime Villa on the Sorrento Peninsula

When Real Estate Does Not Make Financial Sense

Annalisa Marzano

Abstract

Wealthy Romans owned a large portfolio of properties, encompassing commercial and residential real estate in both urban and non-urban settings. Ownership of several rural and maritime villas in different geographic locations was the norm for the moneyed elite, and such properties, as can be appreciated from the ancient texts, were continuously bought, sold, confiscated, and auctioned off.

The location of luxury villas was dictated primarily by either the desirability of the area (e.g. vicinity to Rome, as in the case of the maritime villas on the Laurentine coast south of Ostia; vicinity to the emperor, as in the case of the villas in Tibur; a beautiful landscape, thermal waters, and proximity to Neapolis and Puteoli, in the case of Baiae) or by the availability of natural resources that could be exploited. In this chapter, I examine the case of the luxury maritime villa of Positano, on the Amalfi side of the Sorrento Peninsula. The villa, whose existence has been known since the eighteenth century, but which has only recently been partially investigated, does not appear to conform to these criteria. It was a luxury residence built in a location that, however beautiful its natural landscape, was difficult and very challenging in antiquity: it had no relevant natural resources; it presented very little land, which could afford only limited agriculture; and it could be reached only by sea. However, someone decided to build a villa on this spot. What were the reasons? What motivated the owner to invest in the high-quality décor and in the shipping of building material from Rome to erect a residence that was entirely isolated? The archaeological identification of a late Republican phase in this building indicates that the answer cannot simply be that the villa developed *after* Tiberius retired to the island of Capri because someone desired geographic proximity to the emperor. In this chapter, I will discuss the Positano villa in the context of the real estate market along the Bay of Naples and Sorrento Peninsula, and offer some considerations on the possible reasons it came into existence.

***

Villas as Real Estate Investment

The Roman elite bought and sold properties relatively frequently, particularly villas.[1] For instance, we know that one villa in Tusculum changed owners five

DOI: 10.4324/9781003187806-12

times within 50 years, starting with the freedman Sotericius Marcius and ending with L. Cornelius Balbus.[2] The anecdotal information recorded in the written sources shows that the buying and selling of villas could sometime bring considerable financial rewards. Sulla's daughter Cornelia had purchased Marius' villa at Misenum for only 300,000 sesterces and later sold it on to L. Licinius Lucullus for 10 million sesterces.[3] This property changed owners four times in less than 25 years.[4] Although the low purchase price was likely the result of the proscriptions of 82–81 BC, Cornelia must also have enhanced the property to be able to later sell it for the staggering amount of 10 million.

Improvements could indeed greatly increase the value of villas; these improvements could range from substantial new buildings and renovations, to furnishing the villas with works of art. The needs of villa owners in terms of statuary required to decorate their properties must have been considerable. The aristocratic but impoverished Damasippus, mentioned in some of Cicero's letters, seems to have become a dealer in ancient statues, catering to the elite's needs in furnishing their villas and town houses.[5] Later, at the time of Pliny the Younger, we learn of Domitius Tullus, who left to his wife *amoenissimas villas* and had numerous ancient works of art (original pieces, not copies) in his storehouses, ready to be used for furnishing newly bought properties.[6] Acquired in advance as a result of wholesale purchases, auctions, or appointments held in the provinces, Domitius Tullus' supply of extra works of art indicates the frequency with which he bought (and sold) properties and the necessity of being able to furnish the villas appropriately and quickly. A workshop that produced statuary for the luxury villas in the area of Baiae must have existed there, as can be inferred from the discovery of plaster casts of Greek statues, intended for the manufacture in series of bronze statuary.[7]

The Bay of Naples and the agricultural fertility of Campania had attracted the interests of Rome from quite early in the Republican period. Many senators and other prominent Romans had financial interests in the region and owned a variety of properties there: land, farms, and luxury villas. Luxury maritime villas were a characterising feature of the whole Bay and its islands. In an oft-quoted passage, Strabo described the shores of the Bay of Naples as being dotted with "villas and cultivated fields so close to each other to appear as one continuous city."[8] The earliest luxury maritime villas in this region were built in the northern part of the Bay of Naples, clustering particularly in the area of Baiae, Misenum, Posilipum, and Bacoli.[9] These spots had become popular with elite Romans since the mid-Republic. We are told, for instance, that Cornelia, the mother of the Gracchi, owned a villa at Misenum and that she had retired there after the murder of her son Gaius in 121 BC.[10] By the late Republic, the most prominent members of Rome's political aristocracy – Marius, Sulla, Licinius Lucullus, Pompey, Caesar, and so on – had properties in this area.[11]

Baiae stood out as the most famous location of the Bay of Naples, sought after for its mild climate, thermal waters, and beautiful landscape.[12] Baiae became the epitome of luxury and pleasures, as embodied by the degustation of the quality wines and gourmet food produced locally, such as the famous oysters farmed in the Lucrine Lake. In the imperial period, "living on Lucrine oysters and drinking Falernian wine" was still proverbial for having lived a good life.[13] In short, Baiae was synonymous with life pleasures and relaxation of morals.[14] One may recall Propertius' jealousy and his poetic exhortation to the beloved Cynthia, who was enjoying a retreat in Baiae, to leave that corrupt town as quickly as possible (*corruptas desere Baias*).[15]

Considering the attraction of the area for wealthy Romans, it is no surprise that a healthy real estate market for luxury villas developed in the region already in the Republican period. C. Sergius Orata, possibly an *eques* from Campania or a member of the Roman elite, according to a more recent hypothesis,[16] was the individual credited with starting a successful oyster-farming business in the Lucrine Lake to satisfy the demand of wealthy villa owners for high-quality fresh food.[17] He is also said to have invested in real estate in Baiae, acting with considerable business acumen. He would have bought and sold villas along the Lucrine's shores, after improving and refurbishing them to higher standards. It seems that Sergius Orata enhanced such properties by the addition of bath suites. On the basis of ancient sources declaring him the inventor of *pensiles balineae* or "hanging baths," he is thought to have been the "inventor" of the hypocaust system used to heat up Roman baths – the baths would have been defined as "hanging" because with the hypocaust system the floor of the hot rooms rests on *suspensurae*.[18] In other words, Orata built villas equipped with the latest conveniences in order to sell them at a profit.

Many years later, during the reign of emperor Claudius, the imperial freedman Posides is mentioned in the literary sources for his investments in real estate around the Bay of Naples. Posides too is remembered for his intensive building activity in the area of Baiae. He built there the Aquae Posidianae, a bath complex, and villas that were so luxurious to even surpass the opulence of the imperial palace on the Capitoline in Rome.[19] It is assumed that all this building activity was for profit, and part of the financial strategies pursued by Posides.

The maritime villas of this part of the Bay of Naples were indeed grand and luxurious, responding to the demands of a wealthy clientele engaged in competitive display with one another. The grandeur and architectural excesses of these luxury villas are alluded to by Strabo when he equates them to royal palaces.[20] An earlier passage in Strabo's account clearly reveals the remarkable terms of refence he had in mind in the case of the villas of the Roman elite: the Persian royal palaces, a paramount example of luxury.[21]

However, for some people, investment in luxury residential real estate in the fashionable region of the *crater delicatus* was simply a means to increase social standing and prestige. Cicero, who owned properties at Pompeii, Puteoli, and Cumae, wrote, in reference to his Cuman villa, that the property gave him greater *dignitas*.[22] He also famously observed that the number of notable individuals from Rome who owned properties in Cumae was so high that an apt name for this town was "little Rome" (*pusilla Roma*).[23] Elegant architecture and scenic settings were important features for a luxury villa, but equally important were the social contacts that one would continue to entertain and develop while in residence at the villa. In other words, completely isolated villas, far from other villas and nucleated settlements, were not that attractive. It is worth remembering that luxury Roman villas known on small islands such as Pandateria (Ventotene, in the Pontine archipelago) were in the early imperial period used as places of confinement for disgraced members of the imperial family.[24] The *relegatio ad insulam*, by completely curtailing the social interactions, freedom of movement, and assertion of one's status in society typical of a "normal" villa retreat, negated the very essence of villa life.

'A Lofty Villa Looking Out upon the Dicarchean Deep': Luxury Villas on the Sorrento Peninsula[25]

In antiquity, as today, the Bay of Naples had a high population density. It is therefore natural that, over time, considering the high demand for securing a prime stretch of coastline on which to site a luxury villa with panoramic views, impressive maritime villas should appear also outside of the immediate area of Baiae and Misenum.[26] From the second half of the first century BC onwards, maritime villas were being built also on the other side of the Bay of Naples, in Stabiae (modern Castellammare di Stabia) and on the north shore of the Sorrento Peninsula.[27] An important watershed moment for the spread of luxury maritime villas along the south-eastern coast of the Bay of Naples was the siege and destruction of Stabiae carried out by Sulla in 89 BC, during the Social War, which seems to have resulted in the *ager Stabianus* being assigned, at the conclusion of the war, to Nuceria.[28] Several magnificent villas were built on the Varano plateau, which today overlooks the dense urban agglomeration of Castellammare di Stabia. Most of the building phases identified in the villas of Stabiae date to after 31 BC.[29] These huge villas, measuring up to 22,000 m^2, are among the largest maritime villas known and stood at short distance from each other and from the *pagus* of Stabiae. Imperial freedmen are attested in two of the Stabian villas,[30] including the powerful and notorious *ab epistulis* of Claudius, the freedman Narcissus. Scholars have interpreted this evidence as either indicating that these properties were *praedia* owned by the imperial *fiscus* or that Narcissus himself was the proprietor.[31] In the imperial period Stabiae seems to have been a *statio* of the fleet based at Misenum, something that, according to Esposito, further corroborates the presence of imperially owned *praedia* in Stabiae.[32]

On the Sorrento Peninsula proper, several maritime villas are known. From Marina di Equa to Punta della Campanella, which was the ancient Athenaeum Promontory, 17 villas are known; only two are located inland rather than on the coast and can thus be classed as "rural."[33] Occasional references in the literary sources reveal the name of the owners of luxury maritime villas in Surrentum. We have Statius' famous poem, *Silvae* 2.2, which sings of the villa of Pollius Felix, praising its owner and the way in which he has tamed the landscape to create his luxury villa. Pollius' villa is possibly to be identified with the remains at the "Bagni della Regina Giovanna" locality, on the Capo di Sorrento.[34]

Augustus himself owned villas and rural estates in Surrentum, where he relegated his grandson Agrippa Postumus between AD 5 and 7, and several funerary inscriptions attesting imperial slaves and freedmen are known from this area.[35] Necropoleis for imperial servile personnel identified on the Sorrento Peninsula at Fuorimura Chiommenzano, S. Cesareo, and Marano Borgo suggest that the agricultural properties belonging to the emperor were located in the south-eastern part of the peninsula and that the *fundi* were sizeable. The fact that luxury maritime villas along the shoreline of the peninsula were complemented by agricultural *fundi* belonging to the same elite proprietors, including the emperor, reminds us that even in the case of the most luxurious maritime villas of the Bay of Naples these properties were not completely removed from the sphere of production. As already pointed out by John D'Arms, the owners of maritime villas along the Bay of Naples also owned productive agricultural properties inland, making the dichotomy between unproductive maritime villas and productive *villae rusticae* presented in ancient texts and some modern scholarship apparent rather than real.[36] Not only were luxury villas and agricultural estates part of the same real estate portfolio; maritime villas themselves could also be the seat of various types of production activities, such as wine production, fish farming, quarrying, etc.[37]

By the early first century AD at the very latest, villas appeared also on the other side of the Sorrento Peninsula, on the Amalfi Coast. There were various villas in different parts of the Amalfi Coast, but with few exceptions they are only very partially known, and their status of preservation is in most cases poor. Maritime villas were present on the small island of Gallo Lungo, on the Isca islet, at Positano, Amalfi, and Minori, whereas just opposite the Isca islet, at the small fiord of Crapolla, five impressive Roman cisterns and storerooms are known (Figure 9.1).[38] It is *communis opinio* that, as far as maritime villas are concerned, considerable impetus in real estate development on the Sorrento Peninsula was triggered by Tiberius' decision to leave Rome and "retire" on the island of Capri. Individuals who wanted, or needed, to be close to the emperor but who were unable to own a property on Capri – the entire island had become imperial property with Augustus in 29 BC – would have sought out, and invested in, properties on the nearby Sorrento coast instead. Villa Jovis, which is believed to have been Tiberius' main residence on Capri, is located on the north-eastern tip of the island, just opposite the tip of the Surrentum Peninsula, which is almost 5 km away, 3 Roman miles as stated by Tacitus.[39]

As far as the villas on the Amalfi side are concerned, many years ago John D'Arms had suggested that these started to appear only from about the age of Claudius, because by then all the viable spots on the coastline of the Sorrento side had been already built up and were occupied by luxury villas. This idea largely rested on the evidence provided by a handful of inscriptions discovered on the Amalfi Coast attesting imperial freedmen of the reign of Claudius and on the idea that developments in villa real estate in that general area had started with Tiberius, affecting Sorrento first and then, later on, in a sort of rippling

Figure 9.1 The Sorrento Peninsula and the main sites mentioned in the text (M.D. Öz).

effect, also the portion of the Peninsula further afield. However, it has been shown that many of the inscriptions in question do not, in fact, originate from the Amalfi Coast: they were moved in the post-antique era from Rome and Puteoli, as part of the general trade in ready-made building material and/or as ballast taken on by ships.[40] Furthermore, as discussed below, the archaeological evidence suggests that some of the maritime villas of the Amalfi Coast were built at the end of the first century BC/very beginning of the first century AD, so earlier than Claudius' reign and at about the same time when some of the villas on the Sorrento side of the Peninsula were being developed.

Positano and Its Roman Villa

The Roman villa in Positano has been the object of recent, modern archaeological investigations.[41] Its presence, or rather the presence of Roman structures in the general area occupied by the S. Maria Assunta Church and the church's bell tower, was known since the seventeenth century. In the late 1600s, excavations had been carried out to recover and sell coloured marble and architectural elements, to be reused in building projects of the time, for example at the convent of St. Teresa in Naples. In 1758, during works to consolidate the foundation of the bell tower, ancient remains were discovered, and Karl Weber, who was the royal engineer of the Bourbon monarch and who at the time was directing excavations at Pompeii, Herculaneum, and Stabia, was promptly informed of the discovery.[42] Weber conducted excavations in Positano for five days in April 1758, finding remains of wall paintings, a white-tesserae mosaic floor, two brick columns covered with red plaster, water channels, a large peristyle with columns plastered in white, and a rectangular garden measuring c. 52 m on the long side.[43] However, despite these discoveries, Weber concluded that it was not worth continuing the investigations and returned to his much more challenging and exciting endeavour of excavating the Vesuvian cities buried by Vesuvius. This villa too was destroyed by the eruption despite the Monti Lattari range separating it from Vesuvius; the recent archaeological investigations have clarified how the volcanic event of AD 79 affected this side of the Sorrento Peninsula (Figure 9.2).[44] It does not seem that Weber had identified the remains he excavated as belonging to a luxury villa, but rather he wrote in his report of a "templo antiguo," an ancient temple. Part of the large peristyle identified by Weber was rediscovered in the 1920s when excavating to create a storage area at the back of a butcher's shop, and more remains came to light after the serious flood of 1954.[45] By now, Amedeo Maiuri had correctly identified the ancient building as a luxury maritime villa.

Although just a very small portion of the original villa is known, it is clear that this was a sizeable luxury villa, with high standards in its décor: the wall

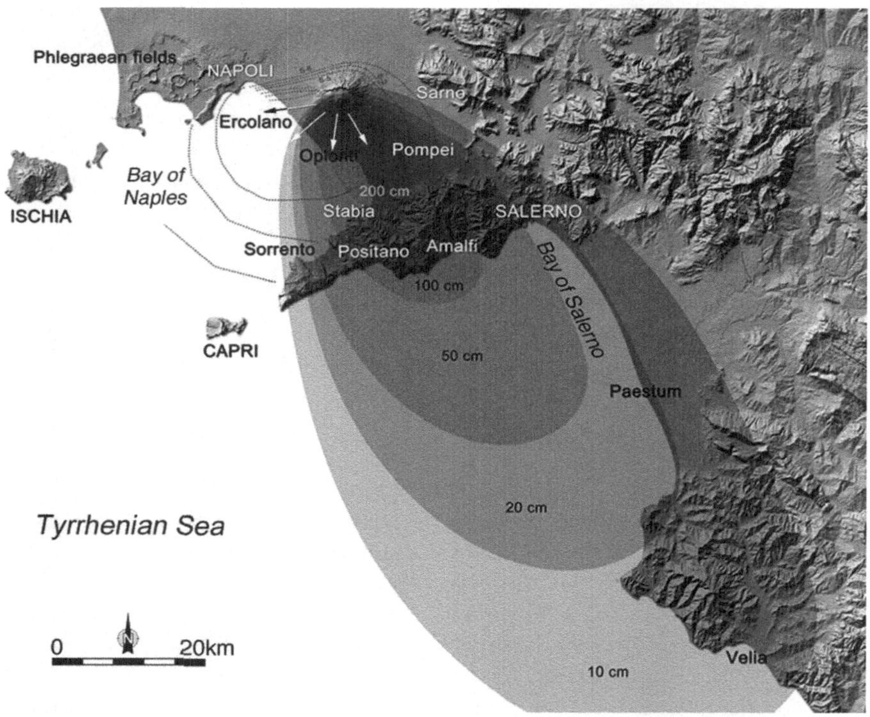

Figure 9.2 The area affected by the eruption of 79 CE – pumice-fall thickness distribution in greyscale; the arrows and associated lines indicate direction and extension of pyroclastic flows (G. Di Maio, GEOMED, courtesy of G. Di Maio).

paintings recently discovered are of high quality, employ rarer pigments, such as blue and a particular type of green, and have key details of the composition rendered in stucco. This "mixed" technique, well attested in bath complexes, is rarer in domestic contexts.[46] The earlier fortuitous discoveries of structures pertaining to the villa indicate that the villa featured a large peristyle garden and that its structures must have occupied much of today's sea front of Positano in the area of the main church of S. Maria Assunta.[47] In terms of the building materials employed in this building, if it was possible to locally produce the lime to be used in the concrete mixture due to the abundant presence of limestone, which characterises the geology of this side of the Sorrento Peninsula, other materials such as the tufa *cubilia* for the *opus reticulatum* walls and the roof tiles had to be transported by sea from elsewhere. Tufa is present on the Sorrento side of the Peninsula and in Naples, areas which have a very different geology from that of the Amalfi Coast; the *cubilia* employed in the *opus reticulatum* walls of the Positano villa were of yellow tufa from the region of the Flegrean Fields.[48] However, it seems that the roof tiles came from much further away, from *figlinae* operating in the area of Rome, and this suggests a wealthy owner from Rome.[49]

We know that the Romans appreciated beautiful natural vistas and panoramas for their villas, and the mild climate of Campania was an additional attraction to own residential properties in the region and visit them regularly. The spot where the Positano villa was built is certainly beautiful – consider the modern fame of the town as the "pearl of the divine Amalfi Coast" – but beautiful landscape was certainly not the only element that was taken into consideration when deciding where to build a luxury maritime villa. How fashionable a location was, ease of access, proximity to secondary urban centres, and natural resources present in the vicinity were very important too. For instance, the maritime villa of Tor Caldara, near Antium, was clearly built in that location because of the presence of important sulphur deposits, which were commercially exploited on the villa estate; connection by land routes in addition to sea and the villa's proximity to Antium completed the attraction and viability of that specific location.[50] Very often, as mentioned above in the case of Baiae or Surrentum, maritime villas clustered along a stretch of coastline, with the nearby properties offering opportunities for social interactions and the towns/villages providing various services, from markets at which to buy supplies to public baths if it was not feasible to get the heating system of one's villa baths going, as observed by Pliny the Younger in reference to his Laurentine villa.[51] But if we consider the Positano villa from these points of view, its existence defies logic.

In antiquity, the area where Positano now stands could be reached *only* by sea and the closest town was Surrentum, about 15.7 nautical miles away,[52] on the other side of the Peninsula. Today, reaching Sorrento by sea takes nearly one hour by fast ferry, several hours if going by small-sized boat with an average overboard engine. The location where the Positano luxury villa stood had no notable natural resources to offer, nor, then as now, was there any sizeable amount of land that could be cultivated, so agricultural exploitation was clearly not among the reasons to have a villa in that location. Indeed, the steep cliffs typical of the local topography have prompted considerable human ingenuity over the centuries to allow for a small settlement to develop. The modern town is known as the "vertical" town, and its houses are built on a series of artificial terraces, closely clustered together. Any agricultural activity consists of vegetable patches and very small vineyards and orchards, the areas for these created with efforts by erecting retaining walls and bringing in additional soil as necessary. I am not suggesting that absolutely no agricultural cultivation took place in the proximity of the Positano villa in antiquity. Indeed, the recent excavations of the villa have brought to light some agricultural tools: a hoe and a spade to tend to horticultural cultivations or to the villa's garden.[53] But it is highly unlikely that any agricultural production here was sizeable enough to lead to any surplus for the market. Therefore, while we can posit with a degree of confidence the local cultivation of vegetables, some fruit trees, probably vines and, maybe, as in modern times, the rearing of chickens and pigs destined for consumption, agricultural productivity was certainly not the reason a villa was built there.

Having excluded agriculture and convenience of location as reasons for erecting a villa in this beautiful but remote spot, one may wonder whether the resources of the sea might have offered substantial reasons to have a property here that would combine the "*luxus*" of refined *otium* with some other form of "*fructus*." This possibility too can be, in my view, firmly excluded for this villa. The area does not offer any particularly bountiful fisheries, barely supporting a small fishing community in more recent historical times. Any systematic and sizeable exploitation of marine resources, whether fishing or fish salting, can thus be discounted. Substantial marine fish farming, which I have in the past argued could be a form of investment for maritime villa owners aiming at producing and commercialising fresh fish, should be discounted too in this case, since commercial fish farming required proximity to *sizeable* urban markets to be viable. The only favourable element that the Positano villa site had in antiquity was the presence of freshwater. So, the question remains, why would someone build a villa here?

In my view, we can disregard the idea that someone who wanted to have a villa in the general area where Tiberius was spending his ruling years, but who could not get a property closer to Capri, chose the bay of Positano instead: the chance discoveries related to the villa structures made in Positano in the 1920s revealed walls built in *opus incertum* together with *opus reticulatum*, a mixed building technique generally dated to the late first century BC.[54] To these we can add the results of the recent archaeological investigations of the villa, which also suggest that the villa already existed in the Augustan period. These archaeological data also allow us to discount the hypothesis, suggested many years ago by Matteo Della Corte on the basis of the toponym Positano, that the villa was built by Posides,[55] the notorious and powerful freedmen of emperor Claudius who, as I mentioned above, was a real estate speculator in the Baiae area. Posides may have, at a certain point, ended up owning the Positano villa, but he certainly did not build it: the villa existed already.

All in all, the more one considers the specific case of this villa and thinks of other examples of luxury maritime villas known on the Tyrrhenian coast of Italy, the more the Roman villa of Positano appears somewhat puzzling. Bearing in mind its location and almost complete lack of connections via land routes in antiquity,[56] the Roman villa of Positano needs to be examined together with the other Roman villas and structures known on the Amalfi side of the peninsula, particularly those someone sailing from the Bay of Naples to the Amalfi Coast would encounter in the stretch of coastline from Punta della Campanella to Positano. As mentioned, there were maritime villas on the islet of Isca and on the small Gallo Lungo Island and large waters cisterns at the Crapolla Fiord (Figure 9.1, nos 2–4). A Roman cistern is also known on the islet known as Vetara or Vivaro (Figure 9.1, no. 5). The hypothesis that I wish to put forward is that as early as Augustus it was the imperial presence and direct ownership of both land and villas in the general area of the Sorrento Peninsula, including the island of Capri (ancient Capreae), that led to the development of luxury villas in these more remote but very scenic locations of the Amalfi Coast. As mentioned above, in 29 BC Capri had become imperial property. Augustus, who still went under the name of Octavian at this time, had visited Capreae on his way back to Rome after the battle of Actium. A favourable prodigy he witnessed when on the island prompted him to ask the city of Neapolis to give him Capreae in exchange for the larger island of Aenaria (mod. Ischia).[57] Augustus spent leisure retreats on Capreae, immersing himself in the local Greek culture, and the presence of trusted friends at other villas on Capreae or nearby islets can be inferred by a comment in Suetonius: Augustus would have named a small island near Capreae "Apragopolis" or "the city of Do-nothings" "from the laziness of some of his company who sojourned there."[58] Which island this might have been is unclear, since there is no island today close enough to Capri to be visible from Augustus' villa there, as Suetonius suggests a few lines later.[59]

In the case of Surrentum, certainly a number of individuals found an incentive to invest in properties there because Augustus and later Tiberius regularly visited the imperial properties of Capreae and Surrentum. However, the idea that those who could not get properties around Surrentum started to build on the other side of the Peninsula in their goal of being close to the emperor does not seem a plausible explanation for the villas that once elegantly stood on the small Gallo Lungo and Isca islands and by the shore at Positano; as noted above, their isolation seems to me to speak against this. A more likely scenario is to think that the first nucleus of the Positano villa was built as a seasonal, subsidiary property for someone who *already* owned a main villa in the Bay of Naples area. Similar considerations apply to the villas on Isca and Gallo Lungo. If the dating of the nucleus of the Positano villa to the Augustan era is correct, it might even be possible to think of Augustus himself, or someone in the entourage of friends close to the emperor, that Suetonius says was at Capreae and its surroundings. Once we reach the reign of Tiberius, the Positano villa and those on Isca and Gallo Lungo[60] must be evaluated together, keeping in mind the emperor's long-term presence on Capreae and the added security put in place in monitoring navigation around the island and in front of the Punta della Campanella to ensure that no one landed on Capreae without imperial authorisation. Visitors wishing to be received by Tiberius presumably had to follow the same procedure adopted by Agrippa I, the son of Aristobulus, when he arrived in Puteoli: sending first a letter to Tiberius to request permission to land on Capreae, then making the sea journey once authorisation was granted.[61] A lighthouse was on the Punta della Campanella, next to the temple of Minerva.[62] This was the end point of the via Minerva coming from Nuceria.[63] Remains of five terraces with retaining walls once belonging to a large building next to the temple and lighthouse have been referred to in the past as either a villa or as housing for soldiers stationed there when Tiberius retired on Capreae.[64] Indeed the lighthouse served not only as a navigational aid but also to exchange visual signals with the lighthouse and signalling tower that stood near Villa Jovis. A similar visual communication system was in all likelihood in place between Capreae and Misenum, where the imperial fleet was.[65] Any scout stationed on Punta della Campanella would have been able to see if a vessel was sailing towards Capreae or in between the stretch of sea framed by Capreae and Punta della Campanella; this is the standard route someone sailing from the Bay of Naples to the Amalfi side of the Sorrento Peninsula (or vice versa) would follow.

Therefore, I believe that for the time of Tiberius the villas of Isca, Gallo Lungo, and Positano and the cisterns at Crapolla and Vivaro need to be considered as part of the same property portfolio which, in all likelihood, belonged to the emperor. The available archaeological data support the possibility of major building phases dated to the Tiberian age. The villa on the Gallo Lungo is very little known, but walls in *opus reticulatum* with corner tufa blocks suggest a dating before the age of Nero.[66] The remains recorded on Isca seem to date to the early Julio-Claudian era,[67] while, as we have seen, structures of the Positano villa date to this period as well. The two villas on the small islands of Gallo Lungo and Isca were without doubt properties occupied only during the good season and not all year round.[68] The islands are little more than rocks in the sea, have no source of freshwater except for what is provided by the rain, and in winter, when the sea is stormy, they can be cut off from the mainland for days. These little islands do not have proper harbours, but only landing points equipped with simple quays and rock-cut steps, so landing there in the case of bad weather and rough sea is not possible, even dangerous, because of the risk the ship would be pushed by the waves against the rocks. Even for short seasonal sojourns during spring/summer, food supplies, water, and anything else that was needed for the refined villa stays of the Roman rich had to be brought in regularly, relying either on a network of redistribution of goods produced and acquired at other properties of the same owner or on purchases at urban markets of the Bay of Naples. Either way, a good level of logistical organisation and regular shipments by sea were needed. The fate of Agrippina the Elder, who may have died of starvation while in exile on Pandateria, is a reminder that a small island could easily be cut off from supplies if someone in power placed strict controls on navigation around it.[69] The fact that the islet of Isca is quite close to the mainland should not be taken as an indication that supplies could easily arrive from there and just be ferried across to the island: the narrow Crapolla Fiord is the only spot where even a small boat could land, as the coastline there features very high rocky cliffs. From the fiord where the Roman remains are, today nearly 700 limestone steps and a long beaten-earth path lead up to the small village of Torca on top of the cliffs' ridge.

Therefore, the hypothesis that these three villas became satellite properties for the use of Tiberius during the years he spent on Capreae should be seriously considered. Tiberius' stay there was not just a seasonal visit to the Bay of Naples like those that the Roman elite had been regularly making since the Republic. Tiberius ended up staying in Capri for many years, from AD 26 to his death in 37, but he was not always on the island.[70] While the emperor never set foot in Rome again, he often left the island to travel to the mainland to stay at various imperial villas, both on the Bay of Naples and closer to Rome.[71] Various trips and stays at Surrentum, Misenum, Antium, Tusculum, and other locations on the mainland can be reconstructed from the available sources, and it was at the imperial villa at Misenum that the emperor died in AD 37.[72] The villas of Isca, Gallo Lungo, and Positano could offer Tiberius a change in scenery and surroundings to break the monotony of his stay on Capreae, while still offering to the emperor total seclusion and a high level of security, which had been for Tiberius important factors in choosing Capreae as his seat.[73] These villas were completely removed from other villas or towns and access to them could be easily controlled: two of the villas stood on tiny islands, making anyone approaching them immediately spottable, while the Positano villa could be reached only by sea or via a long and challenging trek over the mountains. The local topography meant that landing in proximity of the villa was possible only right in front of it. In other words, it is hard to imagine that anyone could have arrived at these properties without the occupiers having ample warnings of someone approaching.

Conclusion

Tiberius had several villas built on Caprae: Tacitus writes that Tiberius had 12 distinctively named villas on the island.[74] On the basis of the mention of a Villa Jovis in Suetonius' biography of Tiberius,[75] it is generally understood that the villas had been named after the 12 Olympian gods. Only four Roman villas have been identified on Capri (Villa Jovis, Damecuta, Gradola, and Palazzo a Mare), in addition to nymphaea attached to them, such as the one of the Grotta Azzurra.[76] The remains of Villa Jovis, with its daring multi-level substructures, are the most impressive of these imperial villas and thought to have been Tiberius' main residence. But what if the 12 villas in question were actually on Capreae *and* also in other isolated locations nearby? Tacitus, in fact, does not unequivocally say that the 12 villas he alludes to were built on

Capreae. After a sentence in which he names the Greek inhabitants of Caprae (*Graecos ea* [i.e. Campania] *tenuisse Capreasque Telebois habitatas fama tradit*), Tacitus simply writes: *Sed tum Tiberius duodecim villarum nominibus et molibus insederat quanto intentus olim publicas ad curas, tanto occultiores in luxus et malum otium resolutus*. This is translated in the Loeb edition as:

> At this time, however, the islet was occupied by the imposing fabric of the twelve villas – with their twelve names – of Tiberius; who, once absorbed in the cares of state, was now unbending with equal zest in hidden vice and flagitious leisure.

It is possible that Tiberius could "have occupied" 12 villas located also in the general, and unpopulated, surroundings of Capreae.[77] The distance between Capri and Positano is c. 11.3 nautical miles. If we assume an average navigational speed of 3 knots, this distance could be covered in less than four hours.[78] However, wind conditions on the Amalfi side of the Sorrento Peninsula are not favourable. The high coastline and mountains, which in the Positano area rise up to more than 1,400 m, means that the wind closer to the coastline is highly irregular, with gusts constantly changing direction. The sailing may have taken longer or required propulsion by oars. In modern times, in favourable conditions, it would take four and a half hours to reach Capri from Positano, sailing by a traditional *gozzo* with lateen sail.[79]

If we accept the possibility that the Positano villa had been part of the emperor's portfolio of residences around Surrentum and Capri, Augustus first, Tiberius later, then its opulence and remote, difficult location, in a landscape void of any significant natural resources and opportunities for production, makes perfect sense. A secondary villa that could be reached by sailing from Capri in half a day, maybe stopping on the way at the villa on the Isca little island first and then on Gallo Lungo to spend a few days in a beautiful natural landscape, is certainly not illogical for Tiberius. The villas were still away from the "crowds" that, according to Tacitus, had pushed Tiberius to leave mainland Campania and retire on the island.[80] However, these properties allowed the emperor to leave Capri and enjoy different views and settings. Such a hypothesis seems to offer a better explanation for the nature of the villas of Positano and of the two small islands I have been discussing than thinking of some wealthy individual wanting to be in close proximity to Tiberius and his entourage.

Notes

1 Rawson 1976 for a study of the Roman aristocracy and the real estate market in the late Republic; Frederiksen 1981: 280–287; Lafon 2001: 181–184.
2 The other attested owners were L. Crassus, Vennonius Vindicius and Q. Metellus; see Valenti 2003: 59.
3 Plut. *Mar.* 34.2.
4 Lafon 2001: 182.

5 Cic. *Fam.* 7.23; *Att.* 12.29, 33 and also Zevi 2004: 23.
6 Plin. *Ep.* 8.18.11.
7 Landwehr 1985.
8 Strabo, 5.4.8.
9 For the architecture of luxury maritime villas of the Bay of Naples see Zarmakoupi 2014. For Roman villa owners along the Bay of Naples. D'Arms' 1970 book, re-published in 2003 (see D'Arms 2003a), remains the fundamental study for the prosopography of villa owners on the Bay of Naples.
10 Plut. *C. Gracch.* 19.1–2.
11 Val. Max. 4.4.1; Plut. *Mar.* 34.2, Sen., *Ep.* 51.11; Cic. *Att.* 4.10.2; 11.6.6; Tac. *Ann.* 14.9.3. Varro, *Rust.* 3.17.9.
12 According to Strabo (5.4.5), Baiae's waters were suited for both "luxury and the healing of diseases"; see also Celsus, *Med.* 2.17 on the benefits of natural saunas. Lafon 2001: 192–193 for the connection between thermalism and villas.
13 E.g. see the epitaph *CIL* 14.914, dated to the second century AD.
14 See for example, the comments in Strabo 5.6; Plin. *HN* 9.169.
15 Prop. 1.11.27; on Baiae's reputation, see D'Arms 2003a: 52–54.
16 Bannon 2014.
17 For oyster farming in the Lucrine see Marzano 2013: 173–189 and 2016.
18 Plin. *HN* 9.168: *ostrearum vivaria primus omnium Sergius Orata invenit in Baiano aetate L. Crassi oratoris, ante Marsicum bellum, nec gulae causa sed avaritiae, magna vectigalia tali ex ingenio suo percipiens, ut qui primus pensiles invenerit balineas, ita mangonicatas villas subinde vendendo.* ("Sergius Orata was the first to create oyster farms in Baiae at the time of the orator L. Crassus, before the Marsian war, not because of his gluttony but because of greed. He derived much revenue from his ingenuity, as he was the first inventor of hanging baths: he used to fit out villas in this way and then sell them."); see also Val. Max. 9.1.1; Macrob. *Sat.* 3.15.2–3; Cic. *Hort.*, cited in Non. 194M (285L s.v. "balneae") and referenced in Fagan 1996: 65. It mentions *balneola: primus balneola suspendit; inclusit pisces.* The expression *pensiles balinae* is thought to refer to baths with hypocaust, but the references in the sources are all very vague and the nature of Orata's invention is not completely clear. See Fagan 1996 for the hypothesis that *pensiles balinae* might have referred to fish-farming activity rather than baths. See also *CIL* 6.29830 for the epigraphic attestation of *aquae pensiles* in a list of various public buildings, including a bath complex.
19 Plin. *HN* 31.2; Juv. *Sat.* 14.91.
20 Strabo 5.7: συνῳκοδομημένων βασιλείων ἄλλων ἐπ'ἄλλοις ("where royal palaces have been built, one next to the other").
21 Strabo 5.2.5: νῦν δὲ τὸ πλέον εἰς τὰς οἰκοδομὰς ἀναλίσκεται τὰς ἐν Ῥώμῃ, κἀν ταῖς ἐπαύλεσι, βασίλεια κατασκευαζομένων Περσικά ("but at the present time most of it is being used up on the buildings at Rome, and also at the villas, now that people are devising palaces of Persian magnificence").
22 Cic. *Att.* 1.13.
23 Cic. *Att.* 5.2.2.
24 E.g. Suet. *Aug.* 65; Tac. *Ann.*1.53.
25 The verse is from Stat. *Silv.* 2.2.3 (*celsa Dicarchei speculatrix villa profundi*), the poem celebrating Pollius Felix's maritime villa near Surrentum.
26 Johannowsky 1986a.
27 Luxury maritime villas were built in Stabiae and on the Sorrento Peninsula after this event; their appearance is generally dated to the second half of the first century BC.
28 Plin. *HN* 3.70; App. *B Civ.* 1.42.186 reports that during the conflict Stabiae had been taken by the Samnite general Papius Mutilus and that the prisoners and slaves were forced to enrol in the army fighting against Rome. About the fate of the *ager Stabianus* see Plin. *HN* 3.62 and Senatore 2001: 30.
29 Howe 2018: 105.

30 Villa S. Marco and Villa del Fauno. This latter villa was only partially investigated in the eighteenth century. The evidence from Villa del Fauno possibly indicating imperial ownership is an inscription on the *lararium* of the villa recording the freedman Antheros and the slave Heracleus, who was *summarum dispensator/vilicus*; the two, who are defined as being *magistri*, evidently of a private religious association, placed a dedication to the *Lares* and *Familia* of the villa owner. Magalhaes (2001: 107–108) cautiously suggests possible ownership by Livia or other members of the imperial family on the basis of various clues, including a bust possibly depicting a young Livia which was found in the same niche as the *lararium*.

31 Esposito 2012: 154; he also observes that Elia (1957: 19) had suggested that the complex of Villa S. Marco had been built by Narcissus as a venue for hospitality / convalescence / health stays, a hypothesis perhaps influenced by the fact that in the nineteenth and early twentieth century Castellammare di Stabia had a prosperous "health tourism" due to the properties of its mineral waters. The evidence attesting Narcissus consists in tiles stamped NARCISSI/AVGVSTI L. from Villa S. Marco and a *fistula aquaria* with the same stamp excavated in a bath complex adjacent to the villa: Ruffo 2010: 186–191; 231; Esposito 2012: 152–153. Another stamp attested on tiles from Villa S. Marco records a home-born slave of Claudius: *Verna Claudi C.S.* See Miniero 1999: 64–65, n. 14 and Magalhaes 2006: 143.

32 Esposito 2012: 159–160; also Parma 2002.

33 The rural villas are located at Cesarano and inland from Massa Lubrense; Russo 2004 and 2006 for the archaeology of the villas known on the Sorrento Peninsula.

34 Russo 2004. This villa is the object of a current archaeological project by Humboldt University. Preliminary reports can be found at www.fastionline.org, s.v. 'Villa del Capo di Sorrento' and in Filser et al. 2017.

35 Suet. *Aug.* 65.1; 92.2. Inscriptions: *NSc* 1928, 208 n. 5, attesting a *vilicus*; Magalhaes 2003, in particular entry n. 28, an inscription attesting a slave who was the administrator of various imperial properties ("*a possesionibus*"). Mingazzini and Pfister (1946: 9) had suggested that the construction of the "imperial" villas of Surrentum had started already with Caesar. On imperial properties in Campania more generally, Camodeca 2007.

36 D'Arms 2003c; Marzano 2007: 13–34.

37 Marzano 2007: 47–81; 2015; 2018.

38 Mingazzini and Pfister 1946 for the remains on the small islands and at Crapolla; for Crapolla, see also De Martino 2014, which largely relies on information from the Mingazzini and Pfister volume. Campanelli et al. 2018 and MAR 2017 for the villa of Positano. For the villa in Minori, Johannowsky 1986b; Di Maio and Iannelli 2017: 134–140; very little has been published on the Amalfi villa; a brief overview of the excavations carried out by the Soprintendenza can be found in Di Maio and Iannelli 2017: 140–144.

39 Tac. *Ann.* 67.3; on Villa Iovis, see Krause 2005.

40 Camodeca 2007: 144–145.

41 For a short overview of the discoveries, see Campanelli et al. 2018; for details of the excavation and the making of the archaeological museum, see MAR 2017.

42 Ruggiero 1888: 453–454, publishing K. Weber's report dated "Portici, April 23, 1758."

43 Ruggiero 1888: 453–454.

44 Di Maio and Iannelli 2017.

45 Mingazzini 1931; Maiuri 1955: 87–98.

46 Jacobelli 2017: 172; for some spectacular photos of the frescoes and the excavation see *Archaeology Magazine* at https://www.archaeology.org/issues/226-1609/features/4758-romans-on-the-bay-of-naples (last accessed 11 March 2021).

47 MAR 2017, 146–147, figs 18–19 for location of identified ancient remains.

48 Guarino 2017: 53.

49 Oral communication by Dr Praianò, who supervised the first phase of the archaeological excavation of the Positano villa in 2003: a tile had a stamp indicating the provenance from such *figlinae*; unfortunately, the find seems to have been subsequently lost.
50 Marzano 2015.
51 Plin. *Ep.* 2.17.26.
52 Calculated using Google Earth and the most convenient straight lines in connecting the various points along the route. Real navigation and what route is taken are however influenced by a number of other factors, especially in the case of boats propelled only by sail and oars.
53 MAR 2017, 179 and fig. 9 at p. 180.
54 Mingazzini 1931: 357–359.
55 Della Corte 1936: Positano has the ending of a place name deriving from a Roman adjective denoting property (e.g. Ottaviano from *octavianum* [*praedium*], derived from the *nomen Octavius*; Marciano from *marcianum*, etc.). Della Corte, a linguist, suggested an original place name Posidaetanum, which over time changed into Positano.
56 The mountain paths that from S. Maria del Castello lead down to Positano and the one called "Sentiero degli Dei," which from just above Positano leads to Agerola, may have existed in antiquity but there is no secure proof. Today, these are very steep, narrow, and uneven hiking paths, probably barely passable by a donkey.
57 Suet. *Aug.* 92; Cass. Dio 52.43.
58 Suet. *Aug.* 98; Apragopolis is mentioned at 98.4.
59 Some scholars, such as Motzo (1957, referenced in D'Arms 2003a: 81 and footnote 10) have suggested that Apragopolis was Punta di Tragara / the famous Faraglioni. It is believed that Augustus' villa was the complex of "Palazzo a mare" but there is no firm proof of this.
60 In addition to the remains of these three villas, Roman cisterns and a landing point are known in the fiord of Crapolla, and cisterns were present also on the Vivaro island, possibly to service the villa on nearby Isca island, since rainwater was the only source of water for this villa.
61 Joseph. *AJ* 18.161–62.
62 For the temple, see, e.g. Strabo 5.4.8, who attributes his construction to Odysseus.
63 Peutinger Table, §IT3.
64 The remains are scant and heavily disturbed by military installations placed by Joachim Murat, the king of Naples from 1808 to 1815, during the hostilities with the English.
65 Houston 1985.
66 Mingazzini and Pfister 1946: 151. Building techniques of the Tiberian period employed at Villa Jovis in Capri are *opus incertum mixtum* and *opus reticulatum mixtum*.
67 Mingazzini and Pfister 1946: 153–157.
68 Marzano 2021.
69 Tac. *Ann.* 6.25; for Julia the Elder's death by starvation while in exile, Cass. Dio 57.18.
70 The fact that Tiberius never returned to Rome attracted negative comments by Tacitus (*Ann.* 4.57) Suetonius (*Tib.* 39), and Cassius Dio (58.72).
71 In AD 26 Tiberius almost entered Rome: he sailed up the Tiber to the *Horti* near the *naumachia*; he must have been at the *Horti Caesaris*, to the south of the Porta Portuensis: Suet. *Tib.* 72.1; Tac. *Ann.* 6.1.1.
72 On Tiberius' travels while in Capri see Rogers 1945 and Champlin 2009.
73 On the isolation and security afforded by Caprae, see Tac. *Ann.* 4.67: *Solitudinem eius placuisse maxime crediderim, quoniam inportuosum circa mare et vix modicis navigiis pauca subsidia; neque adpulerit quisquam nisi gnaro custode* ("I would think that the solitude of the place was its principal attraction, since it is surrounded by a

harbourless sea and has few protected anchorages hardly adequate for small-sized vessels; furthermore, it is impossible to land unobserved by a sentry").

74 Tac, *Ann.* 4.67.

75 Suet. *Tib.* 4.65; actually, the manuscript tradition has "*villa Ionis*", corrected into "*Iovis*".

76 Federico and Miranda 1998; Esposito and Lucignano 2010.

77 Tac. *Ann.* 4.67. Edwards 2011 on how Tacitus presents Tiberius and his retirement to Capri.

78 For navigational speed in Roman time, Casson 1951.

79 Oral communication by the old seaman Giuseppe Grassi of Positano.

80 Tac. *Ann.* 4.67; see also 4.74 for the large crowd gathered presumably at Surrentum in AD 28 when Tiberius and Sejanus returned to the mainland.

References

Bannon, C.J. (2014) Sergius Orata and the Rhetoric of Fishponds. *The Classical Quarterly* 64. 1, 166–182.

Camodeca, G. (2007) Sulle proprietà imperiali in Campania. In: D. Pupillo, ed. *Le proprietà imperiali nell'Italia romana. Economia, produzione, amministrazione. Atti del Convegno, Ferrara–Voghera 3–4 Giugno 2005.* Florence: Le lettere, 143–167.

Campanelli, A. *et al.* (2018) The Roman Villa of Positano. In: A. Marzano and G.P.R. Métraux, eds. *The Roman Villa in the Mediterranean Basin: Late Republic to Late Antiquity.* Cambridge: Cambridge University Press, 120–124.

Casson, L. (1951) Speed under Sail of Ancient Ships. *TAPA* 82, 136–148.

Champlin, E. (2009) "Itinera Tiberi". Princeton/Stanford Working Papers in Classics, version 1.0 (available at https://www.princeton.edu/~pswpc/pdfs/champlin/030901.pdf, accessed 7 March 2021).

D'Arms, J.H. (2003a) *Romans on the Bay of Naples and Other Essays on Roman Campania* (ed. by F. Zevi). Bari: Edipuglia.

D'Arms, J.H. (2003b) Proprietari e ville nel Golfo di Napoli. In: F. Zevi, ed. *Romans on the Bay of Naples and Other Essays on Roman Campania.* Bari: Edipuglia, 331–350.

D'Arms, J.H. (2003c) Ville rustiche e ville d'*otium*. In: F. Zevi, ed. *Romans on the Bay of Naples and Other Essays on Roman Campania.* Bari: Edipuglia, 351–383.

De Martino, G. (2014) The archaeological evidence of the Sorrento Peninsula and Crapolla. In: V. Russo, ed. *Landscapes as Architecture. Identity and Conservation of Crapolla Cultural Site.* Florence: Nardini Editore, 57–64.

Della Corte, M. (1936) Posides Claudii Caesaris libertus – Positano da Posidetanum? *Rivista Indo-Greco-Italica* 20. 1–2, 67–73.

Di Maio, G. and Iannelli, M.A. (2017) Positano e le ville romane della Costa di Amalfi. Il paesaggio archeologico e gli effetti dell'eruzione pliniana del 79 D.C. In: *MAR: Museo Archeologico Romano di Positano. La villa d'ozio. Regione Campania, Comune di Positano, and Parrocchia Santa Maria Assunta* (no ISBN/publisher), 133–162.

Edwards, R. (2011) Tacitus, Tiberius and Capri. *Latomus* 4 (December), 1047–1057.

Elia, O. (1957) *Pitture di Stabia.* Naples: Edizioni scientifiche italiane.

Esposito, D. (2012) Su un possibile *Praedium* imperiale a Stabiae. *Oebalus: Studi sulla Campania nell'antichità* 6, 143–163.

Esposito, A. and Lucignano, A. (2010) Ninfei marittimi imperiali del Golfo di Napoli. *Bollettino di archeologia online,* 1 (Edizione speciale — Congresso di Archeologia A.I.A.C. 2008), 8–16.

Fagan, G.G. (1996) Sergius Orata: Inventor of the Hypocaust? *Phoenix* 50. 1, 56–66.

Federico, E. and Miranda, E., eds (1998) *Capri antica dalla preistoria alla fine dell'età romana*. Capri: La Conchiglia.

Filser, W. *et al.* (2017) Surrounded by the Sea: Re-Investigating the Villa Maritima del Capo di Sorrento. Interim Report. *JRA* 30, 64–95.

Frederiksen, M.-W. (1981) I cambiamenti delle strutture agrarie nella tarda repubblica: la Campania. In: A. Giardina and A. Schiavone, eds. *Società romana e produzione schiavistica. I. L'Italia: insediamenti e forme economiche*. Rome and Bari: Laterza, 265–287.

Guarino, D. (2017) Dall'ipogeo medievale della Chiesa Madre di Positano alla villa romana del I sec. a.C., tra scavi archeologici, restauri e musealizzazione del sito. In *MAR: Museo Archeologico Romano di Positano. La villa d'ozio*. Regione Campania, Comune di Positano, and Parrocchia Santa Maria Assunta (no ISBN/publisher), 43–74.

Houston, G.W. (1985) Tiberius on Capri. *Greece & Rome* 32. 2, 179–196.

Howe, T.N. (2018) The Social Status of the Villas of Stabiae. In: A. Marzano and G.P. R. Métraux, eds. *The Roman Villa in the Mediterranean Basin: Late Republic to Late Antiquity*, Cambridge: Cambridge University Press, 97–119.

Jacobelli, L. (2017) Decorazioni pittoriche e maestranze nella villa romana di Positano. In: *MAR: Museo Archeologico Romano di Positano. La villa d'ozio*. Regione Campania, Comune di Positano, and Parrocchia Santa Maria Assunta (no ISBN/publisher), 162–176.

Johannowsky, W.E. (1986a) Appunti sullo sviluppo delle ville romane in Campania. In: W.E. Johannowsky, M. Laforgia, V. Romito, and V. Sampaolo, eds. *Le ville romane dell'età imperiale*. Naples: Società Editrice Napoletana, 13–20.

Johannowsky, W.E. (1986b). Minori. La villa romana. In: W.E. Johannowsky, M. Laforgia, V. Romito, and V. Sampaolo, eds. *Le ville romane dell'età imperiale*. Naples: Società Editrice Napoletana, 78–86.

Krause, C. (2005) *Villa Jovis: l'edificio residenziale*. Naples: Electa.

Lafon, X. (2001) *Villa maritima: Recherches sur les villas littorales de l'Italie romaine (IIIe siècle av. J. -C./IIIe siècle ap. J.-C.)*. Rome: École Française de Rome.

Landwehr, Ch. (1985) *Die antiken Gipsabgüsse aus Baiae: griechische Bronzestatuen in Abgüssen römischer Zeit*. Berlin: Gebr. Mann.

MAR (2017) *MAR: Museo Archeologico Romano di Positano. La villa d'ozio*. Regione Campania, Comune di Positano, and Parrocchia Santa Maria Assunta (no ISBN/ publisher).

Magalhaes, M.M. (2001) La cd. Villa del Fauno: un possedimento imperiale a Stabiae? In: D. Camardo and A. Ferrara, eds. *Stabiae dai Borbone alle ultime scoperte*. Castellammare di Stabia: N. Longobardi Editore, 105–108.

Magalhaes, M.M. (2003) *Storia, istituzioni e prosopografia di Surrentum romana. La collezione epigrafica del Museo Correale di Terranova*. Castellammare di Stabia: N. Longobardi Editore.

Magalhaes, M.M. (2006). *Stabiae romana. La prosopografia e la documentazione epigrafica: iscrizioni lapidarie e bronzee, bolli laterizi e sigilli*. Castellammare di Stabia: N. Longobardi Editore.

Maiuri, A. (1955) Le vicende dei monumenti antichi della costa amalfitana e sorrentina alla luce delle recenti alluvioni. *RendNap* 39, 87–98.

Marzano, A. (2007) *Roman Villas in Central Italy: A Social and Economic History*. Leiden and Boston: Brill.

Marzano, A. (2013) *Harvesting the Sea. The Exploitation of Marine Resources in the Roman Mediterranean*. Oxford: Oxford University Press.

Marzano, A. (2015) The Variety of Villa Production: From Agriculture to Aquaculture. In: P. Erdkamp, K. Verboven, and A. Zuiderhoek, eds. *Ownership and Exploitation of*

Land and Natural Resources in the Roman World. Oxford: Oxford University Press, 187–206.

Marzano, A. (2016) Sergio Orata e il Lago Lucrino: alcune considerazioni sull'allevamento di ostriche nella Campania romana. *Oebalus. Studi sulla Campania nell'antichità* 10, 131–150.

Marzano, A. (2018) Maritime Villas and the Resources of the Sea. In: A. Marzano and G. Metraux, eds. *The Roman Villa in the Mediterranean Basin: From the Late Republic through Late Antiquity*. Cambridge: Cambridge University Press, 125–140.

Marzano, A. (2021) Maritime Villas and Seasonality. In: R. Raja and A. Lichtenberger, eds. *The Archaeology of Seasonality*. Turnhout: Brepols.

Mingazzini, P. (1931) Positano (prov. di Salerno). Resti di villa romana presso la Marina. *NSc*, 356–359.

Mingazzini, P. and Pfister, F. (1946) *Forma Italiae. Regio I, vol. 2.1: Surrentum*. Florence: Sansoni.

Miniero, P. (1999) Produzione laterizia. In: A. Barbet and P. Miniero, eds, *La Villa di San Marco a Stabia and Other Work on Paintings Buried by Vesuvius*, I–III. Naples, Rome and Pompeii: Centre Jean Berard, École Française de Rome, Soprintendenza Archeologica di Pompei, 63–71.

Parma, A. (2002) Stabiae e la *Classis Misenensis*. In: G. Bonifacio and A.M. Sodo, eds. *Stabiae: Storia e Architettura. 250° Anniversario degli Scavi di Stabiae 1749–1999*, (Studi della Soprintendenza Archeologica di Pompei 7). Rome: L'Erma di Bretschneider, 185–188.

Rawson, E. (1976) The Ciceronian Aristocracy and its Properties. In: M.I. Finley, ed. *Studies in Roman Property*. Cambridge: Cambridge University Press, 85–102.

Rogers, S.M. (1945) Tiberius' Travels, A.D. 26–37. *The Classical Weekly* 39. 6, 42–44.

Ruffo F. (2010) L'insula sud-occidentale del cosiddetto 'impianto urbano' di Stabiae. Nuovi dati dalla recente campagna di scavo (2009). *Oebalus: Studi sulla Campania nell'Antichità* 5, 177–238.

Ruggiero, M. (1888) *Degli scavi di antichità nelle province di terraferma dell'antico regno di Napoli dal 1743 al 1876: Documenti raccolti e pubblicati da Michele Ruggiero*. Naples: V. Morano.

Russo, M. (2004) Alla ricerca della villa sorrentina di Pollio Felice nella baia di Puolo. In: F. Senatore, ed. *Pompei, Capri e la Penisola Sorrentina. Atti del quinto Ciclo di conferenze di geologia, storia, e archeologia: Pompei, Anacapri, Scafati, Castellammare di Stabia, ottobre 2002-aprile 2003*. Capri: Oebalus, 103–177.

Russo, M. (2006) *La villa romana del Capo di Sorrento con i fondi agricoli acquistati dal Comune*. Sorrento: Centro di studi e ricerche multimediali Bartolommeo Capasso.

Senatore, F. (2001) Stabiae: storia dell'insediamento. In: D. Camardo and A. Ferrara, eds. *Stabiae dai Borbone alle ultime scoperte*. Castellammare di Stabia: N. Longobardi Editore, 23–38.

Valenti, M. (2003) Forma Italiae 4.1. *Ager Tusculanus*. Florence: Olschki.

Zarmakoupi, M. (2014) *Designing for Luxury on the Bay of Naples: Villas and Landscapes (c. 100 BCE–79 CE)*. Oxford: Oxford University Press.

Zevi, F. (2004) Cicero and Ostia. In: A. Gallina Zevi and J. Humphrey, eds. *Ostia, Cicero, Gamala, Feasts, and the Economy. Papers in Memory of J.H. D'Arms*. Portsmouth RI: Journal of Roman Archaeology, 15–31.

10 Property Management and Social Patronage

The *gens Neratia* in Rome and Central-Southern Italy between the Second and the Fourth Centuries AD

Maria Letizia Caldelli and Cecilia Ricci[1]

Abstract

The focus of the chapter is on the wealthy gens of the Neratii, which went back to an obscure figure of the Augustan age and achieved senatorial status under Vespasian, between the second and the fourth centuries AD. Our research traces the sources (mainly archaeological and epigraphical) that reveal the wealth of the Neratii; and discusses the developments and transformations of the building activity of the Neratii throughout time and space, between urban and rural areas, in Samnium and in Rome.

In South-central Italy, the extra-urban properties of the Neratii created overtime a network of agricultural land and productive villas that progressively expanded and/or multiplied. The relevant territory, straddling several regions, can be roughly described as a big rectangle with its vertices in Saepinum, Santa Croce di Magliano (Larinum), Beneventum, Aeclanum, and Luceria. From a territorial perspective, a broad chronology emerges, as well as the record of a variety of building initiatives, albeit attestations mainly concentrate on the phase between the second and third centuries.

After a documentary vacuum between the third and the beginning of the fourth centuries, the Neratii appear once again documented in Rome in the 320s, binding (and perhaps not for the first time) the fate of the senatorial *gens* with that of the imperial family. As was always the case for the high-ranking senatorial families, rural land holdings in Italy were accompanied by large urban real estate properties. The family home of the Neratii in Rome was traditionally set to the west of Santa Maria Maggiore's Basilica. In the fourth century AD, whereas Vulcacius Rufinus decided to build his own domus in the Regio VI (Alta Semita), Neratius Cerealis chose once again the Regio V (Esquiliae), where the old aristocratic residence was located, to construct his new housing estate. We can reasonably assume that, in addition to the undoubted political capacity of the family members of the *Neratia gens*, the bulk of their fortune, consisting mainly of immense and widespread real estate property (especially under the form of land holdings) in Samnium, did not experience any crisis, whilst very likely attracting the interest of the imperial dynasty.

***

DOI: 10.4324/9781003187806-13

Introduction

The history of the wealthy *gens* of the Neratii began with an obscure figure from the Augustan age who achieved senatorial status under Vespasian and, in the fourth century, tied the family's fate with that of the imperial family. The aim of the current research is to trace the acquisition, maintenance, and consolidation of the immovable wealth of the Neratii in central-southern Italy throughout the second and third centuries, as well as to discuss to what extent the aedilician activities of the Neratii changed and developed over time and space, between urban centres and rural areas, Samnium and Rome, across a timeframe that spans three centuries.

In the period between the first and the fourth centuries AD, the *gens Neratia*, originating from Samnium,[2] followed an entirely exceptional path. Many of the family members held local and, at a relatively early stage, even central magistrate positions, turning to familial strategies to climb the ladder of social standing. A peculiar element in the context of the history of powerful senatorial families is that the Neratii, despite the great political-social success they achieved, always remained in contact with their birthplace, and with their rural and residential properties in the region, managed by slaves and freedmen.

The sources for the public and private affairs of the *gens* are primarily epigraphic: inscriptions are essential for the reconstruction of careers, familial ties, the topographic distribution of properties, and the family's approach towards the civic community. Several Neratii are mentioned in the *Tabula Alimentaria Ligurum Baebianorum*, an invaluable document for, among other things, understanding estates and their location in central-southern Italy at the beginning of the second century.

There are also other sources, primarily the *Digest* and the *Historia Augusta*. In the *Digest*, the titles and a few extracts of the works of the jurist Lucius Neratius Priscus are brought together, while the *Historia Augusta* specifically addresses the links between the family and the imperial *domus* during the second and, to a lesser extent, the third century. L. Neratius Marcellus, governor of Roman Britain, is also mentioned in Pliny the Younger's epistles, and in a private letter included in the Vindolanda tablets.[3]

Scholarship has given much attention to some of the most prominent members of this family: in Italy, Giuseppe Camodeca, Gianfranco De Benedittis, Marcello Gaggiotti, and Maurizio Matteini Chiari. It is also impossible not to at least mention the works of Anthony Birley, François Chausson, Werner Eck, Marie-Thérèse Raepsaet-Charlier, Begoña Enjuto Sanchez, and Ronald Syme.

Due to space constraints, and in order to maintain coherence with the matter at hand, the origin of the *gens* and its transition from a local to a central political stage, extensively explored elsewhere, are here taken for granted. Instead, it seems appropriate to undertake a brief review of the genealogical framework of the Neratii in question within our chosen timeframe, before bringing our focus onto the specific theme of our discussion.

An Incomplete Family Crest

The first high-profile Neratii in the second century AD are two of the most celebrated and active members of the family (Figure 10.1). These are the sons of the consul of the late Flavian age: Lucius Neratius Priscus iunior, the homonymous jurist referenced earlier, who was consul in AD 97 and member of Trajan's and Hadrian's *consilium principis*[4]; and his natural brother, Lucius Neratius Marcellus, consul in AD 95 and then again in AD 129, adopted by Marcus Hirrius Fronto Pansa and *adlectus inter patricios* under Flavian rule.[5] More so than his brother, and by means of his civic and religious offices, Marcellus followed in the footsteps of his natural father. The *instrumentum inscriptum* of Rome and the onomastics of several freedmen also reveal the existence of a third brother, Caius Neratius (whose *cognomen* is unknown).[6]

Remaining in the second century, the *cognomina Rufinus/Rufina/Rufilla* and *Proculus/Procilla* appear in the following generation, specifically in the onomastics of L. Neratius C.f. Proculus,[7] son of Caius Neratius and brother of Neratia Procilla,[8] wife of a member of the equestrian order in Aeclanum, Caius Betitius Pietas.

In the first half of the third century, a branch of the *gens* associates the *gentilicium* of the Fufidii with that of the Neratii (Figure 10.2). This topic will shortly be revisited when discussing the villa of the Neratii. Interesting figures at this time are Flavia Neratia Septimia Octavilla, mentioned in an urban dedication from the Severan age,[9] and Lucius Neratius L.f. Iunius Aurelius Gallus

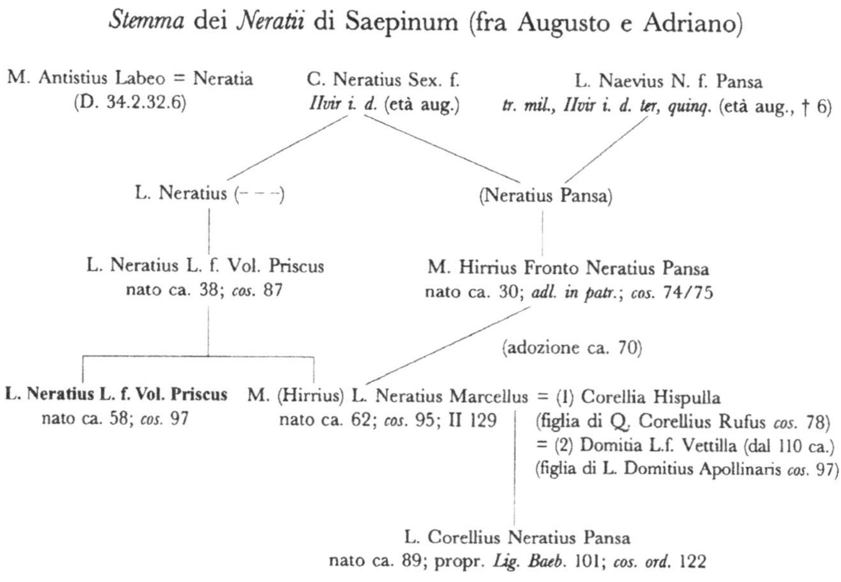

Figure 10.1 Stemma Neratiorum between the first and the second centuries (Gaggiotti 2011, 20).

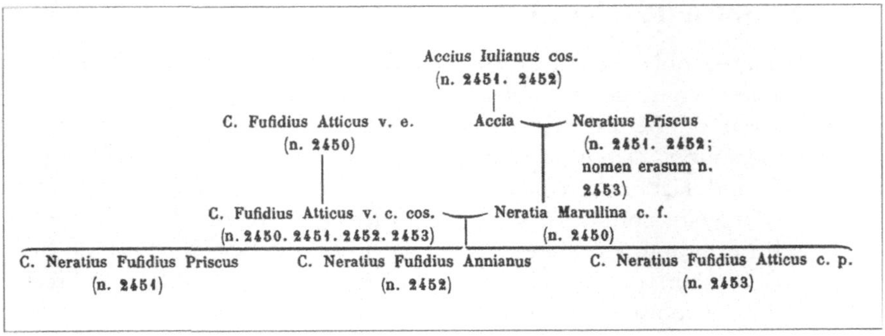

- *Stemma dei* Neratii *tratto dal* CIL *(CIL IX, p. 230).*

Figure 10.2 Stemma Fufidiorum Neratiorum (Gaggiotti 2011, 21).

Fulvius Macer, the last known member of the family around the middle of the third century.[10]

Property Management and Social Patrimony between the Second and Third Centuries

Saepinum

Our starting point is the town of Saepinum, where there are numerous signs of interventions by the Neratii, particularly in the forum.[11] At the beginning of the second century, two Lucii Neratii Prisci, father and son, arranged for the construction of an imposing building, preceded by a monumental honorific arch, on the south-eastern side of the forum; however, it is impossible to infer more from what little remains.[12] The construction of another monumental building in the Forum was due to the initiative (*fecit*) of Priscus' son.[13] We should also not forget the seriously damaged fragment of a (building?) dedication by a Lucius Neratius, whose cognomen is unfortunately not preserved.[14]

Restoration and consolidation works occurred mainly during the fourth century. A series of dedications to Emperor Constantine and his mother Helena, as well as clear signs of a relationship between the Neratii and the imperial household, reveal a renewed attention towards the town's monumental centre. The promoter and agent of numerous initiatives, on behalf of the *rectores* of the new province (the name Fabius Maximus stands out for its recurrence) is Neratius Constantius, the city's patron at the time.[15] Constantius restored, at his own personal expense, the baths of Silvanus and their *porticus*, which had collapsed from use[16]; he also attended to a loosely defined *fabrica* that was clad in marble[17] and, along with Arruntius Atticus, patron of Bovianum and Saepinum, he funded the marble decoration of the *tribunal* and its colonnade.[18]

If it is the case that the powerful urban prefect Neratius Cerealis (see the section below: Neratii in the Fourth Century) lent his support and endorsement to all these works, then there could be various reasons for the construction or reconstruction of these buildings/complexes. They were certainly linked, at least in part, to the effects of the earthquake of 346, as well as to the phase of abandonment or neglect which preceded this and, at the end of the fourth century, to the administrative necessities of the new province.[19]

Saepinum's Territory

The network of Neratii properties outside the urban area, whose details have recently been better clarified, can be divided into agricultural terrains and productive villas which expand and/or multiply, overlapping different regions. A territory-by-territory approach provides a broad chronology, although many cases lie in the phase between the second and the third centuries.

We begin by considering Saepinum's territory, whose limits lie at the crossing of Vinchiaturo, encompassing Ferrazzano and San Giuliano to the north, along the Matese mountain range to the south, and passing in the vicinity of Santa Croce del Sannio to the east, where it is possible to identify the boundary with the Regio II and the territory of the *Ligures Baebiani* (Figure 10.3). The Saepinum area was surely more widespread to the north-east and to the south,

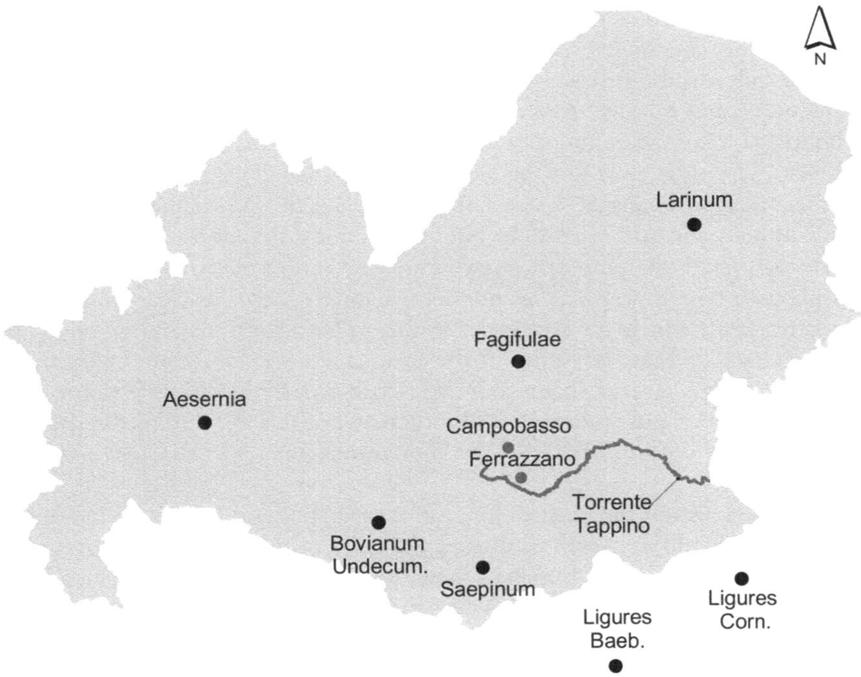

Figure 10.3 Between Saepinum and the Ligures Baebiani (map courtesy of Michele Roccia).

and recent epigraphic discoveries allow us to hypothesise the inclusion of Jelsi, Toro, and Campodipietra within the limits of the *municipium*, although these are traditionally thought to belong to the administrative area of *Fagifulae*.

The Villa in San Giuliano

The identity of the person (or people) behind the initiative to construct the so-called "villa of the Neratii" at San Giuliano, with an original structure that dates to the Augustan era, is still a matter of debate.[20]

While the dating of the villa, which belonged to the Fufidii Neratii family branch, to the third century (above, Figure 10.2) seems unquestionable,[21] the idea that the "family residence" of the Neratii in Samnium was passed down through the generations is nowhere near as certain. The moment of acquisition and management of the properties of San Giuliano needs to be better defined: we hope that the systematic archaeological excavation campaign (in progress, directed by the archaeologist Fulvia Ciliberto) will provide significant clarifications.[22]

The discrepancy in the monumental typology, as well as the textual formulas, of inscribed bases recovered from the surveys undertaken so far does not seem to have ever been explored, and in my view the wider implications of this should not be underestimated.

Two funerary altars, preserved in the walls of the church of San Nicola at San Giuliano, mention the *egregiae memoriae vir* Caius Fufidius Atticus and his grandson, the *clarissimus puer* Caius Neratius Fufidius Atticus. The dedicators, readable only on the first altar, are the son of the *vir egregius*, the *clarissimus vir* and consul Caius Fufidius Atticus, and his wife Neratia Marullina.[23] Two bases of honorary statues were found in the locality of Crocella, in close proximity to the villa. The dedicators are the *Saepinates* (*municipes*), while the beneficiaries are the other two sons of Caius Fufidius Atticus and Marullina: Caii Neratii Fufidii Priscus and Annianus.[24] In both dedications, the father is referred to as *quaestor designatus*: therefore, these two bases are earlier than at least one of the epitaphs mentioned above. The honorary nature is actually clear only in the two latter cases, which are extremely similar, in both formulas and typology, to two honorary dedications found in the forum, respectively offered to a Caius Neratius Fufidius Atticus (namesake of his father, here always referred to as a *quaestor designatus*) and to one of his brothers, whose name, due to the gaps on top of the base, unfortunately remains anonymous (referred to as *legati provinciae Africae filius*).[25]

The dimensions of the bases in honour of Annianus and Priscus, found in the area of the villa, do not seem to suggest the reuse of pieces originally located in Sepino's forum, although this hypothesis cannot be completely excluded. As Marzano correctly suggests, these bases could have been dedicated by the citizens of Sepino to their patrons and positioned in plain view within the residential complex; or, they could be copies of originals present in the forum.[26]

Apart from the aforementioned inscribed monuments, several other inscriptions, of various kinds, come from the area around the San Giuliano's villa.[27]

The epitaph which mentions Primigenius, a *vilicus* of Neratius Proculus, dated at the latest to the second half of the second century, provides a particularly significant insight into the Neratii's interests in the agricultural properties connected to the villa.[28] The naming of a Fisius Sulla, who is the beneficiary of another dedication,[29] suggests a link to Aeclanum and the relationship between Neratius Proculus (the consul of the mid-second century) and the equestrian Caius Betitius Pietas, husband of his sister, who is cited, as we shall see, in other documents.

Ferrazzano and Its Surroundings

Another sizeable group of inscriptions of slaves and freedmen of the *gens* allows us to, as Marcello Gaggiotti states, "understand the extent to which the family was embedded in the territory, its reach and its continuity, its capacity to draw in a workforce and manpower."[30]

The existence of sepulchral inscriptions in areas far-removed from Saepinum cannot always be interpreted as indicators for the Neratii's properties. However, these inscriptions are useful indicators. Most of them come from Saepinum's archaeological area and the sepulchral roads (*viae sepulchrales*), and belong to the end of the first, and especially the second century.[31] We can recall the first-century marble stele, now in a fragmentary state, discovered at Cercepiccola, only 3 km from San Giuliano, which mentions the *libertus* Lucius Neratius Prothymus, patron of Anteros and Tertius[32]; and the epitaph of one or two slaves, named Protus and Proto[genes?], belonging to Neratius Priscus.[33]

Moving towards the northern limit of Saepinum's territory, the epitaph of two freedmen of Priscus and Marcellus, Constans and Potens, seems to demonstrate the existence of a productive villa in this area[34]: it is very unlikely that the two *liberti* could have been buried at a distance from the villa, especially due to the clear emphasis of their functions as *vilicus* and *cellarius* in the inscription, which link them to managerial roles entrusted by the landlord.

Regio II. Circello (*Ligures Baebiani*), Santa Croce di Magliano (*Larinum*), *Aeclanum*, and *Luceria*

A similarly valuable indicator of the progressive multiplication (and extension) of the rural properties of the Neratii and their modes of management is constituted, for the period from the second to the first half of the third century, by epigraphic fragments named as *liberti* or *servi* of the *gens*, discovered in the territory of the Regio II, bordering the Regio IV, and by the already mentioned *Tabula Alimentaria Ligurum Baebianorum* (above, Figure 10.3). Thanks to these clues, the area of interest for the Neratii appears to take the form of a massive rectangle, between Regio IV and Regio II, whose corners are located at Saepinum, Santa Croce di Magliano, Beneventum/Aeclanum (excluding the territory of the *Ligures Corneliani*) and Luceria.

Lucius Neratius Marcellus, consul of AD 95, appears in the *Tabula Alimentaria* of AD 101 as the curator of a *fundus Paccianus* on behalf of Corellius Neratius.[35]

The property was built at the limits or within the territory of the *Ligures Baebiani*, bordering that of *Saepinum* to the east. Corellius, the son of Marcellus' first marriage to Corellia Hispulla and later consul in AD 122 (above, Figure 10.1), was very young at this point, justifying the paternal intervention.[36]

Regarding the forms of property acquisition, it is worth recalling that Lucius Paccius was the name of the husband of a Neratia from the territory of Aesernia (he can be dated between the triumvirate and the early-Augustan period).[37] Around a century (thus perhaps three generations) passed since this first attestation of the Neratii in Samnium, and we lack any knowledge of the fate of the Aesernian branch of the Lucii Paccii. It does not seem entirely unreasonable to imagine that over a few generations, the management of the properties of the *fundus* in the territory of the *Baebiani*, perhaps belonging to the Aesernian *Paccii*, passed into the hands of the Neratii.

Even though the *cognomen* Paccianus is quite common, it is worth remembering that, besides the example of the *Tabula* of Circello, a *fundus Paccianus* is mentioned only once elsewhere, namely on a sepulchral altar in the territory of Luceria (directly bordering that of the *Baebiani*): a certain Tiberius Statorius Geminus, *col(onus) f(undi) Pacciani*, is commemorated by his biological son and by a *Numisia Augusti nostri serva*, whose presence suggests the existence of an imperial property, which coincides with or rather borders on our *fundus*.[38]

Lastly, around ten years ago an epitaph was discovered at Santa Croce di Magliano, a small community that was included, in ancient times, in the territory of *Larinum*. However, it was poorly published and has remained for the most part unknown (Figure 10.4). The deceased was Epictetus, a *tabularius* slave, commemorated by his *coniux* Neratia Sozusa.[39] For palaeographic and formulaic reasons, the slab can be dated to the second half of the second century or later. The text, even in its brevity, is valuable, both as an indicator of the further extension of the interests of the Neratii in the northern area of the neighbouring region, and also for the interesting connections it reveals with professional activities linked with the economic management of productive estates (the job of *tabularius* can be added to those of *cellarius* and *vilicus*, known from the evidence found in Ferrazzano).

Such testimonies for the presence of the Neratii in the Hirpinian hinterland and the northern part of Apulia are not isolated cases: at least three inscriptions of Neratii freedmen were discovered in Luceria's territory (along the route from Lucera to Castel Di Sangro)[40]; while links (and properties) in the territory of Aeclanum appear to date to the first century at the earliest, around the time of the marriage between the biological daughter of Neratius Pansa, Neratia Pansina, and a citizen of Aeclanum of equestrian rank, Lucius Varius Ambibulus.[41] These connections were reinforced in the Antonine age, when Neratia Procilla married Caius Betitius Pietas: in parallel to the merging of these two families, there was also a merging of freedmen of both families, who managed the terrains and related economic activities.[42] A confirmation of this can be found 30 km away, in Benevento's territory, in the epitaph of Neratia Iucunda, a freedwoman commemorated by her husband Caius Betitius Secundus.[43]

Figure 10.4 The new epitaph from Santa Croce di Magliano (private collection, courtesy of G. De Benedittis).

The Neratii in the Fourth Century

After a documentary vacuum between the third and the fourth centuries, the Neratii appear once again on the scene of Rome in the 320s (Figure 10.5), when Galla married Iulius Constantius, son of the emperor Constantius I and Theodora, binding (and perhaps not for the first time) the fate of the family with that of the imperial family.[44]

Prosopographists agree to consider Galla the sister of Vulcacius Rufinus and Neratius Cerealis, the first *cos. ord.* in 347, *PPO Italiae, Illyrici et Africae* between 347 and 353[45]; the second *praefectus annonae* in 328, *praefectus urbi* in 352/353,[46] *cons. ord.* in 358.[47] It is hard to avoid the thought that Galla's marriage influenced her brothers' careers.[48] We know of Cerealis' ascent to the *praefectura annonae* from a letter by Constantinus that is included in the *Codex Theodosianus*, dated to the 1 March 328 and concerning the *mensae oleariae*, the concessions made by the state for the distribution of oil. At this time, Rome was no longer the only city where there was a *praefectus annonae* and, in contrast to the past, this position was now held by members of the senatorial class, the *clarissimi* (Cerealis is the first known). It is unclear if the passage from Symmachus's *Relatio* 40 refers to the *praefectus annonae*.[49] This is a retrospective reference to the measures of Cerealis (the supply of 38,000 *modii* of wheat to Rome, as written in the *Relatio*), detailing – as he was obliged to do – that the Campanian cities were making an exorbitant contribution of grain to Rome.[50] Elio Lo Cascio talks about "part of the Campanian cereal production [...]

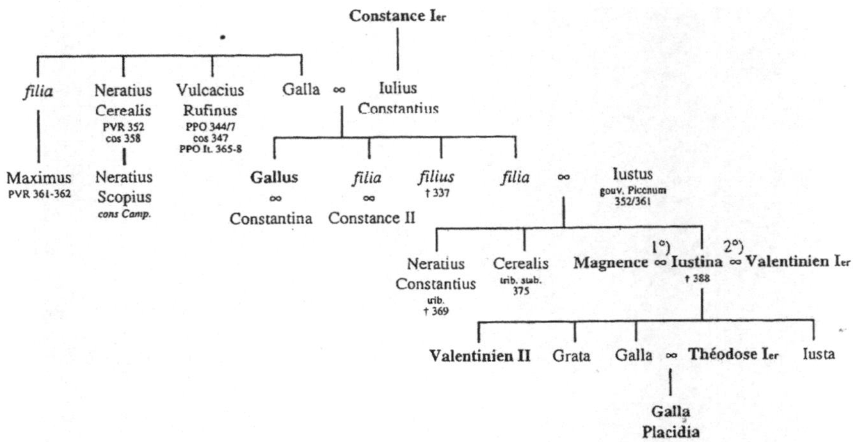

Figure 10.5 Stemma Neratiorum in the fourth century (Chausson 2007, 123).

destined to Rome under the form of a *canon*." He suggests that it would be beneficial to link this measure with the beginning of the organisation of food provisions at Constantinople. The author also considers how grain of non-contributory origin, destined to the *Annona* and coming directly from the estates of the large senatorial Roman *domus*, represented a relatively modest quantity.[51]

Of relevance at this point is Begoña Enjuto Sánchez's theory that the occupation of some of the highest positions by the Neratii in the fourth century was a consequence of their collaboration with imperial powers for the control of the territories of Samnium and Campania.[52] On the contrary, it seems that the renewed fortunes of the Neratii, enough to attract the imperial dynasty's attention, lie in their immense and widespread real estate property (especially under the form of land holdings) in Samnium, a region which was still subject to administration by the province Campania at the time,[53] as well as by a long aristocratic tradition.[54]

As was the case for all high-ranking senatorial families, rural land holdings in Italy were accompanied by large urban real estate properties. The family home of the Neratii, mentioned on two *fistulae* which allow us to locate it to the west of Santa Maria Maggiore,[55] had perhaps become too inappropriate for those descendants who had married into the imperial family. Vulcacius Rufinus, possibly Cerialis' half-brother rather than his real brother, had chosen Regio VI for the erection of his own *domus*. This is suggested by a base with a dedication to Rufinus as prefect, which was set by the *Ravennates* "*in vestibulo domus*," and uncovered in the area of the modern Ministry of Defence (AD 347)[56] (Figure 10.6). The use of precious types of marbles ("*biglio*," "*brocatello*," "*alabastro a nuvoli*") for the wall cladding and pavement gives an idea of the splendour of this urban residence.[57]

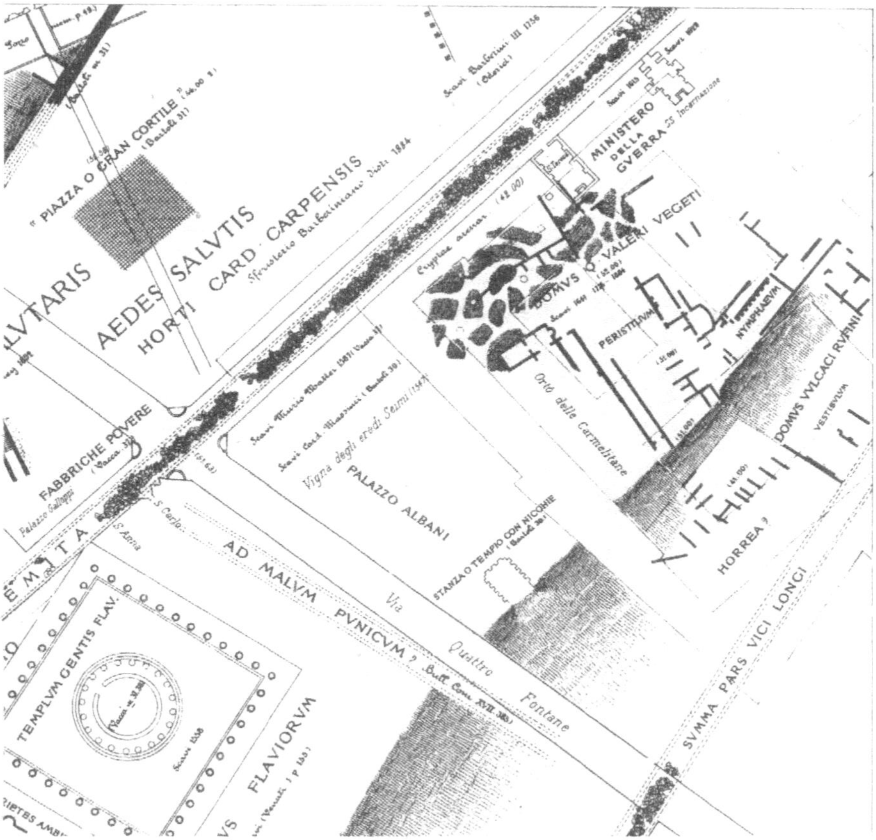

Figure 10.6 Rome, the home of Vulcacius Rufinus (Lanciani, FUR 16).

Unlike his brother, Neratius Cerealis decided to construct his new *domus* within Regio V, where the old aristocratic residence was located (Figure 10.7). His *domus* has been identified with a building in the area between Piazza Esquilina, via Cavour, via Farini, and via Manin (the Bambi-Pistacchi building), thanks to the discovery of two statue bases, both set up by Cursius Satrius for his patrons,[58] one to Cerealis, who was already *praefectus urbi* and *consul ordinarius* in 358,[59] and the other to his son, Naeratius Scopius, *v(ir) c(larissimus)* and *consularis Campaniae*,[60] to whom Satrius refers as *nutritor*.[61] The hypothesis that an earlier *domus* of the Neratii existed in the same area should no longer be considered valid on the basis of *CIL* 6.31917, since we now know with certainty that the inscription refers to Praeneste and to the local magistrate Cnaeus Voesius Aper. The fragment appears to have been moved in a post-antique phase to the Esquiline in Rome, where it was found at the end of the nineteenth century.[62]

Figure 10.7 Rome, the home of Neratius Cerealis (Lanciani, FUR 17).

Therefore, Cerealis, like his brother, had to build a residence for himself *ex novo* even though it was on the family's terrain.[63] In the dedication set up by Cursius Satrius, Cerealis is defined as a *conditor balnearum*. This very same expression, placed after Cerealis' name in the nominative case and the rank of *consul ordinarius*, appears on ten other bases.[64] While it is the case that a large part of these have an unknown origin, at least three come from an area on which the properties of the Neratii were located, although this does not mean that the *balnea* were necessarily made up of part of the *domus*. On the contrary, all this suggests that the *balnea* were open to the public[65] and constructed (or inaugurated) by Cerealis in the year in which he was *consul ordinarius*.[66]

The Roman properties must have remained firmly in the hands of the Neratii. The discovery of a statue of Jupiter on a base inscribed with the name of Neratius Palmatus, *v(ir) c(larissimus)*, defined as *loci dominus conditorq(ue)*, is important in this regard (Figure 10.8).[67] Palmatus dedicated the statue within a sacred space (*sacellum*), which must have stood on his property. The base was discovered, *in situ*, to the north of the building found on the left of the start of via Cavour [as one exits Piazza dei Cinquecento], not far from the place where the bases dedicated by Curtius Satrius were found, and along with at least three other bases which celebrate Cerealis as *conditor balnearum*.

However, the identification of Palmatus is by no means univocal (above, Figure 10.5). The first editor of the inscription, Irene Jacopi, initially followed by Laura Chioffi,[68] identified him as the *praefectus urbi* of AD 412, mentioned in a passage of the *Codex Theodosianus*.[69] This interpretation is followed by Federico Guidobaldi who, ignoring the dedication to Jupiter on the basis of an

Figure 10.8 Statue of Jupiter on a base inscribed with the name of Neratius Palmatus, Rome, Museo Nazionale Romano (Chioffi 1999a, 40 Fig. 4).

excerpt from the *Liber Pontificalis*, recognised him as either Scopius' son or grandson (and so thus Cerealis' grandson or great grandson).[70] Since the *Liber Pontificalis* (I, 233)[71] refers to the act of foundation of Santa Maria Maggiore by Sistus III (432–440), which brought together numerous donations of real estate, Guidobaldi concluded that Palmatus was the final owner and heir of the Neratii's fortune, and that after him the properties passed into the holdings of the church. Recently, Giuseppe Camodeca, examining a theory that Mario Torelli had already proposed (and which was not entirely rejected by Laura Chioffi), has suggested (and in our opinion rightly so) a plausible identification of the Palmatus of the dedication to Jupiter as another brother of Cerealis, or even his own father.[72] The elements that lead to suggest this solution are: a new inscription from Puteoli dedicated to Scopius (in which there could be a veiled reference to Palmatus), combined with its entirely pagan nature, and the close palaeographic and formulaic similarity with the dedication to Jupiter, as well as with the bases of Cerealis (Figure 10.9).[73]

If we accept this hypothesis (which is more than convincing, in our opinion), then the relationship between the *domus Palmati* mentioned in the *Liber Pontificalis*, the AD 412 urban prefect and the *domus* under Santa Maria Maggiore, remains to be determined. Torelli proposed that we should see the latter *domus* as the property that the last Neratii donated to the church.[74] This theory has, however, recently been called into question in the light of the fact that the *domus* underneath Santa Maria Maggiore seems to have had a rather less significant fourth century phase, which would contradict the expectations of a noble house.[75]

Conclusion

A few words to conclude. Torelli's 1982 reflections all remain valid: throughout the Neratii's entire family history there is evidence for, on the one hand, their continued presence in their town of origin, and, on the other hand, of a dense and branched activity in the Capital, where the political power of the family is deployed.[76]

Figure 10.9 *CIL* 6.1744a, base of Cerealis. Rome, Museo Nazionale Romano, Palazzo Altemps (De Angelis d'Ossat 2011, 67).

The history of the Neratii, as has been stated, is exceptional for its continuity over time. The prestigious political career and the political influence of the members of the family of senatorial rank were both assured and consolidated through the acquisition and expansion of rural properties and through the building of strategic family marriages and patronal relationships. Their careers and influence also contributed to the further enlargement of the *res familiaris* and the expansion of their economic influence.

We hope to have successfully drawn a more or less comprehensible picture of the dense web of family relations that emerge from the in-depth analysis of the sources concerning this remarkable family, in particular archaeological and epigraphic documents, some of which are already known, while others have thus far been only partially explored. Tangentially, the fragmentary, yet extensive, mosaic of properties attested in the preserved evidence indicates a successful model of consistent investment in rich rural areas, as well as in municipal politics and patronage, which combined productive and representative villas that were managed by a large number of slaves and freedmen.

Recent excavations, new epigraphic finds and studies, have shown that the third century, previously thought to be a vacuum period in the Neratii's ascent in Rome, was actually a period of intensification of their relationships with other wealthy and powerful senatorial families in the regions I (Campania) and II (Apulia), the latter of which bordering the Saepinum territory, remained the focus of our family's interests. This hypothesis offers a valid and credible explanation for the prominent re-emerging of the Neratii in Rome during the fourth century.

The new and/or renewed relationships of the Neratii, their consolidated power, and the extension of their properties in these regions can be seen as a slow, yet sustained prelude to the final, brilliant phase of the history of this family, the destiny of which became entwined with that of the imperial domus on the grand stage of the late antique city of Rome.

Abbreviations

LTUR	E.M. Steinby (ed.), *Lexicon Topographicum Urbis Romae*, I–VI, Rome 1993–2000.
RE	A.F. Von Pauly and G. Wissowa, *Realencyclopedie der klassischen Altertumswissenschaft*, Stuttgart 1894-.

Notes

1 This chapter is the joint work of the two authors: pp. 167–174; 181–183 were written by C. Ricci and pp. 175–181; 183–185 were written by M.L. Caldelli.

2 On the origin from Samnium, not necessarily from *Saepinum*, we share the opinion expressed by Gaggiotti 2011: 14: "Non è improbabile che la *gens Neratia* ..., in grado di intrecciare rapporti con eminenti famiglie campane, appartenga al novero di quelle genti immigrate da aree limitrofe culturalmente affini che, in epoca augustea (se non da prima), contribuirono alla municipalizzazione di *Saepinum* e costituirono il nerbo della sua classe dirigente."

3 Birley 1991: 87–102: letter addressed by Flavius Cerialis, praefectus of the *cohors VIIII Batavorum* to a certain Crispinus.

4 *PIR*^{2}, N 60. He is the recipient of an honorary inscription from Larinum, reused in the cathedral (*AE* 1969/70.152 = Stelluti 1997: 82 = *EDR*075013; Camodeca 2007: 291 ff., esp. 296 and 310). *Dig.* 33.7.12.43: *Neratius libro quarto epistularum Marcello fratri suo respondit*. See also below.

5 *PIR*^{2}, N 55. See *CIL* 9.6595 = *EDR*081754 (between 117 and 130 AD) and *CIL* 9.2456 = *EDR*133018. From the Saepinum's inscriptions we learn the name of his second wife, Domitia Vettilla. The consul of 95 and 129 has sometimes been identified with the Marcellus who was induced to commit suicide by Hadrian (SHA *Hadr.* 15.4). However, the excellent relationships between the emperor and Neratius Marcellus – who, among other things, in the year following the second consulate, had perhaps dedicated a statue to this emperor in Saepinum (*CIL* 9.6577 = *EDR*133698, between 129 and 130 AD) – have recently made the prevailing opinion that the suicidal person is simply a homonym (Camodeca 2007: 306 with note 52; Gaggiotti 2011: 16–17).

6 *PIR*^{2}, N 51.

7 *PIR*^{2}, N 63. See *CIL* 9.2457 = *ILS* 1076 = *EDR*133040 and *CIL* 9.6596 = *AE* 1990.218 = *EDR*081755.

8 *PIR*^{2}, N 67. See *CIL* 9.1132 = *EDR*132405; Raepsaet-Charlier 1999: 219 and 234. In the Raepsaet-Charlier scheme (at p. 233), Proculus would be L. Neratius Priscus' brother (cos. 97) and Lucius Neratius Corellius Pansa's uncle (for the uncle, see below, notes 36 and 41).

9 *CIL* 6.1415 = 31648 = *EDR*109469; *PIR*^{2} F 430. Octavilla's father was Lucius Flavius Septimius Aper Octavianus (*PIR*^{2} F 365, who was perhaps *patruus* of the emperor Severus); her mother was a *Neratia.*

10 *CIL* 9.2513 = *EDR* 133368 (between late second and third centuries); *PIR*^{2}, I 773, perhaps coinciding with the Lucius Neratius L.f. Iunius Macer of *PIR*^{2}, I 53. This echoes, in the onomastics, the name of Severus' maternal grandfather (Fulvius Macer), further confirming a close link between Neratii and Severans (Chausson 1998, 408–10; Settipani 2000: 311, 327).

11 The basilica with the *tribunal,* on the initiative of Lucius Naevius Pansa, as an original plant dates back to the Augustan age. A first restoration was perhaps undertaken by Marcus Hirrius Fronto Neratius Pansa (Gaggiotti 1978 and 1991).

12 *CIL* 9.2455 = *AE* 1976.195 and 1978.287 = *EDR*076507 (Eck 2003; Camodeca 2007: esp. 292–295, fig. 1 and 2).

13 To which *CIL* 9.6594 = *EDR*077124 must be referred.

14 *CIL* 9.6636 = *AE* 1990.220 = *EDR*081757: Gaggiotti 1987/1988: 136–137, nr. 4, tab. I,I fig. 3 identifies him with Lucius Fufidius Neratius Annianus (third century); perhaps it belongs to an earlier era.

15 Honoured by the community as a patron (possibly) with a statue (*CIL* 9.6591 = *EDR*134322, between AD 354 and AD 375).

16 *CIL* 9.2447 = *EDR*132946 (AD 352–357) and *CIL* 9.6583 = *EDR*133724.

17 *CIL* 9.6587 = *EDR*133728 (AD 361–375).

18 *CIL* 9.6588 = *EDR* 073156 (between AD 353 and AD 375). Constantius as a *vir perfectissimus* promotes an unspecified building activity between AD 351 and AD 375 (*CIL* 9.6590 = *EDR*133731) and has been celebrated as *patronus* (*CIL* 9.6591 = *EDR*134322).

19 Soricelli 2009: esp. 253 s.; Gaggiotti 2011: 25.

20 De Benedittis 2011: 77 believes that an effective attendance of the villa did not occur before the mid-first century.

21 Most scholars think of a property of the *gens Fufidia* (Eck 1996b: 307–308, with note 73; Andermahr 1998: 350–351; Camodeca 2007: 306–307 note 58). *Contra* Gaggiotti 1984–1985 and 2011: 30 note 38, who thinks of the first and second century Neratii and of a property transmitted as a dowry from a Neratia Marullina. Camodeca 2013 also emphasises the Teanense origin of the Fufidii.

22 Ciliberto and Notardonato 2023.

23 The two altars are *CIL* 9.2450 = *EDR*132971 (C. Fufidius Atticus, *egregiae memoriae vir*) and 2453 = *EDR*132988 (C. Neratius Fufidius Atticus, *clarissimus puer*). On the alleged parents of Neratia Marullina, see Gaggiotti 2011.

24 *CIL* 9.2451 = *EDR*132975 with photo (Priscus) and 2452 = *EDR*132984 with photo (Annianus). Gaggiotti 2011: 22 has drawn the attention to the *cognomen Annianus*, already attested in the Neratii's onomastics (*AE* 1990: 220, mid-second century).

25 *CIL* 9.6597 = *EDR*077125 (Caius Fufidius Neratius Atticus); *CIL* 9.6598 = *EDR*077126 (anonymous). The *municipes,* also make the dedications in these cases. On the four inscriptions, see also Muccilli 2010: 53–7, no 1–4.

26 Marzano 2007: 185–186 takes the S. Giuliano's villa as an "esempio calzante di come, in epoca imperiale …lo spazio fisico della villa fosse percepito come pubblico e quindi adatto per la celebrazione dei successi del proprietario nella vita pubblica."

27 In addition to those mentioned in the text, see also the inscriptions: *CIL* 9.2468 = Muccilli 2010: 57 no. 5 = *EDR*133146; *CIL* 9.2505 = Muccilli 2010: 58 f. no. 8 = *EDR*13360; *CIL* 9.2540 = Muccilli 2010: 59 no. 9 = *EDR*133526.

28 *CIL* 9.2485 = Muccilli 2010: 57 s. no. 6 = *EDR*133219.

29 *CIL* 9. 2503 = Muccilli 2010: 58 no. 7 = *EDR*133358: a Fisia Sabina (daughter) and a Fisia Hiusa (freedwoman) offer a dedication to the father and *patronus* Fisius Sulla.

30 Gaggiotti 2011: 20: "A comprendere il radicamento della famiglia nel territorio, la sua portata e continuità, la sua capacità di attrarre forza lavoro e risorse umane."

31 Found along the *via sepulchralis*: *CIL* 9.2510 = *EDR*133365 (perhaps a freedman); from the theater area: *CIL* 9.2511 = *EDR*133366 (a Lucius Neratius Fortunatus together with a Neratia Verecunda); 2512 = *EDR*133367 (Quintus Neratius Q.l. Heracla); 2514 = *EDR*133369 (Lucius Neratius Nikanor and Neratia Secundilla filia). The exact origin is unknown for the following three inscriptions: *CIL* 9.2517 mentions a series of freedwomen (Neratia Tertia, Neratia Daphne, Neratia Sex.l. Isidora, together with a Lucius Neratius Amaranthus); probably a descendant of a freedman, Caius Neratius C.f. Primio, is mentioned together with C. Stellius C.f. Primigenius (*CIL* 9.6637 = *EDR*134574, from Jelsi, but referred to Saepinum); also to be considered is a dedication to the *Genius municipi Saepinatium* by an Augustalis, Caius Neratius C.l. Epinicus, maybe freedman of the Caius Neratius (above, note 6): *CIL* 9.2440 = *EDR*132905 (second century, first mid, see Buonocore 2009: 257, no. 13).

32 *CIL* 9.2515 = *EDR*133370 with photo. However, two other inscriptions discovered in Saepinum surely do not pre-date the third century: one is inscribed on a valuable sarcophagus (*CIL* 9.6635 = *EDR*134572 with photo: Neratius Orphaeus); the other is the *carmen epigraphicum* for Neratius Iustus, a soldier serving first in the urban cohorts, then in the praetorian (*CIL* 9.6604 = *EDR*073037; his parents are freedmen).

33 *CIL* 9.2531 = *EDR*133394.

34 *CIL* 9.2484 = *EDR*133218. See, about it, Ricci and Roccia 2016: 590–592, no. 4.

35 *CIL* 9.1455, col. II, 16, Circello (BN) = *EDR*144345. In the same Tabula is also the name of Lucius Neratius Diadumenus, *curator fundi Rubriani,* in the Beneventum territory (*CIL* 9.1455, col. II, 9).

36 Corellia Hispulla (*PIR*^{2}*C* 1296). On Lucius Neratius Corellius Pansa (*PIR*^{2}*C* 1293), see Vidman 1981: 382 and 384; Eck 1983 (Hispulla as daughter of Q. Cornelius Rufus, cos. suff. AD 78); Camodeca 2007: 299, 306–307, with note 57, and 311; Gaggiotti 2011: 20.

37 *CIL* 9.6806 = *EDR*128426 (first century BC, from Miranda (IS)).

38 *CIL* 9.888 = *ILS* 8555 = *EDR*081737 (here dated to the third century).

39 De Benedittis 2009. The marble slab is currently located in the small town of San Biase (CB). The correct transcription of the text is: *D(is) M(anibus) / Epicteto, tabu/lario. Neratia / Sozusa coniugi.*

40 Three epitaphs come from the Lucerian territory: *AE* 1998.375 = *EDR*153171; *AE* 1998.376 = *EDR*153172 (Neratia Paulina, Neratia Firma, Neratius Faustus, first half of the second century); and *AE* 2006.349 = *EDR*153326 (Neratia Pyrallis). See also Camodeca 2007: 307–308.

41 Ambibulus and Pansina married their daughter, Varia Pansina, to Lucius Corellius Celer Fisius Rufinus (PIR^2 C 1294); he was the brother of Corellia Hispulla, the first wife of Neratius Marcellus (Camodeca 2007: 308 and Gaggiotti 2011: 22). Even in the onomastics of Neratia Marullina (whose name evokes the Eggi Marulli) there is strong insistence on the ties with the families of Aeclanum.

42 Neratia Procilla (*PIR*^{2} N 67 and Raepsaet-Charlier 1987: 251), whose children were Caius Neratius Proculus Betitius Pius Maximillianus (*PIR*^{2} B 119) and Neratia Betitia Procilla, *flaminica* of Faustina the Younger. For family descent in the Severan time, see Raepsaet-Charlier 1999: 234.

43 *CIL* 9.1901, *Beneventum*. On the *gentes Betitia* and *Eggia* of Aeclanum, see Evangelisti 2014.

44 Chausson 2007: 123.

45 *PLRE*, I p. 782 s.v. Rufinus 25; Porena 2003: 366–371, 455 makes a complete revision of the pertinent documentation, particularly regarding the imperial constitutions. Vulcacius Rufinus was very close to Constantius II, especially in organising the logistics to bring down Magnentius.

46 Neratius Cerealis, a partisan of Constantius II, dedicated an equestrian statue to him after the removal of Magnentius from Rome and from Italy, when he was *praefectus urbi: CIL* 6.1158, cf. p. 4330 = *EDR*129241.

47 Chastagnol 1960: 60–61, 301–302, 465 no. 7; Chastagnol 1962: 135–139 no. 58; *PLRE*, I p. 197 Cerealis 2; Pavis d'Escurac 1976: 376–377.

48 Galla probably married Iulius Constantius in the early part of 320, if *Gallus*, who became Caesar in AD 351, was born in 325/6 (Amm. Marc., 14. 11. 27). On Galla see *PLRE*, I p. 382 s.v. Galla I.

49 Symm., *Relat.* 40.4 (AD 384–385): *Exhinc per aliquot annos cucurrit ista praebitio, donec Capuana legatio apud diuum atque inclytum Gratianum germanum Numinis Vestri sua tantum damna deplorans eum frumenti numerum quem Cerealis ex multis urbibus Romano Populo uindicarat restitui omnibus impetraret. Sed occasione rescripti cum sola triginta et octo milia modium quae horreis Aeternae Vrbis accesserant prouincialium recuperasset alimoniae, etiam quinque milia et septingentos modios Puteolani municipes Tarracinensibus abnuerunt.* On the interpretation of this passage see Vera 1981: 303–304.

50 This is the view expressed by Chastagnol 1962: 135–139, followed by Cracco Ruggini 1969: 139, 141; Giardina 1977: 65–66; Lo Cascio 1999: 167 n. 21, whereas Kohns 1961: 70 n. 191A; Camodeca 1980–1981: 71 and more recently Callu 2009: 188 think that the intervention should be ascribed to the period when Cerealis was *praefectus urbi*.

51 Lo Cascio 1999: 168 with reference to Carrié 1975: 1048–1049: "produzione cerealicola campana [...] destinata, in forma di *canon*, a Roma stessa" ... "quella comparativamente modesta quantità che perviene dalle grandi *domus* senatorie romane direttamente dai propri latifondi."

52 Enjuto Sánchez 2006: 115: "una conseguenza della loro collaborazione con il potere imperiale per il controllo dei territori del Sannio e della Campania."

53 The separation of Samnium from Campania and the creation of a special province date back to the mid-fourth century AD. The first known *rector* is Fabius Maximus in AD 352–357 (cited above p. 170), who was also related to the Neratii: see Cecconi 1994: 217.

54 Jacques 1986: 81–226: the scholar highlights how the interest of the Tetrarchs and the Constantinids lay in the search for relationships either with *gentes* of ancient lineage (p. 134), or with families from Southern Italy (or with large properties there), because those regions had been spared from the invasions (p. 111). The Tetrarchs, introducing the tax only in Northern Italy, effectively separated the *Italia annonaria* from the *Italia suburbicaria*, which remained privileged: here the properties of the *clarissimi* were concentrated (p. 136); on Neratii see also 99, 198–220 no. 73.

55 *AE* 1906.133 = *EDR*072133 (found at the corner of via Urbana and via di S. Maria Maggiore): *II Neratiorum C(ai) et Marcelli*; De Caprariis 1987/88.116 e 124 n. 45 = *EDR*170843: *L(uci) Nerati Pr(isci) / Volusius Adiectus fec(it)*. On this *domus* see Eck 1996a: 144.

56 *CIL* 6.32051, cf. pp. 3814, 4807 = *EDR*114762 with photo.

57 Guidobaldi 1996c: 172–173.

58 The dedications refer to the private and domestic sphere.

59 *CIL* 6.1745, cf. pp. 3813, 4750 = *EDR*137195 (seen for the first time at Villa Peretti-Montalto). See Orlandi 2011: 448, no. 58.

60 The date of his magistrature is debated. It essentially depends on the interpretation of a problematic dedication, now lost, from Benevento (*CIL* 9.1566 = *EDR*139124), in which it has erroneously been transcribed *Divo Valeriano*. If we correct it with *Divo Valentiniano*, we must date the dedication after the death of the emperor, which occurred in AD 375: see Cecconi 1994: 215 and n. 19 (AD 375–376), though he is not completely entirely convinced; if we accept the correction *D(omino) n(ostro) Valentiniano*, we can date the dedication as early as 25 February AD 364: see Camodeca and Soldovieri 2018: 292, 294 on the basis of Seek 1921: c. 831, s.v. Scopius. Less specific is Chastagnol 1963, 364 (after AD 358) and M.R. Torelli 2002: 233–234 (the age of Valentinianus). On Scopius, see *PLRE* I, p. 810 Scopius.

61 *CIL* 6. 1746 = 31918, cf. pp. 3813, 4750 = *EDR*137196 (seen for the first time at Villa Peretti-Montalto). On the place of discovery see Chioffi 1999a: 40 and nn. 10–12; Niquet 2000: 29 and n. 100.
62 *CIL* 6.31917, cf. p. 855 ad no. 1744a, pp. 3814, 4793 = *CIL* 14, p. 494 ad no. 3014 = *EDR*114184. See Sabbatini Tumolesi 1984: 31–34; *EAOR*, I 18; *EAOR*, IV, no. 49. De Caprariis 1987/88: 124 n. 45 correctly removes the inscription from the documentation, unlike Guidobaldi 1996a: 79, who continues to consider the inscription from Rome.
63 In this area, wealthy *domus* were built between the fourth and fifth centuries: see Guidobaldi 1986: 213–219.
64 *CIL* 6.1744a = 31916c, cf. pp. 4749–50 = *EDR*126990; 6.1744a = 31916a = *EDR*129313 (S. Maria Maggiore area); 6.1744c = 31916b = *EDR*126992 (Villa Peretti-Montalto); 6.1744g = *EDR*129289 (near the arch of Settimius Severus); 6.1744b = 31916d = *EDR*126993; 6.1744d = 31916g = *EDR*129286; 6.1744e, f, l = 31916f = *EDR*129285; 6.1744h = 31916h = *EDR*129287; 6.1744i = 31916i = *EDR*129288; VI 1744k = 31916e = EDR126991 (ignota).
65 Maréchal 2020: 91–110 (Rome), esp. 102 (S. Maria Maggiore), 228 n. EI-14 (*CIL* 6.31916c).
66 This is the view expressed by Chastagnol 1962: 137–138; see further also Niquet 2000: 209.
67 Jacopi 1980: 15–24 = *EDR*175867.
68 Chioffi 1999b: 252; Chioffi 1999a: 38–42, esp. 39.
69 See *PLRE*, II, p. 824, s.v. Palmatus 1, which does not exclude the fact that Palmatus 1 may be identical to *PLRE*, I, p. 662, s.v. Neratius Palmatus 2, known from *CIL* 10.7124, and debates the identification with the incomplete name which appears in *CIL* 6.37128 = *EDR*071772. See Chastagnol 1962: 269–270, who does not hesitate to identify the *Palmatus* quoted in *Cod. Theod.*, 14. 2. 4 with *Neratius Palmatus, v.c., c[ons. Siciliae?]*, sponsor of the decoration of the Syracuse' theater *frons scaenae* known from *CIL* 10.7124, now lost. Chastagnol also proposes to attribute to *Palmatus* *CIL* 6.37128, cf. pp. 4821–4822 = *EDR*071772, a fragment of an architrave which documents the restoration of the *curia senatus*. However, the reading *Neratius P*[- - -] proposed cannot be accepted because on the stone it is written *Neratius Iu*[- - -] (so formerly CIL) and the palaeography seems be from the fourth rather than from the fifth century: see Orlandi 2013: 341. G. Alföldy, in the commentary on *CIL* 6.37128, p. 4822 proposes to attribute to a certain *Palmatus*, perhaps the *praefectus urbi* of AD 412, the fragmentary architrave from the curia where it's written [- - -]*atus v.* [*c.* - - -]: see *CIL* 6.40803a = *EDR*173068.
70 Guidobaldi 1996b: 151.
71 On Palmatus mentioned in *Liber Pontificalis* see *PLRE*, I, p. 662, s.v. Palmatus 1 (this does not rule out the possibility that he could be Palmatus 2).
72 Torelli 1982: 177–178 puts forward the hypothesis of identifying the Neratius Palmatus from the dedication to Jupiter with the father of Cerealis and with the sponsor of the decoration of the Syracuse theater *frons scaenae* (*CIL* 10.7124).
73 Camodeca and Soldovieri 2018: 294–295 = *EDR*169401 with photo.
74 Torelli 1982: 178.
75 Liverani 2010: 465–466.
76 Torelli 1982: 178: "L'intensa attività edilizia nella capitale, là dove si dispiega il potere politico della famiglia."

References

Andermahr, A. M. (1998) *Totus in praediis: senatorischer Grundbesitz in Italien in der frühen und hohen Kaiserzeit*. Bonn: R. Habelt.

Birley, A.R. (1991) Vindolanda: Notes on Some New Writing Tablets, *ZPE* 88, 87–102.

Buonocore, M. (2009) La *res sacra* nell'Italia centro-appenninica fra tarda repubblica e impero. In: J. Bodel and M. Kajava, eds., *Dediche sacre nel mondo greco-romano: diffusione, funzioni, tipologie* (Acta Instituti Romani Finlandiae 35). Rome: Institutum Romanum Finlandiae, 245–305.

Callu, J.P. (2009) Symmaque, *Oeuvres*, tome V. *Discours. Rapports.* Paris: Les Belles Lettres.

Camodeca, G. (1976) La carriera del giurista L. Neratius Priscus. *Ann. Acc. Napoli* 97, 19–38.

Camodeca, G. (1980–1981) Ricerche su Puteoli tardoromana (fine III–IV secolo). *Puteoli* 4–5, 59–128.

Camodeca, G. (2007) Il giurista L. Neratius Priscus, cos. suff. 97. Nuovi dati su carriera e famiglia. *SDHI* 73, 291–311.

Camodeca, G. (2013) Novità sulle iscrizioni senatorie da Teanum e Cales. In: H. Solin, ed., *Le epigrafi della valle del Comino. Atti del IX Convegno epigrafico cominese*. San Donato Val di Comino: F & C Edizioni, 41–58.

Camodeca, G. and Soldovieri, U. (2018) Un'inedita iscrizione puteolana in esametri per Naeratius Scopius, v.c., consularis Campaniae. *ZPE* 208, 289–298.

Carrié, J.M. (1975) Les distributions alimentaires dans les cités de l'empire romain tardif. *MEFRA* 87, 995–1101.

Cecconi, G.A. (1994) *Governo imperiale e élites dirigenti nell'Italia tardoantica: problemi di storia politico-amministrativa (270–476 d.C.).* Como: Edizione New Press.

Chastagnol, A. (1960) *La préfecture urbaine à Rome sous le bas empire.* Paris: Presses universitaires de France.

Chastagnol, A. (1962) *Les fastes de la Préfecture de Rome au Bas-Empire.* Paris: Nouvelles Éditions Latines.

Chastagnol, A. (1963) L'administration du diocèse au Bas-Empire. *Historia* 12, 348–379.

Chausson, F. (1998) Une hypothèse sur la grand-mère maternelle de Septime Sévère. *Latomus* 57, 391–414.

Chausson, F. (2007) Stemmata Aurea. *Constantin, Justine, Théodose: revendications généalogiques et idéologie impériale au IVe siècle ap. J.-C.* Rome.

Chioffi, L. (1999a) Sulle case delle élites a Roma e dintorni. Supplemento al LTUR. *BCAR* 100, 37–52.

Chioffi, L. (1999b) Domus: Neratius Palmatus. In *LTUR* V, 252.

Ciliberto, F.M. and Notardonato M. (2023) *La ripresa degli scavi della villa romana in loc. Crocella (cosiddetta Villa dei Neratii) presso San Giuliano del Sannio (CB): Aspetti preliminari* (in print).

Cracco Ruggini, L. (1969) Le relazioni fiscali, annonarie e commerciali delle città campane con Roma nel IV secolo. *StRom* 17, 133–146.

De Angelis d'Ossat, M. (2011) Base di statua di Naeratius Cerealis. In: *Museo Nazionale Romano, Palazzo Altemps. Le collezioni.* Milan: Electa.

De Benedittis, G. (2009) Il territorio di Santa Croce di Magliano dal VI secolo a.C. alla tarda antichità. In: C. Ebanista, ed., *Ricerche archeologiche 2007–2008 nel castello di Magliano a Santa Croce di Magliano.* Lucera: Morgan Miller Edizioni, 173–175.

De Benedittis, G. (2011) *I dati di scavo e la villa romana.* In: G. De Benedittis, ed., *San Giuliano del Sannio. La villa dei Neratii.* Campobasso: Palladino Editore, 69–78.

De Caprariis, F. (1987/88) Topografia archeologica dell'area del Palazzo del Viminale. *BCAR* 92, 109–126.

EAOR, I (1988) P. Sabbatini Tumolesi, ed., *Epigrafia Anfiteatrale dell'Occidente Romano, I, Roma.* Rome: Edizioni Quasar.

EAOR, IV (1996) M. Fora ed. *Epigrafia Anfiteatrale dell'Occidente romano*, IV. *Regio Italiae I: Latium*. Rome: Edizioni Quasar.

Eck, W. (1983) Zur Familie der Neratii aus Saepinum. *ZPE* 50, 195–201.

Eck, W. (1996a) Domus: Neratii. In: *LTUR*, II, 144.

Eck, W. (1996b) *Onori per persone di alto rango sociopolitico in ambito pubblico e privato*. In: *Tra epigrafia, prosopografia e archeologia. Scritti scelti, rielaborati e aggiornati*. Rome: Edizioni Quasar, 299–318.

Eck, W. (2003) Suffektconsuln der Jahre 132–134 und Hadrians Rückkehr nach Rom im Jahre 132. *ZPE* 143, 234–242.

Enjuto Sánchez, B. (2006) I Neratii: legami tra Roma e le città del Sannio nel IV secolo d.C. In: M. Ghilardi, Ch.J. Goddard, P. Porena, eds. *Les cités de l'Italie tardo-antique (IVe-VIe siècle). Institutions, économie, société, culture et religion* (CEFR 369). Rome: École Française de Rome, 113–121.

Evangelisti, S. (2014) Le famiglie senatorie dei Betitii e degli Eggii di Aeclanum. In: M. L. Caldelli and G.L. Gregori, eds. *Epigrafia e ordine senatorio, 30 anni dopo*. Rome: Edizioni Quasar, 641–658.

Gaggiotti, M. (1978) Le iscrizioni della basilica di Saepinum e i Rectores della provincia del Samnium. *Athenaeum* n.s. 56, 145–169.

Gaggiotti, M. (1984–1985) La villa dei Neratii nel territorio di Saepinum. *An. Fac. Lett. Perugia* 22, 129–140.

Gaggiotti, M. (1987–1988) Frammenti epigrafici inediti da Saepinum pertinenti alla gens Neratia. *An. Fac. Lett. Perugia* 25, 127–140.

Gaggiotti, M. (1991) "Saepinum" e "La basilica di Saepinum." In: S. Capini, ed., *Samnium. Archeologia del Molise*. Rome: Edizioni Quasar, 243–249.

Gaggiotti, M. (2011) *La gens Neratia*. In: G. De Benedittis, ed., *San Giuliano del Sannio. La villa dei Neratii*. Campobasso: Palladino Editore, 14–31.

Giardina, A. (1977) Sulla concorrenza tra prefettura urbana e prefettura dell'annona, *SycGymn n.s.* 19, 65–74.

Guidobaldi, F. (1986) L'edilizia abitativa unifamiliare nella Roma tardoantica. In: *Società romana e impero tardoantico*, II. *Roma. Politica, economia, paesaggio urbano*. Rome-Bari: Laterza, 165–237.

Guidobaldi, F. (1996a) Domus: Naeratius Cerealis. In: *LTUR* II, 79.

Guidobaldi, F. (1996b) Domus Palmati. In: *LTUR* II, 151.

Guidobaldi, F. (1996c) Domus: Vulcacius Rufinus. In: *LTUR* II, 172–173.

Jacopi, I. (1980) La statua dell'egioco Giove Viminio. *BdA*, s. VI, 65. 6, 15–24.

Jacques, F. (1986) L'ordine senatorio attraverso la crisi del III secolo. In: *Società romana e impero tardoantico*, I. *Istituzioni, ceti, economie*. Rome-Bari: Laterza, 81–226.

Kohns, H.P. (1961) *Versorgungskrisen und Hungerrevolten im spätantiken Rom* (Antiquitas 6). Bonn: Rudolf Habelt Verlag.

Liverani, P. (2010) Osservazioni sulla domus sotto S. Maria Maggiore a Roma e sulla sua relazione con la basilica. *MDAIR* 116, 459–467.

Lo Cascio, E. (1999) Canon frumentarius, suarius, vinarius*: stato e privati nell'approvvigionamento dell'Vrbs*. In: W.V. Harris, ed., *The Transformations of Vrbs Roma in Late Antiquity* (JRA, Suppl. 33). Portsmouth: Journal of Roman Archaeology, 163–182.

Maréchal, S. (2020) *Public Baths and Bathing Habits in Late Antiquity* (Late Antique Archaeology, Suppl. Ser. 6). Leiden: Brill.

Marzano, A. (2007) *Roman villas in Central Italy: A Social and Economic History*. Leiden-Boston: Brill.

Muccilli, I. (2010) Le epigrafi romane della villa. In: G. De Benedittis, ed., *San Giuliano del Sannio. La villa dei Neratii*. Campobasso: Palladino Editore, 53–60.

Niquet, H. (2000) *Monumenta virtutum titulique*. Stuttgart: Steiner Verlag.

Orlandi, S. (2011) *Gli ultimi sacerdoti pagani di Roma: analisi della documentazione epigrafica*. In: *Pagans and Christians in the Roman empire. The breaking of a dialogue (IVth - VIth century A.D.). Proceedings of the International Conference at the Monastery of Bose (October 2008)*. Zurich: Lit Verlag, 425–466.

Orlandi, S. (2013) Le tracce del passaggio di Alarico nelle fonti epigrafiche. In: J. Lipps, C. Machado, Ph. von Rummel, eds. *The Sack of Rome in 410 AD. The Event, Its Context and Its Impact*. Wiesbaden: Reichert Verlag, 335–351.

Pavis d'Escurac, H. (1976) *La préfecture de l'annone, service administratif impérial d'Auguste à Constantin* (BEFAR 226). Rome: École Française de Rome.

PLRE I (1971) A.H.M. Jones, J.R. Martindale and J. Morris, eds., *The Prosopography of the Later Roman Empire*, I. Cambridge: Cambridge University Press.

Porena, P. (2003) *Le origini della prefettura del pretorio tardoantica*. Rome: L'Erma di Bretschneider.

Raepsaet-Charlier, M.-Th. (1987) *Prosopographie des femmes de l'ordre sénatorial (Ier-IIe siècles)*. Leuven: Peeters.

Raepsaet-Charlier, M.-Th. (1999) Matronae equestres. La parenté féminine de l'ordre équestre. In: L'ordre équestre. Histoire d'une aristocratie (IIe siècle av. J.-C. - IIIe siècle ap. J.-C.). *Actes du colloque international de Bruxelles-Leuven, 5–7 octobre 1995*. Rome: École Française de Rome, 215–236.

Ricci, C. and Roccia, M. (2016) Ferrazzano (CB) in età romana. Tra epigrafia e topografia. In: F. Mainardis, ed., *Voce concordi. Scritti per Claudio Zaccaria* (AAAd. 85). Trieste: Editreg, 577–597.

Sabbatini Tumolesi, P. (1984) A proposito di CIL, VI, 31917 da Praeneste (?). *BCAR* 89. 1, 29–34.

Seek, O. (1921) Scopius. In: *RE*, II A 1, c. 831.

Settipani, C. (2000) *Continuité gentilice et continuité familiale dans les familles sénatoriales romaines à l'époque imperiale. Mythe et réalité*. Oxford: Oxford University Press.

Soricelli, G. (2009) La provincia del Samnium e il terremoto del 346. In: A. Storchi Marino, ed., *Interventi imperiali in campo economico e sociale. Da Augusto al Tardoantico*. Bari: Edipuglia, 245–262.

Stelluti, N. (1997) *Epigrafi di Larino e della bassa Frentania*. Campobasso: Lampo.

Syme, R. (1957) The Jurist L. Neratius Priscus. *Hermes* 85, 480–493.

Torelli, M. (1982) Ascesa al Senato e rapporti con i territori d'origine. Italia: Regio IV (Samnium). In: S. Panciera, ed., *Epigrafia e ordine senatorio*, II (Tituli 5). Rome: Edizioni Quasar, 165–199.

Torelli, M.R. (2002) *Benevento romana*. Rome: "L'Erma" di Bretschneider.

Vera, D. (1981) *Commento storico alle Relationes di Q. Aurelio Simmaco*. Pisa: Giardini.

Vidman, L. (1981) Die familie des L. Neratius Marcellus. *ZPE* 43, 377–384.

Part IV

Urban Businesses

11 "Two of My Shops Have Collapsed..."

Real Estate and Predatory Urban Practices in Late Republican Central Italy

Dominik Maschek

Abstract

According to David Harvey, urbanisation is a process which, driven by reckless investors, first and foremost is geared towards the constant absorption of surplus capital. Based upon the analysis of both literary and archaeological sources, this chapter tries to identify and model the nature and scale of what Harvey calls "predatory urban practices" for late republican Italy. Here, we do not find many of Harvey's upstart investors but first and foremost the members of local, landowning elites who were not only interested in financial but also in social capital. Euergetism and conspicuous spending played a key role in their investments; and building projects were high up the list of prestigious donations. Both monumental and vernacular construction projects needed and attracted a large workforce, while at the same time constantly refining the implementation of specific building technologies, modes of property management, and patterns of consumption. By looking at specific data and case studies from Rome and Pompeii, this chapter focuses on the proliferation of dedicated spaces for production, retail, and rental accommodation, commonly subsumed under the term *tabernae*. Through parametric modelling, it becomes clear that rent taking from urban real estate was not only a side-business for late republican investors, but from the later second century BCE onwards it constituted a major sector of the urban economy in densely populated areas. The expected revenue from *tabernae* and lodgings led to large-scale projects of demolition and construction, mainly driven by the members of local elite families and senatorial absentee landlords such as Cicero. As in Harvey's concept of urban predation, it was highly lucrative for late republican property owners to pump capital into property development. This business model transformed the landed municipal elite, the *domi nobiles* of central Italy, into a group of urban investors whose wealth relied to similar degrees on the production of cash crops and urban real estate.

***

On 17 April 44 BCE, Cicero wrote to Atticus from Puteoli, reporting the latest news about the properties he had inherited from the local businessman and banker Cluvius:

> First, I am quite delighted with the Cluvius property. But you ask me why I have sent for Chrysippus: two of my shops [*tabernae*] have collapsed and

DOI: 10.4324/9781003187806-15

> the others are showing cracks, so that even the mice have moved elsewhere, to say nothing of the tenants. Other people call this a disaster, I don't call it even a nuisance. […] However, there is a building scheme under way, Vestorius advising and instigating [*consiliario quidem et auctore Vestorio*], which should turn this loss into a source of profit. […] You ask whether the Cluvian property comes to 100,000 [HS] a year yet. It looks as though it is going to, but in the first year I have cleared 80,000 [HS].
> (Cic. *Att.* 14.9; transl. D.R. Shackleton Bailey)

The Chrysippus mentioned in this letter also features elsewhere in Cicero's correspondence. He was a freedman of a certain Vettius Cyrus, a reputed architect who had worked for Cicero and his brother Quintus on various domestic building projects in the mid-50s BCE.[1] In 45 BCE, Chrysippus had been assessing the state of one of Cicero's gardens and villas, including some suggestions for possible alterations such as converting a bath suite into winter apartments and adding a small *ambulatio* (*Att.* 13.29.1). From this it becomes clear that Chrysippus was not only an expert at estimating, planning, and probably conducting building works, but that he was also at Cicero's disposal for all sorts of projects and tasks. Equally, Gaius Vestorius, who operated alongside Chrysippus in overseeing and managing the restoration of Cicero's shops at Puteoli, could boast substantial expertise in fields like property sales, urban manufacture, and long-distance trade. He is attested to have been an important broker of real estate on the Bay of Naples, alongside operating a lucrative dyeing business whose products were even found on a late republican shipwreck off the coast of Marseille.[2]

Modern scholars have focused on this and other passages in order to demonstrate the intimate links between a late republican Roman senator like Cicero and an extended penumbra of friends and more or less dependent experts who were crucial for the pursuit of his business ventures.[3] Although the existence of a Roman market for urban investment shows signs of capitalist behaviour and economic rationality, its essential reliance on such social networks of dependency and friendship should caution us against understanding and describing it in purely modern terms.[4] Nonetheless, it is clear that Cicero expected a profit from his investments in urban property. The *tabernae* at Puteoli are a case in point, although recent scholarship on the economy of Roman urban centres has mostly focused on production and retail rather than on the potential opportunities of the rental market.[5]

This aligns with a view of the Roman urban economy that is predominantly positive: it is understood as a generator of wealth and concomitant economic growth; as a proxy for the complexity of urban society; and as the culmination of supply chains which criss-crossed the Roman empire and extended well beyond its boundaries. All of this is surely right. However, this chapter will explore another side to urban economies which, so far, has not been fully considered in research on Roman urbanism: the forms of investment and activities which David Harvey has subsumed under the label of "predatory urban practices."

Predatory Urban Practices: Cities for the Few, Not the Many

According to Harvey, urbanisation is a process which, driven by reckless investors, first and foremost is geared towards the constant absorption of surplus capital.[6] Modern capitalist entrepreneurs invest not only in production, but also in rentable real estate in order to maintain their lifestyle and thus their social status. Their investments, for example in construction projects, attract workers, artisans, and craftsmen who in turn have to pay the required rents. Via expenses for rent and subsistence, the workers' wage payments are converted back into revenue for the investors.

In Harvey's view, transfer payments to the working urban population thus

> can be clawed back for the capitalist class as a whole through predatory and exploitative activities in the realm of consumption. For much of the low-income urbanized population, the joint excessive exploitation of their labor and the dispossession of their meager assets constitutes a perpetual drain upon their capacity to sustain minimally adequate conditions of social reproduction.[7]

But, in the long run, this double strategy of the financial elite causes a paradoxical situation: the demand for labour partly leads to higher wages, which in turn increases the demand for cheap workers who live permanently at the subsistence level. At the same time, urban space is becoming denser, leaving less and less room for the capitalists' investments. The result is social conflict. Ultimately, the investors have no choice but to subject their own city and its social structure to a continuous process of "creative destruction."[8]

Based upon the analysis of both literary and archaeological sources, it is obvious that similar processes were also at work in late republican Italy. As demonstrated by the *tabernae* at Puteoli, wealthy investors like Cicero put their money into real estate, demolition, construction projects, and urban development throughout the late second and first centuries BCE, whilst others, such as Atticus and Vestorius, acted as partners and middlemen. Specialised builders and architects like Chrysippus provided the crucial expertise. The speed and intensity of urban development was staggering. Writing in the Augustan period, Strabo states that the construction of houses in Rome

> goes on unceasingly in consequence of the collapses and fires and repeated sales (these last, too, going on unceasingly); and indeed the sales are intentional collapses, as it were, since the purchasers keep tearing down the houses and building new ones, one after another, to suit their wishes.
>
> (Strab. *Geogr.* 5.3.7; transl. H.L. Jones)

Although this description closely matches the definition of "creative destruction" in Harvey's predatory urban practices, the differences to modern capitalism were profound. In Rome and in the towns of late republican Italy we do not find many of Harvey's upstart investors but first and foremost the members of landowning elites who relied on extended networks of friends and dependents to realise their aims. Euergetism and conspicuous spending played a key role in their investments; and building projects were high up the list of prestigious donations.

Perhaps it is due to the prominence and magnitude of the elite's euergetistic activities that the field of predatory urban practices does not figure prominently in historical and archaeological studies of the urban *plebs* in late republican Rome and central Italy.[9] Conventionally, these people's destitution is accepted as a given fact, partly seen as a result of the displacement of small farmers by slave estates in the later second and first centuries BCE.[10] Archaeologists and historians have been more interested in what has been labelled an urban "middle class" of shopkeepers and artisans. Debates mostly revolve around the social composition of this group (freedmen or freeborn, dependent or independent?) and aspects of terminology (is "middle class" an appropriate word?), but generally its emergence is seen as a sign of growing prosperity and social mobility in the late republican and early imperial period.[11]

However, this does not shed much light on the degree to which urban life was conditioned by the conscious choice of elite investors to capitalise on the rest of the urban population. In order to reach a deeper understanding of these dynamics, we have to consider both sides of the coin: how, on a structural level, did investment in urban development create both wealth and destitution, and what, if any, was the systemic link between the two? In order to address these questions, this chapter will focus on one particular aspect of this socio-economic transformation: the proliferation of dedicated spaces for production, retail, and rental accommodation, commonly subsumed under the term *tabernae*.

The Allure of the *taberna*: Real Estate Development and Investment in the Late Second and First Century BCE

From the second century BCE to the Augustan period, the Apennine peninsula experienced a period of remarkable urban growth. Central Italy in particular was at the heart of a development that saw the monumentalisation of many towns in Latium and Campania alongside the intensification of agricultural production and new levels of consumption.[12] Urban centres served as focal points for internal migration across the peninsula, resulting in growing urban populations which increasingly relied on a monetised economy.[13] This created the perfect conditions for rent-seeking elites to generate a new stream of guaranteed income. Most archaeological studies on domestic architecture in central Italy, explicitly or implicitly, reckon with urban populations of home-owners, such as in Pompeii.[14] But given the evidence for the existence of a potent rental market in Roman legal texts, it is fairer to assume that, by the late second and early first century BCE, a substantial part, if not the majority, of the urban population in central Italy would have lived in some sort of rental accommodation.[15] This means that, alongside the sale of wine and other agricultural produce from their estates, the rent generated from shops, bars, and lodgings must have constituted a major source of income for late republican urban elites.[16] It is therefore curious that, so far, this aspect of late republican urbanisation has only been of limited interest to scholars working on the Roman economy and on the socio-political history of the late Republic.

According to Livy, *tabernae* had already been part of the Roman Forum in the sixth century BCE.[17] Allegedly, these *tabernae lanienae* were then transformed into *tabernae argentariae* at some point before 308 BCE.[18] More reliable reports concern the rebuilding of the *tabernae* (*novae*) after a fire in 210 BCE and the existence of *tabernae* in the Forum Boarium by 192 BCE.[19] In the mid-third century BCE, Rome saw the construction of its first permanent *macellum* which contained a number of separate market stalls.[20] Half a century later, buying and selling of goods and services were at the heart of a well-known passage in Plautus' comedy *Curculio*; the *tabernae veteres* on the south side of the Roman Forum feature prominently in it.[21] The construction of the great basilicas in the 170s and 160s profoundly altered the commercial topography of the Forum, whilst also providing space for yet more prominently placed rows of *tabernae*.[22]

At the same time, the archaeological evidence demonstrates the proliferation of *tabernae* that were integrated into elite houses. A number of *domus* on the north slope of the Palatine feature clearly articulated shop fronts alongside the so-called *clivus Palatinus* and the Via Sacra.[23] Their layout, according to the excavators, was defined at some point after the fire of 210 BCE, with modifications in the decades between 70 and 20 BCE, but the most intense building activity seems to date predominantly between the second and the last quarters of the second century BCE.[24] *Tabernae* were also identified in another group of *domus* on the northeast slopes of the Palatine, dating to the mid-second century BCE and perhaps associated with the reconfiguration of urban infrastructure initiated by the censors of 174 BCE.[25] A lavishly decorated monument from the late second century BCE, found in the vicinity alongside the Via Sacra, offers a glimpse into the social world associated with these shops. Its inscriptions mention several *magistri* of artisanal *collegia*, and in particular butchers (*lanii*) and gem-makers (*gemmarii*). The monument's ostentatious and fashionable design shows considerable investment and the desire for representation and recognition amongst these well-organised associations of shopkeepers and highly qualified artisans who operated in a specialised urban market.[26] The revenue generated in these places must have been substantial, as also attested by the growing importance of conspicuous consumption amongst the Roman elite throughout the second and first century BCE.[27]

A similar development has been observed at Pompeii. Here, the second half of the second century BCE saw the construction of a large number of new *tabernae* in Nocera Tufa and grey lava. As opposed to earlier periods, these *tabernae* were no longer confined to the front of larger *domus* but now also appeared on the flanks of urban properties, in an obvious attempt to maximise commercial space. Moreover, the number of *tabernae* integrated into the frontal façades of houses increased significantly, from the traditional two to up to six.[28] Considering the sheer scale of these architectural changes it is difficult not to agree with Miko Flohr's assessment that "investment on a larger scale transformed the functioning of the local economy, with profound socio-economic consequences."[29]

One particularly important aspect of this transformation was the incorporation of *tabernae* into a number of public buildings of late republican Pompeii. Whilst shops did not yet form part of the so-called Republican Baths which were built in the middle of the second century BCE, the design of the slightly later Stabian Baths (around 130/125 BCE) included a row of nine spacious *tabernae* with pillars of Nocera Tufa that lined the Via dell'Abbondanza to the south of the building.[30] This was even surpassed by the Forum Baths at the Via delle Terme, in a prime location north of the Pompeian forum, commissioned in the early years of the Sullan *colonia* (Figure 11.1): here, no fewer than 24 *tabernae* encircled the main bath building, covering nearly 50 per cent of the area.[31] Rather than labelling this complex a bathhouse with *tabernae* it would thus be equally valid to call it a shopping mall with a central bathing suite.[32] Even more remarkably, the construction of the Forum Baths seems to have

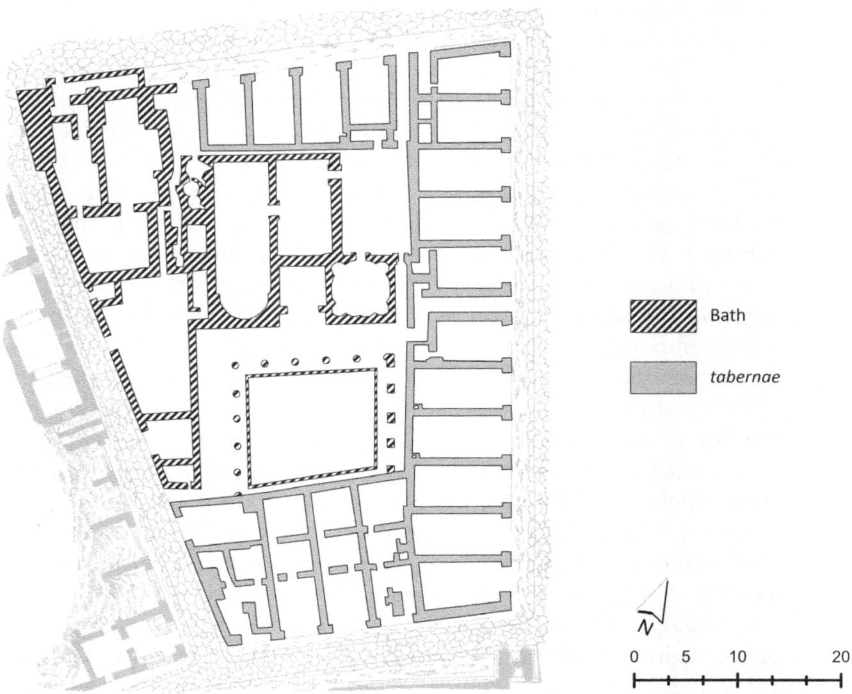

Figure 11.1 Forum Baths at Pompeii, early years of the Sullan *colonia*; drawing: D. Maschek.

responded to a major development project in the adjacent Insula VII 6 across the Vico delle Terme. Here, in the decade leading up to 89 BCE, several properties on the insula's east side were converted into *tabernae* with a façade in Nocera Tufa. These shops replaced a number of older row houses.[33] Given the coherent architectural design and the uniform usage of building materials, it is fair to follow Michael Anderson's suggestion that the entire row of *tabernae* was commissioned by the owner of the "Casa di Secundus Tyrannus Fortunatus," a substantial *domus* to which the first shop had originally belonged.[34]

Rather unsurprisingly, the close link between the owners of wealthy Pompeian houses and the development of real estate into new spaces for retail and rental accommodation also had an eminently political side to it. An Oscan inscription found near the shops at the main entrance of the Stabian Baths and dating to the second half of the second century BCE relates to the erection of a sundial by decree of the assembly and overseen by the *quaestor* Maras Atinius.[35] As already indicated in the comedies of Plautus, time keeping was indeed crucial for shopping and business transactions in an urban environment.[36] The decision by the Pompeians to set up a sundial next to the *tabernae* in the Stabian Baths thus makes perfect sense. After the establishment of the Sullan *colonia*, another inscription tells us about substantial restoration works in the bathhouse that were undertaken by the *duoviri* Gaius Ulius and Publius Aninius.[37] By decree of the decurions, the two leading magistrates of the town let contracts for the construction of a *laconicum* and *destrictarium*, and they also saw to the restoration of the *palaestra* and the porticoes which may have included the row of *tabernae* on the building's south façade.

The epigraphic record from the Forum Baths shows a similar picture. Two building inscriptions which were found in the *tabernae* of the Via del Foro on the east side of the bathhouse attest the agency of the *duovir* Lucius Caesius, followed by another pair of *duoviri*, Gaius Occius and Lucius Niraemius, who used public funds to conduct the building works by decree of the town's decurions.[38] Apart from the limited use of limestone, the walls of this first building phase are mostly faced in quasi-reticulate lava masonry. The same facing technique and stone material was used in two other prominent buildings of the early *colonia*, namely the amphitheatre and the *theatrum tectum* whose commissioners Gaius Quinctius Valgus and Marcus Porcius were probably even the first pair of *duoviri quinquennales* ever elected at Pompeii.[39]

Strategies of Urban Rent Seeking (1): Retail and Consumption

The literary sources and the archaeological evidence from Rome and Pompeii clearly show that, starting in the second century BCE, elite families were increasingly keen on developing urban real estate, either privately or in their role as magistrates. Cicero's considerations regarding his *tabernae* at Puteoli thus reflect certain strategies of investment which by the mid-first century BCE had been around for at least three or four generations. But in order to gauge the degree to which these strategies were intrinsically predicated upon the living conditions of the majority of the urban population, we have to build a more comprehensive model that allows us to understand the systemic link between production, consumption, and rent seeking in late republican central Italy. In the following, I will first explore the potential for predatory urban practices in retail and consumption, before moving to the closely related fields of production, construction, and rental accommodation.

Steven Ellis has rightly emphasised that it is very difficult to arrive at estimates regarding the revenue generated from Roman retail, but this does not mean that some parametric modelling is not feasible as it can help us understand the possible orders of magnitude of the phenomenon.[40] As attested in the literary and epigraphic sources, *tabernae* were regularly leased out to tenants. In two inscriptions from Pompeii, rental agreements of one and two years are attested.[41] This is not dissimilar to the long-term arrangements agreed upon by "upper class tenants" in Rome.[42] Such long-term agreements provided a stable income for the landlord, but they also imply that *tabernarii* were recognised as reliable business partners, and, of course, wealthier families could have rented a *taberna* in order to let it be managed by an *institor*.[43] The archaeological record shows that there was a considerable spectrum of affluence and material means across the range of *tabernae* and, consequently, amongst the group of people running the shops.[44]

Regarding the potential sums of rent charged for *tabernae* we have to rely on somewhat more circumstantial evidence. The banker L. Caecilius Iucundus probably rented a fullery from the town of Pompeii in 58 CE for 1,652 HS a year.[45] This amounts to 4.5 HS per day, and clearly Iucundus would have expected a profit from the business, which implies sales that were higher than this daily rent plus the expenses for materials and staff. The latter are hard to gauge, but a team of two skilled and one unskilled workers could have taken wages of 14 HS per day.[46] Leaving aside the question of the pricing of materials, rent plus wages for his *fullonica* would thus have cost Iucundus up to 20 HS per day. If he reckoned with 5 to 10 per cent net profit then the revenue generated by the fullery would have been in the range of 21 to 22 HS per day (7,665 to 8,030 HS per year), but, given the economic potential of the textile trade, the profit margin was probably more considerable than this.

Further clues are provided by the architectural layout of the shops in the Forum Baths at Pompeii, which, as we have seen, were clearly built with the intention of maximising rental income from retail space. Based on dimensions and spatial organisation, it is possible to distinguish between three types of properties (Figure 11.2): first, the 16 spacious single-room shops lining the Via delle Terme and the Via del Foro, two of the most important urban thoroughfares; second, the three substantial three-room *tabernae* with further lodgings on the first floor on the Vicolo dei Soprastanti; and third, the bar at the southwestern corner of the *insula* which included a *triclinium* for formal dining and presumably also an upper floor with lodgings.

Based on their size and layout, the shops of the first type were definitely geared towards retail, although it is ultimately impossible to establish the nature

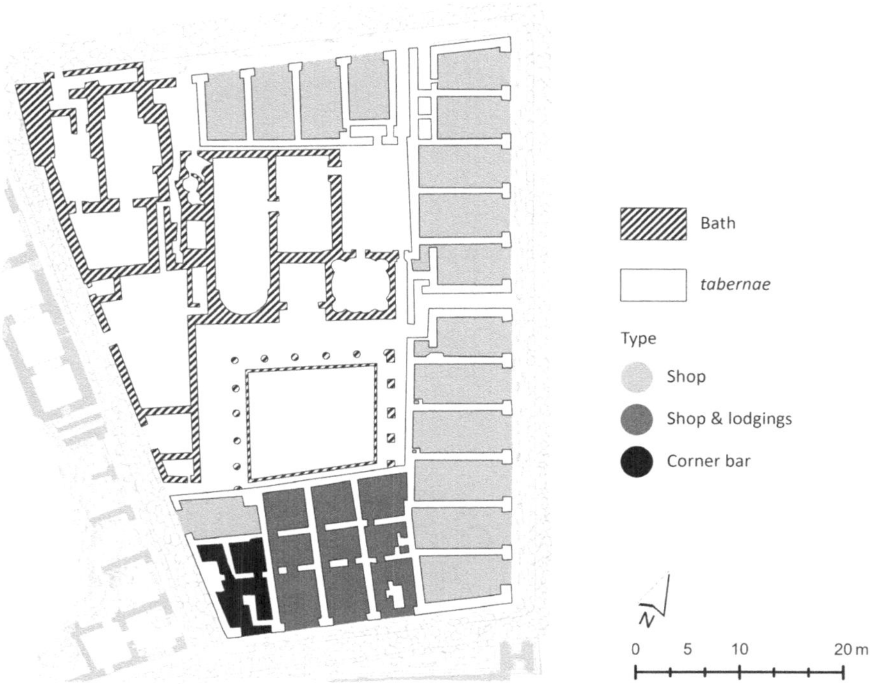

Figure 11.2 Forum Baths at Pompeii, types of (rental) property; drawing: D. Maschek.

of their business.[47] However, the lack of bespoke installations makes it clear that these spaces were not used for the kind of specialised production represented by Iucundus' *fullonica*. Thus, staff numbers could be significantly reduced, and the payment of wages would have been much less of a pressing issue in the case of family businesses. As a consequence, operating costs would have been lower than in a workshop and landlords could have charged more rent for such types of commercial properties. Hypothetically assuming a daily rent of 9 HS (3,285 HS per year) for the one-room *tabernae* (twice as much as for Iucundus' *fullonica*) therefore seems justified, whereas, for the purpose of the model, the more complex three-room *tabernae* shall be costed at 12 HS per day (4,380 HS per year; Figure 11.3).

Estimating the rent-producing potential of the corner bar is further facilitated by a number of attested prices for food and drink.[48] Although these prices are early imperial in date, they still provide useful orders of magnitude for particular items of expenditure. One bar in Pompeii charged 1 to 2 *asses* for hard cheese, 4 *asses* for soft cheese, 2 to 3 *asses* for ordinary wine, 16 *asses* (1 *denarius*) for excellent wine, 5 *asses* for onions, 1 *as* for dates, and 1 *as* for sausages.[49] In another graffito from Pompeii, cheap wine was listed at 1 *as*, Falernian at 4 *asses*[50]; and another bar painting from Herculaneum advertised wine at prices

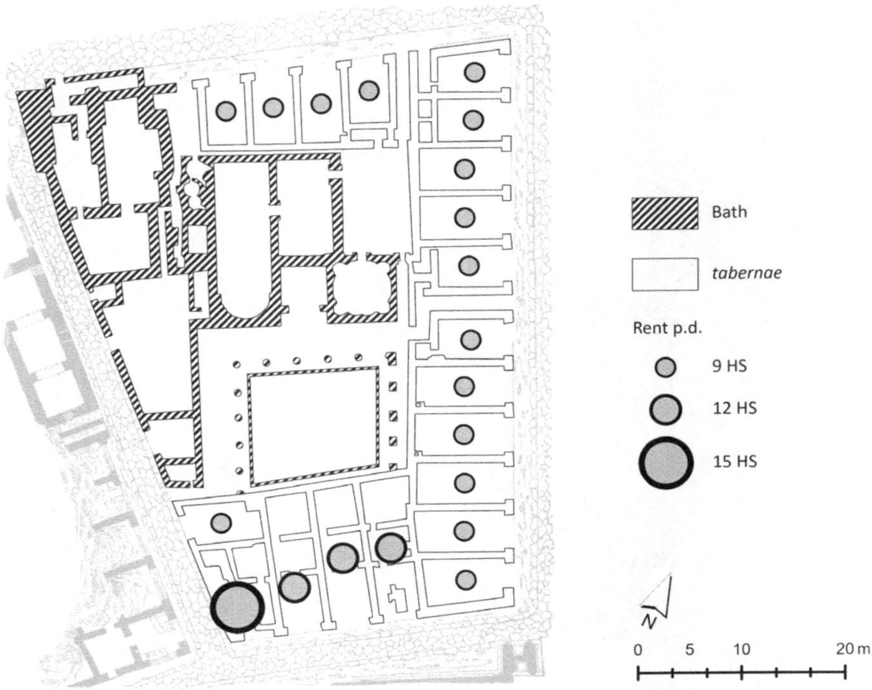

Figure 11.3 Forum Baths at Pompeii, hypothetical rental income per day; drawing: D. Maschek.

from 2 to 4.5 *asses* per *sextarius* (c. 0.5 litres).[51] From this, we can tentatively establish a price range for one serving of wine between 0.5 and 1.125 HS. Twenty customers ordering a *sextarius* of ordinary quality wine thus created a daily revenue of between 10 and 22.5 HS for the *tabernarius*.

In order to gauge the possible margins of net profit, we also have to consider purchasing prices. Available estimates for the minimum wholesale price for wine under the early empire range from 8.5 HS per amphora (25.9 litres equals 0.16 HS per *sextarius*) to 15 HS per amphora (0.29 HS per *sextarius*).[52] Based on the assumption of a family business, the minimum net profit margin for a bar owner with 20 wine-drinking customers per day was therefore 68 per cent, with a net profit of 6.8 HS, and the maximum net profit margin 74 per cent with a net profit of 16.7 HS. Naturally, this was further boosted by the consumption of food and more expensive wines. One serving of soft cheese and sausages (1 HS) per customer would have earned the innkeeper an additional 14 HS per day, if we reckon with a similar profit margin of wholesale price to retail price as for wine (70 per cent). Thus, even a *tabernarius* selling ordinary wine and modest food was able to make significantly more money per day (20.8 HS) than a skilled labourer on a decent wage of 6 HS; if we take the average of the net profit generated by the "low-end" and "high-end" estimates of daily wine and food sales, the resulting 25.75 HS were over four times the daily earnings of a skilled worker.

Given these potential profit margins, it seems reasonable to set the rent for the corner bar at the Forum Baths of Pompeii, in a prime location near to the town's civic centre, at 15 HS per day, which is equally in step with the tiered estimates for the other two types of *tabernae* in the same *insula* (Figure 11.3). Such a sum constituted a substantial deduction from the innkeeper's revenue, but it left them with 11 HS and thus nearly twice the daily income of a skilled worker. From the landlord's perspective (Figure 11.4), the *tabernae* and rental rooms in the Forum Baths were capable of creating an annual income of at least 71,175 HS (52,560 HS for the 16 single-room shops; 13,140 HS for the three shops plus lodgings; 5,475 HS for the corner bar). Further considerable income could have been generated by leasing the baths from the town and running them through an *institor* or subleasing them to a middleman.[53] Interestingly, the annual income calculated for the *tabernae* alone falls into the same order of magnitude as the 80,000 HS of profit Cicero had been able to realise from his unspecified number of shops in Puteoli before the beginning of the renovation works in 44 BCE.[54]

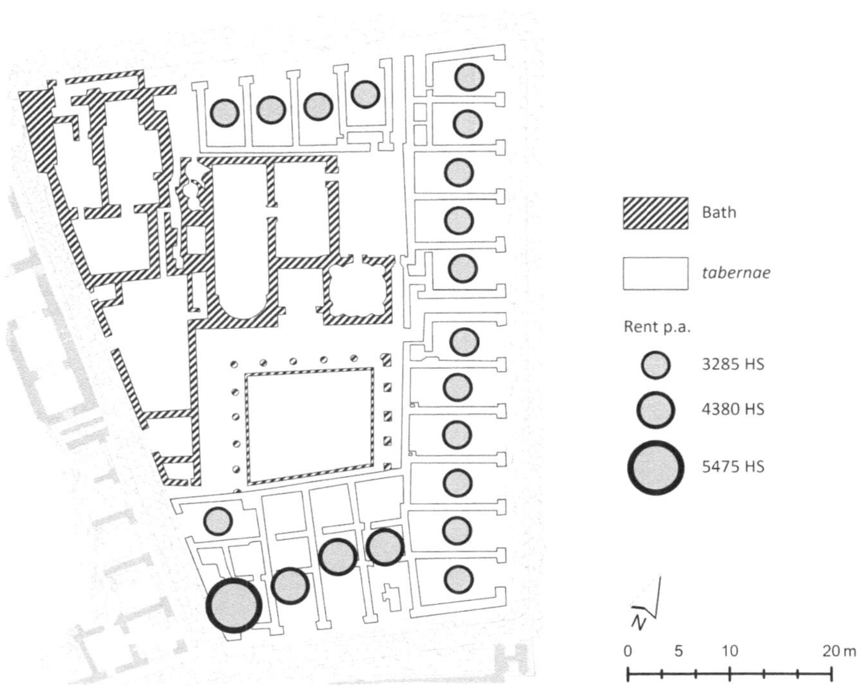

Figure 11.4 Forum Baths at Pompeii, hypothetical rental income per year; drawing: D. Maschek.

Strategies of Urban Rent Seeking (2): Construction and Production

These considerations regarding the potential returns on investment in *tabernae* are naturally linked to other fields of economic activities in which owners and developers like Cicero and Vestorius were involved. The intimate link between *tabernae* and substantial public building projects, such as the Stabian Baths and the Forum Baths at Pompeii, demonstrates the pervasive encroachment of elite interests upon the field of large-scale construction in late republican central Italy. Elite investors could not only expect a steady flow of rent from the letting of urban properties, but also from the sales of goods produced on their extraurban estates which provided a wide range of consumables, from wine and olive oil to foodstuffs.[55] Moreover, through the ownership of quarries, forests, and brickyards, late republican elite families also played a crucial role in the provision of building materials for urban construction sites.[56]

This is further substantiated by the wealth of archaeological and epigraphic evidence from central Italy in the second and first century BCE. In Hélène Jouffroy's extensive but by no means complete gazetteer of 1986, we find no fewer than 165 archaeologically attested monumental buildings such as porticoes, amphitheatres, theatres, infrastructure buildings, city walls, sanctuaries, and temples in central Italy between 150 BCE and the Augustan period, *excluding* the city of Rome.[57] Moreover, there are 100-odd building inscriptions of monumental construction projects from Latium and Campania for the second century BCE and the pre-Augustan decades of the first century, mentioning more than 200 individual magistrates actively involved in public construction works.[58] The acquisition and development of real estate must therefore have been a crucial factor in the economic strategies of urban elites in late republican central Italy.

Both monumental and domestic construction projects needed and attracted a large workforce, while at the same time constantly refining the implementation of specific building technologies and modes of property management.[59] The notorious story about M. Licinius Crassus who entertained 500 servile architects and workers in order to rebuild urban properties in Rome after their destruction by fire can serve as a case in point.[60] In recent years, several quantitative studies, such as by Will Wootton on late Roman mosaics and by Francesca Bologna on Pompeian wall paintings, have started to shed light on the microeconomic dynamics of the Roman construction industry.[61] From their estimates it is clear that urban and rural building and renovation projects could sustain the work of a number of specialised and well-salaried craftsmen across multiple generations.[62]

Depending on the nature of the tasks at hand, and organised by managers like Vestorius, professional *redemptores* or architects like Chrysippus, these specialists were then complemented by a much larger number of workers on an *ad hoc* basis.[63] These workers came from the substantial pool of city dwellers, complemented by seasonal labourers from the countryside.[64] The payment of wages was one of the main pull-factors for such workers to participate in urban development projects. The magnitude of these cashflows is indicated by the first results of a macro-scale study on the expenditure on monumental building projects in late republican central Italy: according to parametric modelling, between 150 and 50 BCE, the construction of sanctuaries, city walls, porticoes, market buildings, and basilicas in Latium led to wage payments of at least 25 million HS; in the same time period, 2 million HS were spent on workers' wages in Campania, and 400,000 HS in Umbria (Figure 11.5).[65] Through the consumption of food and the payment of rent in the respective urban centres, a significant percentage of this money was then absorbed in a cycle of redistribution that benefited the original investors.

Investors or members of their extended elite networks could generate further profit by using building materials which they either owned directly or which came from the estates of their friends or political allies. Public building contracts such as the *lex Puteolana*, drawn up in 105 BCE, prescribed the use of certain building techniques; moreover, they specified the quality of particular materials such as mortar and building stones.[66] Such clauses are important from an economic point of view, as Roman developers had a sound understanding of how the type and qualities of materials could lead to depreciation of a property over time. This becomes clear from Vitruvius, who, referring to walls of "soft rubble" (*e molli caemento*), states that

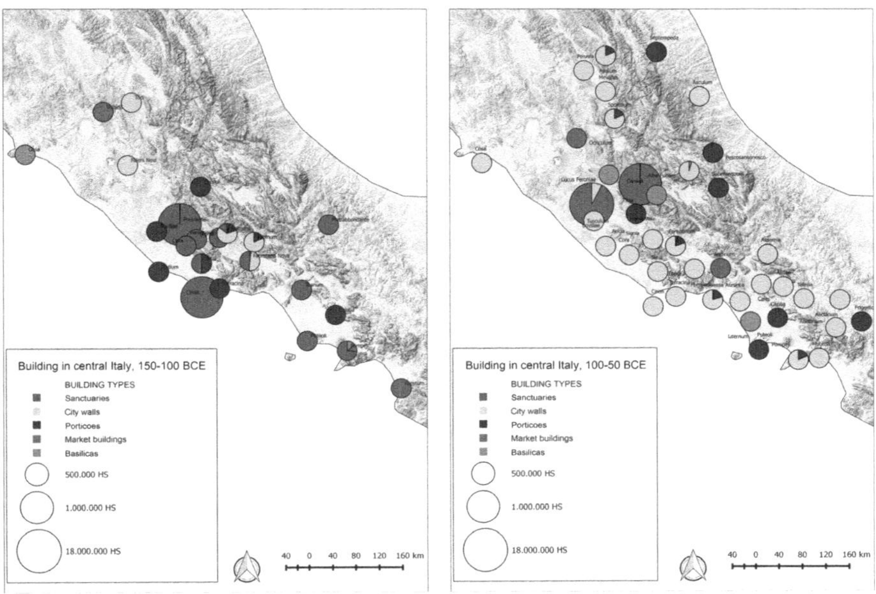

Figure 11.5 Hypothetical costs of public construction projects in central Italy, 150 to 50 BCE; map: D. Maschek.

> when assessors are appointed to evaluate party walls, they never assess soft rubble walls according to their initial cost, but rather, when they look at the price recorded in the original contracts, they deduct one-eightieth of that sum for each subsequent year, and the remaining amount is fixed as the current value of the walls. They have rendered the judgement, in effect, that such walls cannot last more than eighty years.
>
> (Vitr. De Arch. 2.8.8; transl. I. D. Rowland)

Some notion of "amortisation" is implicit in this passage, and it seems fair to assume that it not only played a role in sales but also in the initial choice of building materials for new projects. When drawing up the building contract for a row of *tabernae* or an apartment block, late republican investors would probably already have factored in the anticipated loss over the years of expected service.[67] Similar tendencies can be observed in legislation and archaeological evidence regarding the demolition of old buildings and the salvaging and reuse of their most valuable materials.[68] Such concepts of depreciation also imply that there was a point at which it was more profitable for owners to demolish and rebuild a property than to simply renovate it once again. In this way, the principle of "creative destruction" played a crucial role in the normative framework of the late republican building industry.

All of this makes clear that, by the time of Cicero and Vitruvius, the field of property development in central Italy was regulated by a set of rules which worked in the interests of wealthy and well-connected investors. This institutionalisation relied on the agency of local elite families, inextricably linking their corporate interests with the process of demolition and construction. Overall, late republican urban development rested upon a potent nexus of private economic gain, the investment of public funds, and the fact that many commissioners acted in an official role as magistrates, whilst at the same time presumably cooperating or even colluding with their social peers.

Similar considerations pertain to the elite's opportunities to sell the agricultural produce of their rural estates to the very people who lived, worked, and paid rent in their shops and apartments. In particular, with respect to the production of wine, olive oil, and wheat, wealthy landowners in late republican central Italy were uniquely well placed to make a profit by scaling up and thus dominating urban markets. This vital economic synergy has seen intense research over the last few decades.[69] In this context, some doubt has been raised by Nathan Rosenstein about the overall profitability of agriculture. By tentatively modelling population figures and comparing them with agricultural outputs, Rosenstein tries to show that agricultural production, even of cash crops, did not offer a lot of opportunities for substantial capital gains for republican elites.[70] However, Alessandro Launaro rightly points to the fact that Rosenstein's figures for prices are on the lower end of the attested spectrum.[71] Consequently, wealthy landowners could have realised a much more significant profit margin by selling wine and olive oil to urban markets, in particular with respect to the uneven development of prices and the elite's ability to make strategic usage of storage facilities to sell at the most advantageous moment.

Ultimately, however, an answer to the question of profitability cannot be solely derived from the perspective of the producers but also has to reckon with the possible modes of consumption. There is a real possibility that in newly built bars, restaurants, and *tabernae*, the landlords could have dictated that their tenants should exclusively market the owner's agricultural produce, therefore carving out little outlets for themselves as sellers in the urban marketplace and effectively bypassing the disadvantages of low wholesale prices.[72] As we have already seen in the previous section, purchasing prices for wine are attested in the range from 0.16 HS per *sextarius* to 0.29 HS per *sextarius*. In the case of the bar owner discussed before, the wholesaler's daily revenue for 20 *sextarii* of wine would have been between 3.2 HS and 5.8 HS, leading to a yearly gross profit of between 1,168 HS and 2,117 HS. This is not a trivial sum as it amounts to no less than 21 to 39 per cent of the annual rent we tentatively assumed for the corner bar at the Forum Baths. By selling wine from his own estates, the innkeeper's landlord could thus have boosted his yearly returns by more than one third.

It is therefore not helpful to see the provision of town dwellers with wine, olive oil, and other foodstuffs as an isolated strand of elite economic strategies. Instead it formed part of an integrated system of predatory urban practices. Understood in this way, the total revenue generated from urban wine sales in central Italy is less interesting than the degree to which such sales enabled investors to extract more rent from the urban working population.

Strategies of Urban Rent Seeking (3): Rental Accommodation

The third field in which substantial returns could be realised from real estate was through the letting of rental accommodation. Most evidence for the details of tenancy agreements and for the level of rent comes from the city of Rome where housing was notoriously expensive.[73] The lowest attested annual rent in late republican Rome is 2,000 HS, probably for a *cenaculum* rented by a freedman in the later second century BCE, whilst his neighbour, the future dictator Sulla, lived in the same apartment building for 3,000 HS a year (Plut. *Sulla* 1.6). In the context of a severe credit crisis in 48 BCE, Julius Caesar remitted all rents in Rome up to 2,000 HS a year, and all rents in Italy up to 500 HS a year (Suet. *Caes.* 38.2; Cass. Dio 42.51.1).[74] From this, one can tentatively deduce a ratio of 4:1 in metropolitan versus municipal rents by the time of Cicero.

Larger rental properties were often managed through middlemen who operated on a contractual basis: they paid a lump sum (*aversio*) to the owner in advance and then subleased the individual apartments at a higher price to make a profit. This arrangement appears frequently in the *Digest.*[75] In one case (*Dig.* 19.2.30 pr.), a middleman rented an apartment block (*insula*) for 30,000 HS from the owner and then sublet the individual apartments (*cenacula*) for a total revenue of 40,000 HS, thus creating a profit of 10,000 HS. In general, the legal texts assume a range of profits for middlemen from 20 to 33 per cent per year. Such arrangements must have increased the overall level of rent, as profitability for the middlemen depended on adding a substantial surcharge to an already acceptable fee. Conservative estimates reckon with expenses for accommodation at 30 to 35 per cent of overall income in the late Republic and early Empire, but this could of course have been significantly higher depending on location and type of property.[76]

In his fundamental study on sub-elite housing in Pompeii, Felix Pirson identified 270 *tabernae* as potential rental properties: 31 per cent (85) of these feature a second room, 12 per cent (33) have two additional rooms, and 8 per cent (21) three or more additional rooms. The remaining 48 per cent (131) have a main room and a *pergula*. A mezzanin is attested in 88 per cent (239) of Pompeian *tabernae*. Due to the much smaller excavated area, the overall number of potential rental *tabernae* at Herculaneum (19) looks tiny in comparison. However, the breakdown of layout and size is not dissimilar to the Pompeian record: 26 per cent (5) of *tabernae* had a second room; 26 per cent (5) two additional rooms, and 21 per cent (4) three or more additional rooms; 68 per cent (13) of *tabernae* feature a *pergula*. Moreover, in both Pompeii and Herculaneum, *cenacula* (small apartments) were often located above *tabernae, domus, hospitia*, and workshops on the upper floor of a property. Based on their size and layout, Pirson concludes that the majority of these rental *tabernae* and *cenacula* were most likely inhabited by individuals or "core" families of not more than five people, including slaves.[77]

Depending on the way in which these properties were managed and on the development of the real estate market, rent probably varied considerably, as illustrated by the great divergence between Rome and the rest of Italy in the time of Caesar. Thus, instead of producing estimates per unit of accommodation, the aim of the following parametric estimates is to gauge the potential degree to which late republican landlords could squeeze money out of their tenants, focusing on the group of urban workers who earned wages. The key question is to what extent households in first century BCE central Italy were negatively impacted by the payment of rent for accommodation. This can be tentatively quantified by deducting daily expenses for subsistence and accommodation from household income. The amount of surplus money a household had available at the end of the day can then serve as an indicator for at least two different, but related, aspects: the level of household prosperity or destitution, and the untapped potential for the landlord to increase the rent.

The model considers three different household configurations (Table 11.1): single (adult male), two persons (one adult male, one adult female), and three persons (one adult male, one adult female, one child). These combinations of age and gender are further varied by the assumption of different skill levels amongst the household members (skilled and unskilled) and different employment status.[78] Due to the nature of the evidence, any reconstruction of wage levels in late republican central Italy must rely on a fair degree of conjecture,

Daily wages (HS)			
Skilled (m)	6.5	*Skilled (f)*	2.2
Unskilled (m)	4	*Unskilled (f)*	1.5
		Child (f, m)	1.5

Daily rent (HS; 35% of wage)			
Skilled (m)	2.3	*Unskilled (m)*	1.4

Daily subsistence (HS, per person)			
'Respectability basket'	0.7	*'Subsistence basket'*	0.3

'SUBSISTENCE BASKET'

Household size	Daily surplus (HS) *Skilled (m) / Skilled (f)*	rents as % of household income	Daily surplus (HS) *Skilled (m) / Unskilled (f)*	rents as % of household income	Daily surplus (HS) *Unskilled (m) / Skilled (f)*	rents as % of household income	Daily surplus (HS) *Unskilled (m) / Unskilled (f)*	rents as % of household income
1-person (m)	3.9	39%	3.9	39%	2.3	42%	2.3	42%
2 persons (m, f, 1 working)	3.7	44%	3.7	44%	2.0	49%	2.0	49%
2 persons (m, f, 2 working)	5.8	33%	5.2	35%	4.2	32%	3.6	35%
3 persons (m, f, c, 1 working)	3.4	48%	3.4	48%	1.8	56%	1.8	56%
3 persons (m, f, c, 2 working)	5.6	36%	4.9	39%	3.9	36%	3.3	40%
3 persons (m, f, c, 3 working)	7.1	31%	6.5	33%	5.5	29%	4.8	32%

'RESPECTABILITY BASKET'

Household size	Daily surplus (HS) *Skilled (m) / Skilled (f)*	rents as % of household income	Daily surplus (HS) *Skilled (m) / Unskilled (f)*	rents as % of household income	Daily surplus (HS) *Unskilled (m) / Skilled (f)*	rents as % of household income	Daily surplus (HS) *Unskilled (m) / Unskilled (f)*	rents as % of household income
1-person (m)	3.5	46%	3.5	46%	1.9	53%	1.9	53%
2 persons (m, f, 1 working)	2.8	57%	2.8	57%	1.2	71%	1.2	71%
2 persons (m, f, 2 working)	5.0	43%	4.3	46%	3.3	46%	2.7	51%
3 persons (m, f, c, 1 working)	2.1	68%	2.1	68%	0.5	88%	0.5	88%
3 persons (m, f, c, 2 working)	4.3	51%	3.6	55%	2.6	57%	2.0	64%
3 persons (m, f, c, 3 working)	5.8	43%	5.2	46%	4.2	46%	3.5	50%

Table 11.1 Wages, rent, and subsistence levels of urban households in Italy, first century BCE; elaboration: D. Maschek

but overall it seems reasonable to assume 6.5 HS for one day of skilled labour and 4 HS for one day of unskilled labour by the middle of the first century BCE.[79] By comparison with data from early imperial Egypt, it is assumed that skilled and unskilled female workers earned roughly one third of their male counterparts (2.2 and 1.5 HS per day, respectively); the wage raising potential of children is considered the same as for unskilled female workers.[80]

In terms of annual expenses, the model follows the proposition of a 250-day working year.[81] Regardless of location, it sets rent at 35 per cent of a daily wage, assuming that at least the highest earner of a household was in continuous employment. Although 0.25 to 0.4 HS per night are attested for a bed in a poor neighbourhood in early imperial Rome (Petron. 8.4), the estimates will be based on the assumption of more stable tenancy agreements for those on a decent income. The costs for household subsistence are based on the Roman consumption baskets first defined by Robert Allen and further calibrated by Walter Scheidel.[82] Although the binary contrast of a low-level "subsistence basket" and a slightly more opulent "respectability basket" is of course a stark simplification of a much more complex reality, it nonetheless allows us to model different levels, opportunities, and constraints for late republican household consumption. The "respectability basket" used in my estimates came at a daily 0.7 HS per person, whereas the "subsistence basket" without wine, cheese, eggs and considerably less meat and legumes was affordable at 0.3 per day.[83]

The estimates for the six different households produce remarkable results. Households with only one person in employment were consistently and markedly disadvantaged with respect to their available daily surplus. Surviving on the "subsistence basket" (Table 11.2), unskilled male workers could retain a meagre 2.3 HS per day in a single household, which decreased to only 2 HS in a two-person household and shrunk to 1.8 HS for a family of three.

Even at the basic subsistence level, skilled workers did significantly better, saving 1.6 to 1.7 HS per day more than their lower skilled neighbours. This was the level of surplus income which constituted the baseline for households with two or three people in employment. Those with two skilled workers could save up to 5.8 HS, further boosted to 7.1 HS by the work of children. These margins of household surplus make it clear that coping with price hikes and engaging in consumption from the "respectability basket" must have been within the grasp of many working people and small families in late republican central Italy, although households with only one person in employment must have struggled to make ends meet (Table 11.3).[84]

Taking into account the need for households to cover subsistence for the entire year and thus to establish reserves which also covered the weeks outside the 250 working days, it is useful to look at annual figures as well (Tables 11.4–11.5). Living on the "subsistence basket," households with only one person in employment could expect to generate a small yearly surplus of between 182 and 692 HS, whereas two or three people in work, depending on their skills, could make from 567 to 1,414 HS per year. Although consumption from the "respectability basket" would see many families with only one wage earner run

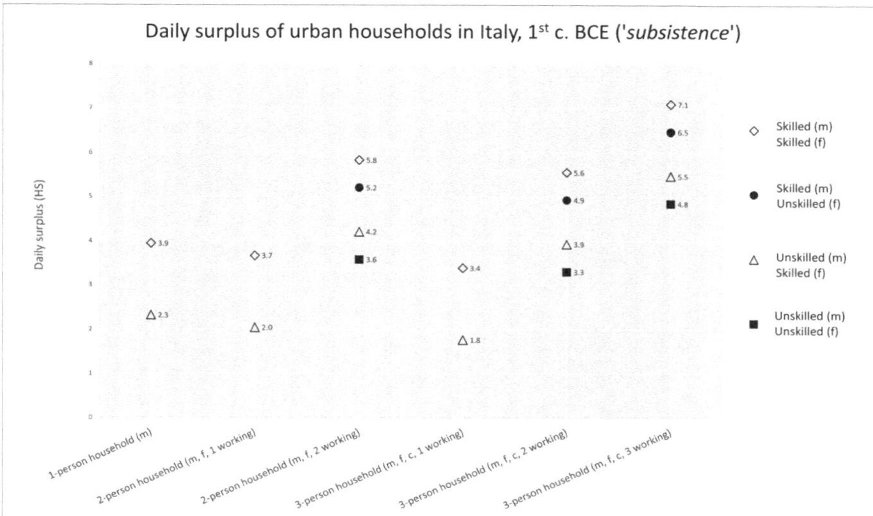

Table 11.2 Daily surplus of urban households in Italy, 1st century BCE ("subsistence basket"); graph: D. Maschek

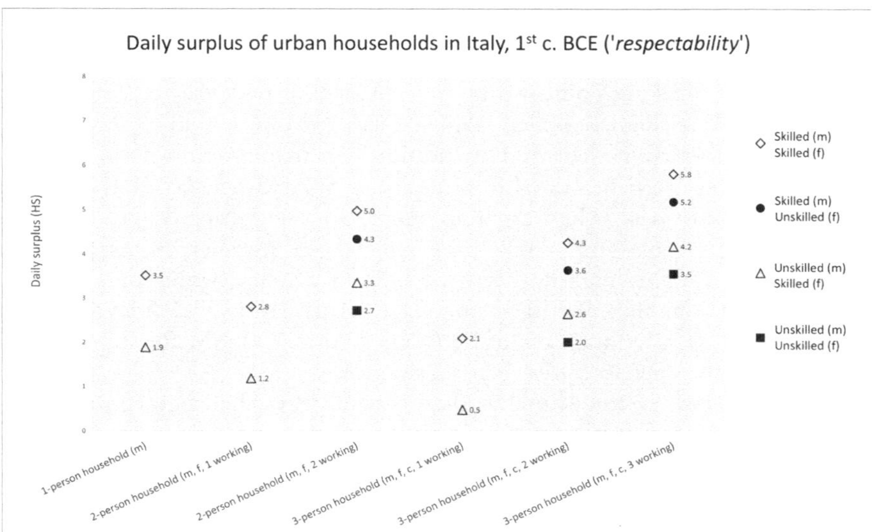

Table 11.3 Daily surplus of urban households in Italy, first century BCE ("respectability basket"); graph: D. Maschek

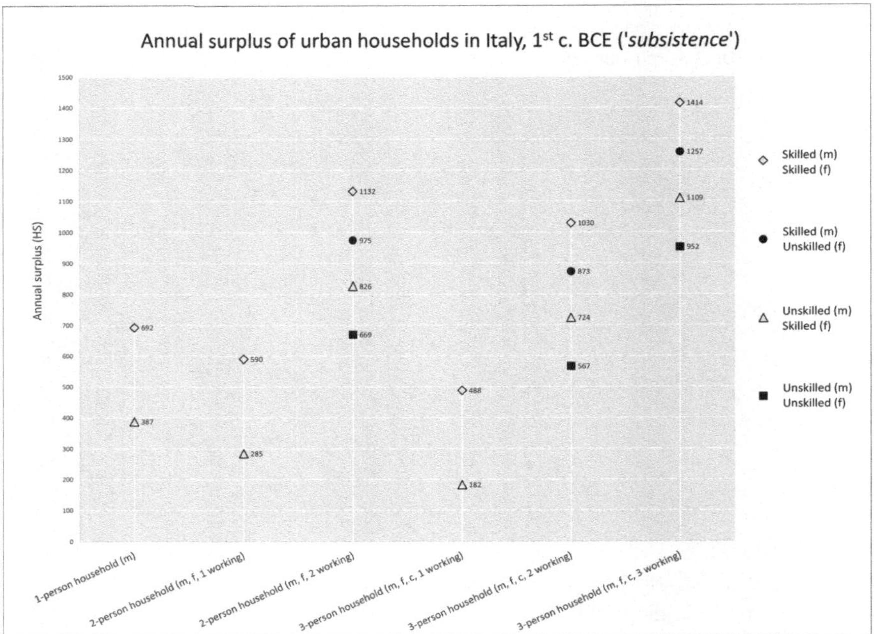

Table 11.4 Annual surplus of urban households in Italy, first century BCE ("subsistence basket"); graph: D. Maschek

into debt, it was still affordable for households with two or three working members. The breaking point was the overall level of rent. Any increase above 50 per cent of the highest skilled wage earner's income would gradually push people into deepening debt and destitution. As mentioned before, Caesar's remittance in 48 BCE pertained to rents up to 5.5 HS per day in Rome and 1.4 HS per day in Italy. The former amounted to a staggering 85 per cent of a skilled worker's wage and would have left a large number of metropolitan households in a highly precarious situation. Even when surviving on the "subsistence basket," families with only one wage earner or lower skill levels would have operated at an annual loss of between 50 and 700 HS, forcing them to take up loans in order to cover their subsistence.

These estimates, as conjectural as they certainly are, shed light on the economic potential of predatory urban practices in late republican central Italy. From the perspective of landlords and investors in real estate, many of the people who lived in rental accommodation, bought goods in *tabernae*, and consumed food and drink in local bars generated a significant amount of surplus capital which was there for the taking. A three-person household with two skilled workers living on the "respectability basket" was able to pay more than half a daily wage's worth (3.3 HS) as rent without falling below 4 HS of surplus per day. This would have amounted to 60 per cent of their daily expenditure,

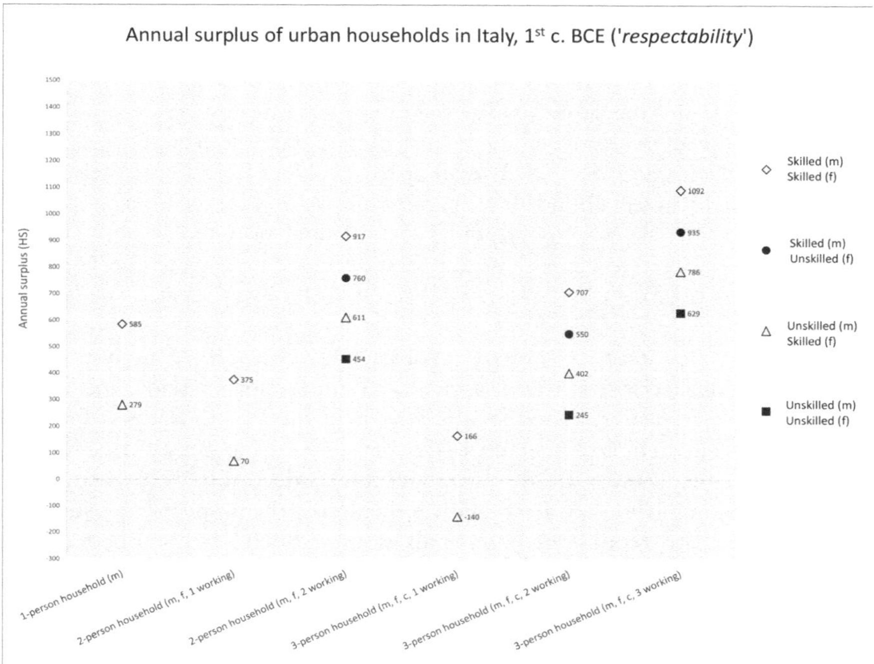

Table 11.5 Daily surplus of urban households in Italy, first century BCE ("respectability basket"); graph: D. Maschek

but it still kept them well above the bare subsistence level. Consequently, landlords in late republican central Italy could easily have realised annual rents for accommodation of 1,200 HS and more from such modest urban households.

Conclusion

The economic significance of these estimates is clear: rent taking from urban real estate was not only a side-business for late republican investors, but from the later second century BCE onwards it constituted a major sector of the urban economy in densely populated areas such as Rome and much of central Italy. The expected revenue from *tabernae* and lodgings triggered large-scale projects of demolition and construction, mainly driven by the members of local elite families and senatorial absentee landlords such as Cicero. As in Harvey's concept of urban predation, it was highly lucrative for late republican property owners to pump capital into property development. The initial investment was then clawed back from tenants through a pyramid-like system of letting and subletting, alongside the sale of wine and foodstuffs, which guaranteed continuous revenue over prolonged periods of time.

This business model transformed the landed municipal elite, the *domi nobiles* of central Italy, into a group of urban investors whose wealth relied to similar degrees on the production of cash crops and urban real estate. Of the wages paid to workers and the profit made by shopkeepers, impressive mean values of 35 to 65 per cent were absorbed by urban rent takers through charges for subsistence, accommodation, and retail space (Table 11.6). Nevertheless, the available capital was still abundant enough to allow for an increase in prices and rents, preying on the surplus created by individual households and pushing many of them closer towards debt and destitution. These were the countless urban dwellers described by Sallust as "those who have no means" (*quibus opes nullae sunt*).[85]

Landlords, by contrast, could expect substantial returns. Even without engaging in any other activities such as agricultural production or trade, the 70,000 to 75,000 HS per year estimated for the *tabernae* at the Forum Baths at Pompeii were already sufficient to cover up to 75 per cent of the census qualification which, by the first century BCE, was required for a decurion.[86] The benefits of urban rent taking were on a par with agriculture, the respectable economic pursuit of the late republican elite. This is underlined by the discussion of annual income from various types of agricultural estates in Book 3 of Varro's *De Re Rustica*, published in 37 BCE but set in the year 50 BCE.[87] The Ostian villa of Marcus Seius who engages in husbandry for the urban market is reported to produce a profit of more than 50,000 HS per year (*RR* 3.2.7–14), whereas Axius' 200 *iugera* farm at Reate makes only 30,000 HS (*RR* 3.2.15). By contrast, Marcus Aufidius Lurco generates over 60,000 HS per year from pea-fowl (*RR* 3.6.1), the same sum brought in by Varro's own aviary in his

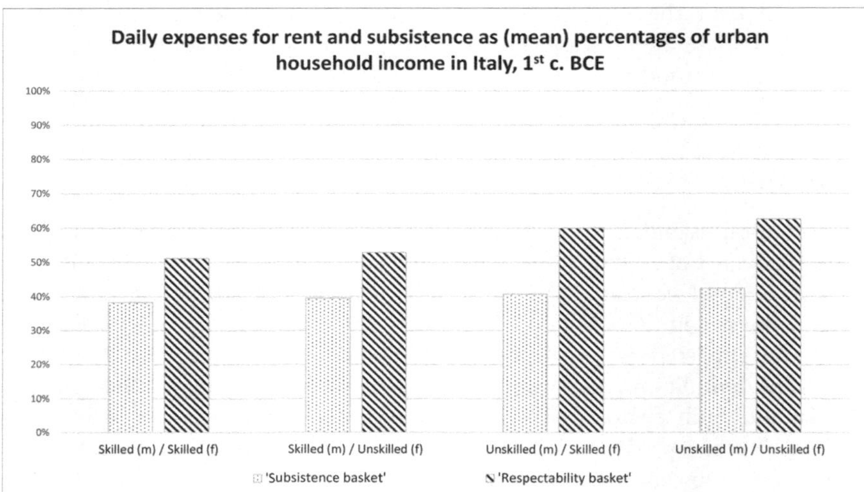

Table 11.6 Daily expenses for rent and subsistence as (mean) percentages of urban household income in Italy, first century BCE; graph: D. Maschek

maternal aunt's villa on the Via Salaria. Lucius Abuccius' villa near Alba makes 10,000 HS from the land and 20,000 HS from the steading, but a maritime villa, so he claims, would have produced more than 100,000 HS of annual profit (*RR* 3.2.17). Moreover, Varro reports that Cato the Younger raises 40,000 HS from his fishpond (*RR* 3.2.17), but it is not clear whether this is for a year's catch or for a one-off sale. As regards the profitability of urban rent, it is revealing that none of these sums, in the vast majority referring to the yields of *pastio villatica*, is higher than the estimated 70,000 to 75,000 HS for the *tabernae* at the Forum Baths in Pompeii or indeed the 80,000 to 100,000 HS for Cicero's *tabernae* at Puteoli.

As with the large-scale production of wine, olive oil, and other goods for the urban market, investment in urban real estate required considerable capital to start with. All such undertakings were longer-term investments as they did not immediately yield returns.[88] Even modest development projects incurred substantial costs for the hiring of workers, the purchase of materials, and the expertise of an architect and other specialists. The necessary capital was either provided from savings or via loans for which landholdings could be produced as collateral, thus very much favouring those who already owned estates or other assets.[89] Belonging to the decurions or being among the elected magistrates would have given investors a significant edge over potential competitors.

It is therefore hardly a surprise that rent seeking in places like Pompeii was connected to changing political fortunes. In the second half of the second century BCE it was obviously driven by old elite families who reconfigured their houses and important public buildings by the addition of new rows of *tabernae*. By contrast, in the years right after the foundation of the Sullan *colonia*, the case of the Forum Baths shows that the new colonial magistrates took full advantage of the situation and converted prime real estate into a bathhouse with substantial spaces for retail and consumption. There are hints that the new elite's takeover led to political tensions. In his speech delivered in defence of P. Cornelius Sulla in 62 BCE, Cicero referred to dissent between the colonists and old inhabitants of Pompeii that had arisen around elections and a rather ill-defined *ambulatio* (Cic. *Sull.* 61.8).[90] As Cicero himself frequently used the word *ambulatio* to describe colonnaded passageways, it is plausible to understand this as a reference to a public *porticus* which may well have included rental spaces for retail and other business.[91]

While real estate investment in late republican central Italy thus could certainly lead to tensions amongst competing investors on the level of the curial class, it is also important to consider its wider socio-political importance. Predation was the one side of the coin, creating bonds of allegiance and dependence the other. Through the construction and letting of *tabernae*, landlords were able to establish and maintain strong vertical links and networks in their respective urban communities. Owning shops enabled elite investors to bind a select part of their following particularly closely to themselves as *institores* or tenants. In this way, the *tabernae* on the street fronts of large *domus* also became a symbol of the political influence of individual leading families.

However, the allocation of living and working space as a method of increasing economic power and social capital was not limited to private houses. As discussed before, members of the local elites also controlled the renting of *tabernae* in public buildings, in the construction of which they were either directly involved or which they could lease from the city as *conductores*.[92] The world of late republican tenants and *tabernarii* was thus a far cry from that of an independent urban middle class. As Henrik Mouritsen pointedly stated, "*tabernae* merely demonstrate the decentralisation of trade and production, revealing little about who profited from these activities. The question is who controlled these spaces and the workers who toiled there."[93]

This sums up the crucial importance of real estate development and predatory urban practices for late republican Rome and central Italy.[94] By the time when Cicero planned the restoration of his crumbling shops at Puteoli, excessive rent taking and pressing urban debt had become virulent problems which fuelled social conflict and, ultimately, the violent eruptions of civil war.

Notes

1 Vettius Chrysippus: Cic. *Att.* 2.4.7; 13.29.1; *Fam.* 7.14.1; Vettius Cyrus: Cic. *Att.* 2.3.2.; *Q. fr.* 2.2.2.; *Mil.* 46. On both architects: Martin 1989: 49–51; J.C. Anderson 1997: 32–35; Bernard 2016: 84–85.

2 Cic. *Att.* 14.10.3; 14.11.2; Vitr. *De Arch.* 7.11.1; Plin. *NH* 33.13.162; Garnsey 1976: 126; D'Arms 1980: 78–81; Andreau 1997: 99–118.

3 On urban real estate and the wider socio-economic background of Cluvius and Vestorius in the context of late republican central Italy: Garnsey 1976; Rawson 1976; Frier 1978; D'Arms 1981: 63. 86–88; Andreau 1983; Rauh 1986, 1989; Rosenstein 2008: 19–21; Craver 2010b; 2010a: 8–23, 29–48; Pina Polo 2016: 170–172.

4 Shatzman 1975: 47–50, 104–108; Wallace-Hadrill 1991; Lomas 1997; Parkins 1997; Andreau 1999: 139–154; Rollinger 2014: 306–334; Mouritsen 2017; Rosillo-López 2021a.

5 E.g. Baratto 2003; 2004; Robinson 2005; Monteix 2010; Holleran 2012; Flohr 2013; Hawkins 2016; Wilson and Flohr 2016; Flohr and Wilson 2017; Holleran 2017; Ellis 2018; Flohr and Monteix 2020.

6 Harvey 2012: 53–57.

7 Harvey 2012: 57. For the Roman urban context cf. Garnsey 1976: 131 who states that "it is also necessary to recognize that there were income-generating transactions taking place in the 'internal' urban economy, as a result of the division of labour within the cities [...]. Property-owners participated indirectly in those activities. For example, they took a rake-off from transactions between private producers and retailers on the one hand, and retailers and urban consumers on the other, through rents charged on premises."

8 Cf. Harvey 1990: 105–106: "The effect of continuous innovation [...] is to devalue, if not destroy, past investments and labour skills. *Creative destruction* is embedded within the circulation of capital itself. Innovation exacerbates instability, insecurity, and in the end, becomes the prime force pushing capitalism into periodic paroxysms of crisis. [...] The struggle to maintain profitability sends capitalists racing off to explore all kinds of other possibilities."

9 E.g. Boren 1969; Yavetz 1969; Treggiari 1980; Scobie 1986; Kühnert 1991; Purcell 1994; Pirson 1999; Van den Bergh 2003; MacMahon and Price 2005; E.-J. Graham 2006a; Ellis and Gray 2008; Mignone 2016: 77–137; 2017; Rosillo-López 2021b.

10 For a critique of this model from various perspectives, see Jongman 2003; de Ligt 2004; Rosenstein 2004: 26–106; de Ligt and Northwood 2008; Rosenstein 2008; Capogrossi Colognesi 2009; Keaveney and Earnshaw-Brown 2009; Launaro 2011, 2015; De Haas 2017; Kron 2017; Launaro 2017; Marzano 2020.

11 E.g. Zanker 1975; Kockel 1993; Petersen 2006; Borg 2012; De Angelis et al. 2012; Mayer 2012; Flohr 2013; Petersen 2015; Hawkins 2016; Wilson and Flohr 2016; Ellis 2018; Flohr 2019a.

12 Cf. Gabba 1972; Torelli 1983; Lomas 1997; Laurence 2001; Lomas 2002; Patterson 2006: 25–71. 115–176; Morley 2008; de Ligt 2012b; Kay 2014: 216–234; Witcher 2017; Smith 2020.

13 On demographic trends in late republican Italy, including the important aspect of internal migration: Broadhead 2002, 2008; Launaro 2011; de Ligt 2012a; Hin 2013; de Ligt and Tacoma 2016; Erdkamp 2016. Monetisation levels in late republican Italy: Hollander 2005, 2007; Kemmers 2016; Crawford 2017.

14 E.g. Wallace-Hadrill 1994: 105: "On the whole we are probably right to assume that a single physical unit belonged to a single owner [...]", but equally ibid. 132: "It is sheer innocence to populate all the houses of Pompeii with owner-occupiers." Implicitly, the idea of owner-occupiers is also present in recent studies on the relation between the size and decoration of Pompeian houses and social status: e.g. Flohr 2017: 2019a, 2019b.

15 The evidence is comprehensively collected and discussed in Frier 1980; du Plessis 2012: 150–172.

16 Garnsey 1976; Parkins 1997; Jongman 2006; Rosenstein 2008: 2–3, 20–22; Monteix 2013; Ellis 2018: 102–125.

17 Liv. 1.35.10. For 458 BCE, Livy (3.27) reports that *tabernae* were ordered to close across the city. Similar closures are attested for 426 BCE (Liv. 4.31.9), 320 BCE (Liv. 9.7.8), and 216 BCE (Liv. 23.25.1–3). Cf. Holleran 2012: 105–107.

18 Varr. *apud* Non. 853 L; Liv. 9.40.16.

19 Fire of 210 BCE: Liv. 26.27.3; 27.11.16; Forum Boarium: Liv. 35.40.3.

20 Val. Max. 3.4.4. Cf. Bernard 2018: 181–185; 2019b, 244.

21 Plaut. *Curc.* 466–484. Cf. Weis 2005: 234–238.

22 Freyberger and Ertel 2016: 45–56.

23 Carandini, Bruno, and Fraioli 2010: 102 Fig. 43: Houses 5, 6, and 7. Cf. Ellis 2018: 129–130.

24 Carandini, Bruno, and Fraioli 2010: 98–111; Mogetta 2021: 84.

25 Liv. 41.27.5. For the excavation results, see Carbonara 2006; Zeggio 2006: 74–75 fig. 8. For a late second/early first century BCE *domus* with three road-facing *tabernae* in the Subura (Santi Sergio e Bacco): Andrews 2014: 65–76.

26 Di Giuseppe 2017. Cf. Treggiari 1980.

27 Wallace-Hadrill 2008: 315–355; Zanda 2011; Maschek 2018: 211–222; 2020b: 38–42.

28 Flohr 2019b: 84–87; 2020: 3–9. For the wider context of the boom in retail infrastructure during the second and early first century BCE: Ellis 2018: 133–149.

29 Flohr 2019b: 88.

30 Trümper 2018: 97–103; Trümper et al. 2019: 119–126. 146; Trümper 2020: 6–8.

31 For the date, see M. Anderson 2015: 81; Trümper et al. 2019: 124.

32 Cf. Pirson 1999: 149: "Mit den Forumsthermen hat die Einbindung vermietbarer Einheiten in öffentliche Gebäude in Pompeji bereits ihren Höhepunkt erreicht."

33 M. Anderson 2015: 78–83.

34 M. Anderson 2015: 83.

35 Vetter 1953: no. 12.

36 E.g. Plaut. Boeot. frg. 1 = Gell. 3.3.5. Cf. Weis 2005: 244–247.

37 *CIL* 10.829; Castrén 1975: 87; Mouritsen 1988: 78; Pobjoy 2000: 80–81. Pirson 1999: 145–147 is certainly right in assuming that the commissioners of the bath building had a vital interest in this kind of rental space and might even have subsequently leased the building from the town as *conductores*.

38 *CIL* 10.819; Castrén 1975: 88; Mouritsen 1988: 28–30, 77; Bispham 2009: 263 n. 88; Monteix 2013: 163.

39 *CIL* 10.844. 852. Cf. Castrén 1975: 88–91; Pobjoy 2000: 78–79.

40 Ellis 2018: 105–108. A fundamental issue of interpretation pertains to the propositions taken by different scholars working on the Roman urban economy, and the economy of *tabernae* in particular. For instance, Ellis 2018: 107 entertains the idea that "a good many" Roman shops "were essentially economically irrational" (and more important for upholding networks of social dependency, such as the patron–client system), whereas Robinson claimed that the bakery in the Casa del Labirinto, built after the 62 CE earthquake, was "undoubtedly [...] a financial asset and should be regarded as part of the economic portfolio of the upper class owners" (Robinson 2005: 97).

41 *CIL* 4.138 (Insula Arriana Polliana, VI 6): "Insula Arriana / Polliana [C]n. Al[le]I Nigidi Mai / locantur ex [k(alendis)] Iulis primis tabernae / cum pergulis suis et c[e] nacula / equestria et domus conductor / convenito Primum [C]n. Al[le]I / Nigidi Mai ser(vum)"; *CIL* 4.1136 (Praedia Iuliae Felicis, II 4): "In praedis Sp. f. Felicis / locantur / balneum venerium et nongentum tabernae pergulae / cenacula ex idibus Aug(ustis) primis in idus Aug(ustas) sextas annos / continuos quinque / s(i) q(uinquennium) d(ecurrerit) l(ocatio) e(rit) n(udo) c(onsensu)." Cf. Pirson 1999: 15–19.

42 Frier 1977: 34–37; 1980: 34–47.

43 Treggiari 1980: 52–57; Aubert 1993; 1994: 9–16. 95–98; Ellis 2018: 113–114.

44 Ellis 2018: 29–83.

45 Andreau 1974: 69–70; Jongman 1988: 173. 213. 216: the pertinent information comes from tablets 141, 142, 143, and 144, which attest that he was in arrears on his annual payments.

46 Assuming a daily wage of 4 HS for an unskilled worker and 6 HS for a skilled worker in the time of Cicero: Kay 2014: 284; Maschek 2016: 325. Of course, Iucundus could also have employed slaves whose daily upkeep would have been somewhat (but not significantly) lower.

47 Cf. the useful discussion of functional markers in Holleran 2017: 153–159.

48 On Roman bar food and drink, including a discussion of the archaeological evidence from Pompeii and Herculaneum: Ellis 2018: 228–238 and, most recently, Bowes 2021b.

49 *CIL* 4.5380 (at IX.7.24–25).

50 *CIL* 4.1679.

51 *AE* 1989, 182a.

52 8.5 HS per amphora: Duncan-Jones 1982: 46–48; 15 HS per amphora: Col. *Rust.* 3.3.10. Frank 1933, 139. 404 sees 20 HS (= 0.39 HS per *sextarius*) as an average price per amphora in the second and first centuries BCE, but this, as Rosenstein 2008: 14 n. 70 notes, seems to be erroneously based on retail prices.

53 For attested business models cf. Meusel 1960: 23–33; du Plessis 2012: 172–173.

54 This shows that also a comparatively small number of *tabernae* could produce significant annual revenue. There is thus no need to assume that 250 or more *inquilini* would have lived in Cicero's property at Puteoli, as estimated by Frier 1978: 5–6 in his otherwise lucid discussion.

55 The literature on late republican agricultural production and its intrinsic links with elite landownership is vast. Useful points of reference are provided by Morley 1996: 88–93; Marzano 2007; Rosenstein 2008; Bodel 2012; Launaro 2015; Kron 2017; Marzano 2020.

56 On ownership and production of building materials (e.g. tile, brick, and *opus doliare*) in republican Italy, see comprehensively Nonnis 2015. On specific materials:

DeLaine 1995; 2000; Lancaster 2005: 12–21; S. Graham 2006b; Lancaster and Ulrich 2014; DeLaine 2015.

57 Jouffroy 1986.

58 Cébeillac-Gervasoni 1990; 1991; Panciera 1997; Cébeillac-Gervasoni 1998; Gregori and Nonnis 2013; Blokzijl 2016–2017.

59 Cf. DeLaine 2001, 2006; Dessales 2011; Maschek 2016; Mogetta 2016; Gerding 2019; Maschek 2020a.

60 Plut. *Crass.* 2.4–5. Cf. Frier 1980: 32–33; Craver 2010b: 135.

61 Wootton 2015; Bologna 2019.

62 For a macro-view of the economics of Pompeian interior decoration cf. Flohr 2019a. Harris 2015 also raises some important questions in this respect, but with less of a focus on the construction industry.

63 Anderson 1997: 3–67, 95–113; 2014; Bernard 2016.

64 Brunt 1980; Skydsgaard 1983; Martin 1989: 69–71; J.C. Anderson 1997: 119–127; Bernard 2016: 64–67; Erdkamp 2016; Maschek 2016: 323–327; Bernard 2018: 171–175; 2019a: 23.

65 Maschek 2020a: 51–55. As this study did neither include all categories of public buildings, nor indeed the sector of private construction, these estimates must be taken as an absolute minimum.

66 *CIL* 1^2.698 = *CIL* 10.1781 = *ILS* 5317 = *ILLRP* 518; Wiegand 1894; Dessales 2016.

67 Cf. Rihll 2013; Shaw 2019a: 18; 2019b: 548–551; Mogetta 2021: 42.

68 On the economic potential of reuse in Roman architecture cf. Barker 2010; Barker and Marano 2017; Barker 2018.

69 E.g. Jongman 1988; de Ligt 1990; 1993; Morley 1996; Erdkamp 1999; 2001; Lo Cascio and Storchi Marino 2001; Patterson 2006; Launaro 2011; Bowman and Wilson 2013; Launaro 2015; Erdkamp 2016; De Haas and Tol 2017; Kron 2017; Launaro 2017; Hollander 2019; Marzano 2020.

70 Rosenstein 2008: 2009.

71 Launaro 2017: 98.

72 Pirson 1999: 168.

73 Exhaustively collected in Frier 1977; 1980.

74 Scheidel 2007: 339 n. 72; Craver 2010b: 150–151, 151–155; Kay 2014: 260–264.

75 Alfen. *Dig.* 19.2.30 pr.; Labeo *Dig.* 19.2.58 pr., 60 pr.; Labeo/Paul. *Dig.* 19.1.53 pr.; Afric./Serv. *Dig.* 19.2.35 pr.; Ulp. *Dig.* 13.7.11.5, 19.2.7; Tryph. *Dig.* 19.2.8. Cf. Frier 1980: 30–31; Rosillo-López 2021a: 123–132.

76 Frier 1977: 34; 1978: 4–6. For widely different profit margins, depending on location: Craver 2010b: 151. In imperial Egypt, 14 to 25 days' worth of wages were sufficient to rent a home for a year: Drexhage 1991: 78–91, 450–452. This is certainly too low for comparison with late republican Rome and central Italy.

77 Pirson 1999: 68–70, 85–86, 165, 167. Cf. Craver 2010a: 127–136. 144; Ellis 2018: 98–100.

78 As for the detailed estimates of the daily and annual surplus of urban working households in late republican Italy, these will be at the heart of a more extensive study which is currently being prepared for publication.

79 Kay 2014: 284; Maschek 2016: 235. By comparison, the daily upkeep for slave in the 70s BCE can be put at 3 HS (Cic. *Rosc. Am.* 28; Frank 1933: 384).

80 Scheidel 2010: 433–435.

81 Scheidel 2010: 432 n. 13.

82 Allen 2009: 332–342; Scheidel 2010: 429–435. For a recent critique of the "baskets" and associated estimates of Roman living standards: Bowes 2021a: 17–18; Bowes 2021b: 577–579.

83 These rates are adapted from Scheidel 2010: 430–434, Tab. 1–2, who uses Egyptian drachms (¼ of the early imperial *denarius*) in his calculations. For the value of the

annual "respectability basket," Scheidel reckons with 209 to >312 drachms (208.96 to >312 HS) per person, which amounts to 0.57 to >0.85 HS per person per day; in the model, I have used the average of 0.71 HS per person per day. The annual "subsistence basket," as established by Scheidel, comes at 102 to 103 drachms (102 to 103 HS) per person, which translates into an average of 0.28 HS per person per day.

84 Cf. Hawkins 2016: 54–58; Bowes 2021b: 576–580.
85 Sall. *Cat.* 37.3.
86 For this requirement and for the date of its most probable introduction (between 140 and 88 BCE): Mattingly 1937: 105–106; Wiseman 1971: 65 n. 7; Rathbone 1993: 127–137; Rosenstein 2008: 12.
87 On the wider moral and cultural context of Varro's account of *pastio villatica*: Spencer 2010: 78–85.
88 E.g. Marzano 2007: 54–75; 2013; Kay 2014: 133–160; Launaro 2015; Kron 2017; Shaw 2019b: 92–102; Van Oyen 2020: 21–22, 42–46. 54–57; Marzano 2021.
89 On loans, collateral, and other financial instruments in republican Rome cf. Andreau 1999: 9–29; Hollander 2007: 31–57; Kay 2014: 113–124.
90 On the Sullan elite and the native *Pompeiani*: Zevi 1995; Lo Cascio 1996; Zevi 1996: 131–134.
91 E.g. Cic. *QFr.* 3.5.8; *Dom.* 44; For this reading cf. Weis 2005: 252–253.
92 Pirson 1999: 169; Hawkins 2016: 167–189; Ellis 2018: 107–125.
93 Mouritsen 2012.
94 Frederiksen 1966; Boren 1969; Hollander 2005: 229–231; 2007: 65–75; Kay 2014: 243–257, 260–265; Rosillo-López 2016: 34–35; Maschek 2018: 134–144; 2020b: 38–42.

References

Allen, R.C. (2009) How Prosperous were the Romans? Evidence from Diocletian's Price Edict. In: A.K. Bowman, A. Wilson eds. *Quantifying the Roman Economy: Methods and Problems*. Oxford: Oxford University Press, 327–345.

Anderson, J.C. (1997) *Roman Architecture and Society*. Baltimore: Johns Hopkins University Press.

Anderson, J.C. (2014) Architect and Patron. In: R.B. Ulrich and C.K. Quenemoen eds. *A Companion to Roman Architecture*. Malden, MA: Blackwell, 127–139.

Anderson, M. (2015) Public Buildings and Private Opportunities: Some Dynamics in Pompeii's Urban Development. *Journal of Roman Archaeology* 28, 71–95.

Andreau, J. (1974) *Les affaires de Monsieur Jucundus* (Collection de l'École Française de Rome 19). Rome: École Française de Rome.

Andreau, J. (1983) À propos de la vie financière à Pouzzoles: Cluvius et Vestorius. In: M. Cébeillac-Gervasoni ed. *"Les bourgeoisies" municipales italiennes aux IIe et Ier siècles av. J.-C.* Paris: C.N.R.S, 9–20.

Andreau, J. (1997) *Patrimoines, échanges et prêts d'argent: l'économie romaine*. Rome: "L'Erma" di Bretschneider.

Andreau, J. (1999) *Banking and Business in the Roman World*. Cambridge: Cambridge University Press.

Andrews, M.M. (2014) A Domus in the Subura of Rome from the Republic Through Late Antiquity. *American Journal of Archaeology* 118. 1, 61–90.

Aubert, J.-J. (1993) Workshop Managers. In: W.V. Harris ed. *The Inscribed Economy: Production and Distribution in the Roman Empire in the Light of Instrumentum Domesticum*, Ann Arbor, MI: University of Michigan, 171–181.

Aubert, J.-J. (1994) *Business Managers in Ancient Rome: A Social and Economic Study of Institores, 200 B.C.–A.D: 250*. Leiden: Brill.

Baratto, C. (2003) Le tabernae nei fora delle città romane tra l'età repubblicana e il periodo imperiale 1. *Rivista di Archeologia* 27, 67–92.

Baratto, C. (2004) Le tabernae nei fora delle città romane tra l'età repubblicana e il periodo imperiale 2. *Rivista di Archeologia* 28, 45–65.

Barker, S. (2010) Roman Builders – Pillagers or Salvagers? The Economics of Deconstruction and Reuse. In: S. Camporeale, H. Dessales, and A. Pizzo, eds. *Arqueología de la construcción II: los procesos constructivos en el mundo romano: Italia y provincias orientales*. Madrid: CSIC, 127–142.

Barker, S. (2018) The Demolition, Salvage and Recycling Industry in Imperial Rome. *Aedificare. Revue internationale d'histoire de la construction* 2. 4, 37–88.

Barker, S. and Marano, Y.A. (2017) Demolition Laws in An Archaeological Context: Legislation and Architectural Re-use in the Roman Building Industry. In: P. Pensabene, M. Milella, and F. Caprioli, eds. *Decor: decorazione e architettura nel mondo romano: atti del Convegno Internazionale Roma, 21–24 maggio 2014*. Rome: Edizioni Quasar, 833–848.

Bernard, S.G. (2016) Workers in the Roman Imperial Building Industry. In: K. Verboven and C. Laes, eds. *Work, Labour, and Professions in the Roman World* (*Impact of Empire: Roman Empire, c. 200 B.C.-A.D. 476*). Leiden and Boston: Brill, 62–86.

Bernard, S.G. (2018) *Building Mid-republican Rome: Labor, Architecture, and the Urban Economy*. Oxford: Oxford University Press.

Bernard, S.G. (2019a) The Economy of Work. In: E. Lytle, ed. *A Cultural History of Work in Antiquity*. London: Bloomsbury Academic, 19–32.

Bernard, S.G. (2019b) Political Competition and Economic Change in Mid-Republican Rome. In: C. Damon and C. Pieper, eds. *Eris vs. Aemulatio: Valuing Competition in Classical Antiquity*. Leiden and Boston: Brill, 230–250.

Bispham, E. (2009) *From Asculum to Actium: The Municipalization of Italy from the Social War to Augustus*. Oxford: Oxford University Press.

Blokzijl, T. (2016–2017) Constructing and Reconstructing City Walls: Responses to Socio-Political Change in Roman Italy After the Social War, ca. 90–30 BC. *Talanta. Proceedings of the Dutch Archaeological and Historical Society* 48–49, 185–214.

Bodel, J.P. (2012) Villaculture. In: J.A. Becker and N. Terrenato, eds. *Roman Republican Villas: Architecture, Context, and Ideology*. Ann Arbor: University of Michigan Press, 45–60.

Bologna, F. (2019) Water and Stone: The Economics of Wall-painting in Pompeii (A. D. 62–79). *Journal of Roman Archaeology* 32. 1, 97–128.

Boren, H.C. (1969) The Urban Side of the Gracchan Economic Crisis. In: R. Seager, ed. *The Crisis of the Roman Republic: Studies in Political and Social History*. Cambridge: Heffer, 54–66.

Borg, B. (2012) The Face of the Social Climber: Roman Freedmen and Elite Ideology. In: S. Bell, and T. Ramsby, eds. *Free at Last! The Impact of Freed Slaves on the Roman Empire*, London: Bristol Classical Press, 25–49.

Bowes, K. (2021a) When Kuznets Went to Rome: Roman Economic Well-Being and the Reframing of Roman History. *Capitalism: A Journal of History and Economics* 2. 1, 7–40.

Bowes, K. (2021b) Tracking Consumption at Pompeii: The Graffiti Lists. *Journal of Roman Archaeology* 34, 552–584.

Bowman, A.K. and Wilson, A., eds. (2013) *The Roman Agricultural Economy: Organization, Investment, and Production*. Oxford: Oxford University Press.

Broadhead, W. (2002) *Internal Migration and the Transformation of Republican Italy*. PhD, University College London.

Broadhead, W. (2008) Migration and Hegemony: Fixity and Mobility in Second-Century Italy. In: L. de Ligt and S. Northwood, eds. *People, Land, and Politics: Demographic Developments and the Transformation of Roman Italy 300 BC–AD* 14, Leiden and Boston: Brill, 451–470.

Brunt, P.A. (1980) Free Labour and Public Works at Rome. *Journal of Roman Studies* 70, 81–100.

Capogrossi Colognesi, L. (2009) Una lunga storia. In: J. Carlsen and E. Lo Cascio, eds. *Agricoltura e scambi nell'Italia tardo-repubblicana*. Bari: Edipuglia, 15–61.

Carandini, A., Bruno, D., and Fraioli, F. (2010) *Le case del potere nell'antica Roma*. Rome: Laterza.

Carbonara, V. (2006) Domus e tabernae lungo la via verso il foro. *Scienze dell'Antichita: Storia, archeologia, antropologia* 13, 15–35.

Castrén, P. (1975) *Ordo populusque Pompeianus: Polity and Society in Roman Pompeii*. Rome: Bardi.

Cébeillac-Gervasoni, M. (1990) L'évergétisme des magistrats du Latium et de la Campanie des Gracques à Auguste à travers les témoignages épigraphiques. *Mélanges d'archéologie et d'histoire de l'École française de Rome* 102, 699–722.

Cébeillac-Gervasoni, M. (1991) Les travaux publics à la fin de la république, dans le Latium et la Campanie du Nord: La place de la classe dirigeante et des familles de notables. *Cahiers du Centre Gustave Glotz* 2, 189–213.

Cébeillac-Gervasoni, M. (1998). *Les magistrats des cités italiennes de la Seconde guerre punique à Auguste: Le Latium et la Campanie, Bibliothèque des écoles françaises d'Athènes et de Rome* Vol. 299. Rome: École Française de Rome.

Craver, Scott E. (2010a) *Patterns of Complexity: An Index and Analysis of Urban Property Investment at Pompeii*. PhD, University of Virginia.

Craver, Scott E. (2010b) Urban Real Estate in Late Republican Rome. *Memoirs of the American Academy in Rome* 55, 135–158.

Crawford, M.H. (2017) Where Were the Coins We Find Actually Used? In: T.C.A. De Haas and G.W. Tol, eds. *The Economic Integration of Roman Italy: Rural Communities in a Globalizing World*. Leiden and Boston: Brill, 407–416.

D'Arms, J.H. (1980) Senators' Involvement in Commerce in the Late Republic: Some Ciceronian Evidence. In: J.H. D'Arms and E.C. Kopff, eds. *The Seaborne Commerce of Ancient Rome: Studies in Archaeology and History*. Rome: American Academy in Rome, 77–89.

D'Arms, J.H. (1981). *Commerce and Social Standing in Ancient Rome*. Cambridge, MA: Harvard University Press.

De Angelis, F., J.-A. Dickmann, F. Pirson, and R. von den Hoff, eds. (2012) *Kunst von unten? Stil und Gesellschaft in der antiken Welt von der "arte plebea" bis heute: Internationales Kolloquium anlässlich des 70. Geburtstages von Paul Zanker, Rom, Villa Massimo, 8.-9. Juni 2007 (Palilia 27)*. Wiesbaden: Reichert.

De Haas, T.C.A. (2017) The Geography of Roman Italy and Its Implications for the Development of Rural Economies. In: T.C.A. De Haas and G.W. Tol, eds. *The Economic Integration of Roman Italy: Rural Communities in a Globalizing World*. Leiden & Boston: Brill, 51–82.

De Haas, T.C.A. and Tol, G.W., eds. (2017) *The Economic Integration of Roman Italy: Rural Communities in a Globalizing World*, Leiden and Boston: Brill.

de Ligt, L. (1990) Demand, Supply, Distribution. The Roman Peasantry Between Town and Countryside. Rural Monetization and Peasant Demand. *Münstersche Beiträge zur antiken Handelsgeschichte* 9, 24–56.

de Ligt, L. (1993) *Fairs and Markets in the Roman Empire: Economic and Social Aspects of Periodic Trade in a Pre-Industrial Society*. Amsterdam: J.C. Gieben.

de Ligt, L. (2004) Poverty and Demography: The Case of the Gracchan Land Reforms. *Mnemosyne: Bibliotheca Classica Batava* 57. 6, 725–757.

de Ligt, L. (2012a) *Peasants, Citizens and Soldiers: Studies in the Demographic History of Roman Italy 225 BC–AD 100*. Cambridge: Cambridge University Press.

de Ligt, L. (2012b) Urban Archaeology, Urban Networks and Population Dynamics in Roman Italy. In: F. Vermeulen, G.-J. Burgers, S. Keay, and C. Corsi, eds. *Urban Landscape Survey in Italy and the Mediterranean*, 184–196. Oxford: Oxbow.

de Ligt, L. and Northwood, S., eds. (2008) *People, Land, and Politics: Demographic Developments and the Transformation of Roman Italy 300 BC–AD* 14. Leiden and Boston: Brill.

de Ligt, L. and Tacoma, L.E., eds. (2016) *Migration and Mobility in the Early Roman Empire*. Leiden: Brill.

DeLaine, J. (1995) The Supply of Building Materials to the City of Rome. In: N. Christie, ed. *Settlement and Economy in Italy, 1500 BC-AD 1500: Papers of the 5th Conference of Italian Archaeology*. Oxford: Oxbow, 555–562.

DeLaine, J. (2000) Organising Roman Building and Space. *Journal of Roman Archaeology* 13. 2, 486–492.

DeLaine, J. (2001) Bricks and Mortar: Exploring the Economics of Building Techniques at Rome and Ostia. In: D.J. Mattingly and J. Salmon, eds. *Economies Beyond Agriculture in the Classical World*. London and New York: Routledge, 230–268.

DeLaine, J. (2006) The Cost of Creation: Technology at the Service of Construction. In: E. Lo Cascio, ed. *Innovazione tecnica e progresso economico nel mondo romano: Atti degli incontri capresi di storia dell'economia antica, Capri, 13–16 aprile 2003*. Bari: Edipuglia, 237–252.

DeLaine, J. (2015) The Production, Supply and Distribution of Brick. In: E. Bukowiecki, R. Volpe, and U. Wulf-Rheidt, eds. *Il laterizio nei cantieri imperiali: Roma e il Mediterraneo: atti del I workshop "Laterizio" (Roma, 27–28 novembre 2014)*. Florence: All'Insegna del Giglio, 226–230.

Dessales, H. (2011) Les savoir-faire des maçons romains, entre connaissance technique et disponibilité des matériaux: La connaissance des roches et son application par les structores: Le cas pompéien. In: N. Monteix and N. Tran, eds. *Les savoirs professionnels des gens de métier: études sur le monde du travail dans les sociétés urbaines de l'empire romain*. Naples: Centre Jean Bérard, 41–63.

Dessales, H. (2016) La *Lex parieti faciendo*: de l'usage du vocabulaire de la construction à sa diffusion. In: R. Robert, ed. *Dire l'architecture dans l'Antiquité*. Paris: Karthala, 381–410.

Di Giuseppe, H. (2017) 11B.4. Un'epigrafe. Lanii e gemmarii nei pressi della Sacra via a Roma. In: A. Carandini, P. Carafa, M.T. D'Alessio, and D. Filippi, eds. *Santuario di Vesta, pendice del Palatino e Via Sacra. Scavi 1985–2016*. Rome: Edizioni Quasar, 468–480.

Drexhage, H.-J. (1991) *Preise, Mieten, Pachten, Kosten und Löhne im römischen Ägypten bis zum Regierungsantritt Diokletians: Vorarbeiten zu einer Wirtschaftsgeschichte des römischen Ägyptens 1*. St. Katharinen: Scripta Mercaturae Verlag.

du Plessis, P.J. (2012) *Letting and Hiring in Roman Legal Thought: 27 BCE–284 CE*. Leiden and Boston: Brill.

Duncan-Jones, R. (1982) *The Economy of the Roman Empire: Quantitative Studies*, 2nd ed. Cambridge: Cambridge University Press.

Ellis, S.J.R. (2018) *The Roman Retail Revolution: The Socio-Economic World of the Taberna*. Oxford: Oxford University Press.

Ellis, S.J.R., Gray, D. (2008) Uncovering Plebeian Pompeii: Broader Implications from Excavating a Forgotten Working-class Neighbourhood. In: P.G. Guzzo and M.P. Guidobaldi, eds. *Nuove ricerche archeologiche nell'area vesuviana (scavi 2003–2006)*. Rome: "L'Erma" di Bretschneider, 309–320.

Erdkamp, P. (1999) Agriculture, Underemployment, and the Cost of Rural Labour in the Roman World. *Classical Quarterly* 49, 556–572.

Erdkamp, P. (2001) Beyond the Limits of the 'Consumer City': A Model of the Urban and Rural Economy in the Roman World. *Historia. Zeitschrift für alte Geschichte* 50, 332–356.

Erdkamp, P. (2016) Seasonal Labour and Rural-Urban Migration in Roman Italy. In: L. de Ligt and L.E. Tacoma, eds. *Migration and Mobility in the Early Roman Empire*. Leiden: Brill, 33–49.

Flohr, M. (2013) *The World of the Fullo: Work, Economy, and Society in Roman Italy*. Oxford: Oxford University Press.

Flohr, M. (2017) Quantifying Pompeii: Population, Inequality, and the Urban Economy. In: M. Flohr and A. Wilson, eds. *The Economy of Pompeii*. Oxford: Oxford University Press, 53–84.

Flohr, M. (2019a) Artisans and Markets: The Economics of Roman Domestic Decoration. *American Journal of Archaeology* 123. 1, 101–125.

Flohr, M. (2019b) Prosperity, Investment, and the History of Pompeii's Urban Economy. In: M. Maiuro and M. Balbo, eds. *Popolazione, risorse e urbanizzazione nella Campania antica. Dall'età preromana alla tarda antichità*. Bari: Edipuglia, 75–90.

Flohr, M. (2020) Commerce and Architecture in Late Hellenistic Italy: The Emergence of the *taberna* Row. In: M. Flohr and N. Monteix, eds. *Shops, Workshops and Urban Economic History in the Roman World*. Heidelberg: Propylaeum, 1–11.

Flohr, M. and Monteix, N., eds. (2020) *Shops, Workshops and Urban Economic History in the Roman World, Archaeology and Economy in the Ancient World*. Heidelberg: Propylaeum.

Flohr, M., and Wilson, A. eds. (2017) *The Economy of Pompeii*. Oxford: Oxford University Press.

Frank, T. (1933) *An Economic Survey of Ancient Rome, 1: Rome and Italy of the Republic*. Baltimore: The Johns Hopkins Press.

Frederiksen, M.W. (1966) Caesar, Cicero and the Problem of Debt. *Journal of Roman Studies* 56, 128–141.

Freyberger, K.S., and Ertel, C. (2016) *Die Basilica Aemilia auf dem Forum Romanum in Rom: Bauphasen, Rekonstruktion, Funktion und Bedeutung*. Wiesbaden: Reichert.

Frier, B.W. (1977) The Rental Market in Early Imperial Rome. *Journal of Roman Studies* 67, 27–37.

Frier, B.W. (1978) Cicero's Management of His Urban Properties. *The Classical Journal* 74. 1: 1–6.

Frier, B.W. (1980) *Landlords and Tenants in Imperial Rome*. Princeton, NJ: Princeton University Press.

Gabba, E. (1972) Urbanizazzione e rinnovamenti urbanistici nell'Italia centro-meridionale del I sec. a.C. *Studi classici e orientali* 21, 73–112.

Garnsey, P. (1976) Urban Property Investment. In: M.I. Finley, ed. *Studies in Roman Property*. Cambridge: Cambridge University Press, 123–136.

Gerding, H. (2019) Public Building and Clientage: Social and Political Aspects of Roman Building Industry. In: D. Möller, ed. *Vetenskapssocieteten i Lund: Årsbok 2019*. Lund: Vetenskapssocieteten i Lund, 17–29.

Graham, E.-J. (2006a) *The Burial of the Urban Poor in Italy in the Late Roman Republic and Early Empire*. Oxford: Archaeopress.

Graham, S. (2006b.) *Ex figlinis: the Network Dynamics of the Tiber Valley Brick Industry in the Hinterland of Rome*. Oxford: Hedges.

Gregori, G.L. and Nonnis, D. (2013) Il contributo dell'epigrafia allo studio delle cinte murarie dell'Italia repubblicana. *Scienze dell'Antichita: Storia, archeologia, antropologia* 19. 2/3, 491–524.

Harris, W.V. (2015) Prolegomena to a Study of the Economics of Roman Art. *American Journal of Archaeology* 119. 3, 395–417.

Harvey, D. (1990) *The Condition of Postmodernity: An Enquiry Into the Origins of Cultural Change*. Oxford: Blackwell.

Harvey, D. (2012) *Rebel Cities: From the Right to the City to the Urban Revolution*. London and New York: Verso.

Hawkins, C. (2016) *Roman Artisans and the Urban Economy*. Cambridge: Cambridge University Press.

Hin, S. (2013) *The Demography of Roman Italy: Population Dynamics in an Ancient Conquest Society (201 BCE–14 CE)*. Cambridge: Cambridge University Press.

Hollander, D.B. (2005) Veterans, Agriculture, and Monetization in the Late Roman Republic. In: J.-J. Aubert, ed. *A Tall Order: Writing the Social History of the Ancient World. Essays in Honor of William V. Harris*. Leipzig: B.G. Teubner, 229–239.

Hollander, D.B. (2007) *Money in the Late Roman Republic*. Boston: Brill.

Hollander, D.B. (2019) *Farmers and Agriculture in the Roman Economy*. London and New York: Routledge.

Holleran, C. (2012) *Shopping in Ancient Rome: The Retail Trade in the Late Republic and the Principate*. Oxford: Oxford University Press.

Holleran, C. (2017) Finding Commerce: the *taberna* and the Identification of Roman Commercial Space. *Papers of the British School at Rome* 85, 143–170.

Jongman, W.M. (1988) *The Economy and Society of Pompeii*. Amsterdam: J.C. Gieben.

Jongman, W.M. (2003) Slavery and the Growth of Rome: The Transformation of Italy in the Second and First Centuries B.C.E. In: C. Edwards and G. Woolf, eds. *Rome the Cosmopolis*, Cambridge: Cambridge University Press, 100–122.

Jongman, W.M. (2006) The Rise and Fall of the Roman Economy: Population, Rents and Entitlement. In: P.F. Bang, M. Ikeguchi, and H.G. Ziche, eds. *Ancient Economies, Modern Methodologies: Archaeology, Comparative History, Models and Institutions*. Bari: Edipuglia, 237–254.

Jouffroy, H. (1986) *La construction publique en Italie et dans l'Afrique romaine*. Strasbourg: AECR.

Kay, Ph. (2014) *Rome's Economic Revolution*. Oxford: Oxford University Press.

Keaveney, A. and Earnshaw-Brown, L. eds. (2009) *The Italians on the Land: Changing Perspectives on Republican Italy Then and Now*. Newcastle: Cambridge Scholars Publishing.

Kemmers, F. (2016) Coin Use in the Roman Republic. In: F. Haymann, W. Hollstein, and M. Jehne, eds. *Neue Forschungen zur Münzprägung der römischen Republik. Beiträge zum internationalen Kolloquium im Residenzschloss Dresden 19.-21. Juni 2014*. Bonn: Habelt, 347–372.

Kockel, V. (1993) *Porträtreliefs stadtrömischer Grabbauten: Ein Beitrag zur Geschichte und zum Verständnis des spätrepublikanisch-frühkaiserzeitlichen Privatporträts*. Mainz: Philipp von Zabern.

Kron, G. (2017) The Diversification and Intensification of Italian Agriculture: The Complementary Roles of the Small and Wealthy Farmer. In: T.C.A. De Haas and G.

W. Tol, eds. *The Economic Integration of Roman Italy: Rural Communities in a Globalizing World*, Leiden and Boston: Brill, 112–140.

Kühnert, B. (1991) *Die plebs urbana der späten römischen Republik. Ihre ökonomische Situation und soziale Struktur*. Berlin: Akademie-Verlag.

Lancaster, L.C. (2005) *Concrete Vaulted Construction in Imperial Rome: Innovations in Context*. Cambridge: Cambridge University Press.

Lancaster, L.C. and Ulrich, R.B. (2014) Materials and Techniques. In: R.B. Ulrich and C.K. Quenemoen, eds. *A Companion to Roman Architecture*, Malden, MA: Blackwell, 157–192.

Launaro, A. (2011) *Peasants and Slaves: The Rural Population of Roman Italy (200 BC to AD 100)*. Cambridge: Cambridge University Press.

Launaro, A. (2015) The Nature of the Villa Economy. In: P. Erdkamp, K. Verboven, and A. Zuiderhoek, eds. *Ownership and Exploitation of Land and Natural Resources in the Roman World*. Oxford: Oxford University Press, 173–186.

Launaro, A. (2017) Something Old, Something New: Social and Economic Developments in the Countryside of Roman Italy between Republic and Empire. In: T.C.A. De Haas and G.W. Tol, eds. *The Economic Integration of Roman Italy: Rural Communities in a Globalizing World*. Leiden and Boston: Brill, 85–111.

Laurence, R. (2001) Roman Italy's Urban Revolution. In: E. Lo Cascio and A. Storchi Marino, eds. *Modalità insediative e strutture agrarie nell'Italia meridionale in età romana*. Bari: Edipuglia, 593–611.

Lo Cascio, E. (1996) Pompei dalla città sannitica alla colonia sillana. Le vicende istituzionali. In: M. Cébeillac-Gervasoni, ed. *Les élites municipales de l'Italie péninsulaire des Gracques à Néron. Actes de la table ronde de Clermont-Ferrand (28–30 novembre 1991)*. Naples: Centre Jean Bérard, 111–123.

Lo Cascio, E., and Storchi Marino, A., eds. (2001) *Modalità insediative e strutture agrarie nell'Italia meridionale in età romana*. Bari: Edipuglia.

Lomas, K. (1997) The Idea of a City: Élite Ideology and the Evolution of Urban Form in Italy, 200 BC–AD 100. In: H.M. Parkins, ed. *Roman Urbanism: Beyond the Consumer City*, London and New York: Routledge, 21–41.

Lomas, K. (2002) Public Building, Urban Renewal and Euergetism in Early Imperial Italy. In: K. Lomas and T.J. Cornell, eds. *"Bread and Circuses": Euergetism and Municipal Patronage in Roman Italy*. London: Routledge, 28–45.

MacMahon, A. and Price, J., eds. (2005) *Roman Working Lives and Urban Living*. Oxford: Oxbow.

Martin, S.D. (1989) *The Roman Jurists and the Organization of Private Building in the Late Republic and Early Empire*. Brussels: Édition Latomus.

Marzano, A. (2007) *Roman Villas in Central Italy: A Social and Economic History*. Leiden: Brill.

Marzano, A. (2013) Agricultural Production in the Hinterland of Rome: Wine and Olive Oil. In: A.K. Bowman and A. Wilson, eds., *The Roman Agricultural Economy: Organization, Investment, and Production*. Oxford: Oxford University Press, 85–106.

Marzano, A. ed. (2020) *Villas, Peasant Agriculture, and the Roman Rural Economy*. Heidelberg: Propylaeum.

Marzano, A. (2021) Capital Accumulation and Production: A View from the Roman World. In: M.J. Kelly and P. Pachá, eds. *Capitalism's Past*. Santa Barbara, CA: Punctum Books, 65–88.

Maschek, D. (2016) Quantifying Monumentality in a Time of Crisis: Building Materials, Labor Force and Building Costs in Late Republican Central Italy. In: J. DeLaine, S.

Camporeale, and A. Pizzo, eds. *Arqueología de la construcción V: Man-made Materials, Engineering and Infrastructure: Proceedings of the 5th International Workshop on the Archaeology of Roman Construction, Oxford, April 11–12, 2015.* Madrid: Consejo Superior de Investigaciones Científicas, 317–330.

Maschek, D. (2018) *Die römischen Bürgerkriege: Archäologie und Geschichte einer Krisenzeit.* Darmstadt: Philipp von Zabern.

Maschek, D. (2020a.) Assessing the Economic Impact of Building Projects in the Roman World: The Case of Late Republican Italy. In: C. Courault and C. Márquez, eds. *Quantitative Studies and Production Cost of Roman Public Construction.* Córdoba: UCO Press, 45–67.

Maschek, D. (2020b) Die vielen Gesichter der Krise: Archäologische und historische Perspektiven auf das spätrepublikanische Italien. In: K. Matijević, ed. *Wirtschaft und Gesellschaft in der späten Römischen Republik. Fachwissenschaftliche und fachdidaktische Aspekte.* Gutenberg: Scripta Mercaturae Verlag, 33–58.

Mattingly, H. (1937) The Property Qualifications of the Roman Classes. *Journal of Roman Studies* 27, 99–107.

Mayer, E.E. (2012) *The Ancient Middle Classes: Urban Life and Aesthetics in the Roman Empire.* Cambridge, MA: Harvard University Press.

Meusel, H. (1960) *Die Verwaltung und Finanzierung der öffentlichen Bäder zur römischen Kaiserzeit.* Diss. Universität zu Köln.

Mignone, L.M. (2016) *The Republican Aventine and Rome's Social Order.* Ann Arbor: University of Michigan Press.

Mignone, L.M. (2017) Wohnintegration im republikanischen Rom. In: M. Haake and A.-C. Harders, eds. *Politische Kultur und soziale Struktur der Römischen Republik: Bilanzen und Perspektiven, Akten der internationalen Tagung anlässlich des 70. Todestages von Friedrich Münzer, Münster, 18.-20. Oktober 2012.* Stuttgart: Steiner, 231–253.

Mogetta, M. (2016) The Early Development of Concrete in Domestic Architecture of Pre-Roman Pompeii. *Journal of Roman Archaeology* 29, 43–72.

Mogetta, M. (2021) *The Origins of Concrete Construction in Roman Architecture: Technology and Society in Republican Italy.* Cambridge: Cambridge University Press.

Monteix, N. (2010) *Les lieux de métier: boutiques et ateliers d'Herculanum.* Rome: École Française de Rome.

Monteix, N. (2013) Espace commercial et puissance publique à Pompéi. In: A. Dardenay and E. Rosso, eds. *Dialogues entre sphère publique et sphère privée dans l'espace de la cité romaine. Vecteurs, acteurs, significations.* Bordeaux: Ausonius Éditions, 161–184.

Morley, N. (1996) *Metropolis and Hinterland: The City of Rome and the Italian Economy 200 B.C.–A.D. 200.* Cambridge: Cambridge University Press.

Morley, N. (2008) Urbanisation and Development in Italy in the Late Republic. In: L. de Ligt and S. Northwood, eds. *People, Land, and Politics: Demographic Developments and the Transformation of Roman Italy 300 BC–AD 14.* Leiden and Boston: Brill, 121–137.

Mouritsen, H. (1988) *Elections, Magistrates and Municipal Élite: Studies in Pompeian Epigraphy.* Rome: "L'Erma" di Bretschneider.

Mouritsen, H. (2012) Review of: Emanuel Mayer, The Ancient Middle Classes: Urban Life and Aesthetics in the Roman Empire, 100 BCE-250 CE. *Bryn Mawr Classical Review.* https://bmcr.brynmawr.edu/2012/2012.09.40/.

Mouritsen, H. (2017) Cicero's *familia urbana* and the Social Structure of Late Republican Rome. In: M. Haake and A.-C. Harders, eds. *Politische Kultur und soziale Struktur der Römischen Republik: Bilanzen und Perspektiven, Akten der internationalen Tagung anlässlich *des 70. Todestages von Friedrich Münzer, Münster, 18.-20. Oktober 2012*. Stuttgart: Steiner, 215–230.

Nonnis, D. (2015) *Produzione e distribuzione nell'Italia repubblicana. Uno studio prosopografico*. Rome: Edizioni Quasar.

Panciera, S. (1997) L'evergetismo civico nelle iscrizioni latine d'età repubblicana. In: M. Christol and O. Masson, eds. *Actes du Xe Congrès international d'épigraphie grecque et latine, Nîmes, 4–9 octobre 1992*. Paris: Publications de la Sorbonne. Histoire ancienne et médiévale, 53–82.

Parkins, H.M. (1997) The "Consumer City" Domesticated? The Roman City in Élite Economic Strategies. In: H.M. Parkins, ed. *Roman Urbanism: Beyond the Consumer City*. London and New York: Routledge, 83–111.

Patterson, J.R. (2006) *Landscapes and Cities: Rural Settlement and Civic Transformation in Early Imperial Italy*. Oxford: Oxford University Press.

Petersen, L.H. (2006) *The Freedman in Roman Art and History*. Cambridge: Cambridge University Press.

Petersen, L.H. (2015) "Arte Plebea" and Non-elite Roman Art. In: B. Borg, ed. *A Companion to Roman Art*. Chichester: Wiley-Blackwell, 214–230.

Pina Polo, F. (2016) Cupiditas Pecuniae: Wealth and Power in Cicero. In: H. Beck, M. Jehne, and J. Serrati, *Money and Power in the Roman Republic*. Brussels: Editions Latomus, 165–177.

Pirson, F. (1999) *Mietwohnungen in Pompeji und Herkulaneum. Untersuchungen zur Architektur, zum Wohnen und zur Sozial- und Wirtschaftsgeschichte der Vesuvstädte*. München: Pfeil.

Pobjoy, M. (2000) Building Inscriptions in Republican Italy: Euergetism, Responsibility, and Civic Virtue. In: A.E. Cooley, ed. *The Epigraphic Landscape of Roman Italy*. London: Institute of Classical Studies, 77–92.

Purcell, N. (1994) The City of Rome and the Plebs Urbana in the Late Republic. In: J. A. Crook, A.W. Lintott, and E. Rawson, eds. *The Last Age of the Roman Republic, 146–43 BC*. Cambridge: Cambridge University Press, 644–688.

Rathbone, D. (1993) The Census Qualifications of the *assidui* and the *prima classis*. In: H. Sancisi-Weerdenburg, H.C. Teitler, and R.J. van der Spek, eds. *De agricultura: in Memoriam Pieter Willem de Neeve (1945–1990)*. Amsterdam: Gieben, 121–152.

Rauh, N.K. (1986) Cicero's Business Friendships: Economics and Politics in the Late Roman Republic. *Aevum: Rassegna di Scienze Storiche, Linguistiche, Filologiche* 60. 1, 3–30.

Rauh, N.K. (1989) Finance and Estate Sales in Republican Rome. *Aevum: Rassegna di Scienze Storiche, Linguistiche, Filologiche* 63. 1, 45–76.

Rawson, E. (1976) The Ciceronian Aristocracy and Its Properties. In: M.I. Finley, ed. *Studies in Roman Property*. Cambridge: Cambridge University Press, 85–102.

Rihll, T.E. (2013) Depreciation in Vitruvius. *Classical Quarterly* 63, 893–897.

Robinson, D. (2005) Re-thinking the Social Organisation of Trade and Industry in First Century AD Pompeii. In: A. MacMahon and J. Price, eds. *Roman Working Lives and Urban Living*. Oxford: Oxbow, 88–105.

Rollinger, C. (2014) *Amicitia sanctissime colenda: Freundschaft und soziale Netzwerke in der Späten Republik*. Trier: Verlag Antike.

Rosenstein, N.S. (2004) *Rome at War: Farms, Families and Death in the Middle Republic*. Chapel Hill and London: University of North Carolina Press.

Rosenstein, N.S. (2008) Aristocrats and Agriculture in the Middle and Late Republic. *Journal of Roman Studies* 98, 1–26.

Rosenstein, N.S. (2009) Aristocrats and Agriculture in the Late Republic: the "High Count". In: J. Carlsen and E. Lo Cascio, eds. *Agricoltura e scambi nell'Italia tardo-repubblicana*. Bari: Edipuglia, 243–257.

Rosillo-López, C. (2016) Cash Is King: The Monetization of Politics in the Late Republic. In: H. Beck, M. Jehne, and J. Serrati, eds. *Money and Power in the Roman Republic*. Brussels: Editions Latomus, 26–36.

Rosillo-López, C. (2021a) *Domum pestilentem vendo*: Real Estate Market and Information Asymmetry in the Roman World. In: C. Rosillo-López and M. García Morcillo, eds. *Managing Information in the Roman Economy*. Cham: Palgrave Macmillan, 117–134.

Rosillo-López, C. (2021b) Destitute, Homeless and (Almost) Invisible: Urban Poverty and the Rental Market in the Roman World. In: C. Courrier and J.C. Magalhães de Oliveira, eds. *Ancient History from Below: Subaltern Experiences and Actions in Context*. Abingdon: Routledge.

Scheidel, W. (2007) A Model of Real Income Growth in Roman Italy. *Historia* 56, 322–346.

Scheidel, W. (2010) Real Wages in Early Economies: Evidence for Living Standards from 1800 BCE to 1300 CE. *Journal of the Economic and Social History of the Orient* 53. 3, 425–462.

Scobie, A. (1986) Slums, Sanitation, and Mortality in the Roman World. *Klio* 68, 399–433.

Shatzman, I. (1975) *Senatorial Wealth and Roman Politics*. Brussels: Editions Latomus.

Shaw, B.D (2019a) Did the Romans Have a Future? *Journal of Roman Studies* 109, 1–26.

Shaw, B.D (2019b) Grape Expectations. In: M. Maiuro, G.D. Merola, M. De Nardis, and G. Soricelli, eds. *Uomini, istituzioni, mercati. Studi di storia per Elio Lo Cascio*. Bari: Edipuglia, 533–551.

Skydsgaard, J.E. (1983) Public Building and Society in Ancient Rome. In: K. de Fine Licht, ed., *Città e architettura nella Roma imperiale: Atti del seminario del 27 ottobre 1981 nel 25° anniversario dell'Accademia di Danimarca*. Odense: Odense University Press, 223–227.

Smith, C.J. (2020) Urban Networks in Latium. *Journal of Urban Archaeology* 1, 85–97.

Spencer, D. (2010) *Roman Landscape: Culture and Identity*. Cambridge: Cambridge University Press.

Torelli, M. (1983) Edilizia pubblica in Italia centrale tra guerra sociale ed età augustea: ideologia e classi sociali. In: M. Cébeillac-Gervasoni, ed. *Les "bourgeoisies" municipales italiennes aux IIe et Ier siècles av. J.-C. Colloque Centre Jean Bérard. Institut Français de Naples, 7–10 décembre 1981*. Paris: Éd. du C.N.R.S, 241–250.

Treggiari, S. (1980) Urban Labour in Rome: *mercennarii* and *tabernarii*. In: P. Garnsey, ed. *Non-slave Labour in the Greco-Roman World*. Cambridge: Cambridge University Press, 48–64.

Trümper, M. (2018) Gymnasium, Palaestra, Campus and Bathing in Late Hellenistic Pompeii: A Reassessment of the Urban Context of the Republican Baths (VIII 5, 36). In: U. Mania and M. Trümper, eds. *Development of Gymnasia and Graeco-Roman Cityscapes*. Berlin: Edition Topoi, 87–113.

Trümper, M. (2020) Logistics of Building Processes: The Stabian Baths in Pompeii. In: C. Recko and M. Heinzelmann, eds. *Quantifying Ancient Building Economy*. Heidelberg: Propylaeum, 5–18.

Trümper, M., Brünenberg, C., Dickmann, J.A., Esposito, D., Ferrandes, A.F., Pardini, G., Pegurri, A., Robinson, M., and Rummel, C. (2019) Stabian Baths in Pompeii: New Research on the Development of Ancient Bathing Culture. *Mitteilungen des Deutschen Archäologischen Instituts, Römische Abteilung* 125, 103–159.

Van den Bergh, R. (2003) The Plight of the Poor Urban Tenant. *Revue internationale des droits de l'antiquité* 50, 443–477.

Van Oyen, A. (2020) *The Socio-Economics of Roman Storage: Agriculture, Trade, and Family*. Cambridge: Cambridge University Press.

Vetter, E. (1953) *Handbuch der italischen Dialekte*. Heidelberg: C. Winter.

Wallace-Hadrill, A. (1991) Elites and Trade in the Roman Town. In: A. Wallace-Hadrill and J. Rich, eds. *City and Country in the Ancient World*. London: Routledge, 241–272.

Wallace-Hadrill, A. (1994) *Houses and Society in Pompeii and Herculaneum*. Princeton, NJ: Princeton University Press.

Wallace-Hadrill, A. (2008) *Rome's Cultural Revolution*. Cambridge: Cambridge University Press.

Weis, A. (2005) Liberalitas and lucrum in Republican City Planning. Plautus (Curc. 466–483) and L. Betilienus Vaarus. In: A. Haltenhoff, A. Heil, and F.-H. Mutschler, eds. *Römische Werte als Gegenstand der Altertumswissenschaft*. München & Leipzig: Saur, 225–258.

Wiegand, T. (1894) *Die puteolanische Bauinschrift: sachlich erläutert*. Leipzig: Teubner.

Wilson, A. and Flohr, M., eds. (2016) *Urban Craftsmen and Traders in the Roman World*. Oxford: Oxford University Press.

Wiseman, T.P. (1971) *New Men in the Roman Senate, 139 B.C.-A.D.* 14. London: Oxford University Press.

Witcher, R. (2017) The Global Roman Countryside: Connectivity and Community. In: T.C.A. De Haas and G.W. Tol, eds. *The Economic Integration of Roman Italy: Rural Communities in a Globalizing World*. Leiden and Boston: Brill, 28–50.

Wootton, W. (2015) Figuring out the Facts: Calculating Mosaic Labour Times in 4th-c. A.D. Britain. *Journal of Roman Archaeology* 28, 261–282.

Yavetz, Z. (1969) The Living Conditions of the Urban Plebs in Republican Rome. In: R. Seager, ed. *The Crisis of the Roman Republic: Studies in Political and Social History*. Cambridge: Heffer, 162–179.

Zanda, E. (2011) *Fighting Hydra-like Luxury: Sumptuary Regulation in the Roman Republic*. London: Bloomsbury.

Zanker, P. (1975) Grabreliefs römischer Freigelassener. *Jahrbuch des Deutschen Archäologischen Instituts* 90, 267–315.

Zeggio, S. (2006) Dall'indagine alla città. Un settore del centro monumentale e la sua viabilità dale origini all'età neroniana. *Scienze dell'Antichita: Storia, archeologia, antropologia* 13, 61–122.

Zevi, F. (1995) Personaggi della Pompei sillana. *Papers of the British School at Rome* 63, 1–24.

Zevi, F. (1996) Pompei dalla città sannitica alla colonia sillana. Per un'interpretazione dei dati archeologici. In: M. Cébeillac-Gervasoni, ed. *Les élites municipales de l'Italie péninsulaire des Gracques à Néron. Actes de la table ronde de Clermont-Ferrand (28–30 novembre 1991)*. Naples: Centre Jean Bérard, 125–138.

12 The *horrea*

How Storage Engaged with Shipping Flows and Made the Roman Economy Bigger[1]

Emilia Mataix Ferrándiz

Abstract

Warehouses were intimately connected to shipping. They acted not only as repositories for cargo waiting to be dispatched, sold, or used as security in relation to a loan, they also formed an integral part of the processing of the cargo. Thus, storage does not imply the final end of the distribution cycle of merchandise, but rather a step within that cycle, which leads to the relocation of these goods to other ships or storehouses. However, the latest excavations carried out in Rome have revealed archaeological evidence for manufacturing activities carried out inside warehouses, in addition to the storage enterprises.

All these different endeavours taking place in warehouses would have implied the use of slight variations of the letting and hiring contract enabled by classical Roman law. For storage activities, the evidence from the Sulpicii archive demonstrates the similarities in legal practices between state-owned and privately owned warehouses, as well as the practice of having a fairly short contract of lease, into which technical rules of law were tacitly incorporated via a set of legal rules displayed in the warehouse. In relation to this, what does the discovery of these manufacturing activities imply in terms of contracting? What does it mean for the role of warehouses within the economic cycles of production and distribution of goods? This chapter will describe the diverse nuances within the frame of the lease and hire contract in order to accommodate the diversity of activities that took place inside warehouses. It will also contextualise the different practices and their associated contracts in relation to the economic and legal contexts of their associated commercial cycles. Finally, the chapter will evaluate how these activities, along with the flexibility of the letting and hiring contracts, managed to integrate these different trading practices, and how this entire process also had an impact on the role and value of these buildings inside commercial cycles.

***

Introduction

The title of this chapter emerges from Levinson's book devoted to the study of the creation, development, and standardisation of the metallic shipping box.[2] Levinson's

DOI: 10.4324/9781003187806-16

volume starts with a similar opening question as does this contribution: what is it about the *horrea* themselves that is so important for the Roman economy? Surely not the thing itself. A soulless brick structure held together with *suspensurae*, doors, and corridors has all the romance of a tin can. The value of this utilitarian structure then does not lie in what it is, but in how it is used. In addition to storing goods, warehouses had multiple functions, as retail and wholesale outlets, as well as other complex operations.[3] In this sense, while the Trajanic warehouses represent the growth of traffic of goods towards Rome and the force of the Empire, the anomaly found in the cell studied in this chapter also speaks for the complexity and multiplicity of uses of these structures. The latter shows the variety of activities taking place in a concrete historical context and place, revealing details of people working in these structures and how they organised their tasks. In addition, the structural changes which later wiped out the anomalous cell to create a homogeneous structure also reveal details about how the cycles of trade and storage were changing at the time.

The property market was key within Roman society, strongly shaped by conceptualisations of ownership, which reflected diverse political agendas and social aspirations.[4] This chapter follows on from the material turn of real estate to study storage's transformations, which are a sensitive indicator of changing mentalities.[5] Roman law and its practice had a socio-economic impact on how buildings were managed and used. The case study in focus allows us to analyse the interaction between public and private concerns and tackle the flexibility of the legal tools available in the Roman west to target the different activities handled in this cell. This chapter provides one key case to explore the effect of material changes on society and the other way around, understanding that agency works for both humans and materials.[6] The work starts from two supposedly constant or regular elements: homogeneous infrastructure and standardly based letting and hiring contracts. However, it is from the concrete case study tackled here that we can shed light on the changes of the "invariable" structures and bring to the fore the unexpected in the study of well-known warehouse complexes. The latter implies that analysing the effect of material changes with respect to legal transactions unravels a wide range of social phenomena, as the relationship between law as it is presented to us in the legal sources available and its practice.[7] In addition, the correlation of human activities with the changes in these warehouses will also be considered in terms of reciprocal agency to categorise the commercial landscape of the areas targeted. This in turn can help to redefine the sometimes rigid distinction between the spheres of public and private trade – official and unofficial, legal, and social – and argue for a more nuanced conception of trade practices and their spaces.

One essential element is that this cell is integrated in a system of storage facilities, which in turn is part of the port system of Imperial Rome.[8] Therefore, storage facilities could not be considered in isolation or only in relation to this complex of warehouses.[9] They occupied positions between land and sea-river routes that cannot be appreciated only by looking at their relationships with the surrounding hinterland and other elements forming the Roman port system (e.g. the Tiber river, the storage houses located around the *portus tiberinus*) and also including the port of Ostia.[10] Overall, the activities taking place in the Trajanic warehouses were part of a distributive cycle that enabled the supply of goods to Rome.[11] However, it is necessary to conceive these warehouses as infrastructures that developed organically, showing significant variations since they were constructed *ad hoc*.[12] Their structural differences have made me wonder about the two main questions around which this chapter is constructed. The first appeals to the title of this contribution, and wonders about how the changes on the concrete case study in focus engage with the flow of the port system of Rome. The second aims to see how the contract used to manage these structures may vary depending on the changes on this cell, to handle the different activities carried out there and the goods handled. The legal tools available will shed light on a wide range of relevant practices in terms of real estate devoted to storage, such as the economic rationale of commercial practitioners with respect to different commodities.

The *Magazzini di Traiano*

The complex of warehouses studied in this chapter could be found at Portus, the maritime port of Imperial Rome, located some 30 km to the southwest of the city, and just under 3 km to the north of Ostia at the mouth of the Tiber.[13] It was an artificial port that begun under Claudius and was substantially enlarged under Trajan, who built the complex of warehouses in the second century CE. The so-called *magazzini cossidetti di Traiano* were constructed and extensively developed during the Antonine period, possibly on the site of earlier warehouses. These warehouses underwent phases of rebuilding during the later second and third century CE.[14] The *magazzini* occupy a strategic position within the port complex, since they are situated between the Claudian and Trajanic basins, they are bordered to the north and to the east by the connecting canal between the two bodies of water and to the south by a small and closed basin (*darsena*) connected directly to the Tiber and therefore to Rome (Figure 12.1).

Respecting some symmetry, the Trajanic warehouses were located partly around the *darsena*,[15] and partly along a land corridor, and opened up in a "u" shape towards the hexagonal Trajanic basin (Figure 12.2).[16] This specific context justifies a detailed quay and mooring system to facilitate the unloading of goods and cargo and their transfer inside the warehouses to be stored before their expedition.[17] As a whole, the setup of these warehouses – as the Trajanic port itself – was geared towards receiving large, bulk loads as efficiently as possible, but carefully controlling their further trajectory.[18] These flows could have also been affected by seasonality, with ships arriving en masse during the seafaring season, forcing the rapid unloading of cargoes, while the other half of the year would have been devoted to preserving cargoes and maintaining warehouses.[19] However, perhaps the constraints of the sailing season affected to a major extent *annona* supplies, especially when the Roman state was assuming the risks for the cargoes shipped,[20] while privately owned cargoes could have

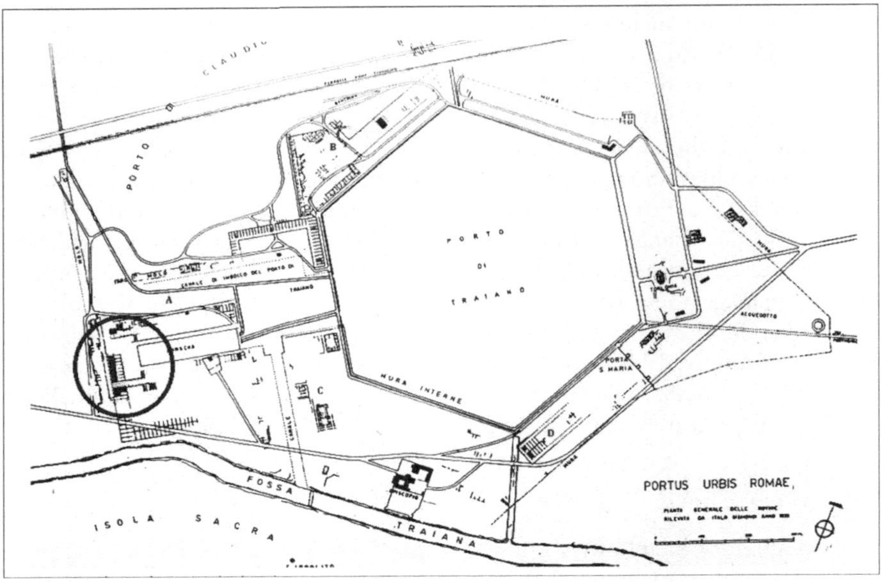

Figure 12.1 The Trajanic basin, with detail from the *magazzini* (Bukowiecki et al. 2018, fig. 5).

been more willing to carry out voyages beyond the seasonal limits.[21] These factors are connected to the management of public food distribution and will help contextualise the infrastructural changes of the warehouse spaces studied in this chapter and their role in the whole complex.

Following the traditional classification of warehouses established by Rickman, the *magazzini* belong to the "spine type," which, in architectural terms, means that these were formed by two rows of rooms installed directly back to back, with cells opening outwards.[22] For that reason, the front walls of these storage cells are systematically oriented towards the exterior, along the axes of the external circulation of the basin. The back walls of the cells of storage delimit, for the north and south buildings, a large central space of traffic, east–west orientation. This space, where it is probably possible to restore many activities related to the daily operations taking place at warehouses (verification, accounting; organisation of the distribution of goods; temporary storage, etc.), communicates with the outside through numerous passages north–south, systematically coupled to the staircases that reach the floor.[23] The latter evidences the large amount of goods that could be stored in these spaces, which makes sense given their role in the port.

Other classifications of warehouses look at the way they are employed and divide them mainly into two kinds: mostly for storage, or for mixed use (storage, sale, eventually distribution), looking to their geographical location, structure, or historical and climatic context.[24] In the cases of most of the cells

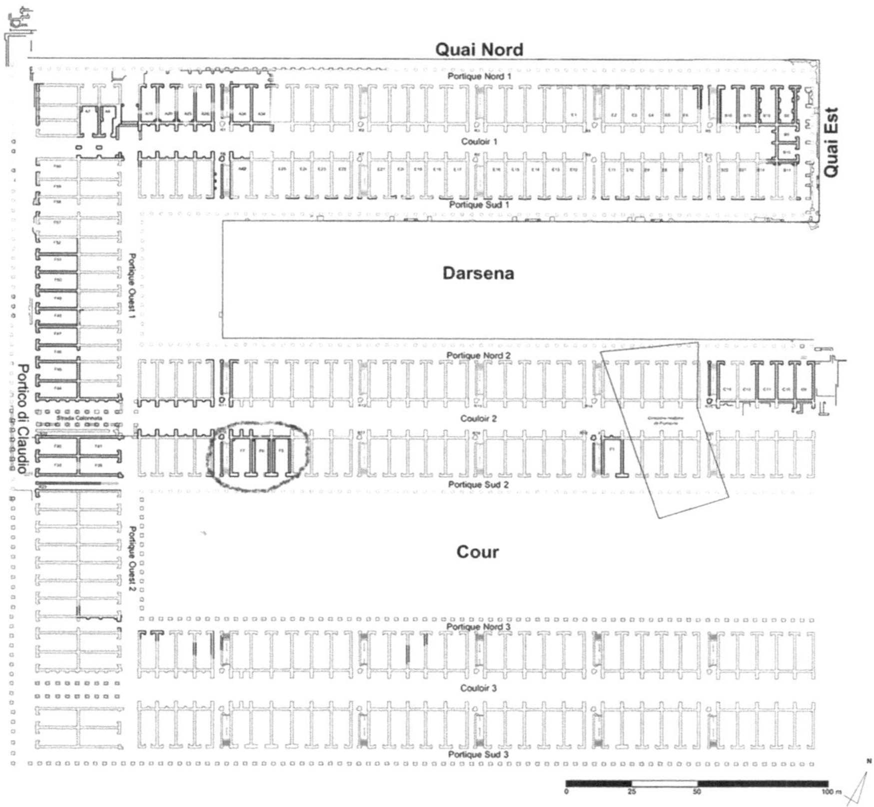

Figure 12.2 The storage complex from the Trajanic warehouses. The F6 cell is highlighted by the shaded round circle (Bukowiecki and Mimmo 2018, fig. 4).

from the Trajanic warehouses, their architectural features allow the labelling of them as being of mixed usage (storage and distribution). Most cells were equipped with *suspensurae* or elevated floors,[25] which traditionally have been associated with grain storage, as they allowed aeration.[26] However, this assumption was inferred on the sole basis of the warehouse size, and assuming that the activities developed there involved the *annona*.[27] Indeed, a recent study carried out by the archaeological team excavating these facilities indicates that there was not only one, but several types of *suspensurae*, evidencing different kinds of activities carried out in the associated warehouses.[28] Moreover, another study on the thermal performances of the Trajanic warehouses proves that the absence of openings would not have allowed the storage of grain for long periods.[29] Other features of these warehouses would be that these *supensurae* allowed the distribution of the weight of storage in bulk, maintained temperature and protected goods from humidity. The latter allows us to formulate hypotheses about the different functions of the cells forming these warehouses, such as short storage and distribution of goods, as well as their possible use to store goods other than wheat. However, even if we can accept the mixed usage of these buildings, given their location in the port and their features, not all these cells were used for the same mixed uses, at least not in all periods, as I will indicate with the example from the next section.

The Mysterious Case of the Anomalous Cells

The *magazzini* are formed by 150 cells, of which only 30 are currently accessible. Concerning the cells located in the southern part of the warehouses, in the zone delimited in a circle on the planimetry (Figure 12.2), the excavation team has noted anomalies in the constructive characteristics of one of the two storage cells that they were able to excavate in this zone (cell F6). One of the technical characteristics of most of the storage cells of the warehouses in the territory of Rome is the presence of two opposing walls, placed perpendicular to the two portions of the front wall that frame the access door and which prevented, in the case of bulk storage of wheat for example, the goods from invading the opening area of the two door leaves. It should be pointed out here that, for obvious reasons of circulation in the passages in front of the cells, the doors of Roman warehouses were systematically opened inwards. The absence of a "retour de facade" in cells F5, F6, and F7 therefore clearly indicates that, originally, in the configuration of the transverse raised floors with the side benches, bulk storage had been excluded for this period.[30]

This group of cells is located far from access to water (dock, harbour basin, and *fossa traianea*), which allows us to say that they were not destined for the unloading and immediate redistribution of cargoes. The F6 cells were equipped with transversal *suspensurae* (Figure 12.3), which principally concerns the storage cells built during the Antonine period, as evidenced by the stamps found in other cells which also have transversal upholding.[31] However, the F6 cell is constructed in a way that does not allow any connection towards the exterior nor the canals. In particular, the first planned layout (the one corresponding to the Antonine period) concerns a very unique transverse raised floor system because the slope of the floor converges towards the centre of the room and powerful and wide side benches seem to have to support large containers (perhaps barrels?).[32] The particular morphology of this floor, which seems predisposed to collect and evacuate liquid substances towards the centre of the cell, coupled with the presence of these lateral benches, indicate the development of a specific activity carried out in this cell, whose exact nature is still unknown. It is possible that not all goods arriving at the port were suitable for redistribution towards the city. Probably, a minimum of processing operations for raw materials,[33] or perhaps simply repackaging in smaller or better adapted containers of raw food, could be carried out within the warehouses, in remote areas to areas of heavy traffic such as wharves or wide corridors.[34] The lack of *tabernae* and openings does not indicate a commercial function of these cells,

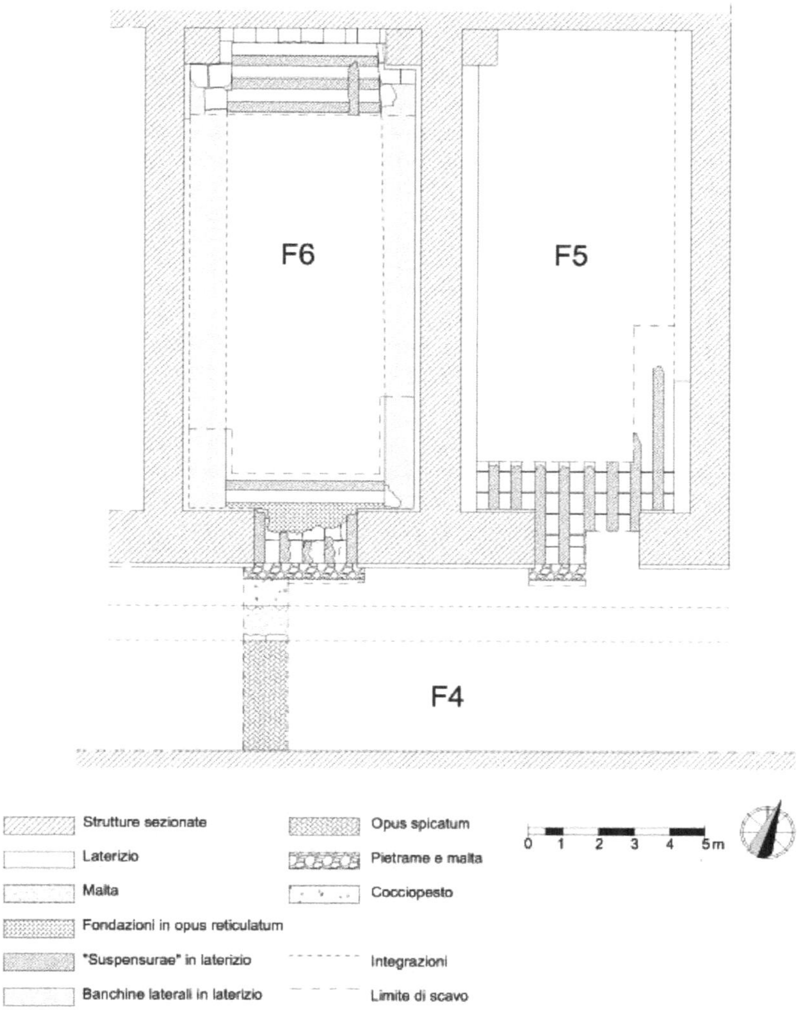

Figure 12.3 Functional changes in the F6 cell from the end of the second century CE to the beginning of the third century CE (Bukowiecki and Panzieri 2013, fig. 2)

especially when comparing them with other warehouses. For example, the *horrea Agrippiana* were located bordering the republican *forum* and their structure included *tabernae*, while in the case of the *horrea Galbana*, even though some inscriptions associated with them refer to commercial professions such as fishmongers, the lack of *tabernae* proves that no retailing activity was developed there.[35] Instead, some buildings associated with retail activities have been identified in a neighbouring area, later occupied by the Basilica portuense.[36]

The end of the history of the F6 cell, of which this phase is already a first reconstruction of the Antonine era, is that this first "artisanal" device will be completely covered during the last stage of Severan restructuring (Figure 12.3).[37] The refurbishment aimed to potentiate maximum storage capacity of warehouses, using a more conventional, longitudinal, raised soil system, characteristic of bulk storage, for example of wheat, seems to be the most possible option. The latter resonates Severus' efforts to increase the supply and speed of turnover of Rome's grain supply, what translates into the developments of Portus' warehouses (including the construction of new ones).[38] The efforts of Severus to promote grain supply for the *Annona* are not only visible in Italy, but also in Africa, with warehouses built for that purpose.[39]

This summary of the excavation reports has contextualised the case study in focus, and briefly outlined the different economic periods during which these cells were in function. The anomaly of these cells, even if it does not allow us to completely challenge the view that Portus was designed as a site without history, not subject to many modifications (contrarily to Ostia),[40] shows that there are some nuances to contradict that vision. Perhaps these cells were managed differently and operated separately from the rest of the warehouses during the Antonine period (as happened with Ostia and Puteoli), even if they probably would not have functioned autonomously from the rest of the warehouse complex, since they are all part of the port system of Rome.

Another issue would be to identify what was repackaged or transformed in these cells that justified the presence of the side benches, presumably used to sustain large containers, and repurpose the liquids into smaller ones. Not all the warehouses at Portus were intended for grain, but temporary storage was also to be provided for oil and wine, and other goods that arrived in bulk.[41] These cells do not resemble architecturally the warehouses that have been identified as *cella vinaria* or *cella olearia*, which normally deal with large containers such as *dolia defossa*.[42] However, it is necessary to bear in mind that these were mainly used for redistributing goods unloaded at the port; one reason why it would not make sense to place containers there for the preservation of liquids.

Wine transport at Portus is attested to in the Torlonia relief, and Meiggs also speaks about a Bacchus statue found at the north-east side of the Trajan harbour, indicating that perhaps some *horrea vinaria* were located there.[43] This introduces the possibility that our F6 cell was devoted for wine, but due to the distance with respect to the location of the supposed *horrea vinaria*, we could perhaps think that either they worked in different periods of time, or, if in the same era, they may have functioned separately from the rest of the cells of the warehouse complex. When thinking about wine, the first thing that comes to mind is wine and barrels, especially considering that between the second half of the first century CE and the Antonine period there is a reduction in the proportion of amphorae in the deposits from Rome, Ostia, other Campanian lands not affected by the Vesuvian eruption, as well as in other frontiers from the Empire.[44] The latter could perhaps point to an increase of wine imports carried out with barrels, but the discourse has been always considered *ex silentio* given their archaeological absence, even if texts and iconographical representations speak highly about their use in this period.[45]

If we consider barrels, then we need to think why repackage wine into smaller containers at Portus if it still needed to get to Rome or Ostia (or to Rome towards Ostia) to be sold? Indeed, there was a *portus vinarius* located near Monte Testaccio from AD 68,[46] and a *forum vinarium* has been identified at Ostia, even if its location is uncertain, as is its relationship with Portus in terms of the transit of merchandise.[47] In addition, barrels were a container easily transportable in river boats, as is attested by later evidence in Rome, or by other cases from the Roman Empire.[48] Therefore, could that have been wine repackaged for consumption at Portus, by the magistrates and people living there and its surroundings? Excavations in the late antique Basilica portuense (fourth to fifth centuries CE) have revealed that prior to the construction of the temple, the area was occupied by several buildings possibly of commercial character, which underwent a continual process of development over the course of the first, second, and third centuries CE.[49] These buildings could perhaps be the places where the repackaged wine was sold. Instead, could it be that it was repackaged at Portus to have it ready to be distributed in Rome? As can be appreciated, this inquiry leaves many questions up in the air, which unfortunately cannot be solved with the actual evidence.

Otherwise, we can consider whether oil could have been repackaged there, even if the evidence is not much more conclusive on that end. Whilst it is true that oil distribution reached its highest peak during the Antonine period, as the existence of several single oil cargoes reveals,[50] the benches seem to be better suited to holding a container such as a barrel rather than oil amphorae such as Dressel 20, used to transport oil from Baetica for the *annona* supply. In addition, we would be facing the same *conundrum* as in the case of wine: why repackage the product at Portus, when it still needed to be transported up to Rome? The infrastructure enabled for the supply of oil in Rome is more than well attested to with the evidence of Mount Testaccio, around the area of *Septem Caesaris* where there were inscriptions recalling the names of oil merchants (e.g. *CIL* IX 4680). Bruzza, who carried out excavations around the *Horrea Seiana* in the *Porticus Aemilia* of Rome (1868–1870), discovered the relief of a Dressel 20 carved on an *opus reticulatum*.[51] This suggests the existence of a warehouse dedicated to the storage of fiscal goods such as oil (*horrea fiscalia*). In addition, the transport of Dressel 20 by boat is also attested to in a mosaic from the Piazzale delle Corporazioni in Ostia (*statio* 51). Therefore, again, was the liquid transferred into smaller vessels to be distributed at the same area of the port? As with the case of wine, we need to point out the commercial buildings located in the area later occupied by the basilica portuense, and also underline the presence of *negotiatotes vinarii et olearii* in the areas of Rome, Portus, and Ostia, who could have been in charge of the redistribution.[52]

These remarks have underlined that, unfortunately, we do not have enough evidence to indicate with any certainty the function and the product stored in cell F6. We will need to wait for further excavations in the area to clarify that function and leave these previous remarks as working hypotheses. However, what seems clear is that, for a certain period, the cell was used for repackaging or transforming goods for distribution, and that later it was used for storage and distribution. Following these observations, the next section aims to examine how to legally address the events happening in these cells in relation to a letting and hiring contract when its functions changed through time. How could the contract of letting and hiring address cells that not only served to store goods, but were also for tasting,[53] repackaging, distributing, and even maybe manufacturing goods? How did the contract change, depending on the circumstances? The latter touches upon the legal taxonomies used to identify these buildings in a contractual framework, and to what extent these determine the legal remedies available to handle the operations carried out in these facilities.

Enquiring Roman Law in Context: *Locatio Conductio* and Storage

Locatio conductio (lease and hire) was one of the commonest contracts employed in trade, and it is the subject of study of a vast amount of literature that is not going to be quoted in detail here.[54] It was a consensual and bilateral agreement that consisted mainly of one person, the lessee, who rented from the other subject, the lessor, an object (*rei*), the performance of a certain task (*opus facere*), or the workforce of that subject to perform a certain task (*operarum*).[55] In sum, it was a single kind of contract which was agreed on the essential terms (object, price, and time) within which the object of that contract will define the liabilities of the parties implied, and therefore the subsequent action to be used in case of dispute.[56] In the case of the warehouses, the frame that governed the lease of a warehouse was the *locatio conductio rei*,[57] which in practice meant that the contract was based on the lease of the building or a space in the warehouse, but it had some legal particularities that qualify this contract as a specific case.[58]

The main aim of the agreement would have been to generate profit for the *horrearius* (person managing the warehouse) and it seems likely that the warehouse would have been let on these terms (*fruenda locata*).[59] The structure outlined in Roman legal texts involves three parties, namely the warehouse owner (*dominus horreorum*),[60] who could be either an individual or a procurator acting on behalf of the Roman state or a local municipality, the *horrearius* (contractual middleman),[61] and the customers who used the warehouse for the storage and safekeeping of goods. Even if warehouses were managed privately or publicly,[62] both activities were "nested," especially in archaeological contexts such as Portus, where there was a strong state presence, but private actors interacted in daily activities.[63]

As their name and location indicates, the Trajanic warehouses were imperial property, which does not forbid that the F6 cell could be located by privates during the Antonine period to shelter goods before their sale or after their acquisition by wholesalers. Indeed, that seems to be the case for the warehouses from Patara and Andriakè, also owned by the emperor (in this case, Hadrian),[64] which were located close but not next to the port quay, as was the case with the F6 cell.[65] The latter would qualify these warehouses as serving different purposes from unloading, similarly to the F6 cell. However, while for example the Lycian warehouses had a system of communicating rooms, the F6 system does not provide for external communication or even between the channels.[66] These features make it more complicated to understand what the specific use for these cells was.

Even though we do not have evidence for these warehouses, it seems that it was usual for elite estate owners to market their produce through their *tabernae* tenants, so perhaps they could have used the same strategy with the help of agents or warehouse subletting.[67] The latter will indicate that the use of these facilities was part of an intricate system of economic practices led by Roman elite owners.

One of the main epigraphic inscriptions that helps reconstruct the *essentialia* of the *locatio conductio* of publicly owned warehouses is the *lex horreorum Caesaris*, which contains a set of legal rules concerning the letting of spaces within a warehouse. The *lex* was found near the *Porta Salaria* in Rome, and dated to the reign of emperor Nerva (96–98 CE).[68] The *horrea Caesaris* have been identified with the *horrea Galbae*, located between the southern end of the Aventine Hill and the Monte Testaccio.[69] Their location far from the Tiber makes it possible to identify these as warehouses for storing goods and not for unloading.[70] The inscription reads:

> In his h]orreis [Imp(eratoris) – C]aesaris Aug(usti) loc(antur) [mercatoribus frument]ar(iis) armaria et loca [cum operis cella]rar(iorum) ex hac die et ex [k(alendis Ianuariis)] lex horreorum / [quisquis in annum futurum retinere volet horreum armarium aliu]dve quid ante Idus Dec(embres) pensione salute renuntiet qui non / [renuntiaverit si volvet retinere et cum horreario aliter pro i]nsequent anno non transegerit tanti habebit quanti eius gener(is) / [horreum armariumve eo anno ibi locari solebit si modo ali locatum n]on erit quisquis in his horreis conductum habet elocandi et / [substituendi ius non habebit – cu]stodia non praestabitur quae in his horreis invecta inlata / [erunt pignori erunt horreario si quis pro pensionib]us satis ei [non fece]rit quisquis in his horreis conductum habet et sua / [–] fuer(it) venia [qu]squis in his horreis conduc(tum) habet pensione soluta chirogr(apho) / [– quisquis habens conductu]m horreum su[a ibi] reliquer(it) et custodi non adsignaver(it) horrearius sine culpa erit.
>
> In the warehouses of the Emperor ... Caesar Augustus are let to grain merchants, chests and spaces together with the *operae* of warehouse attendants from this day and from the 1st of January.
>
> The *lex horreorum*.
>
> Whoever wishes to retain the chest or other space which he has rented for a further year, shall give notice before the 13th of December and once payment has been made. He who has not given notice, if he wishes to retain the chest or other space and has not transacted otherwise with the *horrearius*, shall pay as much as that chest is customary let out for in that year, provided it has not been let to another.

> Whoever has let [a space] in these warehouses, shall not have the right to sublet or to substitute. Custody of the goods brought into the warehouse shall not be vouched for. Those goods which have been brought into the warehouse shall be deemed to be pledged to the *horrearius*, provided that security has not been given for the rents.
>
> Whoever has rented [a space] in these warehouses, ..., has permission. Whoever has rented [a space] in these warehouses and has paid his rent [with proof] by chirograph, shall be freed ....
>
> Whoever has rented a warehouse and has left his goods there and has not handed it to a custodian (attendant?), the *horrearius* shall be without *culpa*.
>
> (transl. Plessis 2012: 177)

These rulings were probably displayed in the warehouse to be seen by everyone, as happened with other regulations to manage and organise public infrastructure.[71] Apart from practical rules relating to the date of payment and the obtaining of a receipt, the *lex horreorum Caesaris* mentions some legal rules, namely the extension of the lease for the upcoming year (that was declared to the lessor by the ides of December), the ban to sublet, the lack of liability for *custodia* of the *horrearius* and the tacit hypothec over movables (*invecta et illata*) brought into the warehouse,[72] and, finally, that any alterations made by a tenant to a hired space must not be dismantled without permission.[73] A survey of other Roman legal texts demonstrates that these contractual clauses were implicit, and therefore indicates that probably the parties will mostly agree that the essentials of the contract (price, time, the exact place where goods were deposited) and clauses concerning the elements referred to in a general *lex* governing the warehouses will be tacitly incorporated in the contract.[74]

One example of a private lease of a cell within a state-owned warehouse can be found in tablet 45 from the *Sulpicii* archive, which was published in a critical edition by Camodeca in 1999 and has received a lot of attention since then.[75]

> TPSulp. 45: C(aio) Caesare Germanico Augusto Ti(berio) Claudio Nerone/ Germanico co(n)s(ulibus), sextum nonas Iulias (2 July 37 AD). Diognetus C(aii) Novi Cypaeri servus scripsi iussu Cypaeri/domini mei coram ipso me locasse Hesycho Ti(berii) Iulii /Augusti l(iberti) Eueni ser (vo) horreum duodecimum in horreis Bassianis publicis Puteolanorum mediis, in quo repositum est triticum Alexandrinum, quod pignori accepit hac die a C(aio)/ Novio Euno, item in iisdem horreis imis intercolumnia, ubi/repositos habet saccos leguminum ducentos, quos pignori accepit ab eodem Euno. Ex k(alendis) Iuliis in menses singulos sestertiis singulis n[u]m (mis). Act(um) P[u]t(eolis.
>
> Under the consuls Gaius Caesar Germanicus Augustus and Tiberius Claudius Nero Germanicus on the 6th day before the Nones of July (2 July 37), I, Diognetus, slave of Gaius Novius Cypaerus, have written with the authorisation of my master Cypaerus and in his presence that I let to Hesychus, slave of Tiberius Iulius Evenus, freedman of Augustus, stall 12

on the middle floor of the Bassian Public Granaries of the Puteolans, in which Alexandrian wheat is stored, which (Hesychus) receives as a pledge today from Gaius Novius Eunus, likewise in the same granaries the lower floor between the columns, which holds in storage 200 sacks of beans, which (Hesychus) receives as a pledge from the same Eunus. From the Kalends of July (1 July) one sesterce each month. Transacted at Puteoli.

(Transl. Jones 2006: 95)

Gaius Novius Cypaerus was a *horrearius* who had rented the entire Bassian public granary from Puteoli (actual Pozzuoli). In sum, Cypaerus was in the storage business and rented individual spaces in these warehouses. His slave Diognetus was his agent and issued this tablet in which storage spaces were leased to Hesychus, freedman of Evenus Primianus. The grain stored there actually belonged to C. Novius Eunus, from whom Hesychus received it as a pledge. Therefore, this tablet recorded the second lease contract, because Primianus could not substitute Eunus in his first lease contract and therefore a new agreement had to be released. The tablet displays a fairly short contract, in which only some elements appear indicated, such as the identification of the space where the goods are stored, of the goods themselves, the date of the contract, and the price. The sum indicated here should be considered as a symbolic sum necessary for the effectiveness of the bilateral contract of letting and hiring and justified by the tight relationship existing between Cypaerus and Eunus.[76] As can be appreciated, the three conditions indicated at the *lex horreorum Caesaris* do not appear to be explicitly mentioned in this tablet; this is one reason why it has been asserted that these were incorporated tacitly in the agreement.

Further evidence on the letting and hiring of the privately owned Ummidian warehouses (second century CE) located in the Aventine,[77] reassesses the vicinity of letting and hiring of public and private *horrea*.[78]

[In his horr]eis Umm[idianis singulis an]nis locan[tur horrea apothecae comp] endiaria ar[maria intercolumnia et loc]a ex hac d[ie et ex kalendis Iuliis.

Quae in his horreis i]nvecta inla[ta importata erunt, horreario pig]nori erunt d[onec satis ei factum non sit aut pensi]o solvatur.

S[i quid in his horreis conductor in]aedi_caverit, [tollendi ius non habebit, nisi dat]a ei reficiendi po[testas fuerit ——————————] idie [——————————].

In these Ummidian warehouses are let for a single year storeroom, chests between the columns [?] and spaces from this day and from the 1st of July. Whatever has been brought into the warehouse, shall be pledged to the *horrearius* for as long as security has not been given to him or the rent has not been paid. If the *conductor* has walled up anything in these warehouses, he shall not have the *ius tollendi*, unless the power to correct it was given to him.

(Transl. Du Plessis 2012: 187)

This document, although shorter than the *lex horreorum*, indicates similar provisions concerning the *hypothecae* over movables, as well as *ius tollendi* (right to withdraw) of the lessor in the case that the warehouses suffer permanent alterations. These inscriptions seem to suggest that letting and hiring contracts would not differ much, whether used for publicly or privately owned warehouses.[79] In addition, the Ummidian warehouses' inscription indicates that the *lex* refers to "whatever was brought into the warehouses" (*quae in his horreis invecta inlata importata erunt*), while the previous sources referred to grain.[80] Therefore, thanks to this evidence, it is possible to imagine the general traits of the contract of letting and hiring that could have been used to handle the different activities taking place in the F6 cell during the Antonine period, in the case that it was leased to private parties. To sum up, the contract could have then indicated the price, the time of the lease, and the identification of the place where the goods were deposited. Elements such as the obligation of safekeeping the goods stored or the exclusion of *ius tollendi* would have been tacitly implied.

However, the documents previously used refer to goods stored which were removed from the warehouse in the same form and kept in the same container in which they were deposited. Instead, for the case of the F6 cell, the goods arriving to these storehouses could be repackaged in different containers. In addition, it is important to consider that arrangements would be different depending on the product and this would also impact the management and contracts linked to those warehouses. Therefore, what about the liability for *custodia* or safekeeping from the *horrearius*? The *lex horreorum caesaris* includes mentions of *quisquis in his horreis conductum habet elocandi et / [substituendi ius non habebit — cu]stodia non praestabitur*. The fragment was reconstructed in turn by Mommsen and Mitteis; the first indicating that *custodia* referred to a mitigation of the *horrearius*' liability in the case that the ban to sublet was not respected.[81] Conversely, Mitteis proposed that this part of the inscription excluded the *horrearius*' liability with respect to concrete objects,[82] inspired by a text from the Digest in which is described the case of someone who stored gold and pearls in a warehouse when the *horrearius* had a rule which expressly indicated that he refused liability for safekeeping precious goods.[83] However, the *locator* stored these goods in the warehouse, and the *horrearius* allowed that, being then liable for the risk of the loss of these objects as if he had not expressed any rule about the matter.[84]

Regarding these reconstructions, Marini indicates that the *custodia non praestabitur* clause from the *lex horreorum Caesaris* had the function of limiting and exempting the *horrearius* from responding to safekeeping goods deposited in *horrea* for which he did not explicitly have a contract with third parties, or when he was unable to verify the quantity or condition before storage.[85] Such a reconstruction would be consistent with the clause from the *Lex*, which alludes to the *adsignatio* (supervision) of the goods by the *horrearius*, at the time of deposit.[86] The *adsignatio* to control the goods deposited in a warehouse is a well-known procedure when referring to storage practices.[87] That said, I think that in the case that the goods were repackaged, it could be considered that these do not correspond to what was supervised by the *horrearius* and therefore, he could refuse liability in that respect.[88] In addition, if the product repackaged in cell F6 was wine, it is necessary to bear in mind its perishability,[89] and the fact that it was not included among the goods publicly distributed in the Antonine period, involved particular procedures for its distribution and sale.[90]

The latter highlights the element of specialisation and skill needed to handle the different products stored, which would have applied to the *locatio conductio* agreed, but that does not appear in the documents previously studied. This element constitutes one key difference in the lease contract employed for our cell in the different periods, because even if we are not certain about what was stored in cell F6, or how it was managed, what is sure is that this space was not only devoted to storing grain as seems to be its function after the Severan refurbishment. Different activities and assemblages of stored goods implied sophisticated skills and knowledge on the part of traders and warehouse operators (*horrearii*) to manage diverse products, appropriate storage times, and other practicalities of storage technology, alongside the vagaries of demand and sale.[91] For the case of wine, several examples from Roman Egypt indicate a specific title to designate the subjects in charge of managing stocks of perishable goods (*ἐκδοχεῖς*), who were in charge of the *horrea vinaria*, and of surveying the wine stored, its pouring, and its sale.[92]

In that sense, we can assume that the goods stored will affect the contract of the lease. If the warehouse was specialised in a certain kind of goods, it is likely that the personnel working in these facilities would be familiar with a product and its peculiarities would be considered in the contract. This fact is self-evident when we think of specialised workers such as the *saccarii* from Portus, who would have deposited grain cargoes in warehouses that presumably counted on people familiar with the particularities of storing grain.[93] One similar phenomenon can be witnessed in the letting and hiring used in the context of shipping. Some products, such as stone blocks and especially columns, would have been an awkward cargo to manage and it seems probable that certain shippers and vessels specialised in transporting stone.[94] The same would have applied to other products such as wine transported in *dolia*, a business carried out by the Pirani family from the south of France over several generations.[95] The merchant specialised in trading with certain goods would know better how to safely maintain specific cargoes, minimise risks in transport, and have suitable tools for (un)loading them.

That said, such variability on the goods stored and the specialisations of the subjects working in these warehouses echoe details regarding compartmentalisation provided by an inscription found in Rome, concerning a notice of lease of the private *horrea* owned by a consul, Q. Tineius Sacerdos.[96] The inscription lists spaces for hire, probably in decreasing order of size, as: *horrea* (an ensemble of rooms, or the entire building), *apothecae* (wine storerooms),[97] *compendiaria* (a sort of safe deposit), *armaria* (chests),[98] *intercolumnia* (space between columns),[99] and *loca armaris* (subdivisions within, or the standing place of, an *armarium*).[100]

The exact interpretation of the different terms matters less for this argument than the importance of these taxonomic classifications in defining the goods stored and the skills of the subjects working there, while it had an obvious impact on the leasing conditions. As can be appreciated in the sources previously included, while the *lex horreorum Caesaris* refers to *horrea compendi]ar(ia) armaria et loca*, the *lex Ummidianis* refers to *apothecae comp]endiaria ar[maria inter]/ [columnia et loc]a*, and the *TPSulp.* 45 to *horrea* and *intercolumnia.* The latter highlights the variety of goods that could be stored in the same warehouse, and therefore, the need to count on specialised personnel to handle these goods. As an example of that, the case of the *Septem Caesares* warehouses is revealing, as we know for sure that it hosted oil, but also wine. We can also imagine that the *negotiator* from the inscription was dealing with other wares, as he was also a trader of products imported by sea.[101]

Following the text of *TPSulp*.45, our F6 cell would be defined as an *horreum*, which was probably identified by a number, as was the case in the tablet (*horreum duodecimum in horreis Bassianis publicis Puteolanorum mediis*). Concerning the two different phases of this cell, the difference between the lease (in the case of letting the space in both periods), would be based on the goods handled, which, as can be appreciated through the evolution of this cell, goes hand in hand with the architectural features of the warehouse. That said, the fact that these warehouses were located in one of the main sites of the port system of Rome, and that these benches were built *ex professo* in this cell strongly suggest that it was managed by people who wanted to devote it to a specific task, and therefore knew how to manage the product stored. The specific activities carried out in there, given its location and context, would have counted in both periods on the specialised personnel, who would have handled their liability when managing these materials, unless a specific exception was provided in the lease.

Conclusion

The current state of research about the F6 cell highlights that storage activities at Portus were more diverse than is generally assumed and registered a wider range of activities than expected, at least during its first period of activity. However, we cannot forget that this cell has been classified as an "anomaly" with respect to the rest of the facilities composing the Trajanic warehouse. The latter, together with the evidence of the Severan refurbishment of the cell, underlines that the reality of these storage facilities is that they were featured as focal and integrated points of both planning and activity due to their role in distribution. This case study provides a new hypothesis for the function of this peculiar cell and raises several important methodological questions to bear in mind when studying storage facilities. These buildings have been sometimes studied with the focus placed upon one single kind of commodity, one single type of work specialisation, and one single kind of contract to manage the activities. However, the case of the F6 cell highlights that these facilities developed over time, and that their function and management could change depending on factors such as location, as well as the kind of product stored. In addition, I would like to underline the possibility that many of the individuals using these facilities could have been specialised in trading with one or more type of goods, and therefore they understood the intricacies implied when trading with a concrete kind of commodity and its impact in the management of a warehouse.

Concerning the variability of the lease contract that could be used to handle the different phases of this cell, this case study underlines the flexibility of the tools facilitated by the Roman *locatio conductio*. As indicated previously, besides the main elements of price, location of the goods, or time, other details related to the specific goods stored and the activities carried out in the facilities seem to be left to the parties in the contract. That said, if the features of a warehouse are determinant for the goods stored, that in turn influenced the labour carried out in one facility, and, consequently, the contract agreed to handle the different risks and liabilities. In that way, storage, and its related facilities, evidence distinct human–object relations and opportunities. The latter highlight that those human interactions with changes in infrastructures need to be considered in terms of reciprocal agency, to categorise the material commercial landscape of places such as Portus. Finally, the combination of the resilience of these buildings together with the flexibility of the tools used to manage the spaces, and the diverse specialisations of the people working there, made warehouses much more than buildings, characterising them as actual actors influencing the real estate market and the cycles of trade.

Notes

1 I would like to thank Dr Marta García Morcillo and Dr Cristina Rosillo-López for inviting me to participate in this volume. In addition, I would like to also acknowledge the help from Prof. Dennis Kehoe, whose comments and suggestions have improved this piece immeasurably, and Evelyne Bukowiecki for her generosity on letting me use the images displayed in this piece and responding patiently to all my doubts concerning the architectural details of the warehouses studied. Finally, I would like to thank Dr Elena Martelli for her suggestions and information concerning the Puteolian warehouses. Any errors that remain are, of course, my own responsibility. This publication was made possible thanks to the generous funding of the Academy of Finland and a fellowship at the Käte Hamburger Kolleg "Legal Unity and Pluralism" at the University of Münster, funded by the Federal Ministry of Education and Research (BMBF).

2 Levinson 2006: esp. 1–15.

3 Virlouvet 2018: 43–44.

4 For a deeper take on this, see Kantor and Skoda 2017.

5 Similarly as does Van Oyen 2020.

6 Van Oyen and Pitts 2017; Van Oyen 2018.

7 I have underlined the importance of considering the flexibility of legal tools for what concerns letting and hiring in Mataix Ferrándiz 2022a.

8 Arce and Goffaux 2011: Van Oyen 2020: 145. On the port system of Rome, Keay 2012b: 33–65, and on the role of these warehouses inside the port system,

Boetto et al. 2010: 307–308. For a general overview on the commercial significance of ports, see Keay 2020: 1–19.

9 On the "multiform" functionality of warehouses, Virlouvet 2018: 57–58 and on their role as "microcosms" of port societies, Virlouvet 2020: 154–156.

10 Indeed, the massive Trajanic investment at Portus triggered a second-century building "boom" at Ostia, and that synchronicity suggests a close relationship between both harbours, which interlocked with a wider port network. See Zevi 2000; Van Oyen 2020: 132.

11 For a general scheme of the cycle of procedures taking place in Roman ports, see Mataix Ferrándiz 2018; and 2022b.

12 Van Oyen 2020: 125; 144–145; as opposed to Rickman 1971, who prioritises the role of the warehouses at Portus as mainly serving the *annona* distribution.

13 For some general references about the archaeology of Portus, see: Keay et al. 2005; Keay and Paroli 2011; Keay 2012a; Keay et al. 2020.

14 Boetto et al. 2010: 307; Bukowiecki et al. 2018: 245–249.

15 See Keay 2012b: 41.

16 Boetto et al. 2010: 304–305.

17 This can be also perceived in other ports such as *Narbo Martius* (Narbonne), that has indeed been qualified as a "port-warehouse," see Bonsangue 2014: 159–175; 2016: 159–160.

18 Van Oyen 2020: 148.

19 Martelli 2013: 15–21; Van Oyen 2020: 148–149; James 2021: 17, 24.

20 For the case of olive oil shipments, see: Broekaert 2008; Mataix Ferrándiz 2022c.

21 Beresford 2013: 23–24; quoting Plin. *HN.* 2.47.125; Veg. *Mil.* 39.

22 Rickman 1971: 87–122. This kind of construction has been initially identified as evidencing a tight control of the operations taking place in its facilities (Keay et al. 2005: 310). However, this argument has been recently contested by Van Oyen 2020: 135, who highlights the need to read beyond planimetric evidence for warehouses into a range of possible activity patterns.

23 Boetto et al. 2010: 305.

24 Virlouvet 2011: 7–22; Bernardos Sanz and Virlouvet 2016: 59–82.

25 See Marzano in this book (Chapter 9) for a different use of *suspensurae* in the context of Roman baths and *hipocaustum*.

26 Rickman 1971: 293–297.

27 Zevi 2002: 217; and contesting the evidence, Van Oyen 2020: 138.

28 Bukowiecki et al. 2018: 254–260; 263–267, also Bukowiecki (forthcoming).

29 Pagliaro et al. 2015: 566.

30 Bukowiecki and Panzieri 2013: 2–4.

31 Bukowiecki et al. 2018: 240 and n. 24.

32 Bukowiecki and Panzieri 2013: 5; Bukowiecki et al. 2018: 242.

33 Evidence of production is attested in other warehouses, such as the *horrea* from the palazzo SIP at Puteoli, where a washbasin was found. See Rossi 2016: 222.

34 Repackaging is a well attested activity taking place in other ports such Arles (Djaoui 2017: 79–80); Berenike (Sidebotham and Wendrich 2007: 258–284) or Narbonne (Bonsangue 2016: 163).

35 Virlouvet 2006: 45, 51–52, indicating the inscriptions. For more details about the construction and function of *tabernae* in Rome, see Maschek in this volume (Chapter 11).

36 Maiorano and Paroli 2013: 11, 22.

37 Bukowiecki et al. 2018: 242–245. The F6 cell was not the only one affected by that refurbishment, but also the cells F44, F45, F46, and F47.

38 Rickman 1996: 281–291; Verduchi 2004: 242; Keay et al. 2005: 286; Brandt 2005: 26–27; Keay et al. 2012: 510.

39 De Romanis 2007: 187–230.

40 Zevi 2000.
41 Meiggs 1973: 282, 288. Also, Rickman 1971: 127.
42 For some examples for oil, see Van Oyen 2020: 192–193; and some examples for wine, see Martí Oliveras 2015 and Carrato 2017; Thurmond 2016: 165–174.
43 Meiggs 1973: 282.
44 Tchernia 1986: 257–299; Panella & Tchernia 1994: 155–157; Rizzo 2003, Rizzo 2014; Łoś and Pietruszka 2016. James 2021: 32–33; 37; 67–68 provides some rates of wine imports in Rome.
45 Tchernia 1986: 290–291, 298, who also indicates that Ulpian's references to barrels serve as *terminus ante quem* and that the use of barrels was extended in Italy to the second century at the latest. See *Dig.* 33.6.3.1 (Ulp. 23 *ad Sab.*) and *Dig.* 33.7.12.1 (Ulp. 20 *ad Sab.*); Baratta 2001; Marlière 2002; Djaoui 2013.
46 *CIL* VI 9189; 9190; 37807, see also Holleran 2012: 79 n. 74. Other locations of wine depots are described in Palmer 1980: 232–233 and Purcell 1985: 12, 17.
47 Coarelli 1999: 156.
48 For later evidence about wine public distributions, the inscription *CIL* VI 1784 = 31931 directly mentions wine being tasted from barrels at Rome. For more details, see Vera 2006: 303–317. For the distribution of goods with barrels in other river contexts, see the case of Arles as described by Djaoui 2015 and 2017.
49 Maiorano and Paroli 2013: 11, 22, 40, 368, 372, 484.
50 Broekaert 2008: 611 fig.11.
51 Aguilera Martin 2002: 96, fig. 17.
52 Fasciato 1947; Panciera 1980.
53 An accumulation of used stoppers was found associated with warehouse installations at Myos Hormos, which points to the fact that tasting was undertaken in front of them, and that the container was then resealed before being transferred to the consumer, see Thomas 2011: 32.
54 For a review of the literature and sources, see Du Plessis 2012.
55 Proportionality of the reciprocal obligation was essential to the contract, see Thomas 1971: 673–689.
56 For some general notions, see Mayer-Maly 1956; Wacke 1980: 299–334; Fiori 1999: 286–90; Du Plessis 2006a: 423–437; 2012: 9–51, for more concrete evidence for warehouses, see Alzon 1965.
57 In the face of previous opinions which sustained that the contract was a *locatio conductio operis* or *operarum*, or even a mixed contract (Alzon 1956: 245–257). For a review of the literature about these debates, see Marini 2015: 168–171.
58 Du Plessis 2012: 173; 187 n. 210, provides the list of sources from the Digest dealing with *locatio conductio* of warehouses. Also, Rickman 1971: 194–209 discusses a series of inscriptions, many of which were discredited.
59 The different statuses and implications for the contract from the *horrearius* and *dominus horreorum* were highlighted by Thomas 1966: 366–368, with the problem that he did not have access to the critical edition of the *Sulpicii* archive, which makes his claims on *custodia* a bit outdated.
60 *Dig.* 19.2.55pr. (Paul 2 *Sent.*).
61 *Dig.* 9.3.5.3 (Ulp. 23 *ad. Ed.*); *Dig.* 19.2.60.9 (Lab. 5 *Post. a Iav. Epit.*).
62 For a summary of these property regimes, see France 2008 and Dubouloz 2008.
63 Using Tchernia's famous definition from his 2011 book, also very present in Virlouvet 2018.
64 *TAM* II, 397.
65 Cavalier 2007: 63–34; Cavalier 2018.
66 Bukowiecki et al. 2018: 239.
67 See Maschek in this volume.
68 *CIL* VI 33747= *ILS* 5914 and *FIRA* III, 455–456.
69 Gatti 1885: 112; Carcopino 1910: 429.

70 On the *horrea galbae,* Rickman 1971: 165–177; Virlouvet 2006: 23–60.
71 e.g. *Lex Malacitana* (*FIRA* I, 215); *Lex Portorii Asiae* (Cottier *et al.* 2008: 215).
72 Also, in Dig. 20.2.3 (Ulp. 73 *ad ed.*).
73 Marini 2015: 164 n.20; Holleran 2012: 85.
74 Du Plessis 2012: 175, 185–186, quoting *Cod Iust.*4.65.6; *Dig.* 8.5.8.5 (Ulp. 17 *ad. Ed.); Dig.* 19.2.60.9 (Lab 5 *Post. a Iav. Epit.); Dig.* 20.2.3 (Ulp. 73 *ad. Ed.); Dig.* 32.1.30.1 (Lab. 2 *Post. a Iav. Epit.*).
75 Camodeca 1999: 121–124. On the tablet, see for example Virlouvet 2000: 132–143; Lintott 2002: 555–565; Jones 2006: 95–97; Du Plessis 2006b: 90–92, 2012, 178–185; Rossi 2014; Jakab 2021, *inter alia.*
76 Fiori 1999: 45–50; Lintott 2002: 557; Jones 2006: 96.
77 Virlouvet 2020: 155 n.5.
78 *CIL* VI 37795; *FIRA* III, 457.
79 Du Plessis 2006a: 434–435; 2012: 186.
80 In the case of the Puteolian *horrea,* that is a partial impression that we got from the evidence available in the *Sulpicii* archive, while the port of Puteoli counted with warehouses destined for different goods and functions. See Rossi 2016: 205–225, esp. 206 n. 5, 6 and 7 for an extensive revision of the literature available.
81 Mommsen in *Fontes iuris Romani antiqui*[5] of K.G. Bruns from 1886, also *FIRA*[7] I, 372.
82 Mitteis and Wilcken 1963: 259 n. 3.
83 *Dig.* 19.2.60.6 (Lav. 5 *Post. a Iav. Epit.) Locator horrei propositum habuit se aurum argentum margaritam non recipere suo periculo: deinde cum sciret has res inferri, passus est. Proinde eum futurum tibi obligatum dixi, ac si propositum fuit, remissum videtur.* (The lessor of a warehouse had as a rule that he did not accept gold, silver, or pearls at his own risk; but then he consented when he knew that these goods were brought in. For that reason, I say that he would be obliged towards you, in the same way as when he had his rule, and so it seems.)
84 *Periculum* was not a technical term in Roman law, but merely meant "risk of loss," as indicated first by MacCormack 1979: 129–172 and Du Plessis 2012: 39–41.
85 Marini 2015: 177–178 (following Mommsen).
86 On *adsignatio,* see Alzon 1965: 120–125; Robaye 1987: 117 n. 8.
87 Some examples of these controls would be the *ostraka* found at the Ilôt de l' Amirauté (Carthage), witnessing the oil cargoes being stored in the warehouses from the Zeugitana province. See Peña 1998: 117–238.
88 *Dig.*19.2.11.3 (Ulpian. 32 *ad Ed.*) refers to goods stored in a warehouse, and highlights the importance of identifying them, which goes in hand with the fact that these goods should be identified in the same container.
89 Some of the texts of the Digest that refer to the sale of wine, *Dig.* 18.1.34.5 (Paul. 33 *ad. Ed.); Dig.* 18.6.1pr. (Ulp. 28 *ad Sab.); Dig.* 18.1.9.pr-2 (Ulp. 28 *ad Sab.); Dig.* 18.6.4pr. (Ulp. 28 *ad Sab.); Dig.* 18.6.18 (Pomp. 31 *ad Quint. Muc.); Dig.* 18.6.2.1 (Gaius 2 *Rer. Cott.); Dig.* 19.1.5.1pr. (Paul 3 *ad Sab.); Dig.* 19.1.3.3–4 (Pomp. 9 *ad Sab.*). See also Frier 1983: 257–295.
90 Yaron 1959; Tchernia 2000; Jakab 1999: 71–111; 2009: 229.
91 Van Oyen 2020: 150, referring to the mix of goods stored at the *horrea Galbana* in Rome.
92 Rossi 2019: 71–75.
93 Rickman 1980: 133; 2002: 359; Martelli 2013.
94 *Dig.* 19.2.25.7 (Gaius 10 *ad ed. prov.*); Russell 2013: 105, 537.
95 Marlier 2008.
96 *CIL* V 33860=*ILS* 5913.
97 *Dig.* 30.47.1 (Ulp. 22 *ad Sab.); Dig.* 9.3.5.3 (Ulp. 23 *ad Ed.); Dig.* 47.2.21.6 (Paul 40 *ad Sab.); Dig.* 33.7.20 1 (Ulp. 20 *ad Sab.); Dig.*19.2.11.3 (Ulp. 32 *ad Ed.*). Columella. *Rust.* 1.6.9; Vitr. *De arch.* 6.5.2.; Plin. *Ep.* 2.17.13.

98 *Dig.* 1.15.3.2 (Paul *Lib. Sing. de Praef. Vigilum*); *Dig.* 32.52.3 (Ulp. 24 *ad Sab.*); *Dig.* 32.52.7pr.-1 (Ulp. 24 *ad Sab.*); *Dig.* 33.10.3.2 (Paul 4 *ad Sab.*); *PS.* 3.6.56; 3.6.67.

99 *CTh.* 15.1.45.

100 Rickman 1971: 197. Other mentioned terms are *capsa* and *arca* in relation to *armaria*, see: *Dig.* 33.10.3.2 (Paul 4 *ad Sab.*); *PS.* 3.6.67; *Dig.* 1.15.3.2 (Paul *Lib. Sing. de Praef. Vigilum*). This division and the consequent need for specialised manpower would have fitted well within the scheme of elite estate owners and their marketing practices through lessees or subletting as indicated in Maschek in this volume for the case of *tabernae* (Chapter 11).

101 *CIL* IX 4680 (*ILS* 7484): *negotiator vinarius a Septem Caesaribus idem mercator omnis generis mercium transmarinarum.*

References

Aguilera Martín, A. (2002) *El monte Testaccio y la llanura subaventina: topografía extra portam Trigeminam*. Madrid: CSIC.

Alzon, C. (1965) *Problemes relatifs à la location des entrepots en Droit Romain*. Paris: Cujas.

Arce, J. and Goffaux, B. (2011) *Horrea d'Hispanie et de la Méditerranée romaine*. Madrid: Casa de Velázquez.

Baratta, G. (2001) Un'alternativa all'anfora: la botte. In: J. Maldonado Rosso, ed. *Actas del I simposio de la Asociación Internacional de Historia y Civilización de la Vid y del Vino*, Vol. I. El Puerto de Santa Maria: Ayuntamiento de El Puerto de Santa María, 149–155.

Beresford, J. (2013) *The Ancient Sailing Season*. Leiden: Brill.

Bernardos Sanz, J.U. and Virlouvet, C. (2016) Formes et fonctions: essai de typologie. In: B. Marin and C. Virlouvet, eds. *Entrepôts et trafics annonaires en Méditerranée*. Rome: École française de Rome, 59–82.

Boetto, G., Bukowiecki, E., Monteix, N., and Rousse, C. (2010) Portus. Les entrepôts de Trajan. *MEFRA* 122. 1, 303–310.

Bonsangue, M. (2014) Narbonne, un port de stockage de la Méditerranée occidentale sous le Haut-Empire. In: C. Apicella, M.L. Haack, and F. Lerouxel, eds. *Les affaires de Monsieur Jean Andreau. Economie et société du monde romain*. Bordeaux: Ausonius, 159–175.

Bonsangue, M. (2016) Les échanges commerciaux autour de Narbonne (IIe siècle av. J.-C.-IIe siècle apr. J.-C.). In: A.F. Baroni, G. Bernard, B. Le Teuff, and C. Ruiz Darasse, eds. *Échanger en Méditerranée. Acteurs, pratiques et normes dans les mondes anciens*. Rennes: Presses Universitaires de Rennes, 143–167.

Brandt, J.R. (2005) "The Warehouse of the World": A Comment on Rome's Supply Chain during the Empire. *Orizzonti: Rassegna di archeologia* 6, 25–47.

Broekaert, W. (2008) Roman Economic Policies during the Third Century AD: The Evidence of the *tituli picti* on Oil Amphorae. *Ancient Society* 28, 197–219.

Bukowiecki, E. (ed.) Forthcoming. *Les entrepôts dits de Trajan à Portus. Etude d'un complexe de stockage en milieu portuaire (Ier - IVe siècle ap. J.-C.)*.

Bukowiecki, E. and Panzieri, C. (2013). Portus. Les entrepots dits de Trajan. *Chroniques des activités archéologiques de l'École française de Rome*. Italie centrale, 1–11.

Bukowiecki, E., Mimmo, M., Panzieri, C., and Sebastiani, R. (2018) Le système des sols surélevés dans les entrepôts d'Ostie, de Portus et de Rome: nouvelles découvertes en cours. In: V. Chankowski, X. Lafon, and C. Virlouvet, eds. *Entrepôts et circuits de distribution en Méditerranée antique*. Athens: École francaise d'Athènes, 231–267.

Carcopino, J. (1910) Ostiensia. II. Le quartier des docks. *MEFRA* 30, 397–446.

Carrato, C. (2017) *Le dolium en Gaule Narbonnaise (Ier s. a.C. – IIIe s. p.C.): Contribution à l'histoire socio-économique de la Méditeranée nordoccidentale*. Bordeaux: Ausonius.

Cavalier, L. (2007) Horrea d'Andriaké et Patara: un nouveau type d'édifice fonctionnel en Lycie à L'époque impériale. *REA* 109. 1, 51–65.

Cavalier, L. (2018) Nouvelles observations sur les aménagements commerciaux du port d'Andriakè. In: V. Chankowski, X. Lafon, and C. Virlouvet, eds. *Entrepôts et circuits de distribution en Méditerranée antique*. Athens: École française d'Athènes, 109–122.

Coarelli F. (1999) Portus Vinarius. In: E.M. Steinby, ed. *Lexicon topographicum urbis Romae* IV, 156.

Cottier, M., Crawford, M.H. and Crowther, C., eds. (2008) *The Customs Law of Asia*. Oxford: Oxford University Press.

De Romanis, F. (2007) In tempi di guerra e di peste: horrea e mobilità del grano pubblico tra gli Antonini e i Severi. *Antiquités africaines* 43, 187–230.

Djaoui, D. (2013) *Le transport en vrac: dolia ou tonneaux? Nouvelles recherches sur les dolia. L'exemple de la Méditerranée nord-occidentale à l'époque romaine (Ier s. av. J.-C. – IIIe s. apr. J.-C.)*, September 2013, Aspiran, France (unpublished conference paper).

Djaoui, D. (2015) Les pipettes en terre cuite: preuve indirecte de l'utilisation des tonneaux sur Arles et Fréjus à la période flavienne. In: Lemaître, S. and Batigne Vallet, C., eds. *Abécédaire pour un archéologue lyonnais. Mélanges offerts à Armand Desbat*. Montagnac: Instrumentum, 207–214.

Djaoui, D. (2017) Circulation et diffusion des marchandises depuis le delta du Rhône. In: P. Cattelain and A. Leblon, eds. *Potins et pots de vins Échange, commerce et transport vers la Gaule du Nord*. Treignes: Editions du Cédarc, 63–95.

Du Plessis, P.J. (2006a) Between Theory and Practice: New Perspectives on the Roman Law of Letting and Hiring. *CLJ* 65. 2, 423–437.

Du Plessis, P.J. (2006b) The Roman Concept of Lex Contractus. *Roman Legal Tradition* 3, 79–94.

Du Plessis, P.J. (2012) *Letting and Hiring in Roman Legal Thought: 27 BCE–284 CE*. Leiden: Brill.

Dubouloz, J. (2008) Propriété et exploitation des entrepôts à Rome et en Italie (Ier-IIIe siècles). *MEFRA* 120. 2, 277–294.

Fasciato, M. (1947) "Ad quadrigam fori vinarii" Autour du port au vin d'Ostie. *MEFRA* 59, 65–81.

Fiori, R. (1999) *La definizione della "Locatio conductio". Giurisprudenza romana e tradizione romanistica*. Naples: Jovene.

France, J. (2008) Les personnels et la gestion des entrepôts impériaux dans le monde romain. *REA* 110. 2, 484–507.

Frier, B.W. (1983) Roman Law and the Wine Trade: The Problem of Vinegar Sold As Wine. *ZSS* 100. 1, 257–295.

Gatti, G. (1885) Frammento dä iscrizione contenendo la lex horreorum. *Bullettino della Commissione Archeologica Comunale di Roma* 13, 110–129.

Holleran, C. (2012) *Shopping in Ancient Rome: The Retail Trade in the Late Republic and the Principate*. Oxford: Oxford University Press.

Jakab, É. (1999) Vinum *effundere* in Ulp. D.18.6.1.3. *ZSS* 116, 71–111.

Jakab, É. (2009) *Risikomanagement beim weinkauf: Periculum und Praxis im imperium Romanum*. Frankfurt am Main: Beck.

Jakab, É. (2022) Loans and Securities: Tracing Maritime Trade in the Archive of the *Sulpicii*. In: E. Mataix Ferrándiz and P. Candy, eds. *Roman Law and Maritime Commerce*. Edinburgh: Edinburgh University Press, 137–170.

James, P. (2021) *Food Provisions for Ancient Rome, A Supply Chain Approach*. London: Routledge.

Jones, D. 2006. *The Bankers of Puteoli*. Stroud: Tempus.

Kantor, G. and Skoda, H. (2017) *Legalism: Property and Ownership*. Oxford: Oxford University Press.

Keay, S.J. (ed.) (2012a) *Rome, Portus and the Mediterranean*. Oxford: Oxbow.

Keay, S.J. (2012b) The port system of imperial Rome. In: S.J. Keay, ed. *Rome, Portus and the Mediterranean*. Oxford: Oxbow, 33–67.

Keay, S.J. (2020) The Context of Roman Port Societies: An Introduction to the Portus Limen project. In: S.J. Keay and P. Arnaud, eds. *Roman Port Societies. The Evidence of Inscriptions*. Cambridge: Cambridge University Press, 1–35.

Keay, S.J. and Paroli L. (2011) *Portus and its Hinterland: Recent Archaeological Research*. Rome: The British School at Rome.

Keay, S.J., Millett, M., Paroli, L., and Strutt, K. (2005) *Portus: An Archaeological Survey of The Portus of Imperial Rome*. Rome: The British School at Rome.

Keay, SJ., Millett, M., Strutt, K., and Germoni, P. (eds.) (2020) *The Isola Sacra Survey Ostia, Portus and the port system of Imperial Rome*. Cambridge: Cambridge University Press.

Levinson, M. (2006) *The Box: How the Shipping Container Made the World Smaller and the World Economy Bigger*. Princeton: Princeton University Press.

Lintott, A. (2002) Freedmen and Slaves in the Light of Legal documents from first-century AD Campania. *CQ* 52. 2, 555–565.

Łos, A. and Pietruszka, W. (2016) Le vignoble campanien sous les Antonins. *MEFRA* 128-2 (online).

MacCormack, G. (1979) Periculum. *ZSS* 106, 129–172.

Maiorano, M. & Paroli, L. (2013) *La Basilica Portuense. Scavi 1991–2007*. Rome: All'insegna del giglio.

Marini, R. (2015) La custodia di merci dell'horrearius: a proposito di *CIL* VI 33747. *ZSS* 132, 154–180.

Marlier, S. (2008) Architecture et espace de navigation dans les navires a dolia. *Archeonautica* 15, 153–173.

Marlière, E. (2002) *L'autre et le tonneau dans l'occident romain*. Montagnac: Instrumentum.

Martelli, E. (2013) *Sulle spalle dei saccarii. Le rappresentazioni di facchini e il trasporto di derrate nel porto di Ostia in epoca imperial*. Oxford: Oxford University Press.

Martí Oliveras, A. (2015) Arqueología del vino en época romana: el proyecto Cella Vinaria y el complejo vitivinícola de Vallmora (Teià-Maresme-Barcelona). Nuevas aportaciones a la investigación. *Anales de Prehistoria y Arqueología*, 113–139.

Mataix Ferrándiz, E. (2018) *Explaining the Commerce of Roman Mediterranean Ports: The Evidence from scripta commercii and Law* (PhD Dissertation). Southampton-Lyon.

Mataix Ferrándiz, E. (2022a) Goods, Law and Trade. *Locatio conductio*'s Material Evidence. In: K. Verboven, ed. *Law and Economic Performance in the Ancient Economy*. Leiden: Brill, 131–157.

Mataix Ferrándiz, E. (2022b) "As I Went Down to the River to Trade" Trust along the Rhone River (1st cent. BC- 2nd cent. AD). In: C. Rollinger and P. Reinard, eds. *Scripta Mercaturae Beihefte* 3. Munich.

Mataix Ferrándiz, E. (2022c) On Dressel 20 and Beyond. Management, Punishment and Protection in the context of Roman Imperial Oil Distribution. In: E. Mataix Ferrándiz and P. Candy, eds. *Roman Law and Maritime Commerce*. Edinburgh: Edinburgh University Press, 77–108.

Mayer-Maly, T. (1956) *Locatio conductio: eine Untersuchung zum klassischen römischen Recht*. Vienna and Munich: Herold.

Meiggs, R. (1973) *Roman Ostia*. Oxford: Clarendon Press.

Mitteis, L. and Wilcken, U. (1963) *Grundzüge und Chrestomathie der Papyruskunde*, vol. 1. Leipzig and Berlin: Teubner.

Pagliaro, F., Bukowiecki, E., Gugliermetti, F., and Bisegna, F. (2015) The Architecture of Warehouses: A Multidisciplinary Study on Thermal Performances of Portus' Roman Store Buildings. *Journal of Cultural Heritage* 16, 560–566.

Palmer, R.E.A. (1980) Customs on Market Goods Imported into the City of Rome. *MAAR* 36, 217–233.

Panciera, S. (1980) Olearii. *MAAR* 36, 235–250.

Panella, C. and Tchernia, A. (1994) *Produits transportés en amphores: l'huile et surtout le vin. In: L'Italie d'Auguste à Dioclétien, Actes du colloque international de Rome (25–28 mars 1992)*. Rome: École française de Rome, 145–165.

Peña, J.T. (1998) The Mobilization of State Olive Oil in Roman Africa: The Evidence of the 4th Century Ostraca from Carthage. In: The Carthage Papers. The Early Colony's Economy, Water Supply, A Public Bath, And The Mobilization Of State Olive Oil. *JRA* 91, 117–238.

Purcell, N. (1985) Wine and Wealth in Italy. *JRS* 5, 1–19.

Rickman, G. (1971) *Roman Granaries and Store Buildings*. Cambridge: Cambridge University Press.

Rickman, G. 1980. The Grain Trade under the Roman Empire. Memoirs of the American Academy in Rome 36. *The Seaborne Commerce of Ancient Rome: Studies in Archaeology and History*, 261–275.

Rickman, G. (1996) Portus in Perspective. In: A. Gallina Zevi and A. Claridge, eds. *Roman Ostia Revisited: Archaeological and Historical Papers in Memory of Russell Meiggs*. London: British School at Rome, 281–291.

Rickman, G. (2002) Rome, Ostia and Portus: The Problem of Storage. *MEFRA* 114, 353–362.

Rizzo, G. (2003) *Instrumenta Urbis I: ceramiche fini da mensa, lucerne ed anfore a Roma nei primi due secoli dell'impero*. Rome: École française de Rome.

Rizzo, G. (2014) *Ostia VI. Le Terme del Nuotatore. Le anfore Ostia e i commerci mediterranei*. Rome: L'Erma Di Bretschneider.

Robaye, R. (1987) *L'obligation de garde: essai sur la responsabilité contractuelle en droit romain*. Brussels: Publications Fac St Louis.

Rossi, L. (2014) Les *frequentissimi mercatores* de Pouzzoles et le blé égyptien à Rome à la fin de L'époque républicaine. *MEFRA* 126. 2. doi:10.4000/mefra.2536

Rossi, L. (2016) Horrea et granaria à Pouzzoles (République- Haut-Empire). In: A.F. Baroni, G. Bernard, B. Le Teuff, and C. Ruiz Darasse, eds. *Échanger en Méditerranée. Acteurs, pratiques et Normes dans les mondes anciens*. Rennes: Presses Universitaires de Rennes, 205–225.

Rossi, L. (2019) Entrepôts et commerce: études de case en Égypte hellénistique et Romaine. *Cahiers du centre Gustave Glotz* 30, 53–79.

Russell, B. (2013) *The Economics of the Roman Stone Trade*. Oxford: Oxford University Press.

Sidebotham, S.E. and Wendrich, W. (eds.) (2007) *Berenike 1999–2000: Report on the Excavations at Berenike including Excavations in Wadi Kalalat and Siket and the Survey of the Mons Smaraggus Region*. Los Angeles, CA: University of California.

Tchernia, A. (1986). *Le vin de l'Italie romaine. Essai d'histoire économique d'après les amphores*. Rome: Bibliothèque des Écoles françaises d'Athènes et de Rome.

Tchernia, A. (2000) La vente du vin. In: E. Lo Cascio, ed. *Mercati permanenti e mercati periodici nel mondo romano*. Bari: Edipuglia, 199–209.

Tchernia, A. (2011) *Les romains et le commerce*. Naples: Publications du centre Jean Berard.

Thomas, J.A.C. (1966) Return to "horrea." *RIDA* 13, 353–368.

Thomas, J.A.C. (1971) Reflections on Building Contracts. *RIDA* 18, 673–689.

Thomas, R. (2011) Roman Vessel Stoppers; Terracotta Figurines; Ships and Ships' Fittings. In: L. Blue, J. Whitewright, and R.I. Thomas, eds. *Myos Hormos - Quseir al-Qadim: Roman Vessel Stoppers; Terracotta Figurines; Ships and Ships' Fittings*. Southampton: Oxbow, 11–34.

Thurmond, D.L. (2016) *From Vines to Wines in Classical Rome A Handbook of Viticulture and Oenology in Rome and the Roman West*. Leiden: Brill.

Van Oyen, A. (2018) Material Agency. In: S. López Varela, ed. *The Encyclopedia of Archaeological Sciences*. Hoboken, NJ: Wiley-Blackwell, 1–5.

Van Oyen, A. (2020) *The Socio-Economics of Roman Storage: Agriculture, Trade, and Family*. Cambridge: Cambridge University Press.

Van Oyen, A. and Pitts, M. (2017) What Did Objects Do in the Roman world? Beyond Representation. In: A. Van Oyen and M. Pitts, eds. *Materialising Roman histories*. Oxford: Oxbow, 3–12.

Vera, D. (2006) Un' iscrizione sulle distribuzioni pubbliche di vino a Roma (*CIL*, VI, 1785=31931). In: M. Silvestrini, T. Spagnuolo Vigorita, and G. Volpe, eds. *Studi in onore di Francesco Grelle*. Bari: Edipuglia, 303–317.

Verduchi, P.A. (2005) Some Thoughts on the Infrastructure of the Port of Rome. In: S. Keay, M. Millet, L. Paroli, and K. Strutt (Eds), *Portus. An Archaeological Survey of the Port of Imperial Rome*. London: BSR Archaeological Monographs, 248–257.

Virlouvet, C. (2000) Les denrées alimentaires dans les archives des *Sulpicii* de Pouzzoles. *Cahiers du Centre Gustave Glotz* 11, 131–149.

Virlouvet, C. (2006) Encore à propos des *horrea Galbana* de Rome: Entrepôts ou ergastules? *Cahiers du Centre Gustave Glotz* 17, 23–60.

Virlouvet, C. (2011) Les entrepôts dans le monde Romain antique, formes et fonctions. Premières pistes pour un essai de typologie. In: J. Arce and B. Goffaux, eds. *Horrea d'Hispanie et de La Méditerranée Romaine*. Madrid: Casa de Velázquez, 7–22.

Virlouvet, C. (2018) Bâtiments de stockage et circuits économiques du monde romain. In: V. Chankowski, X. Lafon, and C. Virlouvet, eds. *Entrepôts et circuits de distribution en Méditerranée antique*. Athens: École française d' Athènes, 43–60.

Virlouvet, C. (2020) Warehouse societies. In: S.J. Keay and P. Arnaud, eds. *Roman Port Societies. The Evidence of Inscriptions*. Cambridge: Cambridge University Press, 152–177.

Wacke, A. (1980) Rechtsfragen der römischen Lagerhausvermietung. *Labeo* 26, 299–324.

Yaron, R. (1959) Sale of Wine. In: D. Daube, ed. *Studies in the Roman Law of Sale: Dedicated to the Memory of Francis de Zulueta*. Oxford: Oxford University Press, 71–77.

Zevi, F. (2000) Traiano e Ostia in Gonzalez, J. *Trajano emperador de Roma*. Rome: L'Erma di Bretschneider, 509–547.

Zevi, F. (2002) Inquadramento storico relativo ai porti di Roma. In: A.M. Gallina Zevi and R. Turchetti, eds. *Le strutture dei porti e degli approdi antichi*. Soveria Mannelli: Rubbettino, 211–219.

Part V

Properties Beyond Italy

13 Imperial Properties in the North-Western Provinces

Possible Patterns of Acquisition and Sale

Sofia Piacentin

Abstract

Through inheritances, donations, or confiscations, the emperor accumulated an impressive amount of property throughout the provinces of his empire, including land, villas, woods, mines, quarries, and slaves. The emperor's property (*patrimonium Caesaris*) obviously played a crucial role in the legitimisation and maintenance of his power and prestige, but also in regulating economic activities such as the real estate market.

In this work I examine the role of the emperor in the real estate market of the north-western provinces of the empire (Gauls, both Narbonensis and the Tres Galliae – Lugdunensis, Aquitania, and Belgica), Germania inferior, Germania superior, and Britannia. First, I deal with the challenges of detecting imperial properties in such provinces, then I examine a number of property transactions which suggests some general patterns of property acquisition and sale adopted by the emperor. Such analysis would seem to corroborate the imperial tendency of exploiting pre-existing resources, i.e. mines, rather than playing an active role in the land ownership patterns of these provinces.

***

Introduction

In her study about imperial estates published in the collective volume *Studies in Roman Property* edited by Moses Finley in 1976, Dorothy Crawford [Thompson] includes a "working list" of imperial landed property for each province of the empire.[1] It is not surprising that Gaul and Britannia do not appear in such a list. North-western provinces notoriously lack clear evidence for imperial landed properties; however, reasoning about the scattered sources attesting imperial properties in these territories could shed more light on the role that the emperor played in the real estate market of these provinces. Indeed, the focus of this discussion is the provinces of Gauls, both Narbonensis and the Tres Galliae (Lugdunensis, Aquitania, and Belgica), Germania inferior, Germania superior, and Britannia. These provinces have been conveniently grouped under the label of "north-western provinces" to simplify the discussion when I will refer to them throughout this chapter. On one hand, this

DOI: 10.4324/9781003187806-18

label does not imply any unifying features, each of these provinces has a geographical, cultural, social, and economic history which cannot be thoroughly illustrated in this discussion. On the other hand, the choice of examining a broad geographical area should help to gain a fuller picture of the imperial policy adopted in a number of territories traditionally regarded not as central as Italy, Africa, Egypt, and Asia in the scholarly debate about imperial property.[2] In the following discussion, I will first address the difficulty of tracking down imperial estates in north-western provinces, which is often related to the paucity of epigraphic sources found in these territories. I will then examine a number of property transactions (i.e. confiscations and inheritance) between the emperor, his property (*patrimonium*), and individuals, which presumably took place in the north-western provinces of the empire. Finally, I will discuss whether we could detect any general patterns in the acquisition and sale of property by the emperor in the provincial real estate market. I hope that these few remarks may contribute to our understanding of the *patrimonium* in general.[3]

Imperial Properties and Epigraphic Habit in the North-Western Provinces

A dedication slab to the welfare of the emperor Caracalla found at Combe Down, a village near Bath, England, says that the imperial freedman and procurator's assistant Naevius restored from the ground some ruined headquarters (*principia*).[4] The slab was re-used to cover a coffin, and found near the remains of a Roman villa, where also a leaden inscribed sealing interpreted as *p(rovinciae) Br(itanniae) S(uperioris)* had been discovered.[5] The inscription deserves attention for a number of reasons. First, it attests procuratorial activities far from Londinium, the provincial capital and from any legionary camp. Indeed, the term *principia* would seem to refer to an administrative headquarter rather than a military building.[6] Second, the presence of a freedman assistant (*adiutor*) strongly suggests that he was supervising some imperial activities in a delimited area, whose existence might be corroborated by the attestation of a *centurio regionarius* at Bath, a centurion responsible for a particular geographical and administrative region.[7] This area of interest might have included the oolite limestone quarries that were extensively exploited for the construction of the nearby Aquae Sulis, modern Bath.[8] However, imperial ownership of quarries is not to be taken for granted. Alfred Hirt has shown that only a few granite quarries were under direct imperial control, whereas ownership and exploitation of quarries and mines by privates and municipalities is well attested by epigraphic evidence.[9] However, procurators, imperial freedmen, and slaves could be placed in charge of managing not only land but also mines and quarries owned by the emperor in both public and imperial provinces. In a public province like Gallia Narbonensis, a dedicated equestrian procurator looked after the *patrimonium*, whereas in imperial provinces such as in the Tres Galliae, Germaniae inferior, Germania superior, and Britannia, provincial procurators were responsible for both the collection of revenue and the management of *patrimonium*.[10]

Though caution is required, as it is impossible to determine with certainty the imperial interests in the area, the inscription of Combe Down, which attests the activity of a procurator's assistant in a relevant archaeological context, in the proximity of quarries and Roman remains, could be a plausible marker of imperial property in Britannia; unfortunately, it is also one the few examples of such finds in the north-western provinces. Procurators in charge of these provinces are usually attested by honorific dedications found in their home town.[11] Our knowledge is mostly limited to the title of these procuratorships (e.g. *procurator provinciae Narbonensis, procurator provinciarum Lugudunensis et Aquitanicae*), and the series of posts listed in their "career" inscriptions. This hinders any further attempts to identify their tasks and the context in which they operated. Similarly, the majority of inscriptions of imperial freedmen and slaves found in these provinces do not reveal anything about posts related to the management of imperial estates.[12] When known, they were archivists (*tabularii*), treasurers (*dispensatores*), or often employed in the collection of revenues such as the *XL Galliarum* and the *XX hereditatium*.[13]

The difficulty of identifying the original setting of these documents is also increased by the general low rate of surviving inscriptions in these territories. With the exception of Gallia Narbonensis, the number of inscriptions found in these provinces is generally low and surpassed only by inland Hispania Raetia, and Mauretania Tingitana.[14] Clusters of inscriptions are recorded around centres of imperial administration (i.e. Lugdunum, Narbo, Augusta Treverorum) or along communications networks. This is also worsened by the frequent reemployment of Latin inscriptions in the constructions of late antique city walls, so much that epigraphy in Gaul has been often described as "épigraphie des murailles."[15] Many inscriptions have been removed from their original contexts over the years, making it extremely difficult to estimate their real distribution in the territory. Any considerations about provincial epigraphic habit should then be treated with caution.[16] However, the low number of surviving inscriptions remains a central factor to consider when approaching the study of imperial properties in the north-western provinces.

Confiscations and the Real Estate Market: The Case of Gaul

If a survey of epigraphic sources cannot improve much our knowledge of imperial estates in the north-western provinces of the empire, we might explore different lines of enquiry. The history of imperial property would seem to be often entangled with a number of property transactions between the emperor and individuals, usually rich landowners such as senators and *equites*, the best represented social classes of our sources.[17] One would expect to find a strong body of evidence for such transactions in Gallia Narbonensis, where is attested the highest number of known senators and *equites* after Italy.[18] The most comprehensive work on this topic are the four volumes of Yves Burnand, *Primores Galliarum*, a thorough prosopography of senators and *equites* from Gaul, with a collection of sources about their property.[19] Burnand assembled a varied range of sources about rich landowners in Gaul including literary accounts, inscriptions recording acts of euergetism, and toponyms allegedly created after the *gentilicium* of prominent proprietors.[20] Although it is plausible to assume that land must have been a fundamental part of the Gallic élite wealth, sources do not explicitly record any passage of private property into the *patrimonium*, between individuals coming from these territories and the emperor or members of the imperial household.[21] As the emperor's property in the provinces mainly grew by inheritances, confiscations (*bona damnatorum*), and property with invalid testamentary dispositions (*bona caduca* and *vacantia*), we may attempt to track down such property transactions in the scattered literary accounts that deal with the north-western provinces of the empire. First of all, we should remember that although we cannot quantify the number of transactions of property which went into the *fiscus* due to invalid testamentary dispositions, the highest concentration of Roman citizens coming from southern Gaul suggests that the *fiscus* had to manage a considerable amount of such properties, which were presumably sold and must have generated a considerable cash inflow. The great number of these types of property transactions may be inferred by the demographic analysis and discussion of social practices examined by Marco Maiuro, who has convincingly stressed the central role of the *fiscus* in the management and re-sale of *bona caduca* and *vacantia*.[22] Narratives of massive confiscations in the Julio-Claudian age are attested in Gaul under Tiberius and Gaius.[23] These literary accounts are rather vague; we do not know the identity and the number of individuals who suffered confiscations, what was confiscated (real estate, movable objects or cash), or the procedure carried out to seize their properties. Their significance, however, can still be reassessed. Let us consider the first account of such confiscations as reported by Suetonius:

> *praeterea Galliarum et Hispaniarum Syriaeque et Graeciae principes confiscatos ob tam leve ac tam impudens calumniarum genus, ut quibusdam non aliud sit obiectum, quam quod partem rei familiaris in pecunia haberent; plurimis etiam civitatibus et privatis veteres immunitates et ius metallorum ac vectigalium adempta*
>
> that besides this the leading men of the Spanish and Gallic provinces, as well as of Syria and Greece, had their property confiscated on trivial and shameless charges, some being accused of nothing more serious than having a part of their property in ready money; that many states and individuals were deprived of immunities of long standing, and of the right of working mines and collecting revenues.
>
> (Suet. *Tib.* 49.2, Loeb translation)

Suetonius does not employ the standard Latin expressions (*bona publicare, bona vendere*) to describe confiscations imposed on convicted men which implied that property was seized, sold off, and proceeds deposited into the public treasury (*aerarium*). Instead, the use of *confiscare* deserves more scrutiny. In his book on early imperial finances, Michael Alpers has rightly stressed that Suetonius does not employ the verb *confiscare* as a synonym of *publicare* but rather to mean the process of seizing property for personal enrichment.[24] I would also add that Suetonius is the only (non-legal) Latin author to use frequently this verb and most of the time he does so with the meaning of seizing money rather than confiscating landed property.[25] Suetonius claims that some of these individuals were accused of possessing part of their property in money (*quam quod partem rei familiaris in pecunia haberent*). It is not clear whether such accusations responded to an old Caesarian law which set up a limit to the money to be possessed or if it was a preventive measure to avoid hoarding money for revolutionary purpose, following the rebellion led in Gaul by Iulius Sacrovir and Iulius Florus in AD 21.[26] Hence, the charge of owning too much liquidity and the employment of *confiscare* with the meaning of seizing money would seem to suggest a rather different picture from that of confiscations of property imposed after a judicial trial. We may relate this episode to Cassius Dio's account of the emperor Gaius who, playing at dice, had put to death the wealthiest Gauls on the census list and cashed in 150,000,000 denarii.[27] Again, the idea that the richest of the Gauls were killed to extort their money does not really mirror any practice of judicial confiscations which are well documented, especially under the charge of *maiestas*, in the Julio-Claudian age.[28] Such a sum could simply be a conventional representation of a high number, and when compared with other available figures, such as the annual income of revenue collected in Gaul at the time of Caesar, it gives some ideas of the scale of such extortions or at least of the anecdotical value attached to these episodes of imperial rapacity.[29] It also shows to what extent the historiographical representation of the emperor's attitude towards private property shaped his good or bad reputation, and became a *topos* in the subsequent narratives of Nero and Domitian.[30] Whatever the real size and nature of these confiscations was, properties were not automatically taken into the *patrimonium* but were often sold soon after. This sale pattern may partly explain the absence of evidence for imperial estates in Gaul.

Moving on to a different provincial context, exceptions to this paucity of sources are to be found in Gallia Belgica and Germania inferior, where lands were presumably confiscated to defeated people and there is no involvement or, at least, the explicit reference to property belonging to local aristocrats. A couple of inscriptions attest *coloni* in Gallia Belgica, although it is unclear whether or not they worked in an imperial estate. Their presence is documented by two dedications which do not add information about the management of imperial estates.[31] However, the existence of an imperial domain, the *saltus Sumelocennensis*, modern Rottenburg am Neckar, located not far from the German *limes*, is well documented by epigraphy.[32] The *saltus* was managed by an imperial procurator between the reigns of Domitian and Trajan, and must have had the purpose of ensuring the survival and good function of a production centre to supply the army in one of the most critical borders of the western empire.[33] Besides the evidence for an imperial estate along the Rhine border, it is helpful to note that the general absence of imperial landed property in the north-western provinces could be compared to similar patterns of sales and land ownership attested in other provinces such as Greece. A reference to the property sale of the convicted Ti. Claudius Hipparchus in the oil law passed by Hadrian at Athens refers to "those who bought the land of Hipparchus which had been sold by the *fiscus*," showing that confiscated land was re-sold soon after and this would seem to have been a common practice even in Greece.[34] Both land, especially around the most densely inhabited cities of the empire, and imperial agents employed to supervise estates were limited resources. Marco Maiuro sensibly suggests that the emperor might have consciously chosen not to seize too much land because of such material constraints.[35] This point has been further explored by Alberto Dalla Rosa who has recently stressed to what extent an excessive accumulation of imperial land around cities would have hindered the interests of the local landowners, damaging the good functioning of the land market and the fragile balance between imperial administration and city finances.[36] Whereas individual acquisitions were usually sold off, a significant amount of land owned by the emperor seems to have been located mainly in Africa, Egypt, Asia, and Syria far from the most populated territories, where the local concentration of big estates, part of them previously "royal," had a pre-existing system of management which made them easier to be exploited.[37] When we look at the economic features of Africa, Egypt, Asia, or Syria it is clear that their crucial role in the production of grain, oil, wine, and luxury products must have contributed to the emperor's choice of controlling and possessing land in such strategic territories, either to supply the imperial court or to generate revenue.[38]

From this preliminary overview, there seems to be a lack of imperial intervention in the real estate markets of the north-western provinces and their pre-existing land ownership patterns. Though the role of the *fiscus* in selling and cashing the proceeds of properties taken from Roman citizens by the imperial finances should not be underestimated, the scattered narratives of confiscations and property transactions in Gaul would seem to confirm this picture and point to other kinds of provincial exploitation.[39] Tiberius might have extorted cash (or bullion) for the imperial mint, as perhaps Licinus did in 16 BC when Augustus moved the mint in Lugdunum.[40] The relocation of the mint under Augustus in Lugdunum, a crucial settlement placed in a network of streets and navigable rivers would have facilitated the payment of the army and was also located in the proximity of mines. In the account of Tiberius' confiscations considered above, Suetonius also adds that the emperor deprived many communities and individuals of their old privileges (*immunitates*), including the *ius metallorum ac vectigalium*.[41] Imperial exploitation of mines under Tiberius is attested by a dedication set up to honour the *vilicus* Zmaragdus, who seems to have supervised a lead argentiferous mine in the territory of the Ruteni, well known for the richness of their natural resources.[42] It is generally accepted that the dedication of Zmaragdus, set up by an association of imperial slaves (*familia Tiberii Caesaris*) proves the existence of a mine taken into the *patrimonium* soon after Tiberius' alleged confiscations in AD 33.[43] There are, however, other possibilities. Augustus could have donated the mine to Tiberius in an earlier time, as he similarly did with some copper mines in Gaul to Livia (the so-called *aes Livianum*) and to C. Sallustius Crispus in the Alpes Graiae (*aes Sallustianum*).[44] The emperor's practice of assigning properties, out of his generosity, to members of the imperial family and *amici Caesaris* is well attested by sources, as the *saltus* in Illyricum which was repossessed by Tiberius in AD 19 after the condemnation of Cn. Calpurnius Piso.[45] This is to say that despite confiscations and extortions of cash that may have been carried out in Gaul to meet some shortage of liquidity or expenses, the inscription of Zmaragdus does not necessarily fit in the narratives of the financial crisis of AD 33, and could have been ascribed to other forms of exchange of property within the imperial family, such as a revocable "gift-estate," which could have been bestowed to the adoptive prince to enhance his status and earn revenue.[46]

Inheritance and Pillage in Britannia

Among other property transactions attested in the north-western provinces of the empire, Tacitus records that Prasutagus, the client king of the Iceni of Norfolk, East Anglia, appointed Nero co-heir with his two daughters. By including the emperor in his will, Prasutagus had adopted a defensive strategy to spare at least part of his family fortune. According to Tacitus, such arrangement did not prevent the Iceni from suffering a brutal pillage by the Roman army in their territory.[47] They were deprived of their property and treated like slaves, their territory was subdued in the *forma provinciae*, an escalation of events that triggered the revolt led by Queen Boudica between AD 60 and 61.[48] This is a clear example of the sort of circumstances in which real estate might have come into the *patrimonium* in an imperial province, through the right of conquest. Tacitus' account has been often considered as unquestionable proof of the presence of imperial property in Norfolk.[49] Such a view has been frequently adopted to interpret the archaeological evidence of the nearby site of Stonea Grange, located in the Fenlands, a fertile territory with a long-standing salt production industry attested from the Iron Age up to the fourth century AD.[50] Excavations at Stonea Grange have brought to light an exceptional large stone building, not far from a Romano-Celtic shrine of Hadrianic or Antonine age dated to AD 130–150. The site would seem to have been embedded in a large-scale network of roads and canals.[51] These factors combined with Tacitus' testimony have led scholars to assume that Stonea Grange should be seen as an administrative centre of an imperial estate through which salt, wool, meat, and dairy products could have easily been exploited and traded.[52] The view of an imperial domain can be easily challenged. As Jeremy Taylor points out, in the absence of epigraphic evidence, archaeological remains cannot be related to the existence of imperial property with certainty. There are no specific "imperial" land exploitation patterns, and the regional variety of land cultivation and rural settlements do not help to clarify this issue.[53] Although it is plausible to assume that part of the Icenian land was taken into the *patrimonium*, it is very likely that a great part of it was sold soon after the submission of this area or assigned perhaps to other loyal communities after the Roman pillage and the Boudican revolt.[54] It is also worth noting that under the procuratorships listed in the Western empire, the *Notitia Dignitatum*, a list of civil and military posts dating to the fourth or fifth century AD, includes a *procurator gynaecii Ventensis*, a procurator responsible for wool production based at Venta Icenorum, a market town of the Iceni, modern Castor-by-Norwich.[55] This reference would attest a late imperial production unit and would confirm a continuity with one of the pre-existing economic activities of this territory.[56] Any further discussion about the land status of the Iceni is purely speculative but this sketchy overview on the ongoing debate about archaeological evidence in the area suggests a more nuanced picture, and ultimately leads us to question more critically the role of the emperor in the provincial real estate market.

Conclusion

In the wide range of cases presented above I hope to have shown that despite the great regional variety of north-western territories, the emperor seems to have followed some general patterns of acquisition and re-sale of landed property. If inscriptions do not shed much light on such land transactions, literary sources reveal the general imperial reluctance under the Principate of seizing property "en bloc," and the more common practice of re-selling property or extorting cash to create an income. It is not by chance that the only trace of an imperial estate in Narbonensis had probably belonged to the *gens* of the emperor Antoninus Pius, the Aurelii Fulvi from Nemausus, for generations.[57] Moreover, the majority of inscriptions related to imperial administration found in these regions deals with the management of mines (such as the *procuratores ferrariarum* of Gaul and the numerous stamped ingots from Gaul, Britain, and Germany, *plumbum Germanicum*), and would seem to confirm the imperial willingness of exploiting pre-existing economic activities, i.e. rich mineral resources, rather than interfering much with established land ownership patterns.

Notes

1 I would like to thank Alberto Dalla Rosa and Dominic Rathbone for their insightful comments on earlier versions of this chapter. All mistakes are my own.
Crawford [Thompson] 1976. An updated study of imperial property of each province has been recently carried out under the project PATRIMONIVM (ERC-StG 716375) directed by Dr Alberto Dalla Rosa at the Ausonius Institute, Université Bordeaux Montaigne. The final outcome of this teamwork will be a collective volume and an online database. For further information about the project see https://patrimonium.huma-num.fr/

2 Italy: Maiuro 2012; for a focus on luxury maritime villas in Campania see also Chapter 9 in this volume by Annalisa Marzano. Africa: Kehoe 1988; 2007; Kolendo 1991. Egypt: Parassoglu 1978. Asia: Broughton 1934; Dalla Rosa 2014 for a discussion of the most important works on the theme and research methodology.

3 A classic discussion of the meaning of *patrimonium* is Lo Cascio 2000: 97–149.

4 RIB 179: *Pro salute imp(eratoris) C(a)es(aris) M(arci) Aur(eli) | Antonini Pii Felicis Invic| ti Aug(usti) Naevius Aug(usti) | lib(ertus) adiut(or) proc(uratorum) princi|pia ruina op(p)ress (a) a solo res|tituit.* From Combe Down, parish of Monkton Combe, AD 212–222. Full commentary at https://romaninscriptionsofbritain.org/inscriptions/179

5 For the leaden sealing see RIB 2411.37 with previous bibliography.

6 For the use of the term *principia* cf. also RIB 1092; 1912; 3027; *principia TLL* 10.2.2. coll. 1317–8.
7 Whether this *regio* was patrimonial or not remains unclear. The *centurio regionarius* is attested at Bath by a votive altar set up to commemorate the restoration of a holy place. RIB 152. On the *regio*, which could have included the villas of Combe Down, Hambledon and Boxmoor, see Branigan 1973: 90–92.
8 Now confirmed by recent geological analysis in Tucker et al. 2020.
9 Hirt 2010: 82–93.
10 For evidence of ducenary procurators in Narbonensis see Pflaum 1978: 111; 125–129; Haensch 1997: 138–141; 456–457. Cf. Burton 1993 for a discussion on the role of procurators in public provinces. A ducenary procurator was in charge of Lugdunensis and Aquitania and had his headquarters at Lugdunum: Haensch 1997: 133–135; 461–464. Another procurator of the same rank was responsible for Belgica and the two Germanies and had his headquarters at Augusta Treverorum (Germania inferior: Haensch 1997: 65–76; Germania superior: Haensch 1997: 149–153; 470–447; Belgica: Haensch 1997: 130–133; 461). For the financial procurator of Britannia and his headquarters at Londinium see Haensch 1997: 120–130; 457–460; Birley 2005: 298–315.
11 See for example the case of Gallia Narbonensis: only two out of the thirteen known procurators are attested by inscriptions found in the province. Cf. *AE* 1962, 183, the well-known inscription of M. Domitius Marsianus *procurator patrimonii provinciae Narbonensis* found at Bulla Regiae in Africa Proconsularis. M. Domitius Marsianus spent a considerable number of years holding posts in Gaul; however, the only surviving dedication was set up by his brother in his hometown in Africa. For a recent discussion of his career see Rossignol 2010, with previous bibliography on this inscription.
12 For a thorough discussion on sources and methodology used to identify imperial property, and the value of inscriptions of imperial slaves for the identification of imperial estates see Maiuro 2012: 159–169, with a focus on Italy.
13 Detailed discussion of imperial freedmen and slaves in Gauls and the Germanies in France 2000: 196–197, who rightly points out that even in the public province of Narbonensis, where imperial freedmen and slaves should have been employed solely to look after imperial properties, the attestations of a *procurator annonae* of Liguria and Narbonensis and of *procuratores XX hereditatium* of Narbonensis and Aquitania make it very difficult to know their tasks in the province. On the *XL Galliarum* France 2001; on the *XX hereditatium* Günther 2008.
14 This general assessment is based on Woolf 1998: 77–91.
15 Among the many examples of such phenomenon see the introductory pages dedicated to the city walls of Mediolanum Santonum (Saintes) in *ILA*, Santons 45–51.
16 For a recent discussion of epigraphic habit see Beltrán Lloris 2015, esp. 137, where he emphasises to what extent the total number of inscriptions of some provinces is inflated by the number of *instrumentum inscriptum,* which represents the 45.3 per cent of total inscriptions in Gallia Narbonensis and 72 per cent (!) of total inscriptions in Britain.
17 Maiuro collects approximately 300 property transactions between Augustus and Septimius Severus, Maiuro 2012: 27.
18 Goudineau 1996: 474. Similarly to Sicily, senators could travel to Narbonensis without special authorisation (*commeatus*) Tac. *Ann.*, 12.23.1; Cass. Dio 52.42.6–7; 60.25.6–7. Cf. also Chastagnol 1992: 164–165; Christol 2009: 261.
19 Burnand 2005; 2006; 2007; 2009; 2010.
20 Burnand 2007: esp. 206–288.
21 The most emblematic cases are D. Valerius Asiaticus (*PIR* V 26), and Sex. Afranius Burrus (*PIR*[2] A 441, *PCR* 552). D. Valerius Asiaticus, originally from Vienna, was the first Gallic senator to reach the consulate in AD 35. We know nothing about his

property in Gaul but other transactions between his property and the *patrimonium* are recorded at Rome and in Egypt. According to Tacitus, Messalina wanted to take possession of the great *horti Luculliani* which Asiaticus owned in Rome. The *horti* eventually passed to the *patrimonium* and were probably resold to the *gens* Acilia at the beginning of Trajan emperorship, see Tac. *Ann.*11.1.1; Cass. Dio 60.27.2–3. Three papyri attest also that Asiaticus owned some *ousiai* in Egypt, which had probably been donated to him by the emperor Gaius: a petition under Gaius: *P. Lond.* III 894, January 24, AD 39–41, Sijpesteijn 1989; a tax record in which he is mentioned as former owner of an estate *P.Mich.* inv. 876 v I.13, AD 50–51, and in *P. Schoyen* 2, 27, which attests that his property passed to Seneca under Nero. For a recent work on Valerius Asiaticus see Jolivet 2015. Sex. Afranius Burrus, originally from Vasio Vocontiorum, praetorian praefect and procurator of Livia, Tiberius and Claudius named Nero his heir but we do not know anything about his property in Gaul. *CIL* XII, 5842; Tac. *Ann.* 14.60.4.

22 Maiuro 2012: 53–69, esp. 60.

23 Accounts of confiscations in Gaul under Tiberius: Suet. *Tib.* 49.2; Gaius: Suet. *Calig.* 39; Cass. Dio 59.22.3–4. In order to keep a focus on the early Principate I deliberately do not discuss here the confiscations carried out by Septimius Severus: Hist.Aug. *Sev.* 12.1–4, which involved massive confiscations of property of Pescennius Niger, Clodius Albinus, and their supporters and had a great impact on the management of the *bona damnatorum.* Cf. Maiuro 2012: 86–88.

24 Alpers 1995: 32, esp. n. 108; 33; 90 esp. 282; 98; 237, with discussion of previous bibliography on the matter.

25 See Suet. *Aug.*15.1; 101.2 with the meaning of *reponere in arcam; Calig.* 16.4; 41.2; *Dom.* 12.2. The other occurrence is Flor. 1.44.6, who uses the expression *confiscationem mandaverit.* For the use of *confiscare* in legal texts see: *Dig.* 27.3.9.6.2; *Dig.* 48.21.3. pr. 6, 48.21.3.8.1.

26 The danger of hoarding money for revolutionary purposes is one of the excuses allegedly used by the procurator Licinus to justify his abuse when faced with accusations of extortion by the Gauls, see Cassius Dio 54.21.8. According to Tacitus, in AD 33 there was a shortage of currency provoked by a sudden call in of loans and a fall of real estate's prices in Italy, following an upsurge of cases brought to court of people who disregarded an old law about usury and the amount of lands to be possessed in Italy passed by Caesar in 49 BC, Tac. *Ann.* 6.16–7. The senate granted an 18-month extension period to allow landowners to sort out their financial assets, while Tiberius put an end to the crisis, disbursing 100,000,000 sesterces without interest to increase liquidity for three years, resembling what today is known as quantitative easing. On the same point cf. Dennis Kehoe's chapter in this volume (Chapter 4). Further works on the financial crisis of AD 33 in Mrozek 2001: 28–40; Tchernia 2003.

27 Cass. Dio, 59.22.3–4. Cf. also Suet. *Calig.* 41.2, who reports a slightly different version: Gaius was playing at dice in Rome and seized the property of two Roman knights. Cf. also *Cal.* 39, which records a sale that the emperor carried out in Gaul in which jewellery, precious furniture, and also imperial slaves and his sisters' freedmen were sold.

28 On the political implications of the charge of *maiestas* see Baumann 1974; Rivière 2002: 279–294.

29 Suetonius recalls that 40,000,000 sesterces was the annual revenue collected in Gaul at the time of Caesar, Suet. *Iul.* 25.1.

30 Among the many discussions of imperial rapacity see the punctual comments of Levick 1999: 104.

31 *AE* 1919, 85: *I(n) h(onorem) d(omus) d(ivinae) | deae I[u]|noni | colo|ni Ape|rienses | ex iussu.* A fragmentary altar found in the proximity of the train station at Kalhausen (in the territory of the Mediomatrici) in 1914. It is an altar broken on the right side.

First half of the third century AD. *CIL* XIII, 4228: *Deo Mercurio c|oloni Crutisio|nes fe(ce)runt de | suo per Dann|um Giamillum.* It is a small limestone slab found in 1847 in the ancient *vicus* of *Contiomagus*, now Pachten, in the neighbourhood of Dillingen, Saarlouis, Saarland. On the meaning of *dannos*: Pailler 2015. On Gallia Belgica see in general Wightman 1985.

32 *AE* 2010, 1073; *CIL* XIII, 6365. The *saltus* was located nearby the *civitas Sumelocennensis*, epigraphic attestations: *CIL* XIII, 2506, 6358, 6384, 9084, 11726, 11727. On the coexistence of these two entities see Künzl 2010.

33 *I.Prusias* 56, the unknown procurator is honoured by Pompeia Antipatris as [ἐπίτροπον? – – –] | [Σεβαστ]ο̣ῦ χώρας Σ[ου] | μελοκεννησίας καὶ ἐ̣[παρ(χείας) | Γερ(μανίας) Λιμιτανῆς. Under Domitian or Trajan. See Künzl 2010: 501–503. Cf. *AE* 1987, 783; *AE* 1989, 567–568 a dedication set up on 30 March AD 188, from Roman Walheim, a military garrison built to secure the Neckar-Odenwald *limes*. The inscription attests a dedication of a shrine (?) *in solo Caesaris*. Whether it refers to imperial land is highly uncertain. Mehl has proposed that the territory of Roman Walheim, known as a central market town, could have taken over the function of the imperial domain of the *saltus Sumelocennensis* in supplying the army along the border but there is no further epigraphic evidence attesting imperial property in the area, Mehl 1986: 266; Wiegels 1989 with summary of previous debate on the matter. Cf. On the role of imperial properties to secure the continuity of production in less inhabited places see also the case of southern Numidia, Jacques 1992, esp. 130–132.

34 *SEG* 15, 108 = *IG* II2 1100, ll. 1–5: κε(φάλαιον) νό(μου) θε(ιοτάτου) Ἁδριανοῦ | οἱ τὸ ἔλαιον γεωργοῦντες τὸ τρίτον | καταφερέτωσαν, ἢ τὸ ὄγδοον οἱ τὰ | Ἱππάρχου χωρία τὰ ὑπὸ τοῦ φίσκου | πραθέντα κεκτημένοι. On this passage see the comment of Dalla Rosa 2021: 128–129.

35 Maiuro 2012: 108–109.

36 On this last point see Dalla Rosa 2019: esp. 106.

37 Dalla Rosa 2021; esp. 127.

38 For the importance of imperial taxation and revenue see the discussion in this volume by Dennis Kehoe (Chapter 4).

39 See n. 22 above.

40 For a possible link between Licinus' extortions and the relocation of the mint at Lugdunum see Rathbone 1993: 109, n. 72. On the deeds of Licinius "who reigned for many years in Lugdunum": Sen. *Apocol.* 6.1; Cass. Dio 54.21.2–8. On his anecdotical wealth see Sen. *Ep.* 119.9; 120.19; Pers. 2.36; Juv. 1.109; 14.305–8; Mart. *Ep.* 8.3.6. According to the scholiast of Juv. 1.109 he died under Tiberius (*decessit sub Tiberio*), Wessner 1967: 11–12.

41 Suet. *Tib.* 49.2. Cf. *Dig.* 27.3.9 (Ulp. 25 *ad ed.*); Hirt 2010: 84, n. 162.

42 *CIL* XIII, 1550 (4, p. 20); *AE* 1999, 71, found in 1890 at Puech de Serre, a mining district nearby La Bastidie-l'Evêque (Canton of Aveyron et Tarn), AD 33? *Zmaragdo Vilico | quaest(ori) magistro | ex decurion(um) decr(eto) familiae Ti(beri) Cae[sa]ris | quae est in me[ta]llis.* Cf. also the confiscation of the Spanish gold and copper mines of Sex. Marius in AD 33, the year of the financial crisis, Tac. *Ann.* 6.9.11.

43 See Pailler 2011 with previous bibliography.

44 Plin. *HN.* 34.3–4.

45 *Excepto saltu qui esset in Illyrico SCPP*, ll. 84–86, cf. also Eck, Caballos and Fernández 1996: 202–207.

46 On the origin of this practice see Rathbone 1993: 110; for a later example of the practice of bestowing estates to the adoptive prince see the case of a potential property of Aelius Caesar in Mauretania *CIL* VIII, 21663, Dalla Rosa 2017.

47 *Rex Icenorum Prasutagus, longa opulentia clarus, Caesarem heredem duasque filias scripserat, tali obsequio ratus regnumque et domum suam procul iniuria fore. Quod contra vertit, adeo ut regnum per centuriones, domus per servos velut capta vastarentur.* "The Icenian king

Prasutagus, celebrated for his long prosperity, had named the emperor his heir, together with his two daughters; an act of deference which he thought would place his kingdom and household beyond the risk of injury. The result was contrary – so much so that his kingdom was pillaged by centurions, his household by slaves; as though they had been prizes of war." Tac. *Ann.* 14.31. Cf. Tac. *Agr.* 43.4 for another well-known episode of this kind, C. Iulius Agricola, originally from Forum Iulii (*PIR*^{2} I 126) named Domitian co-heir with his wife and daughter.

48 Tac. *Ann.* 14.31–9, cf. Tomlin 2018: 37–38.

49 Mattingly 2006.

50 See for example the works of Salway and Phillips 1970, esp. 1–21; Potter 1989; Jackson, Cameron, and Potter 1996.

51 Jackson, Cameron, and Potter 1996.

52 For evidence of livestock butchered in the site of Stonea Grange see again Jackson, Cameron, and Potter 1996. For a reassessment of the role of Venta Icenorum in the narratives of the Boudican revolt see Bowden 2013.

53 Taylor 2000, esp. 648. Cf. also Todd 1989: 14–16.

54 The toponym of *villa Faustini*, recorded in the *Itinerarium Antonini* 40 km south of Venta Icenorum. Castor-by-Norwich (the town of the Iceni) could be a hint of the presence of private estates in the area. *It. Ant.*, Iter V (474.1–476.6) cf. Rivet and Jackson 1970. About the status of land and its potential assignment to other community in the area see the fragmentary boundary stone which reads *publicum* found a Sawtry RIB 230. The stone might refer to public land belonging to a community.

55 *Not. Dign.*, Occ. X.

56 For a reassessment of the role of Venta Icenorum in the narratives of the Boudican revolt see Bowden 2013.

57 See Chulsky 2018: 197–201 for a study of the *gens* Aurelia in the territory of Nîmes and the relevant toponyms. For the building activity sponsored by Antoninus Pius in Narbonensis see: CIL XII, 4342, *Imp(erator) Caes(ar) divi Hadr[iani fil(ius) divi] | Traiani Parthici n[epos divi Nervae] | pronepos T(itus) Aelius H[adrianus Antoninus] | Aug(ustus) Pius pont(ifex) maxim[us tribun(icia) potest(ate) —] | imp(erator) II co(n)s(ul) IIII p(ater) p(atriae) ther[mas incendio] | consumptas cum por[ticibus et —] | et basilicis et omni [apparatu impensa] | sua r[estituit]*. Cf. Horster 2001: 369. Full discussion and collection of evidence in my upcoming chapter of imperial property in Gaul, Piacentin 2023. On policies of imperial interventions following natural disasters see in this volume the work of Cristina Rosillo-López (Chapter 2).

References

Alpers, M. (1995) *Das nachrepublikanische Finanzsystem. Fiscus und Fisci in der frühen Kaiserzeit.* Berlin: De Gruyter.

Baumann, R.A. (1974) *"Impietas in principem." A Study of Treason against the Roman Emperor with special reference to the first century A.D.* München: Verlag C.H. Beck.

Beltrán Lloris, F. B. (2015) The "Epigraphic Habit" in the Roman World. In: C. Bruun and J. Edmondson, eds. *The Oxford Handbook of Roman Epigraphy*, Oxford: Oxford University Press, 131–148.

Birley, A.R. (2005) *The Roman Government of Britain.* Oxford: Oxford University Press.

Bowden, W. (2013) The Urban Plan of *Venta Icenorum* and its Relationship with the Boudican Revolt. *Britannia* 44, 145–169.

Branigan, K. (1973) *Town and Country: Verulamium and the Roman Chilterns.* Bourne End: Spurbooks.

Broughton, T.R.S. (1934) Roman Landholding in Asia Minor. *Transactions of the American Philological Association* 65, 207–239.

Burnand, Y. (2005) *Primores Galliarum: sénateurs et chevaliers romains originaires de Gaule de la fin de la République au IIIe siècle. Méthodologie*. Brussels: Latomus.

Burnand, Y. (2006) *Primores Galliarum. Sénateurs et chevaliers romains originaires de Gaule de la fin de la République au IIIe siècle. II. Prosopographie*. Brussels: Latomus.

Burnand, Y. (2007) Primores Galliarum. *Sénateurs et chevaliers romains originaires de Gaule de la fin de la République au IIIe siècle. III. Étude sociale. 1. Les racines*. Brussels: Latomus.

Burnand, Y. (2009) *Primores Galliarum. Sénateurs et chevaliers romains originaires de Gaule de la fin de la République au IIIe siècle. III. Étude sociale. 2. Les horizons de la vie*. Brussels: Latomus.

Burnand, Y. (2010) *Primores Galliarum: sénateurs et chevaliers romains originaires de Gaule de la fin de la République au IIIe siècle. IV. Indices*. Brussels: Latomus.

Burton, G. P. (1993) Provincial Procurators and the Public Provinces. *Chiron* 23, 13–28.

Chastagnol, A. (1992) *Le Sénat romain à l'époque impériale: recherches sur la composition de l'Assemblée et le statut de ses membres* (Vol. 19). Paris: Les Belles Lettres.

Christol, M. (2009) Provinciaux nîmois à Rome: l'apport de l'épigraphie locale. In: M.L Bonsangue, and Ch. Hoet-van Cauwenberghe, eds. *Une histoire provinciale: La Gaule narbonnaise de la fin du IIe siècle av. J.-C. au IIIe siècle ap. J.-C.* Paris: Publications de la Sorbonne, 259–279 = Provinciaux nîmois à Rome: l'apport de l'épigraphie locale. In: J. Desmulliez and Ch. van Cauwenberghe, eds. (2005) *Le monde romain à travers l'épigraphie, méthodes et pratiques*. Lille: Éditions du Conseil scientifique de l'Université Charles-de-Gaulle-Lille 3, 145–170.

Chulsky, C. (2018) Notables nîmois: Magistrats, chevaliers et sénateurs issus de la cité de Nîmes à l'époque romaine (milieu du Ier siècle av. n. è. - début du IIIe siècle de n. è.). Montpellier: Supplément *Revue Archéologique de Narbonnaise* 47.

Crawford [Thompson], D.J. (1976) Imperial Estates. In: M.I. Finley, ed. *Studies in Roman Property*. Cambridge: Cambridge University Press, 35–70.

Dalla Rosa, A. (2014) Prolegomeni allo studio della proprietà imperiale in Asia Minore: la questione dell'imperatore come acquirente. *Studi Classici e Orientali* 60, 329–348.

Dalla Rosa, A. (2017) Les successeurs désignés du prince et leur patrimoine. À propos de la délimitation d'Er-Rahel en Maurétanie Césarienne (CIL VIII 21663). *Cahiers du Centre Gustave Glotz* 28, 197–212.

Dalla Rosa, A. (2019) Imperial Properties and Civic Territories: Between Economic Interests and Internal Diplomacy. In: F. Luciani and E. Migliario, eds. *Boundaries of Territories and Peoples in Roman Italy and Beyond*. Bari: Edipuglia, 105–120.

Dalla Rosa, A. (2021) Inimicizia e *cupido pecuniae*. A proposito dell'acquisizione o della rivendita del patrimonio dei nemici del principe. In: F. Pina Polo, F. Marco Simón and J. Remesal Rodríguez, eds. *Enemistad y odio en el mundo antiguo*. Barcelona: Universitat de Barcelona, 125–134.

Eck, W., Caballos, A. and Fernández, F. (1996) *Das Senatus consultum de Cneo Pisone patre*. München: C.H. Beck.

France, J. (2000) Le personnel subalterne de l'administration financière et fiscale dans les provinces des Gaules et des Germanies. *Cahiers du Centre Gustave Glotz* 11, 193–221.

France, J. (2001) *Quadragesima Galliarum: L'organisation douanière des provinces alpestres, gauloises et germaniques de l'Empire Romain:(Ier siècle avant J.-C.-IIIe siècle après J.-C.)*. Rome: École française de Rome.

Goudineau, C. (1996) Gaul. In: A. Bowman, E. Champlin and A. Lintott, eds. *The Cambridge Ancient History vol.* XI, Cambridge: Cambridge University Press, 462–502.

Günther, S. (2008) *Vectigalia nervos esse rei publicae: die indirekten Steuern in der Römischen Kaiserzeit von Augustus bis Diokletian* (vol. 26). Wiesbaden: Harrassowitz Verlag.

Haensch, R. (1997) Capita provinciarum. *Statthaltersitze und Provinzialverwaltung in Der Römischen Kaiserzeit*. Mainz am Rhein: von Zabern.

Hirt, A. M. (2010) *Imperial Mines and Quarries in the Roman world: Organizational Aspects 27 BC-AD 235*. Oxford: Oxford University Press.

Horster, M. (2001) *Bauinschriften römischer Kaiser: Untersuchungen zu Inschriftenpraxis und Bautätigkeit in Städten des westlichen Imperium Romanum in der Zeit des Prinzipats* (No. 157). Stuttgart: Franz Steiner Verlag.

Jackson, R., Cameron, F. and Potter, T.W. (1996) *Excavations at Stonea, Cambridgeshire, 1980–85*. London: British Museum Press.

Jacques, F. (1992) Propriétés impériales et cités en Numidie Méridionale. *Cahiers du Centre Gustave Glotz* 3, 123–139.

Jolivet, V. (2015) Les affaires de Monsieur Asiaticus. *Dialogues d'histoire ancienne* 42. 2, 71–86.

Kehoe, D.P. (1988) *The Economics of Agriculture on Roman Imperial Estates in North Africa* (Vol. 89). Göttingen: Vandenhoeck and Ruprecht.

Kehoe, D.P. (2007) *Law and the Rural Economy in the Roman Empire*. Ann Arbor: University of Michigan Press.

Kolendo, J. (1991) *Le colonat en Afrique sous le Haut-Empire*. 2nd ed. Paris: Les Belles Lettres.

Künzl, E. (2010) Die Zwölfgötter von Rohrdorf. Ein Heiligtum im Saltus Sumelocennensis von Marcus Aurelius bis Caracalla. *Fundberichte aus Baden-Württemberg*, 31.

Levick, B. (1999) *Tiberius the Politician*. London and New York: Routledge.

Lo Cascio, E. (2000) *Patrimonium, ratio privata, res privata. In: Il princeps e il suo impero: studi di storia amministrativa e finanziaria romana*. Bari: Edipuglia, 97–149.

Maiuro, M. (2012) Res Caesaris. *Ricerche sulla proprietà imperiale nel Principato*. Bari: Edipuglia.

Mattingly, D. (2006) *An Imperial Possession: Britain in the Roman Empire, 54 BC-AD* 409. London: Penguin Books.

Maurin, L. (1994) *Inscriptions latines d'Aquitaine (I.L.A.), Santons*. Bordeaux: Éditions Ausonius.

Mehl, A. (1986) Eine private Weihung auf kaiserlichem Boden in Walheim am Neckar, *Fundberichte aus Baden-Württemberg*, 11, 259–267.

Mrozek, S. (2001) Faenus. *Studien zu Zinsproblemen zur Zeit des Prinzipats*. Stuttgart: Franz Steiner Verlag.

Pailler, J-M. (2011) Étapes et conséquences de l'exploitation minière et métallurgique. Monnaies gauloises, monnaies romaines. Le cas Zmaragdus. In: Ph. Gruat, J.-M. Pailler and D. Schaad, eds. *Les Rutènes, du peuple à la cite*. Bordeaux: Aquitania, 209–228.

Pailler, J-M. (2015) Dire la mesure en Gaule, IIe s. av. J.-C.- Ier s. apr. J.-C. Le *-dannos/dannus*, garant public des poids, mesures et qualités. *Pallas* 97, 159–179.

Parassoglu, G.M. (1978) Imperial Estates in Roman Egypt. *American Studies in Papyrology*, 18. Amsterdam: A.M. Hakkert.

Pflaum, H. G. (1978) *Les Fastes de la province de Narbonnaise*. Paris: Editions du CNRS.

Piacentin, S. (2023) Gaul. In: A. Dalla Rosa and M. Maiuro (eds.), *The Emperor and His Properties in the Roman World (44 BC-284 AD)*. Bordeaux. In preparation.

Potter, T.W. (1989) Recent work on the Roman Fens of eastern England and the question of imperial estates. *Journal of Roman Archaeology* 2, 267–275.

Rathbone, D. (1993) Egypt, Augustus and Roman taxation. *Cahiers du Centre Gustave Glotz* 4, 81–112.

Rivet, A.L.F. and Jackson, K. (1970) The British section of the Antonine Itinerary. *Britannia* 1, 34–82.

Rivière, Y. (2002) *Les délateurs sous l'empire romain*. Rome: École française de Rome.

Rossignol, B. (2010) Ens, mines et patrimoine, intégrité, zèle et expérience: Domitius Marsianus et ses missions administratives en Gaule durant le règne de Marc Aurèle. In: F. Chausson, ed. *Occidents romains. Sénateurs, chevaliers, militaires, notables dans les provinces d'Occident (Espagnes, Gaules, Germanies, Bretagne)*. Paris: Éd. Errance, 277–300.

Salway, P. and Philipps, C.W. (1970) *The Fenland in Roman Times: Studies of a Major Area of Peasant Colonization with a Gazetteer Covering All Known Sites and Finds*. London: Royal Geographical Society.

Sijpesteijn, P.J. (1989) Another οὐcία of D. Valerius Asiaticus in Egypt. *Zeitschrift für Papyrologie und Epigraphik* 79, 194–196.

Taylor, J. (2000) Stonea in Its Fenland Context: Moving Beyond an Imperial Estate, Review: "P.J Jackson and T.W. Potter, Excavations at Stonea, Cambridgeshire, 1980–85 (British Museum Press 1996)". *Journal of Roman Archaeology* 13, 647–658.

Tchernia A. (2003) Remarques sur la crise de 33. In: E. Lo Cascio, ed. *Credito e moneta nel mondo romano. Atti degli Incontri capresi di Storia Economica Antica, Capri 2000*. Bari: Edipuglia, 131–146.

Todd, M. (1989) Villa and fundus. In: K. Branigan and D. Miles, eds., *The Economies of Romano-British Villas*. Sheffield: University of Sheffield Department of Archaeology and Prehistory, 14–20.

Tomlin, R. (2018) *Britannia Romana: Roman Inscriptions and Roman Britain*. Oxford and Philadelphia: Oxbow Books.

Tucker, M., Brisbane, M., Pitman, D. and Kearn, O. (2020) Source of Roman stone for Aquae Sulis (Bath, England): Field Evidence, Facies, pXRF Chem-data and a Cautionary Tale of Contamination. *The Geological Curator* 11. 3, 217–230.

Wessner, P. (1967/1931) Scholia in Iuuenalem Vetustiora. *Collegit recensuit illustravit P. Wessner*. Leipzig: Teubner.

Wiegels, R. (1989) Solum Caesaris. Zu einer Weihung im römischen Walheim. *Chiron* 19, 61–102.

Wightman, E.M. (1985) *Gallia Belgica*. Los Angeles – Berkeley: University of California Press.

Woolf, G. (1998) *Becoming Roman: The Origins of Provincial Civilization in Gaul*. Cambridge: Cambridge University Press.

14 The Real Estate Markets in Roman Egypt

Paul V. Kelly

Abstract

This chapter describes the real estate markets of Roman Egypt, dealing with both agricultural land and housing. The nature of the real estate concerned and the institutional constraints on their markets, including taxes, are described. The market data on the demographics and locations of the participants, the seasonality of transactions, the formats of prices and rents, the transactional costs and the likely investment return to the owner are examined. The degree to which markets operated through social networks is assessed and the investment return to the owner of leased land is calculated using a stochastic model. Trends over time are also discussed. The market data is then used to assess the degree to which the markets were driven by financially rational actions, as opposed to actions based on reciprocity and redistribution. For the housing market it is concluded that the preconditions for the exercise of financial rationality did not exist and there is little evidence for its use. However, for agricultural land, on the balance of the evidence, both the sale and rental markets were driven by financial rationality.

***

This chapter describes the nature of the real estate markets in Roman Egypt from the perspective of the individual who owned or bought property. The period concerned is that from AD 1 to 274. The start of the period allows for sufficient time to have elapsed since the Roman conquest of 30 BC to enable Roman institutions to have become established. The end point was chosen to avoid the distortion caused by the jump in prices in the 270s, which is described by Rathbone as a "brusque leap in price levels around 274 by a factor of ten or more."[1] The period from AD 1 to AD 274 was generally a period of low inflation and this allows rents and sales amounts from different dates to be compared and recalibrated to a common real value as at AD 150.[2] This recalibration is key since it expands the data available for comparison and allows trends over time to be identified. The markets examined will include those for sale and lease, and for both housing and land. Much of the information presented in this chapter, including the statistics, derives from the author's doctoral thesis, which in turn was based on papyrological data.[3]

The aim of the chapter is to describe the features of the markets and to assess the degree to which they were driven by financially rational actions, as opposed

DOI: 10.4324/9781003187806-19

to actions based on reciprocity and redistribution and it thus has the following structure. First, the nature of the real estate concerned and the institutional constraints on their markets will be described. Market data for gender, ages, family connections, and locations of counterparties will be examined to identify potential social networks within those markets. The price formats adopted, particularly the degree to which prices were rounded, will be analysed. This rounding information, when combined with data on relative market liquidity and the involvement, or lack of activity, of intermediaries, will be used to consider the price formation mechanisms and their likely efficiency. The net return on investment, after taxes and costs, will be assessed, using where possible, a stochastic model to allow for the risk of non-payment of rent. A stochastic model is one whose inputs and outputs are probability distributions rather than discrete values and which "calculates the implied uncertainty about the outcome measure – a method called the forward propagation of uncertainty."[4] A recent example of the use of stochastic modelling is the advice provided to governments on the probable course of the current pandemic. In this particular case it produces a range of possible outcomes rather than a single, deterministic, average return number, which would be misleading since it would not reflect the range of possible returns, some positive, some negative. Conclusions as to the nature of the markets are then reached separately for housing and agricultural land, by combining the financial outcome results with the data on networks and price mechanisms.

The Nature of the Real Estate

Dealing first with the nature of housing, the constraints imposed by the availability of papyrological data means that the housing stock analysed is essentially that in the rural areas and the towns and cities of Middle Egypt. Few documents have survived from other areas in Egypt, notably from Alexandria. The stock largely consists of houses rather than apartment blocks. These houses were sometimes used for mixed commercial and domestic purposes and there is clear evidence from census documents for shared occupancy of houses between owners, renters, and lodgers.[5] Indeed, in general, houses were occupied by relatively large numbers of people.[6] The houses are in villages, towns, or cities and we have little data from isolated farmsteads. However, even if the houses were in settlements, many families were farming the land. Importantly for tenant and landlord relationships, we have little evidence from land leases of housing being provided within the land lease, thus the housing and land leasing markets may be considered separately. The nature of the properties varied in the number of storeys and the size of their footprint, but most houses were of mud-brick construction with timber used for framing and roof beams.[7] Husson notes that there are only three cases where houses are stated to have been built in stone in the papyri from the Roman era.[8]

Within settlements we also see sales of "vacant lots." These lots could have been put to a number of purposes, other than being simply land suitable for building, including market gardening and commercial activity such as donkey or camel pens. However, the fact that we have no examples of leases of vacant lots, but many of sales, would suggest that the primary intended use of these lots was for building housing. If a vacant lot was an asset generally used for gardening or commercial activity it would be likely that owners would lease out such an asset in the same way as they leased agricultural land. However, if the primary use of such lots was for building, then it would not be practicable for someone to lease a lot, invest in building upon it, and then lose the investment at the expiry of the lease.[9] The prices of lots are generally considerably lower than the prices of houses including the ground itself. Unfortunately the measure of area most often cited in the documents for vacant lots, the *bikos*, does not have any generally agreed value and this means it is difficult to conduct any numerical analysis. However, the average price for a vacant lot, recalibrated for inflation, is 202 drachmas, which is one third of the average price of a house at 600 drachmas.[10] Assuming one house per vacant lot, this one-third ratio is, by curious coincidence, exactly the same as the rule of thumb used in the UK residential building market for the price of land compared with the price of a completed house and its land.[11]

In contrast to vacant lots, agricultural land was generally priced for sale and rented per *aroura*, a measure which was equivalent to 2,760m^2.[12] Plot sizes were generally small and even larger estates had plots which were dispersed over wide areas.[13] Most agricultural land was planted in cereal or vegetable crops.[14] A peculiarity of Egypt is of course, the dependence of the harvest on the state of the Nile flood and the extensive irrigation networks designed to maximise the benefits of the flood. Most leases required crop rotation to allow the land to rest once every two or three years and rents were payable in both cash and kind.[15]

Institutional Constraints

Turning to the institutional constraints on the markets, these came in various forms. The partible inheritance system meant that property became fragmented on inheritance and this posed a problem when fractions of a house became too small to be marketable. If you were the inheritor of a fraction of a house, such as the five brothers who each inherited a fifth share of a seventh share of half a house and courtyard in Arsinoe in the first half of the first century, you could possibly find a *modus vivendi* to share living space with other family members. However, to seek to rent out or sell such a small and ill-defined portion to a third party would be highly problematic.[16] By contrast, relatively small plots of agricultural land were capable of commoditisation and definition by area and could be sold on or leased to a third party. There were few legal constraints on who could, or could not, own or rent a property and indeed the Roman state, by the establishment and maintenance of property registers and the *bibliotheke enkteseon*, would have encouraged the real-estate sale markets through the exchange of information which confirmed ownership.[17] It should be noted that joint-holders and then neighbours were in theory given prior rights by the state over other buyers when private land was put up for sale and this will have constrained competition to some degree.[18]

Another significant institutional constraint on real estate markets is the level of taxes and other frictional costs, such as legal or registration fees. If these fees were too high they would dampen market activity and reduce turnover. In the case of housing, the landlord could be subject to taxes even when the house was leased as is the case in *P.Oxy.* III 502 (AD 164) when the police and brick taxes are still at the landlord's expense, or water tax as appears to be the case in *P.Marm.* r (AD 190–191). However, whether a general tax applied to house ownership, or there was a tax on income on house leases, is currently unknown.[19] Registration and legal costs were relatively low as a percentage of the purchase price in sales, but would typically have been very high as a percentage of the rent in the case of leases, which may have led to housing agreements being more of an informal nature than for the equivalent land leases. In fact we have fewer house leases than house sale documents, whilst the opposite is true for agricultural land.[20]

Turning to land taxes and charges, there were complex conveyancing charges which varied according to the gender and the status of the individual and which Yitfach described as "potentially quite heavy," and this could well have acted as a brake, to some degree, on market activity.[21] There were also ongoing taxes payable by the owner, and Rowlandson stated that, in almost all cases, these taxes remained the landlord's responsibility when the land was leased, and this is indeed the case for the vast majority of the leases reviewed.[22] The annual one artaba land tax rate applied throughout the province at the start of the Roman period and though the rates of taxation changed under Diocletian, for the period under consideration the one artaba land tax may be assumed to be applicable.[23] Although there are variations in the taxes payable on private land, a supplement could also be payable, and typically this supplement was one seventh of an artaba of wheat per aroura.[24] The tax on land raising grain, the *dikoinikia*, of one twentieth of wheat per aroura was also payable.[25] Finally, another tax normally payable by the landlord is the *naubion* tax, which may be estimated at around half a silver drachma per aroura.[26] The most difficult tax to estimate is the crown tax. Wallace sees evidence for this tax applying to real estate as being relatively scarce before the late second century when he views it as an annual rather than exceptional extraction and related to land.[27] There were also exceptional demands by the state for requisitions, and additional costs arising from *epibole*, an obligation which could apply to ownership of a privately owned piece of land to farm some other, presumably less fertile, plot of public land.[28] Although these multiple ongoing taxes seem heavy, I believe that these would not have been sufficient to make land ownership or leasing an unattractive option given the overall levels of return, which will be discussed below.

Market Participants

Turning to the nature of the participants in the marketplaces, transactions clearly passed through social networks and there is a tendency in all the transaction types for women to prefer transacting with other women, men with other men.[29] The social networks which helped create markets were thus gendered spaces. The proportions of women acting within the various markets are shown in Table 14.1, where the most striking feature is that women were essentially unable to act as tenants of agricultural land. There is no known legal barrier to women acting in this way and the reason for this feature is thus likely to be that it was socially unacceptable for women either to farm the land solely with their own labour, or to be seen to direct males to do so.

Transactions which were clearly within the same family are low, but generally higher for housing than agricultural land.[30] It is difficult to identify any strong consistent trends across markets as to the ages of the participants, however, there appears to be a peak in vendor activity for land sales for people in their thirties. This could be interpreted as reflecting the sale of inherited land, which was surplus to immediate requirements, by more mature individuals.[31] As regards land leases, there is a relatively high proportion of younger participants, under the age of 23, reflecting their inability to farm their land directly and thus the need to lease it out to a third party.[32] For housing sales, it seems that individuals were particularly active in the housing market both as buyers and vendors at the relatively advanced ages of the mid-forties and early fifties. At these ages it is unlikely that these market participants would have recently benefitted from parental inheritance given mortality rates by age, and this is thus unlikely to be an explanation for this type of market activity. A possible explanation for these relatively aged market participants may have been that transactions resulted from the re-organisation of domestic space as children matured, married, and had children of their own.[33] Although we must, of course, be careful of projecting our social practices into the past, perhaps this was equivalent to modern "downsizing"? There are too few data to comment on age structures in the housing lease and vacant lot markets.

The vast majority of transactions were local, between counterparties from the same village or city. This can be seen in the proportion of "closed" transactions which are known to have occurred between people in the same location compared with the proportion of those "open" transactions known to have been between people in different locations. This is shown in Table 14.2.

In all cases except land leasing, it was more common for people to transact with people within their immediate geographic circle, than to seek to strike a deal in a geographically wider network. This is particularly marked in the

Table 14.1 Proportion of women by activity

House buyers *n=293*	*Land landlords* *n=959*	*House landlords* *n=183*	*Vacant lot buyers* *n=78*
37%	24%	30%	23%
House vendors n=338	*Land tenants* n=1088	*House tenants* n=172	*Vacant lot vendors* n=93
40%	3%	16%	27%

Table 14.2 Localisation ratios

	Land sales	*House sales*	*Land leases*	*House leases*
Proportion of "closed" to "open" transactions	1.3	3.7	0.5	1.9

housing markets. The exception is land leases, which reflects the concentration of ownership of land, available for leasing, in the city "elites".[34]

Price Formats

Whilst the demographics of the participants in the markets provide valuable information on how they were structured, another source of information is the format used for prices. "Prices" in this context does not only mean sale prices but can be extended to include rents as the price of occupation. I would draw a distinction between "conventional" and "marginal" pricing. In conventional pricing, prices are rounded, which may reflect institutional constraints or market inefficiency. In marginal pricing, the number format is not rounded and this can be considered as evidence for negotiation and competition. Another associated aspect of prices is the degree to which they are variable, since as Temin noted, "variable prices then can be used as markers for the presence of market exchange."[35] Certainly, a relatively small degree of variability in prices would be an indicator of the presence of market forces, but a very high degree of variability may indicate a failure in the pricing mechanism within the market, where participants lack the comparative data to make a rational decision.

Prices for sales of houses were very often rounded, and for land sales, to a lesser extent.[36] I believe this indicates that, given the relative infrequency of these transactions and the consequent lack of available information, this meant that meaningful, reasoned negotiation was very difficult. If neither side had sufficient data upon which to base their negotiating position it is more likely that prices would have been rounded. It might be asked whether larger landowners had an advantage in having better information on prices and likely profitability of a purchase or sale. However, land markets show no difference in average pricing per aroura for large or small deals, which suggests participants across the wealth spectrum used similar, generally inefficient, pricing mechanisms.[37]

In the land rental market, prices were variable, with rent levels for different plots within the same leases differing according possibly to the level of expected yield.[38] Rounding in this market is more difficult to assess given the rates per aroura are relatively low, but some rounding does occur. Both parties would have been able to assess the rent for individual plots, given their local knowledge of the geographic conditions and previous harvests or rent levels. Even absentee landlords could rely on their estate manager or agent to provide this local knowledge. The fact that rents in the Arsinoite nome (a nome being an administrative district) are much more variable than in the Oxyrhynchite logically reflects, I believe, the greater geographic diversity in the Arsinoite.[39] These features indicate the use of reason rather than guesswork. By contrast, house rents appear very heavily rounded and extremely variable, even after allowing for the diversity of housing stock.

Intermediation

As regards how deals were struck, I have determined the percentages of all transactions which definitely involved a third party such as an agent or manager, and these ranged between 4 per cent and 14 per cent.[40] None of the intermediaries concerned appear to have been professional real estate brokers. Overall, I would suggest that these levels are low and that the vast majority of transactions were carried out directly, face to face, between the principals. The highest levels of intermediation are for land leases and this reflects the geographical dispersion of landlord and tenant noted above and the tendency for the landlord to delegate leasing to estate managers. One curious feature of the Egyptian private real estate markets is that there is no evidence for auctions as a sales channel, although there is plenty of evidence for their use when the state sold land.

Investment Returns

Turning to rates of return, or the profitability of owning land, Carrié calculated the return to the owner from leasing land, working from best estimate ranges, which provided results that are consequently vague.[41] His rates of return are also higher than those I show below since he did not take account of the lower returns when land was under fodder.

Leases varied in their term from one to multiple years, and the one-year leases, unless the leased land was split into different plots, would often be for a single crop. When the return to the landlord from renting is analysed, single crop or mono-culture, one-year leases cannot be used directly to assess sustainable investment returns, since the return from land in fodder was much lower than land under cereal crops. Leases frequently required crop rotation, and thus only leases with more than a one-year duration, or one-year leases where part of the land was sown in cereals and partly in fodder can be used to estimate directly a smoothed sustainable investment return to the landlord. I used the leases of this nature which pre-date AD 274 to determine the return on investment in land. The date terminus of AD 274 is to avoid distortion caused by the jump in prices of around that time and the high inflation of the fourth century. In total there are 105 leases which can be used to estimate the likely sustainable return on the land concerned.[42]

Having identified the leases which can legitimately be used, the returns can be calculated by dividing the likely annual financial gain by the amount of the capital employed. Thus, the return from a land or housing lease was equal to the net rent received, after taxes and expenses, divided by the value of the real estate. These calculations were first completed on the basis of my best estimate of each component within the calculation. All monetary values are expressed in AD 150 terms, re-calibrating the amounts to allow for the relatively low inflation after that date up to AD 274.This approach is a "deterministic" one since a single answer is determined for each investment.

However, one problem with a deterministic approach is the reliance that it places on the single best estimates of the components of the calculation. Another difficulty with using a deterministic approach is that while it can provide an estimate of likely returns on an investment it provides no information as to risk. The first problem can largely be alleviated by modelling different possibilities so as to obtain a distribution of likely returns and plot these on a graph and describe the variability in a mathematical way. This methodology is known as a "stochastic" approach.

The returns produced are shown in Figure 14.1, which show the results of 1,000 simulations for an individual lease, Figure 14.2, which are the aggregated results formed by adding together all the 105,000 results for the 105 available individual leases, and Figure 14.3 and Table 14.3, which summarise these results.

When different nomes are compared, it is clear that the distribution of returns for the Oxyrhynchite nome compared with the Arsinoite nome is tighter and lower. In general, I believe that the Oxyrhynchite nome may be a better indicator of the return from leasing land in Roman Egypt than that derived from using the larger data set from all nomes, for two reasons. First, the Oxyrhynchite nome lies in the Nile valley itself, as does much of the exploitable land of Roman Egypt, and is therefore more typical than the Arsinoite nome with its peculiarities of geographical position and irrigation techniques. Second, I have made a necessary assumption that the price of land per aroura is the same within any particular nome at a given date. This is clearly untrue,

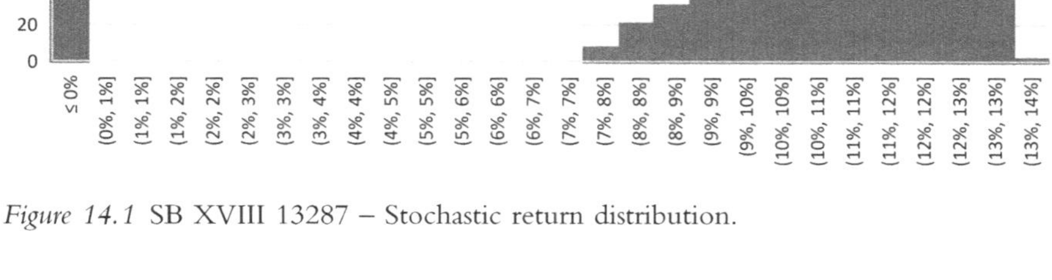

Figure 14.1 SB XVIII 13287 – Stochastic return distribution.

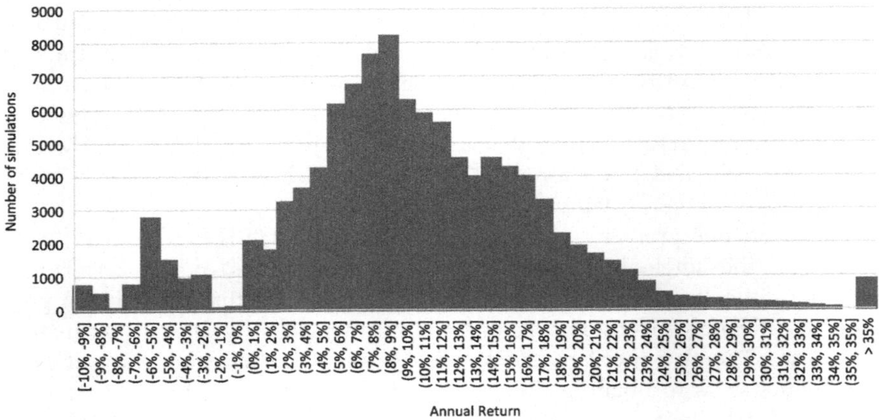

Figure 14.2 All land leases – Stochastic return distribution.

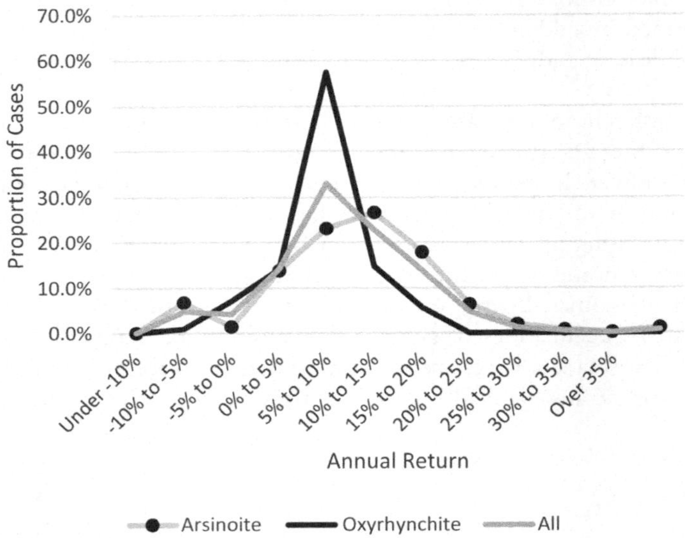

Figure 14.3 All land leases – Stochastic return distribution.

Table 14.3 Median and average stochastic returns p.a. per nome.

Nome	*Median*	*Average*
Arsinoite	11.0%	10.8%
Oxyrhynchite	7.4%	7.2%
All	8.9%	9.6%

since land prices are likely to have varied according to their quality, and although it might not impact significantly on the medians and averages, it will tend to widen the distribution of both deterministic and stochastic results. In the model, the lower the assumed value of land, the higher the calculated return. Thus, the return on fertile plots is exaggerated, since the value of land used is probably too low, and vice versa for poor-quality land. The greater the variability in the land in the nome concerned, the greater this effect. Land prices are less variable in the Oxyrhynchite nome than elsewhere and thus the impact of this effect is less pronounced.[43]

Given the diversity of housing stock and the relative lack of documentation on rent levels, it is difficult to model returns in the same way as in the previous section for land leases. However, median rents and house prices can give some indication of a typical return from leases overall.[44] The return on a house investment based on these medians is 8.2 per cent per annum assuming no ongoing frictional costs to the landlord. This is similar to the returns achievable for investment in land derived above, but the landlord would in reality also face significant depreciation costs over time as the fabric of the building would need renewal.[45] Also the landlord could be subject to taxes even when the house was leased. In addition, whilst if land could not be leased to a third party it could be made productive by direct farming, a house that could not be leased was a wasting asset and thus the risks to the landlord were higher than investment in land.

Diachronic Trends

Some comments may be made as to the development of the markets over time despite Rowlandson's statement that there is "no reliable means of assessing the volume of land sales in Roman Egypt at any period, and certainly not whether the volume increased at any particular time."[46] On the contrary, by comparing the number of land sale documents, as a proportion of all documentary papyri, a pattern can be seen. The proportion of documents is 3.7 per cent in the first century, falling to 2.0 per cent in the second, 1.9 per cent in the third and 0.6 per cent in the first half of the fourth.[47] It would thus appear that market activity in land sales declined over time, which may indicate economic contraction or a failure in market confidence. However, no such reduction is evident in the proportion of land lease documents, suggesting that the land leasing sector was relatively immune from any economic contraction. Van Minnen has suggested that the size of plots decreased "significantly" in the third century and uses this feature as a support for his contention that the third century was a period of agricultural contraction.[48] My data do not support van Minnen's proposition since no significant reduction is apparent.[49] What does happen however, is that the duration of leases declines, which would indicate a decline in confidence rather than activity per se.[50] There is not enough data to make similar comments on the housing markets.

Financial Rationality?

Roman attitudes to agrarian investment have been the subject of a long-standing academic debate. The contrary positions are exemplified by these oppositional statements from Finley and Harris, respectively: "Investment in land, in short, was never in antiquity a matter of systematic, calculated policy, of what Weber called economic rationality" contra "Roman methods of calculating the profitability of an estate were as effective as those practiced by a progressive landowner in the seventeenth century AD."[51] Understanding the nature of the markets and the degree to which decisions were driven by financial rationality is key to resolving this debate. Financial rationality in this context may be understood to involve a comparative decision, a choice between two, or more, options which have different expected outcomes, and the use of reason to make that decision. Individuals exercising financial rationality must also have self-defined financial goals that they wish to achieve, and which they use to make the choice between the available options. If, when making this choice, they have due regard to maximising return and minimising risk, then I would consider that they have made their choice in a financially rational way. However, to enable financial rationality to be exercised, certain pre-conditions must be met. The costs of the transaction must be low enough to allow a reasonable financial return to be achieved and both sides should have sufficient information to be able to assess their options. If the pre-conditions exist then we can use indicators within the market data, such as price formats, to make a judgement as to whether it was likely that financially rational assessments were made.

Turning to the housing market I believe that the evidence shows that the pre-conditions for the exercise of financial rationality did not exist. The relatively high frictional costs would have made house leasing a less attractive investment proposition than leasing land. In addition, we have noted that the difficulties with regard to information exchange, notably the intangible variability of the experience of sharing living spaces, would have made it difficult to commoditise a portion of a house for sale or rent. Even if the pre-conditions did exist, the evidence for a liquid competitive market is slim. House rents were heavily rounded and look conventional in structure. The liquidity in the market, at least that recorded in the papyri, was low compared with other financial transactions. When we consider the relatively high level of intra-familial transactions and lack of formal leasing documentation, this seems to point to a market which was not primarily driven by financial rationality but rather by familial concerns. Of course, it should be noted that the data come from the rural nomes of Roman Egypt, and it may well be that in Alexandria there was scope for commoditisation of the housing market with a larger peripatetic population and larger housing units which could be broken down into standard units and thus commoditised more easily than in the smaller urban sites in the rural nomes. However, the evidence suggests that the housing market in the rest of the province was not driven by financial rationality.

In contrast to the housing market, the markets for buying and renting land seem to have all the necessary pre-conditions for the exercise of financial rationality to take place, with relatively low frictional costs and sufficient information exchange, and there are clear indications of financial rationality actually taking place within the market. Land sale and purchase documents and leases are complex. The land sale contracts go some way to protect the buyer against any information deficits they may have as to the nature of the land they are buying, whereas land leases are more balanced between the two parties. These contractual features indicate an understanding of the risks faced by the parties and try to mitigate these risks in a fashion that is entirely consistent with the exercise of financial rationality. This impression of rational behaviour is reinforced by the rational diversification of crops and plots seen within lease documents. There are no signs of conventional pricing in either land sales or leases, and within both types of documents we can see the exercise of judgement by the fact that in some cases the price of land or the rent applicable may vary for different plots of land within a single lease. Outcomes are financially rational in that land ownership is an attractive financial proposition which produces returns which are comparable to those within the only other market available for investment with a similar risk profile, the secured credit market.[52]

It must, however, be noted that a rational financial outcome is not, in itself, proof of the exercise of rationality by the principals. Financially rational outcomes may arise from conventional behaviours which through social pressures evolve into best practices. For instance, landlords who charge excessive rents will not flourish if tenants frequently default or those who charge inadequate rents will fail since they cannot cover their costs. Rents may then settle at evolutionally determined equilibrium rates. The establishment of this equilibrium level does not necessarily require, at any point, the exercise of financial rationality on the part of the principals. This argument is part of the evolutionary efficiency school within economic theory.[53] However, financially rational outcomes over the medium to long term are a necessary, but not sufficient, indicator of the exercise of financial rationality.

Land sales show no seasonality of activity, suggesting that buyers and sellers were not driven to transact by poor or good harvests. This would have allowed the exercise of financial rationality after due consideration, rather than the principals being rushed into a decision. However, as may be expected, land leases follow the farming year and leases were generally contracted prior to sowing and rents paid after the harvest.[54] This is also entirely financially rational from the perspective of both the landlord and the tenant. There are relatively few intra-familial transactions which might have been transacted on terms that were financially irrational if family ties and needs played a part. Finally, the land markets reacted to changing conditions in a manner which appears financially rational. In times of instability, such as the later third century, the term of leases decreases as individuals seek to ensure that they have greater flexibility to deal with potentially fast changing circumstances. In times of high inflation, there is a shift away from payment of rents for fodder land in cash towards other more inflation-proof commodities including cereals.[55] Thus I believe that on the balance of the evidence, the agricultural land markets were driven by financial rationality.

I hope that these conclusions will assist in answering the central question as to the nature of the markets, which Scheidel described as vital to our understanding of "the dynamics of Roman economic development and especially its limits and decline," since, even allowing for the cultural and geographic peculiarities of Egypt, many of the conditions and institutions that supported these markets also existed in other provinces of the Roman world.[56]

Notes

1 Rathbone 1997: 215.
2 This recalibration assumes that retail prices were stable in the period from AD 1 to AD 150, and then grew at an average level of 1 per cent per annum between AD 150 and AD 274. For the derivation of this approach see Kelly 2020: 30–58.
3 Kelly 2020.
4 Lavan 2016: 21–22.
5 Bagnall and Frier 1994: 69–70.
6 Alston calculated an average number of occupants per house at 7.61 to 7.78 and an average number of people per family group or household at 5.40 to 5.52 based on 11 texts mostly from the Arsinoite nome ranging in date from the first to the third century: Alston 2002: 70.
7 Bagnall 1993: 49; Alston 2002: 59.
8 Husson 1983: 310 citing *P.Oxy.* III 489 l.7 and l.15 (AD 116–117) and *P.Oxy.* XIV 1634 (AD 222).
9 There is no evidence for the separation of the ownership of the land and the housing built upon it, and the subsequent payment of ground rent, as occurs in some modern countries. Thus essentially all houses were held freehold rather than leasehold.
10 Kelly 2020: 156.
11 https://www.savills.co.uk/research_articles/229130/188996-0 downloaded 18 January 2021.
12 See Rathbone 1991: xvi.
13 The median sizes of plots sold or leased was 5.0 arouras (Kelly 2020: 78, 111), which is just under the area of two football pitches. See Rathbone 1991: 23 for comment on large estates.
14 Bowman 2013: 234–239.
15 Kelly 2020: 113.
16 In *P.Mich.* V 276 (AD 47) the solution that the five brothers came upon was to combine their portions into a single share of one seventh of half a house, which they sold to their sister.
17 There is a theory developed by Tomsin, that ownership of catoecic land was, at least in theory, restricted to members of the gymnasial group but this was rebutted by Yitfach who stated that this restriction was lifted with the Roman occupation, Yitfach 2015: 137.
18 See *P.Oxy.* XLI 2954 (third century) for a discussion of the Edict of Avidius Heliodorus. Another example of the interest of the state in land transactions is the requirement, attributed to a rescript of Diocletian, that land be sold at its true value: CJ 4.44.2.
19 Wallace 1938: 75–76.

20 The ratio of the number of leases to sales is 0.4 for housing and 2.6:1 for land, Kelly 2020: 168.
21 Yitfach 2015: 146.
22 See Kelly 2020: appendices 3.2.1–3.2.3
23 Wallace 1938: 11–19 details the levels of land taxation by nome, and a useful summary of taxation rates for private land is provided in Rowlandson 1987: 292.
24 See Wallace 1938: 38–41, where he notes that such a surcharge is prescribed in the *gnomon* for taxation of land in the Arsinoite nome and Rowlandson 1996: 54 for a confirmation of a similar surcharge applying in the Oxyrhynchite.
25 Wallace 1938: 12. I have assumed that this is payable only when the land concerned is under wheat and at the same time and under the same conditions as the main one artaba land tax.
26 Based on *P.Heid.* Inv.G 24 l.10–3 gives 14 drachmas as the cash public charges for two years for 13 arouras, and of the same order of magnitude as that within *P.Achm.* 9 (late second century) where the rate is 2.25 obols per aroura.
27 Based on Wallace 1938: 282–284, where he stated that private land in the Oxyrhynchite nome, in the third century, paid at a rate of eight drachmas per aroura. See also Bowman 1967 for a description of the documents then known to contain references to crown tax and Johnson 1936: 576 for a general description, and for an updated list see *P.Koeln.* II 91 to which add *BGU* XV 2503–9 and subsequent publications. Note that there is no specific mention of crown tax in any of the 105 leases upon which our estimates of sustainable term return are based but this is not surprising since when taxes are mentioned generally there is only an over-arching reference to public dues.
28 See Rowlandson 1996: 88–90. I have also ignored the *catoecic arithmetikon*, on the grounds that is a form of capitation tax rather than a land tax, following Wallace 1938: 176.
29 Kelly 2020: 239.
30 Kelly 2020: 253, the percentages of transactions involving family members are 0 per cent land leases, 1 per cent house leases, 6 per cent land sales, and 9 per cent house sales.
31 Kelly 2020: 85.
32 Kelly 2020: 110.
33 Kelly 2020: 149–150.
34 See Kelly 2020: sub-section 3.2.4.
35 Temin 2013: 8. See also Rathbone 2013: 136–137, "the more expensive goods and those bought in quantity were subject to fluctuations in price which imply the operation of a free local market." And for an excellent summary of pricing theory in economics see Weber 2012.
36 The degree of rounding to tetradrachmas for the cash rents per aroura and house rents is 57 per cent and 88 per cent respectively. For the capital acquisitions of housing and land, the percentages of land and housing transactions between 100 drachmas and 1,000 drachmas that were rounded to the nearest 100 were 47 per cent and 70 per cent respectively. As a comparison for the 70 per cent rounded figure for housing, to a competitive but by no means perfect market, recent equivalent figures for the housing market in England and Wales show that only 5 per cent of all sale prices between 100k and 1,000k were rounded to 100k and 35 per cent were rounded to a multiple of 10k or 100k (Kelly 2020: 155).
37 Kelly 2020: 95.
38 See Kelly 2020: appendices 3.2.2 and 3.2.3 for examples of rental variation. The relative standard deviation, which is a mathematical measure of variability, for each of the markets is as follows: house prices 132 per cent, house rents 99 per cent, land prices 40 per cent, and land rents 65 per cent. In order to reduce heterogeneity, and thus distortion caused by geographical factors, the land rents referred to are from the

Oxyrhynchite nome only, and the house rents are those for village properties only. All prices are re-calibrated to AD 150 general price levels to ensure comparability.

39 Kelly 2020: 122.

40 Kelly 2020: 246.

41 Carrié arrived at a conclusion that in the first and second centuries the effective return on leased land varied between 11.7 per cent and 15.8 per cent and for the third century between 7.0 per cent and 15.8 per cent, Carrié 1997: 132.

42 See Kelly 2020, appendix 3.2.3.

43 See Kelly 2020: Fig. 3.1.19 which shows the "R^2" coefficient for Oxyrhynchite nome prices is much higher than for other nomes, indicating that the typical price of land is more tightly distributed than elsewhere.

44 The median rental income for village houses is 40 dr., where the median house price is 400 dr. The median rental income for city houses is 84 dr. where the median house price is 680 dr. For all houses the median rental income is 49 dr., and the median house price is 600 dr. All figures have been re-calibrated to AD 150 levels.

45 Though tenants were sometimes required to ensure the house was in a clean state at the end of the lease as in *P.Erl.* 72 (fourth century), most houses were relatively insubstantial mud-brick constructions with a relatively short lifetime.

46 Rowlandson 1996: 187.

47 Kelly 2020: 77.

48 Van Minnen 2000: 213. Van Minnen does not present or reference the data which support this suggestion.

49 Kelly 2020: 111.

50 Kelly 2020: 116.

51 Finley 1999: 116 and Harris 1993: 25.

52 Kelly 2020: 228.

53 See Ogilvie 2007: 656–658, for a discussion of evolutionary efficiency and economic institutions.

54 Kelly 2020: 118.

55 Kelly 2020: 115.

56 Scheidel 2012: 9.

References

Alston, R. (2002) *The City in Roman and Byzantine Egypt*. London: Routledge.

Bagnall, R.S. (1993) *Egypt in Late Antiquity*. Princeton: Princeton University Press.

Bagnall, R.S. and B.W. Frier (1994) *The Demography of Roman Egypt*. Cambridge: Cambridge University Press.

Bowman, A.K. (1967) The Crown-Tax in Roman Egypt. *Bulletin of the American Society of Papyrologists* 4, 59–74.

Bowman, A.K. (2013) Agricultural Production in Egypt. In: A.K. Bowman and A. Wilson, eds. *The Roman Agricultural Economy: Organization, Investment and Production*, Oxford: Oxford University Press, 219–254.

Carrié, J.-M. (1997) L'arithmétique sociale de l'économie agraire: Prix de la terre, rente foncière et prix des céréales dans l'Egypte romano-byzantine. In: J. Andreau *et al.* eds. *Économie antique: prix et formation des prix dans les économies antiques*. Saint-Bernard-de-Comminges: Musée archéologique départemental, 121–146.

Finley, M.I. (1999) *The Ancient Economy*. Berkeley: University of California Press.

Harris, W. (1993) Between Archaic and Modern: Some Current Problems in the History of the Roman Economy. In: W. Harris, ed. *The Inscribed Economy*. Ann Arbor: University of Michigan, 11–29.

Husson, G. (1983) *O ϰ α: Le vocabulaire de la maison privée en Égypte d'après les papyrus grecs*. Paris: Publications de la Sorbonne.
Johnson, A.C. (1936) *Roman Egypt to the Reign of Diocletian, Volume II, An Economic Survey of Ancient Rome*. Baltimore: The Johns Hopkins Press.
Kelly, P.V. (2020) *Risk and Return in Roman Egypt. Were Markets in Roman Egypt Driven by Financial Rationality?* PhD Thesis, King's College London.
Lavan, M. (2016) The Spread of Roman Citizenship, 14–212 CE: Quantification in the Face of High Uncertainty. *Past and Present* 230. 1, 3–46.
Ogilvie, S. (2007) Whatever Is, Is Right? Economic Institutions in Pre-Industrial Europe. *Economic History Review* 60, 649–684.
Rathbone, D. (1991) *Economic Rationalism and Rural Society in Third-Century AD Egypt: The Heroninos Archive and the Appianus Estate*. Cambridge: Cambridge University Press.
Rathbone, D. (1997) Prices and Price Formation in Roman Egypt. In: J. Andreau *et al.*, eds. *Économie antique: Prix et formation des prix dans les économies antiques*. Saint-Bernard-de-Comminges: Musée archéologique départemental, 183–244.
Rathbone, D. (2013) Village Markets in Roman Egypt. The Case of First-century AD Tebtunis. In: M. Frass, ed. *Kauf, Konsum und Märkte: Wirtschaftswelten im Fokus - Von der Römischen Antike bis zur Gegenwart*. Wiesbaden: Harrassowitz Verlag, 123–144.
Rowlandson, J. (1987) P. Oxy. XLII 3047, VII 1044, and the Land Tax in Kind. *Zeitschrift für Papyrologie und Epigraphik* 67, 283–292.
Rowlandson, J. (1996) *Landowners and Tenants in Roman Egypt: The Social Relations of Agriculture in the Oxyrhynchite Nome*. Oxford: Oxford University Press.
Scheidel, W. (2012) Approaching the Roman Economy. In: W. Scheidel, ed. *The Cambridge Companion to the Roman Economy*. Cambridge: Cambridge University Press, 1–21.
Temin, P. (2013) *The Roman Market Economy*. Princeton: Princeton University Press.
Tomsin, A. (1964) Les continuités historiques dans le cadre des mesures prises par les Romains en Egypte concernant la propriété de la terre. *Actes du Xe Congrès International de Papyrologie*. Warsaw: Zakład narodowy imienia Ossolińskich, wydawnictwo Polskiej Akademii Nauk, 81–95.
Van Minnen, P. (2000) Agriculture and the Taxes and Trade model in Roman Egypt. *Zeitschrift für Papyrologie und Epigraphik* 133, 205–220.
Wallace, S.L. (1938) *Taxation in Egypt from Augustus to Diocletian*. Princeton: Princeton University Press.
Weber, T.A. (2012) Price Theory in Economics. In: Ö. Özer and R. Phillips, eds. *The Oxford Handbook of Pricing Management*. Oxford: Oxford University Press, 281–339.
Yitfach, U. (2015) Metepigraphê: Ptolemaic and Roman Policies on the Conveyance of Allotment Land. In: E. Jakab, ed. *Legal Documents in Ancient Societies V. Sale and Community Documents from the Ancient World*. Trieste: Edizioni Università di Trieste, 133–151.

Index of People

Index of Places

Index Rerum